DYNAMICS OF INDIAN POLITICS

DYNAMICS OF INDIAN POLITICS

[For UGC-NET, M.A., UPSC and State Public Service Commission Examinations]

By

MANOJ SHARMA

ANMOL PUBLICATIONS PVT. LTD.

NEW DELHI - 110 002 (INDIA)

ANMOL PUBLICATIONS PVT. LTD.
4374/4B, Ansari Road, Daryaganj
New Delhi - 110 002
Ph.: 23261597, 23278000
Visit us at: www.anmolpublications.com

Dynamics of Indian Politics

First Published, 2004

ISBN 81-261-1809-1

PRINTED IN INDIA

Published by J.L. Kumar for Anmol Publications Pvt. Ltd., New Delhi - 110 002 and Printed at Mehra Offset Press, Delhi.

Contents

Preface

Dynamics of Indian Politics as a paper is being taught at the graduate and post graduate level in Political Science syllabus in almost all the Indian Universities. The various courses conducted by various institutions at the Central and State level too have been considered in respect of their syllabus, course contents and requirements. Thus the material presented here would be of interest as well as great use to the students of Political Science. This book has been especially designed for UGC-NET Examination, M.A. (Political Science) Students and other competitive examinations by UPSC and Public Service Commission of various States.

The major topics dealt in this book are—Study of Indian Politics; Governability in India; Rights and Duties; National Integration; Centre-State Relations; Regionalism and Politics; Linguistic Reorganisation; Caste and Class System; Indian Political Process; Foreign Capital and Indian Politics etc.

Manoj Sharma

1

Study of Indian Politics

LEGACIES OF INDIAN POLITICS

The term political system includes two words political and system. Political allocation, as defined by Marion Levy, JR, a political sociologist refers to the distribution of power and responsibility for the action of the various members of the concrete structure concerned. It involves, on the one hand, compulsive sanctions of which use of force is the extreme form and on the other, accountability to the members of the concrete structure. Since state is the centre of all that is regarded as political, it has the legitimate right to use force. Max Weber, an eminent sociologist says that state is a human community that (successfully) claims the monopoly of the legitimate use of physical force within a given territory and adds that the right to use physical force is ascribed to other associations or individuals only to the extent to which state permits it. It is the element of force that gives essential unity to the political system. Then system means an 'organisation' or connected body of things. System, thus implies interdependence of parts, and a boundary of some kind between it and its environments. Interdependence means that when the properties of one component part change, all other components and the system as a whole are affected. By 'boundary' in a political system we mean that there exit points where other system end and the political system begins. In this way political system is 'a structure that performs a certain function for a society'. The political system produces certain output for the society—legitimate policy decision, the goals at which these decisions aim at. These goals may be precise programmatic or only meagre and general. They may be obeyed readily a reluctantly by many or by a few. But when we call them policy decisions, it is only to stress that these decisions have some consequences for the society.

The most acceptable definition of political system has been given by G.A. Almond. He says, "What we propose as that the political system is that system of interactions to be found in all independent societies which performs the function of integration and adoptation (both internal and vis-a-vis other societies) by means of the employment, or threat of employment of more or less legitimate, order maintaining or transforming system in the society.

LEGACIES OF THE INDIAN POLITICAL SYSTEM

We have the legacy of a long tradition. Legacy means all that is left to one by will. Here, in the case of Indian political system, it means all that has come to us through historical development and has its impact on the present system. None can deny that what we find in modern India, is a product of centuries. What we find today has not developed suddenly. According to Rajni Kothari, there are real historical factors which have shaped India of today. The first of these factors is the impact of Hinduism, the second that of the British rule, and the third that of nationalism in the pre-independence days. in Kothari's own words, "Modern India in its political aspects is a product of a variety of influences spread once a long period of time. Three historical strand stand out distinctly and substantial influences. The first is Hinduism, the social bedrock and unifying framework of Indian society. The second is the British impact of rational legal authority welded by a central power that managed to consolidate the whole sub-continent under it. Although operating mainly in the legal and administrative spheres, the British Raj also effected fundamental political belief and relationships.

LEGACIES OF HINDUISM

The Hindu period refers to the days roughly between the fifteenth and tenth centuries before Christ, when the Aryans came to India and the tenth century A.D. when such big empires as that of the Mauryas, the Guptas, The Harsha in the north and that of Cholas and Pallavas in the south was established. Then began the attacks of the Muslims into India but the same continued to be resisted by the

Rajputs and Marathas, though with little success. Still, the great Epics continued to inspire the Hindus in their glorious ancestory and past culture.

1. Caste System. The first and the most important legacy of Hinduism is the caste system. With the passage of time the Aryans came to be divided into four castes—Brahmins, Kshatriyas, Vaisyas and Sudras. Caste system corresponded to the four functions of knowledge, defence, wealth and labour respectively. Though functional in its origin the caste system became hereditary and grew into very complicated pattern of sub-castes and sub-groups within each sub-caste. Importance to caste began to be given not as a Varna but as a Jati. "The sub-division became the division", says Morris Jones, "and the fact that each Jati can be allocated to one of the large Varna groups is of reduced significance." In this sense, castes are not four but thousands. Then there is the lowest caste of Harijans.

Rajni Kothari says, "Each individual not only was born in a particular station by virtue of his caste and kinship, his position in the large social system was also determined by the occupation to which he was sentiled, his relationship to customary authority, and his obligation as a family man or a respondent." Duties were elaborately defined and obligatory. The individual was well protected in return for his compliance of the duties. "Lacking in larger political identities and given the remote and intermittent nature of political authority, Indian society assumed over the centuries a small group orientation that has not been seriously eroded even to the present."

Many people came to believe that the role of caste in free and modern India will be gradually reduced. But this has not come true. Rather, caste has assumed more importance. Politics has in modern India started making use of caste. Votes are sought in the name of caste; candidates are given tickets to contest election keeping well in view the fact as to which caste is in majority in a particular constituency. In turn, caste has also begun taking advantage of politics. People of a caste throw their lot with a particular party keeping in view as to what benefits it would draw from that party.

2. Secular Culture. In spite of the fact that India was socially rigid, it was ideologically liberal and secular. Invaders such as Huns,

Hushaus and Muslims came to India with different religions and cultures but in the liberal and secular atmosphere of India, they got absorbed into Indian culture giving it a composite nature. The culture of India of today is not a Hindu culture but a composite culture.

Due to the degeneration of rigid orthodoxy, there appeared Mahavir and Buddha as the leaders of dissent. They have been followed by dissenting and reformist movements in India upto the present day. These movements have played a great role in the enrichment of Indian civilisation and paradoxically enough in its survival. They not only gave vitality but also lent flexibility. Bhakti movement in the modern time comprised of saints coming from the highest to the lowest of castes, embracing all religions of India without distinction of birth, status and caste.

3. Element of Essential Unity. India is without doubt a country of different religions, castes and languages. It has accommodated diversity. So, ideologically and culturally, it has been very liberal in spite of the fact that we do not find in history an instance to show when India was one. But it has achieved unity in diversity. In spite of various differences, the people of India in its culture have always felt unity and oneness. It is this sense of unity that displayed itself at the time of the invasion of India by China in 1962 and by Pakistan many a time. In the words of Rajni Kothari. "The social system, the doctrines enshrined in the Hindu Epics, the Brahminic elite, and the great dissenting movements, together gave to Hinduism a unified character and a sense of continuity.

Legacies of the British Raj

The second most important source of the legacies of the Indian political system is the British Raj:

(1) Communalism. Communalism in India is essentially legacies of the British Raj. It is the Britishers who played the game of divide the rule. They began to patronise the Muslims after Sir Saiyyed Ahmed Khan pleaded in his book *Causes of the Revolt*, published after the mutiny of 1857 that not the Muslims but the disgruntled elements in India on the whole were responsible for the uprising. It was in Sir Saiyyed that the Britishers found a Muslim who would serve their purpose and began to shower official recognition upon him and through him upon the Muslim community.

The Muslims came as raiders only occasionally in the eighth century but massively in the tenth and eleventh centuries and established the Delhi Sultanate. The local rulers offered resistance and were brought under Muslim domination after long and hard battles. on the religious front, the Muslims found Hinduism with a different system. This led to repression against the Hindus who were converted in lakhs. Akber, however, stands out as an exception. The repression let lose with a view to achieving conversion considerably disturbed the Hindu system. Orthodoxy came to be practised more than ever in order to protect and safeguard the Hindu values and ways of life. According to Rajni Kothari, "This state of affairs threw Hindu society into a state of confusions and defeatism. Hindus responded by withdrawing into the web of exclusiveness provided by caste and kinships, and thus managed to survive. Caste now became a protective shell, a mechanism of isolation and withdrawal from an unkind environment..."

2. Parliamentary Democracy. It would be far fetched to say that we had democratic governments in the past, but the democratic tradition had continued to persist even in the ancient times. It does not in any way suggest that there was no politics in traditional India. There was definitely no absence of politics in village India where village assemblies worked. But it was essentially a politics of different order. "Traditional India", says Morris Jones, "is not non-political, only it contains different kind of politics from that of the modern state. This politics was basically and manifestly a politics of village dominance of local groups and factions in which family and linear ties played the distinct role."

3. English Language. English language is yet another very important legacy of the British rule. It proved one of the most unifying factors in India which has dozens of languages and hundreds of dialects. A Bengali could not understand a Madrasi. A Punjabi could not understand a Southern Indian and so on and so forth. It was English language that forged the links of unity among Indians speaking different languages. The very birth of the Indian National Congress in 1885 could be possible only because the participants to the conference called for giving birth to the Congress could communicate with one another through English. In spite of the fact that Hindi is spoken by a majority of the people of India, it has not proved to be a unifying factor. It has rather brought in antagonism and regionalism into play in the Indian political system.

4. Political and Administrative Unity. We find no instance in ancient Indian history when India was politically or administratively united. Even the reign of Asoka did not cover all the areas what we term India. It was the British authorities which developed a highly effective administrative system and gave political unity to India. Only the British authorities succeeded in establishing a central authority which not only restored law and order but also developed and implemented new administration and justice quite alien to the Indian people.

6. Bureaucracy. A network of highly professionalised bureaucrats is very important for the efficient administration of a country we inherited from the British Raj this system. According to Morris Jones, the political leader of India inherited the more tangible equipment and machinery of government having original structure and composed to trained personnel. Some of the political leaders of India including Jawaharlal Nehru distrusted the bureaucracy being bequeathed by British because they had always served the government against Indian nationalism. It was Sardar Patel who realised the importance of this trained personnel and pleaded for their retention.

5. Birth of Middle Class. In his book 'The British Impact on India' Griffiths holds that the great expansion of the middle class may be one of the most significant contribution of the British in India. The middle class, we know, consists largely of educated who were recruited into the British bureaucracy. It was this educated middle class which gradually out itself off from the masses and became subordinate and loyal to the ruling class.

7. Federalism. The federal structure of Indian government is also a legacy of the British Raj. Morris Jones says, "But, as is evident, this was a large development of the British rule." It was in the Govt. of India Act, 1919 that the element of federalism was introduced for the first time in Indian administration. The provinces were granted independent subjects to legislate upon. But this was on all accounts federalism in its rudimentary form. It was in the Govt. of India Act, 1935 that the concept of federalism was truly envisaged although it could not be put into practice on account of native states to respond to this system. All the sections of people of India found in fedealism a true solution to their problems.

8. Ordinances. The ordinance-making power of the Government is also one of the most important colonial legacies of the British raj. Under the British rule, the Governor-General was given the power to promulgate an ordinance "for the peace and good government of British India." The proposal to vest this power with the Govt. of free India came in for severe attack in the Constituent Assembly from Dr. H.N. Kunzru, H.V. Kamath and others and put Nehru and the top leaders on the defensive. Nehru and other top leaders felt that this extra-ordinary power was necessary in India's special circumstances, at least initially.

9. Role of the Governor. Even the role of the Governor is a British legacy. The position of the Governor right form the Govt. of India Act of 1909, 1919 to that of 1935 was that of an administrator at the provincial level who was responsible to the central government for the administration at the provincial level. He enjoyed a great deal of discretionary powers to run the administration efficiently and effectively. This is what we find in the present Constitution. The role of the Governor assumed particular importance in 1967 when non Congress parties assumed power in more than half of the States while the Centre was ruled over by the Congress. The Governor, it is alleged, helped the Congress its master at the Centre, in toppling non-Congress ministries. Various Governors acted differently in various states in similar circumstances.

LEGACIES OF INDIAN NATIONAL MOVEMENT

The third source of legacies of the Indian political system is the Indian national movement. We can study the legacies of Indian national movement under the following heads:

1. Compromise between Extremes. Indian national movement bequeathed upon us the spirit of compromise between contradictory and opposing view. It is this spirit of compromise that has enabled party system with different ideologies to flourish in India. Rajni Kotharis says that the Indian National Congress was a compromise between two contradictory characteristics of Indian nationalism; conservatism and radicalism...when the Congress turned away from strictly constitutional lines, it get into a direct tussle with colonial authority. By throwing both approaches alternatively, the Congress achieved its aim.

2. Linguistic Regionalism. The linguistic regionalism that we find working so powerfully in Indian Political system today is a legacy of the Indian national movement. It was as late as in 1920 that the Congress advocate for the organisation of states on linguistic basis. It pleaded that demarcation of boundaries of various provinces was done by the British rulers only by the fact of conquest. Whenever a part of the territory of another provinces was conquered, it was added to the province already under its occupation. This plea of the Congress was re-affirmed by it at various occasions.

After the attainment of independence certain self-seeking politicians within the Congress itself sought to have positions and of power at the regional level. Their dream could come true only if a particular state was carved out of the already existing state. So, they began to advocate creation of new States under the plea of promotion of a particular language. They demanded reorganisation of states on linguistic basis. The top central leadership had since realised, after coming into power, the potential dangers in this move but could not help. Andhra was the first state to the carved out of Madras in 1953. Bombay was divided into Maharashtra and Gujarat in 1959. Punjab was bifurcated in 1966.

3. Socialism. Socialism that we intend to bring about in India is also a legacy of national movement which was aimed at getting freedom. Freedom has, however, three aspects—political, economic and social. Independence from foreign rule meant political freedom alone. Economic freedom could, in the Indian context, be brought about, our national leaders like Nehru thought, only through socialism.

So, it was at the Karachi session of the Congress held in 1931 that Nehru declared socialism as the aim of the Congress. It was keeping this pledge in view that the Congress at its Avadi session in 1954 pledged for a socialistic pattern of society as the goal of the Congress. The Congress is working towards the realisation of the goal.

4. Removal of Untouchability. Social freedom means treatment of equality to all persons at the social level irrespective of sex, caste, colour, race, or any other such consideration. Biggest bane of Indian society is the practice of untouchability against the Harijans. The Congress has consistently worked against this practice. Untouchability has also been made a cognisable offence. Not only Congress, rather all the national level parties in India swear against untouchability.

FEDERAL FEATURES OF INDIAN CONSTITUTION

There is a great controversy among the writers on Indian Constitution as regards its nature. Some call it federal whereas others regard it as 'quasi-federal' or 'unitary with subsidiary federal features' or 'federal with strong centralising tendency. As a matter of fact this controversy has developed because the Indian Constitution has sought to blend the American federal system with the British. Parliamentary system in the light of the peculiar conditions prevailing in India. These conditions peculiar to India led the constitution makers to give to the country a constitution most fitted in the circumstances without however caring for any strict theory of constitution making. Their approach was practical and they sought to have a constitution appropriate for the conditions in which India was put in.

Its Federal Features. Let us study A.V. Dicey as to what is a federal constitution. According to him, there are four, essential marks of a federation. *(i)* A written constitution. *(ii)* Distribution of powers *(iii)* A Supreme Court with a power to interpret the constitution and *(iv)* two sets of Government. About the first essential mark Dicey wrote. "To base an arrangement of this kind (federation) upon understanding of conventions would be certain to generate misunderstandings and disagreements." Writing about the second mark he writes. "Federation means the distribution of force of the state among a number of co-ordinate bodies each organising in and controlled by the constitution."

All these three marks are present in Indian constitution. Ours is a written constitution no doubt. There is a clear demarcation of the central and state spheres, each authority being supreme within its own sphere. Enactments in excess of the powers of Union or the State Legislatures are invalid. The Supreme Court is there to decide the disputes arising between the Union and the States. Thus though the word 'federation' is nowhere used in the constitution, yet the constitution has all the marks of a federation.

Its Unitary Features. But there are certain features of the constitution which have led the critics to deny its federal character. On account of these features the constitution has been called a 'quasi-federal', 'a unitary with subsidiary federal features', 'a federation with strong centralising tendency'. The following are those features which give to our constitution a unitary character:

(1) Under Article 249 the Parliament of India can make a law on any matter in the State List, if the Council of States passes a resolution by two-thirds majority declaring that it is necessary or expedient in the national interest to make a law on a particular subject.

(2) If the President declares an Emergency in the country, the Union Parliament can make law in relation to the matters in the state list and give directions to the states as to how they should exercise their executive authority in matters which are within their purview. During the proclamation of Emergency the Union Government may empower the union officials to execute matters mentioned in the state list and suspend the financial provisions of the constitution.

(3) If the President is satisfied that the Government cannot be carried in accordance with the constitution, he can under Article 356 issue a proclamation to the effect and can thereby assume all the powers of the State Government.

(4) In case the President declares financial emergency in the country, he can issue necessary directions, including orders for reduction of salaries and allowances of public servants. He may also direct that all the money bills passed by the

State Legislatures during the period of emergency will be subject to the control of the Union.

(5) Under Articles 256 and 257 the Union Government may issue administrative directions to the states in relation to certain matters and it shall be the duty of the states to carry out such directions.

(6) Under Article 371 the President has been empowered to provide, by order, for the constitution and functions of the Regional Committees for the states of Andhra, Maharashtra and Gujarat.

(7) Certain bills under Articles 31(3), 286(3) and 288(2) are to be reserved for the assent of the President and the same will not come into effect unless the President assents to them. Certain Bills passed by the State legislature necessitate final approval of the President.

In addition to the above provision the following ones are worthy of note:

(1) The Governors of the States are appointed by the President and in the exercise of their powers are answerable to him.

(2) The states cannot initiate amendments to the constitution. This power belongs to the centre alone.

(3) The powers have been so divided as to make the centre strong. The Central Government has power to make laws on 97 subjects enumerated in the Union List, 47 matters in the Concurrent List and on residuary matters. In case of concurrent matters, the central law prevails over the state law even if the former is a later in time and repugnant to the state law. In matters of State List, the Union can legislate under certain conditions and moreover it has full power to legislate on such subjects under Article 253 if a law is needed to implement any treaty, agreement or convention with another country.

(4) There is one constitution. The states unlike the states of the United States cannot have their separate constitution.

(5) There is only one citizenship recognised by the constitution. There is no citizenship of the states as it is in the United States.

(6) There is a single judiciary. There is no system of separate federal courts for the interpretation of federal laws. The High Courts and district courts take cognizance of central laws and the Supreme Court supervises the work of High Courts and hears appeals from them.

(7) The Council of States is not exclusively representative of the states. It has 12 members nominated by the President. The States are not equally represented in the Council. Unlike USA where senate accords equal representation to each state big or small.

(8) Though there are two sets of services—All India Services and State Services but there is no clear-cut demarcation of state laws and union laws. The state services administer the central as well as the state laws.

(9) The Election Commission is a centralised electoral machinery which superintends, directs and controls elections not only to the Parliament but also to the State Legislatures. The Commission is appointed by the President.

(10) The Comptroller and Auditor-General is appointed by the President who keeps vigilance not only over the union finances but also on the finances of the states.

There are other provisions which the critics point out in support of their contention and say that the Indian Constitution is more unitary than federal in nature. They not only look to the theory of the constitution but also point out to the practice adopted so far by the federal Government. The Chief Ministers of the States receive directions from the centre as to whom to include in their cabinets. The composition of the Ministry in the States is really the choice of the Government at the Centre. The Governors are party choices. On more than one occassion the Governors. Chief Ministers, Food Ministers, Education Ministers and others are called at Delhi to confer with the central bosses and receive instructions. The dominance of a single party both at the centre and in the states further adds to the centralised structure. The Central Government treats State Governments as subordinate Governor heading the states as their boy-errands and this habit has sufficiently entrenched itself. The Planning Commission has become a part of the Government.

These facts of the constitution and the realities of its working led Dr. K.C. Wheare to remark that "the new constitution establishes, almost devolutionary in character: a unitary state with subsidiary federal features". Our constitution has only the form of federation, but a mere form does not make it a federation, whatever may be the reasons for the constitution-makers to make the centre so strong and powerful as to make the states appear subordinate, the fact cannot be denied that to vest the centre with such vast powers as the Constitution of India has done, is a negation of the accepted theory of federation. D.D. Basu stressing the uniqueness of the Indian federal small system said, "The Constitution of India is neither purely federal nor purely unitary but is a combination of both. It is a union or composite state of a novel type".

SALIENT FEATURES OF CONSTITUTIONS

The Constitution of India is a native gift to the Indian people. It is the result of the deliberations of the Constituent Assembly—a representative body of the Indian citizens established in 1946 under the Cabinet Mission Plan. The Members were elected indirectly by Provincial Legislatures by the System of Proportional Representation by means of single transferable vote. The constitution-makers have given us a constitution unique in several respects. Its main features are the as follows:

(1) A Written and Comprehensive Document. The first feature which strikes a student of the Indian Constitution is its written and bulky nature. It contains 395 articles divided into twenty two parts and nine schedules. It is the bulkiest constitution in the world. There is hardly any constitution of the world which is so lengthy and so comprehensive as the Indian Constitution. Our Constitution is five times lengthier than the American Constitution. There are a number of reasons which explain the comprehensiveness of our constitution. Among these are:

(a) The Constitution of India includes provisions relating tot he governmental machinery of the States. In this respect it differs from the Constitution of United States and follows the example of Canada.

(b) The vastness of the country and the peculiar problems—social, linguistic, communal and geographical, led the founding Fathers to provide special provisions to meet these problems.

(c) The constitution carries a full chapter on the Directive principles of State Policy. This is novel. Besides it incorporate a detailed chapter on Fundamental Rights. Later through an amendment (42nd) fundamental duties were also added.

(d) Many provisions are of transitional nature. Part XXI only carries such provisions.

(e) The constitution makers have provided not only the structure of the government but also have provided matters of administrative detail.

(f) The provisions relating to the distribution of powers are more detailed than those of the Canadian and American Constitutions.

(2) Sovereign Democratic Republic. The Constitution of India establishes a Sovereign Democratic Republic in the country. It means that the country is sovereign in its internal and external matters. Internally, it is supreme, and externally, it is independent. Our membership of the Commonwealth of Nations and the United Nations is purely voluntary. The emphasis on Democracy is noteworthy, Ours is a democracy where the voice of the people is supreme. Our constitution is for the people, their welfare and prosperity. The word "Republic" also is significant in as much as it lays emphasis on the fact that the head of our state cannot be a king. He alone can be the President who is elected by the people in an indirect way. Justice, Liberty, Equality and Fraternity are the four pillars of Indian Democracy. The Preamble to the Constitution clearly emphasizes the fact that India is a democracy in form as well as in substance. Democracy, Socialism and Secularism are our ideals.

(3) Fundamental Rights. Another main feature of the Constitution of India is the incorporation of fundamental rights in it. A full chapter-Part III-including twenty-four Articles have been incorporated defining the rights of Indian citizens and those living in India. The main rights included under this chapter are:

(a) Right to Equality.

(b) Right to Freedom.

(c) Right against Exploitation.

(d) Right to Freedom of Religion.

(e) Cultural and Educational Rights

(f) Right to Property, and

(g) Right to Constitutional Remedies.

These rights are not only on paper but they are inviolable and justiciable. The Constitution by Article 32 has recognised the right of every person to move the Supreme Court for the enforcement of any of these rights. No law, ordinance, custom or usage or administrative order can abridge or take away any of these rights. A law which violates any of the fundamental rights is repugnant. It may, however, be mentioned that our rights are not absolute. The State may impose reasonable restrictions upon the enjoyment of these rights and may suspend their enforcement under conditions of grave emergency. It may also be important to note that during the British regime in India no Parliamentary Act had ever contained a list of fundamental rights. It is for the first time that the rights of the Indian citizens have been given a constitutional recognition. At a later stage according to 44th amendment Right to Property ceased to be a Fundamental Right; (See chapter on amendments). So these are six fundamental rights.

(4) Directive Principles of State Policy. A new and an important feature of the Indian Constitution is the incorporation of what have been called the Directive Principles of State Policy in Part IV of the Constitution. Dr. Ambedkar described it as a "novel feature" of the Constitution of India. These principles are those which seek to make economic and social democracy in India real. Some of these principles are; adequate means of livelihood, equal pay for equal work, fair distribution of wealth, employment for all, free and compulsory primary education, social security, adequate wages for all, organisation of village panchayats, introduction of prohibition and separation of Judiciary from Executive.

(5) Independent Judiciary. The constitution establishes the Supreme Court which is independent of the influence of the executive. The High Courts also may be said to be independent. The constitution includes a number of provisions like Articles 124, 221, 360, 112, 211, which guarantee the independence of Indian judiciary. The Supreme Court has the power of judicial review. In other words, it can determine the validity of any law passed by the State and declare it unconstitutional in case it violates any of the provisions of the constitution.

(6) Parliamentary Government. The constitution establishes a parliamentary form of Government for India. Under a parliamentary government, the head of the state is nominal. The real authority is vested in the cabinet which is collectively responsible to Parliament and remains in office so long as it enjoys the confidence of the latter. All the requisites of the parliamentary government exist in the Indian Constitution. The head of the state, i.e., the President is the nominal head. The real power is exercised by the cabinet. The provision of a President does not make India a Presidential Government. The position of the Indian President is analogous to the position of the British King or Queen.

(7) Partly Rigid and Partly Flexible. The constitution of India may be said to be neither rigid nor flexible. It is partly rigid and partly flexible. It is less flexible than the British Constitution and less rigid than the American one. There are certain provisions like Articles 4, 169, 240 which can be amended by a simple majority in Parliament. Some provisions, for example, 73(2); 75(6); 97; 125(2); 148(3) are of a transitional nature which shall remain in force only so long as Parliament otherwise provides. No article of the constitution is unamendable. However, there are certain provisions of a federal nature whose amendment requires not only a special majority in Parliament but also ratification by not less than half of the legislatures of the States.

(8) Single Citizenship. The Constitution of India recognises only one citizenship, i.e., Indian citizenship. In the U.S. and Switzerland there is double citizenship, citizenship of the Union and the citizenship of the state to which the citizen belongs. In India we are the citizens of the Union of India. This is unlike of true federation.

(9) A Secular State. The constitution of India establishes a secular state, although the world secular never occurred in the constitution in the original constitution. At a later stage it was added in the Preamble. The state is not to be guided by any particular religion in the discharge of its functions. There is no official or state religion. All religions are of equal significance and the people are free to profess and practise any faith. The state is wholly detached from religious dogmas and activities and is neutral in religious matters. No religion is to be given priority or preference over the other. All citizens enjoy equal rights without any distinction of religion, caste or creed. As a step towards secularism the constitution has abolished communal electorates and rights since the inception of the constitution introduced joint electorates.

(10) Other Features. In addition to the above main features there are some other features which may be discerned in the Indian Constitution. The constitution provides for Universal Adult Suffrage and abolishes communal electorates. The Introduction of adult suffrage", writes Prof. Srinivasan, "without any qualifications of any kin is the boldest step taken by the Constituent Assembly and is an act of faith". Hindi is devnagri script has been prescribed as the national language of India. It shall be the duty of the union to promote the spread of the Hindi language.

FUNDAMENTAL RIGHTS

It has always been a baffling problem for the constitution-makers as how to reconcile law with liberty, authority with freedom. If power is necessary for the maintenance of order in society, the abuse of power by those in authority is also likely. This likelihood of misuse of power has been sought to be minimised in modern constitution-making by incorporating certain rights as fundamental in the constitution of a country. The Indian constitution also carries as elaborate and comprehensive statement of fundamental rights. It covers an entire Part (Part III) of the constitution containing twenty-four (12-35) Articles. The provisions are detailed. They not only define the different rights but also minutely add to each right an elaborate set of limitations and reservations. The 42nd amendment of the constitution added a new part to chapter IV as IV A. It incorporates the fundamental rights of every citizen under article 51-A.

The fundamental rights as contained in our constitution are grouped under seven categories, they are:

1. Right to Equality. Articles 14-18 of the constitution deal with the right to equality. Article 14 guarantees to all persons equality before the law and equal protection of laws within the territory of India. In other words this Article assert the supremacy of the same law or Rule of Law. Every man irrespective of his status is subject to the same law and is amenable the same courts. No law will be held constitutional if it is discriminatory in its character. Article 15 provides that the state shall not discriminate against any citizen on grounds only of religion, race, caste, sex or place of birth; nor will any citizen be subject to any disability on any one of the above grounds in regard to access to shops, hotels, places of public entertainment or the use of wells, tanks ghats, roads and other public places wholly or partly maintained out of state funds. Article 16 guarantees equality of opportunity in matters relating to employment or appointment to public services to all citizens irrespective of religion, race, sex, descent, place of birth or residence. Under Article 17 untouchability in any form has been declared unconstitutional. Article 18 lays down that "no titles, not being military or academic distinction shall be conferred by the State."

2. Right to Freedom. Articles 19 to 22 cover the right to freedom. Of these Articles, Article 19 is the most significant. This Article guarantees seven fundamental freedoms. These are:

(a) freedom of speech and expression;

(b) freedom to assemble peaceably and without arms;

(c) freedom to form associations or unions:

(d) freedom to move freely throughout the territory of India;

(e) freedom to reside and settle in any part of India;

(f) freedom to acquire, hold and dispose of property; and

(g) freedom to practise any profession, or to carry on any occupation, trade or business.

However, the enjoyment of these freedoms is subject to certain conditions. Limitations may be imposed in the interest of security of state, friendly relations with foreign states, public order, decency or morality or to prevent contempt of courts, defamation, incitement to an offence. The right to assemble peaceably is subject to the conditions that the assembly must be peaceable and unarmed. The state may always impose reasonable restrictions in the interests of public order. It may be worthy of note that the seven freedoms guaranteed by the constitution are not absolute. The state has power to impose reasonable restrictions on their enjoyment.

Article 20-22 protect the individual's life and personal liberty,. Under Article 20 "no person shall be convicted of any offence except for violation of law in force at the time of the commission of the act charged as an offence, nor be subject to a penalty greater than that which might have been inflected under the law in force at the time of the commission of the offence. "The constitution prohibits the enactment of ex-post facto laws. Article 21 secures the most cherished of all fundamental rights. Under the said Article "no person shall be deprived of his life or personal liberty except according to the procedure established by law." The phrase 'procedure established by law' is a technical one and it is not the place to examine the phrase at length here. One thing, however, may be noted that the phrase 'procedure established by law' carries a meaning different from 'due process of law' - a phrase used in the American Constitution. By adopting the phrase 'procedure established by law' the Constitution makers have limited the authority of the courts in the matter of judicial review and placed supreme authority in the hands of legislature to lay down any procedure subject of course to the limitations in Articles 14, 20 and 22. Preventive Detection Act is sometimes considered an encroachment on personal liberty but in fact it is just like a loaded gun which can kill the people and also safeguard them. The gun must therefore be used safely.

3. Right to Freedom of Religion. This right is dealt under Article 25 to 28. Article 25 gives freedom of conscience and freedom to profess, practise and propagate any religion subject, of course, to public order, morality and health. The freedom of religion guaranteed by this Article has two aspects. in its positive aspect this Article safeguards the free exercise of religion by all persons. Negatively it prohibits the state to compel by law the person to accept any particular creed or religion. Article 26 allows everyone the right to establish and maintain institutions for religious and charitable purposes, to manage its own affairs in matters of religion, to own and acquire movable and immovable property and to administer such property in accordance with law. Under Article 27 "no person shall be compelled to pay any taxes, the proceeds of which are specifically appropriated in payment of expenses for the promotion or maintenance of any particular religion or religious denomination." Under Article 28 "no religious instructions shall be imparted in any educational institution wholly maintained out of state funds.

4. Right against Exploitation. Articles 23 and 24 deal with this right. Article 23 prohibits traffic in human beings including traffic in women for immoral purposes, begging and other similar forms of forced labour, Article 24 provides that "no child below the age of fourteen years shall be employed to work in any factory or mine or engaged in any other hazardous employment." However, the state may impose compulsory service for public purposes, but in doing so "the state shall not make any discrimination or grounds only of religion, race, caste or class or any one of them." it may be remarked that in prohibiting the employment of children below the age of fourteen years our constitution has gone in advance of that of the United States where there is no constitutional prohibition against employment of children in any industry.

5. Cultural and Educational Rights. Article 29 and 30 ensure to every section of citizens the protection of their language, script or culture. Article 29 also provides that "no citizen shall be denied admission into any educational institution maintained by the state or receiving aid out of state funds on grounds only of religion, race, caste, language or any of them." Article 30 "guarantees to all minorities whether based on religion or language the right to establish and administer educational institutions of their choice and declared that in granting aid to educational institutions, the state shall not discriminate against any educational institution on the ground that it is managed by a religious and linguistic minority." It is a matter to be considered if these provisions guaranteeing protection to linguistic minorities are not likely to hinder the growth of national unity, a national language and national culture in India.

6. Right to Property. Article 31 states that no person shall be deprived of his property except by authority of law and on payment of compensation. This right, however, will not prevent a state from making a law for the purpose of imposing or levying any tax or penalty for the promotion of public health or the prevention of danger to life or property or for fulfilling objections in regard to what is Declared to be evacuee property.

Article 31 was amended for the first time in 1951 and two additional Articles 31A and 31B were inserted. Article 31A was further amended in 1955 by the Fourth Amendment Act which added four new categories of legislation which shall not be open to challenge on the ground that they are inconsistent with or take away or abridge any of the rights conferred by Article 14, 19 or 31. The said Amendment also added a new clause (2A) to Article 31 to make away the jurisdiction of the Supreme Court in respect of the determination of compensation.

7. Right to Constitutional Remedies. Article 32 of the constitution confers upon every person the right to move the Supreme Court by appropriate proceedings for the enforcement of his fundamental rights. The appropriate proceedings or remedies are applications for the issue of directions or orders or writs including writs in the nature of Habeas Corpus, Mandamus, Prohibition, Quo-Warranto and Certiorari. These writs can be issued by the High Courts for protecting fundamental rights. Thus the jurisdictions of the Supreme Court and High Court is concurrent.

The provision relating to constitutional remedies was aptly described by Dr. Ambedkar as "the heart and soul of the constitution". And in fact it is so because it gives the assurance that the fundamental rights given by the constitution of India are not merely rights on paper but on the contrary are justiciable and that the Supreme Court cannot refuse to entertain applications seeking protection against violation of fundamental rights.

Before this discussion of fundamental rights is concluded it may be remarked that the fundamental rights to move the Supreme Court may be suspended by the President during the proclamation of an emergency by him. Secondly, it may also be noted that our fundamental rights are not absolute. They are subject to certain restrictions and we can enjoy them only within certain bounds. The critics have pointed out that so many limitations of such a wide import have been placed on enjoyment of fundamental rights that nothing substantial is left in them. The phrase like 'decency', 'morality', 'public order', 'health', 'security of state' etc. are so general and of so wise import that it would be simple to invoke them to curtail the rights guaranteed by the constitution.

However, it may be said that the limitations imposed upon the enjoyment of fundamental rights make a sense and are in a way necessary to ensure the security of state and equal enjoyment of rights by all. Absolute or unrestricted rights are not possible in a civilised society. In every country the rights of individuals are restricted directly or indirectly. In spite of the several limitations on our rights the fact remains that these rights are fundamental as they have been incorporated in the fundamental law of the land and are justiciable.

Significance of Fundamental Rights. Although the fundamental rights can be suspended in times of national emergency, the very fact that they have been incorporated in the constitution and backed with judicial safeguards gives them a unique importance for the people of our country. Their enjoyment has been assured to all under the normal circumstances. In Motilal Vs. Uttar Pradesh Government. Mr. Justice Sapru observed, "the object of these Fundamental Rights as far as I can gather from a reading of the Constitution itself, was not merely to provide security to and equality of citizenship of the people living in this land and thereby helping the process of nation building, but also, and not less important, to provide certain standards of conduct, citizenship, justice and fair play. In the background of the Indian Constitution, they were intended to make all citizens and persons appreciate that the paramount law of the land has swept away privileges and has laid down that there is to be perfect equality between one section of the community and another in the matter of all those rights which are essential for the material and moral perfection of man."

Fundamental Duties. The 42nd amendment of the constitution added fundamental duties in the Chapter on Fundamental Rights. It is a sort of code of conduct which every citizen is required to follow in his action and conduct. Following are the Fundamental Duties:

(i) to abide by the constitution and respect the ideals and institutions, the National flag and the national anthem;

(ii) to cherish and follow the noble in deals which inspired our national struggle for freedom;

(iii) to uphold and protect the sovereignty, unity and integrity of India;

(iv) to defend the country and render national service when called upon to do so;

(v) to promote harmony and the spirit of common brotherhood amongst all peoples of India transcending religious linguistic and regional or sectional diversities, to renounce practices derogatory to the dignity of women;

(vi) to value and pressure the rich heritage of our composite culture;

(vii) to protect and improve the natural environment including forests, lakes, rivers and wildlife and to have compassion for living creatures;

(viii) to develop a scientific temper humanism and the spirit of inquiry and reform;

(ix) to safeguard public property and abjure violence; and

(x) to strive towards excellence in all sphere of individual and collective activity so that the nation constantly rises to higher levels of endeavour and achievement.

The critics point out futility of mere enumeration of duties, in the absence of effective provisions for enforcing them.

MARXIST APPROACH

Marxian approach offers a complete approach to international politics in so far as it explains what is happening, How it is happening. To which goal is it heading for; and what would be the final stage of its development? To Karl Marx and his followers International politics is an extension of class war at the international level. In it the capitalists (states) are exploiting the poor (states) and for safeguarding their interests are resorting to wars and imperialism. The way out is that workers, who have no country of their own except the class to which they belong, must unite and throw off the chains (capitalism and all the evils that it contains). The immediate goal is the over throwing of capitalism and the final goal is the establishment of an international communist community free from exploitation, war, imperialism, inequalities and all the evils which characterise the existing capitalist dominated system.

The Marxian approach, as able supplemented by Lenin, enjoys support in all the socialist countries, China, however, accepts it only along with the thoughts of Mao Tse Tung. The popularity of this approach has been increasing ever since 1917 when Socialist Revolution came in Russia and the class struggle between the bourgeoise and the proletariat extended to the international arena encompassing the sphere of inter-state relations. In fact Marxism is a theory of internationalism since it has firm faith that class war between the rich and the poor extends from National to the international level and that the final shape of world is destined to be a communist international community.

Marxian View of International Politics. Marxian view of international politics is identical with its view of politics. Just as politics within a state involves a continuous struggle between the two contending classes. The rich (Owners of means of production, and having monopoly over production, distribution and exchange) and the poor (the workers; the under-dogs who suffer exploitation at the hands of the Rich) likewise international politics is a struggle between the capitalist states and the victims of capitalistic exploitation-the poor and backward states. International relations involve the exploitation of the poor states by the rich states through devices like imperialism and war. The end of this era is destined to come through the spread of socialism to all states. Workers revolutions against their internal exploiters would convert the states to socialism and then the forces of socialism would join hands to do away with capitalism at the global level. Finally international relations would get established on the basis of socialists brotherhood of all. The workers of the world would then live together as equal and participating members of the international community, free from exploitation.

PHILOSOPHICAL FOUNDATIONS OF MARXIAN APPROACH

Marxian approach to international politics is based upon several philosophical theories, concepts and assumptions.

(1) Marxian approach that class struggle between the two economic classes is historically and eternally a true fact. Each society is divided between two economic classes—the rich i.e., haves and exploiters who own and use the material means of production for their selfish (profit) ends, and the poor i.e., have nots and exploited class of worker which toils and yet suffers all exploitation at the hands of the rich. Likewise the international society also stands divided between capitalists (Bourgeoise) states-i.e., rich, developed and powerful states who hold a monopoly over the economic power and thereby over the political power, and the poor and down trodden underdeveloped states suffering exploitation at the hands of the Bourgeoise states. The former constitute the dominant and the latter the dominated part of the International society.

(2) Marxists advocate the view that all political relations, domestic as well as international are determined by material factors. They interpret politics and international politics as a process of evolution of material production forces. The material conditions and the class structure that these produce at a given time determine the nature and course of all politics as well as international politics.

(3) The socialist states have become strong. The worker shave come to consolidate power in these states. They have got rid of their exploitation at the hands of the bourgeoise. Yet exploitation of the

workers in capitalist states and in the Third World states continues and hence the relevance of Marxian call for throwing off exploitation is still there.

(4) The imperial-bourgeoise states are involved in strife and struggle among themselves and yet are united in maintaining and extending their control over the poor and developing states. They are maintaining a sort of a balance of power for preserving their system that suits them. The working class in these country is not yet in a position to over throw the capitalists rule either through the assertion of democratic instruments like elections or through revolutionary means. It however derives strength from the power that their counter parts enjoy in the socialist systems and the improvement in their condition that has given them power to limit their exploitation at the hands of the bourgeoise.

(5) Presently, the capitalist-bourgeoise states are maintaining their power through neo-colonial control over the people of the Third World countries These constitute the exploiting class in contemporary international relations. The other class is the working people, not only the industrial workers who are struggling hard to end exploitation. Their power to do so now stems from their capacity to resist the exploitation by their employers in the capitalist countries and the successes the working people have been able to register in the socialist countries where they exercise power. Working people of all countries are uniting in accordance with the call given by the communist manifesto.

FUNDAMENTALS OF MARXIAN APPROACH TO THE STUDY OF INTERNATIONAL FEATURES

Prof. Arun Bose in his article the Marxian Theory of international Relations, lists the following four features of the basis framework of Marxian view of international politics:

(1) Proletarian Internationalism. Marxian view of international politics is based upon the concept of Proletarian Internationalism which in itself is based upon the concept of unity of the working class at the international level. Marxism believes that the final objective to be secured is International Socialist Order. It stands for proletarian internationalism against bourgeoise nationalism.

The concept of Proletarian internationalism includes:

(i) the world proletariat have a common interest, independent of all nationality;

(ii) united action by the proletariat is one of the first condition for the emancipation of the proletariat;

(iii) in proportion as the exploitation of one individual by another is put an end to the exploitation of one nation by another will also be put an end to and hostility of one nation by another will come to an end; and

(iv) working men have no country, since the proletariat of each country must first acquire political supremacy; must first constitute itself in a nation, it is itself nationa.

(2) Self-Determination. Marxian approach accepts self-determination as the principle of organising the international society. It advocates that all nations of the world must be free to determine their political destiny. Colonial system must go. Self-determination by all the nations alone can give an enduring and strong basis to international relations.

(3) Anti-Imperialism. Marxian view of international politics believes that the break up of the bourgeoise world order is inevitable. Capitalism has reached its final imperialism. Wars, militarism and armed conflicts have becomc the ways of the imperialists. The contemporary era of international relations shows that:

(i) Capital has become international and monopolistic.

(ii) Hence, the proletariat revolution is possible not only in several countries of Europe, but even in onc capitalist country which would form the nucleus, the base, the hegemon, of world socialist revolution attracting to its cause the oppressed classes of other countries.

(iii) Uneven political economic development is an absolute law of capitalism.

(4) Peaceful Coexistence. The Marxists advocate that all nation-states of the world must live peacefully without criticising or undermining Orther's social economic and political systems. It implies:

(i) Proletarian Revolution would be victorious first in several countries, or even in one country;

(ii) It has to survive capitalistic encirclement by relying on anti-imperialist contradictions; and

(iii) The best way to achieve this is to try to work at the relations of peaceful coexistence between socialist states and, at least, some if not all the capitalist states.

The acceptance of peaceful co-existence however does not mean that the limits of socialism have been achieved; that capitalism and imperialism will continue to prevail and shall never be over thrown. It only means that the struggle between the labour and capital, between the social systems, will continue in different forms till such time as the ideas and achievements of scientific socialism triumph over capitalism.

Marxian approach to international relations as such is based upon the concepts of Proletariat internationalism, anti-imperialism, self-determination and peaceful co-existence. It believes in the onward march of international relations towards its logical and destined conclusion—end of capitalism-imperialism, withering away of state, unity of the proletariat as one nation and true internationalism. Emphasising full relevance of Marxian approach to contemporary international relations, the 27th congress of the Communist Party of the Soviet Union observed "World development confirm the fundamental Marxist Leninist conclusion that the history of society is not a sum of fortuitous elements, that it is not a disorderly 'Brownian motion' but a law-governed onward process. Not only are its contradictions a verdict on the old world, on everything that impedes the advance, they are also a source and motive force for social progress. This is progress which takes place in conditions of a struggle that is inevitable so long as exploitation and exploiting classes exist."

The Marxian approach to international relations is regarded by the socialists as the approach to international politics which can fruitfully explain its past, present and the future. The increased importance of international economic relations and the emerging struggle between the forces of colonialism (neo-colonialism) & anti-colonial Third world and former socialist states is quoted by the supporters of the Marxian Approach to observe that these facts fully bring home the utility of Marxian approach for analysing international relations. However, the critics describe it as a utopian approach which cannot realistically explain the realities of politics and international politics. The exploitation of workers by the workers in the 'Socialist Countries', the continued presence of powerful national sentiments even in the hay days of socialism in the former socialist states of Eastern Europe and Russia, the acceptance of peaceful co-existence instead of open and total support for class struggle and revolution, the strength of nationalism against proletarian or class internationalism etc., cannot be really explained by the Marxists. In this last decade of the 20th century non-communist regimes have been established in almost all the former socialist states of Eastern Europe and the Republics of the former Soviet Union. These states have now abandoned Marxism in favour of Democratic Liberalism.

CRITICAL EXAMINATION OF MARXIST APPROACH

Karl Marx is indeed the greatest political thinker of all times. No other political thinker has aroused greater controversy or exerted greater influence on future generations as did Marx. It is because he devised a new method of analysing social reality and all the processes—social, political and economic going on within it. His method is what we term as Dialectical and Historical Materialism. It is through this method that Marx explained the laws of social and historical development.

Marxist Methodology. Marx borrowed the dialectical method from Hegel. Hegel applied that method for giving a rational explanation for the philosophy (development) of history. Hegel claimed that progress or development in the world occurs as a result of the dialectical clash of ideas. Instead of ideas, Marx applied dialectics to the field of matter. In this way, Marx, no doubt, borrowed the dialectical method from Hegel, he turned it upside down. He, infact, reversed it. Hegel held the view that conflict lies in the world of ideas, and material forces are only reflections thereof. Marx, on the contrary, asserted that there is a clash of material forces and ideas are only the products of material environment in which men live. In this way, Marx believed that it was the material conditions which provide momentum to social history. He considered matter to be the primary substance round which everything revolves. He emphasised that history was not the unfoldment of the divine spirit but, on the other hand, the product of human interaction that is guided and controlled by matter.

In the process of their day-to-day social activity, men enter into specific economic relations with one another—economic relations with a view to satisfying the essential needs of human existence. Essential needs are satisfied through production. Production necessitates the use of some instruments or forces of production. The forces of production are the raw-materials or natural resources and the techniques with the help of which those materials are converted into consumable goods. The forces of production give rise to certain Relations of production. (Relations of production mean the relations into which men enter for the purpose of production.) It is with reference to the forces of production and the relation of production that the essential nature of society can be understood. The history of development of society can be analyzed only with reference to the history of the development of production processes in that society. A change in forces (modes) of production occurs by the discovery of some new raw-materials or by the incorporation of certain technological innovations in the instruments or techniques of production. A change in the forces of production leads to a change in the relations of production. The new relations of production come in conflict with the old relations leading to a revolutionary social change.

Change is thus the essential principle of both the social and natural phenomenon. Society is always in a state of flux. It is always in movement bringing about change and development. Engles says, "All Nature from the smallest thing to the biggest, from a grain of sand to the sun, from protista to man, is in a constant state of coming into being and going out of being, in a constant flux, in a ceaseless state of movement and change."

Consequently, there is a change in society also that brings about its movement of progress. But this change is not unlinear (gradual, in a straight line). It is in the shape of dialectical movement—development through clash between opposite and anti-thetical forces.

For the purpose of analysis, it is essential to study the relationship between the existing form of society with its earlier form. On the one hand, it is to be a historical analysis in which the past, the present and the future would be linked. On the other hand, it would require analysis of the political structures in relation to the economic structures. The study of the linkage (relationship) between these institutions and structures is the most important to Marx. Only this approach gives a proper understanding of society.

It is why Marx linked the dialectical view of reality with a materialist conception of history. But, unlike Hegel, he believed in the primacy of matter and its ultimate reality. The intellectual and political life of society has to be studied and analysed in relation to the existing mode of production and the relations of production. Consequently, he sought to find the determinants of social and political developments in the material conditions of the life of the people. He stressed that social environments are not created by people.

The forces of production constitute a base on which grows a superstructure which enables this system to endure. The superstructure is represented by thoughts and practices of man manifested through economic, political, religious and other institutions. In simple words, superstructure is represented by laws, moral codes, religion, art, governmental forms, police, bureaucracy, schools, mass media, the supporting theories and the like.

Certain scholars have termed the materialist conception of history as economic determinism. It means Marx tried to reduce the richness and variety of historical events to the single factor-economics. Marx did not regard economics as the only factor.

It was within this framework of dialectical and historical materialism that political structures, institutions and processes had to be studied and examined. According to Marx, it was essential that political science should concern itself with questions regarding the State and Government within this wider context of historical development and the specific nature of relations of production within that society. It was in the 'Communist Manifesto' that Marx gave the general pattern of historical development in the world in terms of four stages—primitive Communism, ancient society, Feudalism; and

Capitalism. Capitalism is the fourth and the final stage through which we are passing at present. The capitalist stage would lead to the socialist stage which in turn to the Communist stage in which there would be no class.

States not Actors of International Politics. In this way, the States are not actors of international politics. They rather reflect the deeper and wider historic-economic forces. The States could not, therefore, be the primary units of analysis.

State, according to Marx, is not an independent or autonomous political unit. It is rather an instrument of exploitation in the hands of the exploiting class against the exploited class. All human history, according to Marx, is a history of class struggles in which State has been used as a political weapon to suppress the exploited class. Accordingly, State is but an instrument of class and not that of nation. It pursues not national but class interest. A worker has no motherland. They must unite on international basis to throw off the chains of slavery imposed upon them by their respective feudal or bourgeois masters.

On the other hand, we find that the dominant approaches of both the Traditional and the Behavioural variety take nation-State as the actors in the drama of international politics with a view to achieving their national interest They always aim at the enhancement of national power and influence. The Realist School advocates that the proper study of international politics involves the study of interest defined in terms of power as distinct and autonomous from other fields.

The Marxian Approach rejects the role of State as an autonomous political unit aimed at the achievement of national interest. The Functional Approach of international politics is, however closer to the Marxian Approach in so far as they visualise an international community transcending national—geographic unit. Still, there are two marked differences between the Marxian and Functionalist Approach. First, the Marxian Approach regards contradictions as the moving force in history but Functionalists believed in complementarily. Secondly, the achievement of truly Communist and just international society would be possible as a result of historical forces and not depend upon the good sense and good offices of national decision—making agencies as the Functionalist advocate.

Critical Appreciation. We find, however that the classical Marxian Theory of international politics is far from satisfactory in explaining the phenomenon of international politics. As envisaged by Marx, the nation-States have not perished. On the contrary, they have not only shown a tendency of survival but of further consolidation. And Nationalism, instead of class affinities, continues to be the pattern of international relations. The Third World countries have gained freedom by dint of the concept of Nationalism itself. Not only that, even the countries claiming to be Marxist have to evoke nationalist sentiment. Instead of getting unity in the socialist movement over the world, there has been a serious split as we find between the Soviet Union and China. More than that, Communist parties in almost all the countries have been split into various factions—in India it is split at least into three broad divisions. The Communist regimes are fighting out in between themselves but at the same time practising peaceful co-existence with the capitalist systems.

Marxism and Internationalism. Marxism is international in approach. It appeals workers of the world to unite against capitalist exploitation going on in the whole of the world. For the abolition of explaitation is required what is exactly international socialist revolution. Lenin also pleaded that the Russian Revolution was only the first in a series of revolutions that were yet to come in European countries. Revolution in Russia is, according to Lenin, the first stroke at the weakest link in the chain of Capitalism.

It was Stalin who gave a radically different interpretation. He advocated the idea of 'Socialism in one country' meaning thereby that Socialism should first of all be consolidated in one particular country and then work for bringing about revolution in other countries. Mao remarked that Stalin was never keen on bringing Communist Revolution in China. He wanted the Communist Party of China to continue helping and playing a secondary role to the Chiang Kai Shek's K.M.T.

The concept of 'Peaceful co-existence' cannot be explained in Marxian terms. It was Khruscheve who brought this concept into being by collaborating with the capitalist world. Peaceful co-existence means existence of both Socialism and Capitalism side by side. Marxism advocated bringing about revolution in the whole of the world.

Marxism, Imperialism and Neo-colonialism. On finding that the Marxian prediction that Communist Revolution will occur in highly inindustrialised countries has not come true. Lenin gave a new interpretation. He pleaded that Imperialism is the highest stage of Capitalism. He sought to justify that revolution will come in the world when the capitalist countries reach the stage of Imperialism. Marx could not, according to Lenin, foresee that imperialism will be the highest stage of Capitalism. Accordingly, any force that cut at the root of colonialism is progressive.

Anti-colonial and nationalist movements in countries what we term today as Third World was regarded by the Soviets as progressive or aligned with Socialism. Even the introduction of public sector economy in these countries was seen as a good sign. But the concept of mixed economy in these countries turned out to be more favourable to private investment and thus opposed to Socialism. Even then Soviet Russia began to develop closer relations with the countries not on account of ideological reasons but out of gaining alliances and friendships against the Amerian bloc.

The Chinese policy towards the Third World countries is no less contradictory. The lent support to moves against regimes which were not friendly. At the same time, China gave support to many regimes which were not socialist but otherwise inclined favourably towards China.

China played a rival to Soviet Russia in giving leadership to the Third World countries. Out of this rivalry China condemned Soviet Russia for pursuing a policy of Social Imperialism. They further accused Soviet Russia of hegemonism (creating areas of influence and dominance). She accused Russia as a neo-imperialist (Imperialism practised in a new form) with respect to the East European and Third World countries. This charge is not wholly unfounded but we can also not deny that Soviet Russia has helped many countries in a way that none could.

Scholars like Sweezy, Baran, Galtung and Gunder Frank have brought out the fact that the Western pattern of aid helps only the better off classes in the Third World countries. It is why in spite of so many development Plans the condition of the poor goes from bad to worse. It widens still further the gap between the poor and the rich. So long as the present political structure remains infact, there is no possibility of development. In Marxism there is no such thing as 'non-capitalist' mode of development other that Socialism. The attitude of Russia on this aspect is nothing other than what may be termed in power politics terms. The Soviet and Chinese stand that they are not interested in 'exporting revolution' and their support to the demand of the New World Order within present political structures is nothing other than leading a support to status quo.

It is thus clear that all countries pursue foreign policies to gain their own national interest irrespective of the fact whether they are capitalist or socialist. Fore the achievement of this interest even socialist States like Soviet Russia tried to adjust to the? Western Capitalism. It is explained that Soviet Russia entered into detente with the West to gain Western technology. The same is true is case of China which has sought American help. She is securing massive foreign investments much against the principles of Socialism.

No denying the fact the Soviet Russia compected with U.S.A. in terms of areas of strategic influence yet it did not succeed in breaking the chain of Capitalism in the Third World countries.

In this way, we find that the Classical Marxian Theory of international politics where State has no role to play, has totally come out to be untrue. State has assumed more important role and this role is getting strengthened with the passage of every day. Modern Communist States are following a policy that is against the fundamental principles of Marxism. Clearly, the international socialist movement has failed.

FASCISM

Fascism is derived from the Roman word, fasces, which means a bundle of rods and an axe. This represented the authority of the state. As a political philosophy, fascism glorified the state and exalted the nation above all individual interests. Like Russian

Communism, it was a product of the conditions generated by the first World War. In fact, these two philosophies have certain superficial resemblances. Both are critical of the parliamentary system of democracy, and are alike in their insistence on establishing a one-party state, and on the exclusion of all hostile elements from any share in the control of the state. Both have established dictatorship. But in spite of these, the two doctrines are fundamentally different. Unlike the communists, the fascists have not tried to provide a theoretical basis for their doctrines. They have not created a whole philosophy of thought; rather they have picked up suitable ideas from a number of sources.

Like the Hegelians, the fascists conceive the nation as the ultimate thing in evolution. The nation is not a mere aggregate of individuals. It is an organism representing the ultimate synthesis of all moral and spiritual values of the race. Fascism is opposed to all forms of individualism. The individuals are completely subordinate to the state. "Everything within the state, nothing against the state, nothing outside the state."

Fascism is also strongly imperialistic. The nation, as it grows strong, must have the means of expansion and self-expression. It must have room to expand. To the fascists, an empire represents an inspiration and a duty.

Fascism has put forth the theory of the corporate state. The state does not consist of individuals, but of groups, or corporations. Labourers, employers and all other interests are to be organised into corporations which are to serve as electoral colleges for the election of members to the fascist legislature.

The notion of the totalitarian state which fascism seeks to build up is opposed to the liberty of the individuals. The state may be a brilliant organisation, but it is not the end. It is only a means for promoting the development of the personality of individuals. Its appeal to force and to war will mean ultimately the destruction of civilisation. The fascist dictatorship is a poor substitute for democracy which believes in equality and freedom. All these tenets of fascism show that it has tried to create more uniformity than unity.

LIBERALISM AND PRINCIPLES

Liberalism is an outstanding ideology of the modern world. The European countries have been greatly affected by this ideology. But it is extremely difficult to define Liberalism exactly as it is not a certain and systematic concept. The ideals and thoughts of several thinkers are included in it and they have changed with the passage of time.

Max Learner has called it, "Perhaps the most disputed term of our generation".

Sartori has gone to the extent of saying that Liberalism is so prone to change what it should be left to the self-styled restrictions.

True Meaning of Liberalism. The word 'Liberalism' originated from Latin word 'Liberalis' which means Free Man. This principle basically believes in the freedom of an individual. According to Encyclopedia Brittanica, freedom is the very basis of Liberalism. In the words of MacGovern," Liberalism as a political creed is a compound of two separate elements. One of these is democracy, the other is individualism." Liberalism is deadly opposed to all the forms of Dictatorship. Sartori has defined Liberalism in simple words, "Very simple, Liberalism is the theory and practice of an individual liberty, judicial defence and the constitutional State."

Hallowell has summed up the meaning of Liberalism in the beliefs given below:

1. Supremacy of individual's personality and spiritual equality of all individuals.
2. Freedom of individual's will.
3. Welfare of an individual.
4. Existence of rights connected with life, freedom and property.
5. Law should be above the administrative order.
6. An individual should be independent in the political, social, economic and religious spheres.
7. Creation of State to safeguard natural rights.
8. An individual can revolt against State in case of violation of conditions stated in the agreement.

9. Existence of supreme reality based on reason and when an individual can posses it through contemplation.

MAIN PRINCIPLES OF LIBERALISM

Liberalism is an amalgam of several ideologies, yet it has a few fundamental principles, mentioned below:

1. **Faith in Human Reason.** The basic principle of Liberalism is faith in human reason. The Liberals like John Locke and Thomas Paine, in seventeenth and eighteenth centuris, emphasised the fact that man should not accept any tradition which is useless if tested by reason. Liberalism attaches more importance to reason than feelings.
2. **Opposition to History and Tradition.** Superstitions, traditions and blind faith were prevalent in middle ages and Liberals opposed it. Liberalism led to the revolutions in England, America and France.
3. **The Purpose of State is to Develop the Personality of the Individual.** According to Liberals, development of individual's personality embodies the development of State.
4. **Man is the End, State is the Means.** The liberals consider man to be end and State to be a means. The object of State is to fulfill man's aims.
5. **Supporter of Human Freedom.** Liberalism supports man's freedom and believes that freedom is his birth-right. According to Laski, "Liberalism is directly related to freedom for it came as a foe of privileges by virtue of birth or creed".
6. **Faith in Secularism.** The Liberals stressed man's religious freedom and suggested that religious institutions should be kept apart from State. Thus the liberals have faith in secularism.
7. **State is Artificial.** The libeals believe that State is an artificial institution and not a divine and natural one.
8. **Support of Democracy.** Liberalism is an inseparable part of Democracy, and Democracy is the very basis of Liberalism. Liberalism believes in people's sovereignty.

9. **Constitutional Government.** Liberalism originated as a reaction of absolute rule and it supports Constitutional Government.

10. **Belief in the Concept of Natural Rights of Man.** Liberalism believes in the concept of natural rights of man which he possesses since birth. According to Locke, the main natural rights are right to life, liberty and property.

CRITICISM OF LIBERALISM

Liberalism has been criticised on the basis mentioned below:

1. **Man is not Selfish Only.** Liberals like Bentham regard man to be selfish, but this conception is wrong. No individual can be wholly selfish or wholly selfless. It is improper to propound a concept on the basis of one feeling.
2. **State is not a Necessary Evil.** Several Liberals consider state to be a necessary evil, but this is incorrect. State is not an evil; rather it is a natural expression of man's social consciousness. Modern State is a welfare state and is responsible for satisfying the needs of individuals.
3. **It is Incorrect to Say that the Individual is the Sole Judge of His Interests.** This view point of Liberals that man judges his interests better is correct to some extent. But there are certain matters in which society and state understand individual's interests in a better manner.
4. **Conception of Liberty is Wrong.** Liberals' conception of liberty is wrong. The Liberals wrongly think that State's functional sphere and individual's Liberty are opposed to each other. In fact Liberty can be positive and constructive only when it is under some control.
5. **Not a Clear Concept.** The concept of Liberalism is vague. It can not be defined in certain terms and all the Liberals don't support all the principles.
6. **Individual is not a Separate Unit from Society.** According to Liberals, society is a group of free individuals. But in fact, society and individual are not opposed to each other and their interests are the same.

❐

2

Governability in India

BUREAUCRACY, EVILS AND REMEDIES

There are many distorted versions of the true meaning of Bureaucracy. The word 'bureaucracy', which literally means "desk government" management by bureaus, is sometimes used with contempt as is taken to imply irresponsibility, arbitrariness, officiousness and regimentation.

Technically, the term is used in two senses. In its larger sense bureaucracy is used "to describe any personnel system where the employees are classified in a system of administration composed of a hierarchy of sections, divisions, bureaus, departments and the like." In its narrow sense it is used to a describe "a body of public servants organized in a hierarchical system which stands outside the sphere of effective public control." In other words we may say that bureaucracy is a system of administration in which professional class of expert civil servants administer the affairs of the state in an impartial manner and it is organized in an hierarchical way, Bureaucracy is an expert professional class of civil servants. These servants administer on the basis of rules and regulations rather than on grounds of favouritism. They are recruited on the basis of merit.

Some Views on Bureaucracy. Bureaucracy "signifies the concentration of administrative power in bureaus or departments and undue interference by officials in matters outside the scope of state interference." —Encyclopedia Brittanica

"A system of government the control of which is so completely in the hands of officials that their power jeopardises the liberties of ordinary citizens." —Harold G. Laski

"Bureaucracy is the systematic organization of tasks and individuals into a pattern which can most effectively achiever the ends of collective efforts." —Pfiffner & Presthus

Max Weber's View on Bureaucracy. Max Weber has given the following three characteristics of bureaucracy:

1. The regular activities required for the purpose of the bureaucratically-governed structure and distributed in a fixed way as official duties.
2. The authority to give the commands required for the discharge of these duties is distributed in a stable way and is strictly de-limited by rules concerning the corrosive means, physical or otherwise, which may be placed at the disposal of officials.
3. Methodical provision is made for the regular and continuous fulfilment of these duties and for the execution of the corresponding rights.

Thus it may be said that bureaucracy is a system wherein the officials are servants of the king in the fullest sense of the term and are organized as a distinct branch of the government. They constitute a distinct official class with its own etiquette, powers and privileges.

Evils of Bureaucracy. The bureaucratic system of administration has been vehemently criticized by writers of eminence. Some times the civil servants are contemptuously labelled 'Bureaucrats'. Prof. Laski defined bureaucracy as "a system of government the control of which is so completely in the hands of the officials that their power jeopardises the liberties of the ordinary citizens." The American President Hoover observed, "There are three implacable spirits in bureaucracy—self-perpetuation, expansion and demand for more power." Prof. W.A. Robson has summarized the defects of bureaucracy in these words : "The maladies from which bureaucracy most frequently suffers are an excessive sense of self-importance of their office; and indifference towards the feeling or the convenience of individual citizens; an obsession with the binding and inflexible authority of the departmental decisions, precedents, arrangements or forms, regardless of how badly or with what injustice they may work in individual cases; a mania for regulations and formal procedure, a preoccupation with the activities of particular units of administration and inability to consider the government as a whole: a failure to recognize the relations between the governors and the governed as an essential part of democratic process." The evils pointed out by Robson may be briefly stated as follows:

1. ***Circumlocution.*** The severest criticism against bureaucracy is levelled due to its lengthy and round about way of doing work. The bureaucrat cares very much for formal rules and regulations. Every case has to run up the full course of going up and down. The officers care more for routine than for results. In the words of Burke "They think the substance of business not much more important than the forms of it." Charles Dickens in his famous novel 'Little Dow' it describes the circumlocution office in the words, "Boards sat upon them; Secretariat minuted upon them; commissions gabbled about them, clerks registered, entered, checked and ticked them off, and they melted away. In short, all the business of the country went through the circumlocution office, except the busines that never came out of it, and its name was legion."
2. ***Red Tapism.*** Closely allied with circumlocution is the defect of red tapism. Red tapism means blindly following the formal rules and regulations though following the prescribed rules is not itself bad but the dogged and blind attachment to them certainly kills the efficiency of work. The civil servants are trained in rules and regulations.
3. ***Formalism.*** Bureaucracy makes too much use of forms and formalities which makes the official lose his sense of judgement and initiative. The language and the form of official letters and the method of putting note on the file are fixed beforehand, each officer acts mechanically. W. Bajehot describing the life of an official writes, entering the office young, he copied letters for five years, he made an index of papers for nine years, he made an analysis of

documents for five years; more when he commenced at last to transact business it was strictly of a formal character and he was upwards of twenty years in the public service before he ever decided on anything of special importance no wonder that he was unwilling to decide anything, that he refferred everything to somebody else, that he corresponded in his best handwriting, with another public officer; his entries were most correct but the transactions were normally wrong; the book-keeping was admirable but affairs recorded feeble or inefficient."

4. ***Unresponsiveness.*** Bureaucracy follows routine procedures which breed inflexibility. The official becomes specialist, oriented towards techniques rather than people. In the words of Lord Russel, "Bureaucracy tends to develop a negative psychology perpetually prone to prohibitions." The vision of the public servants become myopic due to their training and experience in one particular institutionalized activity.

   There is no gainsaying in the fact that the evils mentioned above are there in the bureaucratic system. In popular sense bureaucracy is understood as the negative of liberty and popular sovereignty. But we cannot afford to do away with it. The defects of bureaucracy are not incurable.

5. ***Despotism.*** Lord Hewart believed that the individuals will lose their liberties under the despotism of the bureaucrat. Today the ardent bureaucrat has usurped the legislative and judicial powers of the government. Ramsay Muir has attacked the growing powers of the civil servants.

6. ***Empire Building.*** Bureaucracy perpetuates the evil of dividing the work of government into isolated and independent sections each blowing its own trumpet. There units cease considering themselves as part of a bigger whole—the government. They start considering their little empires as ends in themselves. The following are some of the safeguards which are worthy of attention:

(i) Decentralizaiton of authority.

(ii) Effective political control of the Parliament and the Cabinet.

(iii) Good leadership and management control.

(iv) Just and efficient personnel management.

(v) An effective and flexible organization.

(vi) Research into administrative methods.

(vii) A continuous internal review of means, objectives and results.

(viii) A professional morale antipathetic to bureaucratic methods.

(ix) Effective participation of the layman or non-official in the administration.

In conclusion, we may say that bureaucracy is a necessity to the modern age and its outright condemnation is irrational. To quote John A. Veig, "Granted that the government bureaucracy contains its share of droves and dullards self servers, and time servers, of minor tyrants and soulless automatons, these comprise all told but a fraction of the total. Man for man and woman for woman, there is not now and there never has been any reason for believing them to be different from their fellow citizens who are self-employed or work in private industry. The bureaucracy is now so numerous that no citizen can indict it without indicting the nation itself."

BUREAUCRACY AND PROBLEMS

Bureaucracy refers to the set of officials working under the ministerial responsibility and providing clerical as well as administrative help to the cabinet in various aspects of the administration. Bureaucracy if let loose, may over-shadow the cabinet itself but it is not to be presumed that bureaucracy is something beyond the control or even without control. Much of the haughtiness of the bureaucrats depends upon the Ministers under whom they work.

Modern view is that, bureaucracy must not be considered as 'a political' institution. Ramsay Muir defined the Civil Officials i.e. the bureaucrats as the band of high graded personnels, and "neutral in politics, that they serve every government faithfully and sincerely, work in anonymity and have no ambitions or political affiliations is totally false."

It is evolved from what has been said and what is being said of bureaucracy is that, only a dynamic, strong and able Minister can keep the civil servants under his control. Though it is much expected, but not found, that bureaucracy is not politicised Ministers are non-permanent executive whereas bureaucracy constitutes the permanent executive. It has been found that when the bureaucrats have found their grievances unsolved, they have approached the parliamentarians to seek help. In India, instances are there to prove that even the defence bureaucracy is politicised. It is stressed that, "When the officials became dissatisfied with promotion policies, they established a liaison with Ministers of parliament for the redressal of their grievances. The military officials supplied facts to the Press and Members of Parliament, and canvassed for their case of candidatures, and went to Parliament where they sat in the galleries to hear their cases being discussed. Thus, in the process higher echelons of military bureaucracy were politicised. If Menon was accused of creating cliques in the Military, many military officials were in no way less cliques."

Pandit Nehru kept control over bureaucracy hence he, accepted General Thimayya's resignation when he cast aspersions of Krishna Menon the then Defence Minister regarding promotion policy. Nehru kept bureaucracy completely under control, Lal Bahadur Shastri finding it difficult, depended more on the bureaucrats like L.K. Jha. Shastriji was under the impression that Jha had got a control over the administrative and political machinery of the country. Thus, Shastri "created an instrument, on which he could rely completely." Jha was instrumental in drafting Kutch Agreement and papers on the Cairo Conference and so they came quite close to the nucleus of the power-sphere. It has been commented rightly that : "Soon Jha was found everywhere-whether on government committees or with foreign delegations led by Shastri, Jha was present. Key foreign ambassadors, who came to know things quitely, started calling on Jha, and Jha went on spreading his tentacles to foreign policy, defence negotiations with foreign countries and all economic matters."

Bureaucracy, that thrived under Shastri became more spearheaded when Mrs. Gandhi assumed the office of the Prime Minister of India. She preferred bureaucrats to the Home Minister Gulzarilal Nanda who resigned owing to the indifferent attitude of his Secretary L.P. Singh, in November 1966. This weakness of the Home Minister Nanda and Prime Minister Mrs. Indira Gandhi was obvious when they failed to suppress the growing unrest among the Delhi police as well as the violence that occurred when protest-demand against the slaughtering of cow was staged before Parliament.

Though Mrs. Gandhi continued to rely upon the bureaucracy operating in the Secretariat, yet she was choosy in depending on only seasoned bureaucrats like D.P. Dhar and P.N. Haksar. The Prime Minister's too much reliance on the seasoned bureaucrats led Michael Brechar to comment that Indian bureaucracy has become, "an interest group in its own right." The role of ministers declined due to the importance shifted in the court of bureaucrats. Dharam Vira, a retired ICS Officers commented that the Ministers "have initially been reached to the position of mere camp followers-as far cry from the concept of first among equal."

Cases have been found when, "Politicians flirted with some of the ICS Officers. Department secrets and files have been supplied to factional leaders by the civil servants to be used against the Ministers."

Thus the Indian bureaucracy is a sensitively politicised group. It has been established, that "Civil Servants have interests, and self-projection of interests is undertaken by highly placed individual officials, and this self-projection of interests brings them into contact with the Members of Parliament, especially, those who can articulate their interests in the democratic system. This fact has been under scored because Indians have been fed on the British theory of 'neutrality of civil service in politics', a fact which has been exploded by this case. All organised have their political activity; bureaucracy cannot be an exception."

In the modern era a civil servant who is keen for a stay at a station of his choice or who aims at promotion through underhand means is supposed to have political God fathers who should keep his interests safeguarded. Evidently in this age of 'give and take' the ministers of effective M.Ps/M.L.As will like to have pound of flesh.

INDEPENDENCE OF BUREAUCRACY

Elaborate provisions have made in the Constitution of India to make the public services independent. The Union Public Service Commission has been created "with a view to removing all possibility of temptation likely to compromise the twin principles of objectivity and non partisanship which have to be constantly kept in view by the Chairman and members of the commissions in the performance of their duties."

The following arrangements have been made to ensure the independence of the civil servants:

(i) Appointment is made by the head of the State for a fixed period of time.

(ii) Salary is drawn from the Consolidated Fund of India, and it cannot be varied against them during their service period.

(iii) A civil servant is promoted on the basis of the length of his service and efficiency.

(iv) They cannot be re-employed in any government service except the Public Service Commission.

(v) A civil servant is selected on the basis of merit.

(vi) Removal or suspension can take place only after a thorough enquiry made by a Judge of the Supreme Court.

(vii) He has been debarred from taking part in politics.

From the point of view of political participation, it is clear that Indian bureaucracy is uncommitted if looked from the angle of the system prevailing in Communist Countries; but our bureaucracy can be called 'committed' to the constitution only. The term committed bureaucracy is being misused. The bureaucrat remain committed to a particular party whatever their policy and way of thinking. Hence the party in the opposition suffers at their hands if the latter comes in power the committed civil servants are uprooted and degenegrated.

PROBLEM OF COMMITTED BUREAUCRACY

The issue of committed bureaucracy got impetus towards the end of 1969, when Mrs. Indira Gandhi called the administrative machinery as an obstacle in the way of national development. The Congress saw its split, and Mrs. Gandhi heading a minor government strongly felt that bureaucracy needed to be infused with the feelings of commitment.

The civil servants, thus were accused of being conservative and reactionary. The government felt that there was a need to evolve a bureaucracy that would be committed to the policies and resolutions framed for the development of the country. It was concluded that a recruitment policy should be evolved to select the personnels who could be helpful in implementing the social and economic transformation requiring to be done for creating a secular and socialist society in India.

However, the supporters of the committed bureaucracy avoided to give any specific explanation on what they meant by the term the committed bureaucracy. Referring to this vague term, Ashok Mehta reacted, "It is not easy to understand what a committed bureaucracy means in a democratic policy. In a democratic set-up governments change, their political complexions latter, and it is difficult to understand to what set of ideas the bureaucracy is to be committed."

Due to the lack of proper explanation the meaning of the term 'Committed Bureaucracy' was taken in the Communist sense and thus the critics pointed out that if it is so, the country might be thrown into an era of totalitarianism. It was feared that if the system of committed bureaucracy prevailed it would lead to the gross administrative misuse and a state of awfulness and chaos. The danger arising out of it were pointed out as, "If the civil servant is to be committed of Mrs. Gandhi's Government and its policies, then by the same definition, he will have to be committed to a Jana Sangha administration in Delhi, to a Mr. Jyoti Basu is West Bengal, to a Swatantra administration in Orissa, the DMK in Madras, Akali administration in Punjab and so on". The idea of committed bureaucracy has been criticised as a grave notion in a democratic society as it means committed to the ideology of the ruling party and not the constitution.

CRITICAL APPRECIATION OF INDIAN BUREAUCRACY

The ghost of committed bureaucracy disappeared with the landslide victory of Mrs. Gandhi in 1971 elections. Though constitution makes specific provisions to guard the independence of bureaucracy yet in practice following lacunae are present in the system:

1. The Regulation Act, titled, the UPSC (Exemption from consultation) Regulation 1958 (as amended up to 1974) provides that the government is not bound to consult the Service Commission in the case of certain category of officials. But it is doubted that with this regulation the centre as well as States, "are free in cases where the considered the matter of sufficient importance to follow their own judgment provided they are prepared to justify their action before the legislature."
2. It has been found that most of the civil servants try to help the leaders in power in order to win some favours. In this context it is commented, "Indian bureaucracy during Congress Party rule was in collusion with Congress Party leaders and even factional leaders actively worked for the personal or the party interests of the Congress leaders. This was done in return for the benefits of promotion and better jobs."
3. The evil of political patronage spoils the integrity of the intelligent and spirited class of bureaucrats. Honest work does not win them as much laurels as the political patronage. Hence we find brain drain. The talented leave government jobs and take to business or migrate to alien lands.
4. It is stated that there is a deep rooted evil of corruption among the Indian bureaucrats. Often the stories of public scandals are brought to the surface (for instance the recent Antulay Trust Affairs which sparked noisy scenes in Parliament in the Monsoon as well as winter Session in 1981 and more recently even the Supreme Court of India

upheld lower courts version regarding Antulay's Trust affairs) A.D. Gorawala hints out, "Corruption in all its guises stalks the land unashamed. It is... cities, towns, villages, all acknowledge its presence and admit its power."

5. Lack of integrity pervades the whole bureaucratic organisation committing "yesmanship". As Bhalerao opines, yesmanship, "also pervades the Indian bureaucracy. The young public servant soon realises that a realistic and disinterested assessment and outspokeness are not received very warmly by his immediate superiors and may even lead to his relegation to unimportant work. " In Gorewala Report it has been pointed out that, "Most men are too anxious to court the pressure of those who are above them."

POLICE ADMINISTRATION

District administration is primarily responsible for maintaining law and order in the district. If this is not maintained, the very basis of having district administration will be shaken from the foundations. In maintaining law and order, the police plays a big role and such it is essential to study police administration at the district level.

Nature of Police Administration. At the district level police administration is expected to act in accordance with the provisions of the law and most obey all laws in true spirit in which these were enacted. The police must aim at educating the people so that the public becomes an active participant in running district administration. The police should not interpret or ignore laws simply because these do not suit its convenience.

Police Administration in Operation. It was as early as in 1861 that the First Police Act was passed envisaging the system for the running of police administration. This Act was subsequently amended in 1895. Subsequently changes were brought in the Act in 1925, 1946 and 1949. After independence this Act has been modified several times to suit the aspirations and expectations of the people. Briefly speaking policy administration is as under:

Senior Superintendent of Police.

Superintendent of Police.

Additional Superintendent of Police.

Deputy Superintendent of Police.

Assistant Superintendent of Police.

Inspector of Police.

Sub-Inspector of Police.

Head Constable.

Constable.

Duties and Responsibilities. The Senior Superintendent of Police is incharge of the District police. In police administration he exercises almost the same powers as the District Magistrate. He maintains law and order and also ensures that laws passed by the government are enforced. He also carries out inspection of the police stations and takes steps for the protection of life and property of the people. He also ensures proper police arrangements at the time of festivals and visits of V.I.P's. He listens to the complaints made against subordinate Police Authorities.

Next to Him Comes Superintendent of Police. For Smaller districts he is incharge of police administration. He performs all the duties of Senior Superintendent of Police in his District. He works under the guidance of District Magistrate. In his work Superintendent of policc is assisted by one or more Additional Superintendents of Police. They are assigned particular areas and jobs and are expected to finalise certain cases at their own level. In addition to Additional Superintendent of Police a Superintendent of Police, is also assisted by other officers.

Then Comes Deputy Superintendent of Police. In smaller districts he is only next to Superintendent of Police. He is incharge of general police administration of the staff working under him. He is put incharge of an administration circle.

The District is divided into circles and each circle is put under the charge of Circle Inspector. In a circle there may be more than one Circle Inspector. A Circle Inspector is assisted by Sub-Inspectors.

There are Senior and Junior Circle Inspectors. The routine duties in the Circle are carried out by Head Constables. But the lowest in the rank is constable who ensures that the laws are not violated. The police is also assisted by village chowkidar in the performance of its duties.

Methods of Recruitment. All high posts in the police organisation are filled up by the people belonging to Indian Police Service. The officers down below the rank of Deputy Superintendent of Police can be either recruited direct or are promoted from the employees already working in the department on the basis of their service records. The constables are however, recruited direct from the market.

Central Bureau of Investigation and Police. There are many cases which cannot be investigated by the police in normal way. For that the help of Central Bureau of Investigation is sought. It is the responsibility of police to assist the C.I.B. in the discharge of its functions without any hindrance and influence.

Other Police Agencies. In addition to what has been said above there is reserve police which helps the police in times of emergency. Then there is provincial armed constabulary which is semi-military type organisation and helps police only in crisis. There are also public prosecutors who process cases falling under Indian Penal Code and prosecute the people who violate provisions of Indian Penal Code. In addition, in the district we have women police and traffic police as well.

An Assessment of Police Administration. Police administration in the district has come much under criticism. It is said that the police is usually violent and undermines the dignity of citizens. It harasses the people and puts pressures to get its own point of view accepted. It is also said that the police uses too much force which is quite often useless and coercive. On the other hand, the police argues that it must use with the criminals, if it is to get information from them. The use of excessive force is only a relative term. It is also argued on behalf of the police that it is over-burdened with work and ill-paid. It is also not well equipped to deal with latest crime techniques.

CENTRAL VIGILANCE COMMISSION

Central Vigilance Commission is primarily responsible for keeping a vigil on the activities of the public servants who fall within the purview of the central government. It has extensive jurisdictions.

Central Vigilance Commission. The Government of India has always been keen that the public servants in India should maintain high degree of integrity which should be beyond all doubts. It was with this end in veiw that in 1955, an Administrative Vigilance Division was created in the Ministry of Home Affairs at the Centre. In 1962 Santhanam Committee was set up by the Central Government which was knwon as 'Committee on Prevention of Corruption'. It was on the recommendations of this Committee that a Central Vigilance Commission headed by Central Vigilance Commissioner was set-up. The Commission extends its jurisdiction and powers in respect of all matters to which the executive powers of the central government extend. This includes public undertakings and corporate bodies.

The Function of the Commission. It can investigate into every alleged understand transaction in which public servant is involved or in which his integrity is doubted. It can call reports from concurred agencies to properly investigate into cases and can refere the matter to CIB. It can also initiate review of procedure and practices being following in administration for maintaining national integrity. The Commission sends its report to the Ministry of Home Affairs, which in turn places that before the Parliament.

It undertakes an enquiry into any transaction in which a public servant is alleged to be involved. It can also take over under its direct control complaints for further action. It also initiates review of procedure and practices of administration.

Modes of Corruption. The Commission has identified serveral modes of corruption which include acceptance of sub-standard stores, mis-appropriation of public money, borrowing money from contractors, showing favors firms/contractors, claiming false allownaces, possession of disproportionate assets and abuse of official position. Some other modes of corruption include acceptance of illegal gratification in recruitment or missue of government employees for personal work, moral turpitude and acceptances of gifts.

Appointment of Commission. Central Vigilance Commission is appointed by the President for a period of 6 years or till he attains to age of 65. His status has been equated with that of the Chairman of UPSC. The Commission consists of Commissioners, an officer on special duty, a Chief Technical Commissioner, Six Technical Commissioners and three Commissioners for Departmental Enquiries. In addition to this, there are number of persons in the lower staff. It is not a statutory body but has set up with an executive resolution. It has advisory functions which are similar to those of the UPSC. Its enquiries are based on complaints received from the individuals as well as from other sources such as press. MP's or reports of Parliamentary Committees and so on. It also receives complaints direct from the people. A definite procedure has however, been laid down for the disposal of complaints received so that these are attended immediately and promptly. When a complaint is received the matter can be referred for enquiry to the concerned department and the Commission may advise that on the future course of action.

The Commissioner has power to call for all papers and documents.

Vigilance Organisation in the Ministry. Each ministry has a vigilance organisation. Head of the office/ministry will be the chief vigilance officer and a link between his ministry and also Chief Vigilance Commissioner. In each public undertaking there will be a vigilance officer. In some cases these officers are full time while in other cases they are part-time. The Commissioner will assess the work of officers. There is also an officer of public sector undertaking which looks after vigilance affairs. In some cases they are whole while in other officers they are part-time officers. Every such officer is appointed in consultation with central vigilance officer. Central Vigilance Officers in the ministries are usually of the rank of Deputy Secretary and vigilance officers are of the states of Under Secretary. Central Vigilance Commissioner assess the work of vigilance officers. Chief Vigilance Officers and vigilance officers are required to review the work of the progress of vigilance work of their respective ministries, department.

Assessment of the Work of Vigilance Commission. Vigilance Commission was set up with a view to check corruption among public servants. Though the Commission was setup with all the good intentions, but it appears that it has not been as active as its was expected when suggestion was made for its setting up. Though it has brought several officers and other categories of public servants in its network, yet corruption among public servants has as yet not come to an end. Many public servants manage to escape out of its network. One possible reason for this could be that whereas number of public servants has very much increased staff of the commission has not proportionately increased. Therefore, much remains to be done, if it is desired that the Commission may effectively work.

Every effort is being to ensure that integrity of public servants is fully maintained. Efforts are being made to ensure that public servants are not corrupted or bribed. The methods have proved very useful and effective and none has a doubt that if attempts are contained to be made the day is not far off when the nation will have pure administration.

REMEDIES AGAINST ABUSE OF POWER

Judicial control can be in the form of suing the State or the Government itself or the public official concerned for this wrongful acts. The system regarding the suibility of the Government and public officials differs in the countries following the system of Rule of Law or the Administrative Law. The Rule of Law system prevails in England and her Dominions and other Commonwealth countries including India, the U.S.A. and Belgium. The Administrative System is practised in France and other countries of continental Europe. The system of Rule of Law implies that everybody, high or low, official or private citizen is subject to the same ordinary law of the land and that the official cannot take shelter behind the State sovereignty in committing mistakes in his official capacity. In the words of Dicey. "With us (English) every official, from the Prime Minister down to a constable or a collector of taxes is under the same responsibility for every act done without legal justification as any other citizen." That means that the State cannot be held liable for the wrong acts of its officials even if they had done an injury to a citizen while working in their official capacity and that the officials themselves are personally liable for their wrongful acts. The State thus enjoys immunity from liability in torts i.e., it cannot be used for damages and a suit can be brought for damages only against the official responsible for inflicting an injury.

This remedy is hardly or any use, because the damage decreed by the courts cannot usually be recovered due to the impecunious condition of officials. An agitation has therefore, been going on to so reform this system as to make the remedy effective.

Suability of State in India. In India the suability of the State is governed by Article 300 of the Constitution, which in a nut shell provides that the State is suable for contracts i.e., trading functions. In practice, however, the State is ordinarily held responsible for the tortuous acts of its servants. In the case of Rao vs. Khusal Chand the Bombay High Court has held that the Government cannot claim any immunity from illegal sets under S. 176 of the Government of India Act, 1935, when it illegally requisitions land under the Bombay Land Requisition Ordinance. Except in case of strictly 'sovereign' acts, the Government of India is liable for all unlawful acts of its servants. Recently, the question of liability of the State Government arose when the Supreme Court upheld the Rajasthan High Court's Order, allowing compensation of Rs. 15,000 against the State for the tortuous act of one of its employees (driver of a Government jeep who knocked down a person on the foot-path, causing him multiple injuries, which resulted in his death). The State's main contention was that it was not liable for the tortuous act of its employee. Dismissing the appeal of the State of Rajasthan, the Chief Justice, Mr. B.P. Sinha of the Supreme Court, in his judgment delivered on February 2, 1962 held that a state would be as much liable for the tortuous acts of its employees, committed during the course of employment, as any other employer. 'The immunity of the Crown of the United Kingdom was based on the old feudalistic notions of justice, namely that the King was incapable of doing a wrong and therefore he could not be used in his own courts.

Administrative Law System. On the other hand in the countries where the system of Law prevails, the liability of the State for the wrongful acts of its official is fully established. There the officials are tried not in the ordinary courts of law but in the administrative courts which award damages from the public funds to the aggrieved individuals. The State may later deal with its officials at fault as it thinks fit but so far as the citizen is concerned he uses and obtains damages from the State.

The protagonists of this system contend that firstly, it frees the administrative authorities from the jurisdiction of the law corrupts and hence secures promptness, fearlessness and efficiency in administrative action. Secondly, Judges they believe who are only experts in the law and know nothing about the technicalities of administration or executive exigencies should not be entrusted with the task of settling administrative disputes. Administrative disputes should be decided from the point of view of public policy and not from the legal point of view. Hence, the necessity of administrative law which ensures decisions of administrative actions by administrative experts. Thirdly, the system provides remedies to the citizens against the wrongful acts of the officials, whether high or low, at a very low cost and rather with greater case than is possible under the Rule of Law System.

Certain Exceptions of the Rule of Law. It may be mentioned here that even in countries following the Rule of Law system, there are certain officials like the Heads of the State who enjoy legal immunity and are not amenable to the ordinary courts of the land. For example, the British Monarch is completely immune from legal liability in respect of any of his or her acts done in public or private capacity. "The King can do not wrong" is a legally accepted phrase in England. The American President is also immune from any legal proceedings during the term of his office. He can only be impeached by the Congress and it is only after his removal from office that he can be tried in ordinary courts for crimes committed by him as President. In India personal immunity from legal liability is granted to the President of the Union and Governors of the States for any act done in exercise of their powers and duties as laid down in the constitution. During their term of office they are immune from any criminal proceedings even in respect of their personal acts.

The other officials can be used both in civil and criminal cases. Civil proceedings can be instituted against an official for anything done in his official capacity after the expiry of two months notice. No such notice, however, is necessary when the official is to be proceeded against for an act done outside the scope of his official duties. When criminal proceedings are to be instituted against an official for the acts done in his official capacity, previous sanction of the President or the Governor as the case may be is to be obtained.

ADMINISTRATION LAW

As we see in the countries where the system of Administrative Law prevails, the liability of the State for the wrongful acts of its official is fully established. There the officials are tried not in the ordinary courts of law but in the administrative courts which award damages from the public funds to the aggrieved individuals. The State may later deal with its officials at fault as it thinks first but so far as the citizen is concerned he uses and obtains damages from the State.

The protagonists of this system contend that firstly, it frees the administravite authorities from the jurisdiction of the law courts and hence secures promptness, fearlessness and efficiency in administrative action. Secondly, it is contended that the Judges, who are only experts in the law and know nothing about the technicalities of administration or executive exigencies should not be entrusted with the task of setting administrative disputes. Administrative disputes should be decided from the point of view of public and not from the legal point of view. Hence, the necessity of administrative law which ensures decisions of administrative actions by administrative experts. Thirdly, the system provides remedies to the citizens against the wrongful acts of the officials whether high or low, at a very low cost and rather with greater ease than is possible under the Rule of Law System. The French Council of State has been working with perfect smoothness, independence and impartiality and people look upon it with respect, pride and confidence. Accroding to Mr. C.K. Allen.

CERTAIN EXCEPTIONS TO THE RULE OF LAW

It may be mentioned here that even in countries following the Rule of Law system, there are certain people like the Head of the State who enjoy legal immunity and are not amenable to the ordinary courts of the land. For example the British Monarch is completely immune from legal liability in respect of any of his or her acts done in public or private capacity. "The King can do no wrong" is a legally accepted phrase in England. The American President is also immune from any legal proceedings during the term of his office. He can only be impeached by the Congers and it is only after his removal from office that he can be tried in ordinary courts for crimes committed by him as President. In India personal immunity from legal liability is granted to the President of the Union and Governors of the States for any act done in exercise of their powers and duties as laid down in the Constitution. During their term of office they are immune from any criminal proceedings even in respect of their personal acts. Civil proceedings in respect of their personal acts are permissible even during their term of office but only after two months written notice stating the nature of the proceedings the cause of action, name, address etc. of the party concerned, and the relief claimed. The Ministers have however, no such immunity and they are therefore, liable for crimes and torts and are amenable to thc ordinary courts.

EXTRAORDINARY JUDICIAL REMEDIES

In addition to the judicial remedies of suing the Government or its officials, citizens have the following extraordinary remedies also against the excesses of public officials:

1. **Habeas Corpus.** Hebeas Corpus literally means "to produce the body of" The writ of Habeas Corpus is accordingly issued by the courts in the nature of an order calling upon the person who has detained another to produce the latter before it in order to let in know on what grounds he has been confined and to set him free if there is no legal justification for the confinement.

   The writ of Habeas Corpus is granted as a matter of right and not at the discretion of the court. *i.e.*, the court is obliged to issue it if there is prima facle case for supposing that the person is unlawfully deprived of this liberty. It is something very peculiar that our Constitution declaring India to be a Sovereign Democratic Republic and providing a lengthy chapter on Fundamental Rights of the citizens should authorize the Parliament and State Legislatures to pass laws providing for the preventive detention of a person in times of peace. It is indeed a great limitation on the citizens right to liberty. But it cannot be helped as there are still some anti-social and subversive elements in our country and to prevent them from becoming a serious danger to the welfare of society or to the security of the state, it is necessary to exercise detention power under the Preventive Detention Act. It is worth mentioning here that this power cannot be used arbitrarily by the executive. A person cannot be detained for more than 3 months unless the cause of his detention is investigated by an Advisory Board consisting of persons of the status of the judge of a High Court within that period and the Board has reported that there is, in its opinion, sufficient cause for such detention. In a democratic country, Preventive Detention Act providing restriction on the liberties of the people, seems most obnoxious. The earlier it is scrapped. the better it would.

2. **Writ of Mandamus.** Mandamus literally means "a mandate" or "a command". The writ of Mandamus is a command issued from a common law court of competent jurisdiction directing any person, corporation on inferior court requiring him or them to do some particular thing specified therein which appertains to this or that office and is in the nature of public duty. In short, it is a writ issued to a public official to do a thing which is part of his official duty but which he has so far failed to do. This writ cannot be claimed as a matter off right.

This writ can, therefore, be issued on the fulfillment of certain conditions. Firstly, the petitioner must prove that the has a legal right to the performance of a legal duty by the respondent.

Secondly, the right must be a public right and duty sought to be enforced as a public duty.

Thirdly, the petitioner should ordinarily be the same person whose right is being infriged.

3. **Prohibition.** The writ of prohibition is a judicial writ issued by a superior court to an inferior court for the purpose of preventing it from usurping jurisdiction with which it is to vested. This writ then commands Lower Court not to do a thing which it is not legally competent to do . This writ can be claimed as a matter of right. Prohibition should be differentiated from Mandamus.

   Firstly, a Prohibition writ can be claimed as a matter of right while the Mandamus cannot.

   Secondly, Mandamus can be available against any public authority or official, but Prohibition can be issued only against judicial and quasi-judicial tribunals. It is not available against purely administrative or legislative authorities or acts.

   Thirdly, Prohibition does not require any personal right or interest on the part of the applicant but in the case of Mandamus he must prove his personal legal right.

4. **Injunction.** Injunction is a writ issued by the Court requiring a person to do or refrain from doing a thing. It is called "mandatory" when it requires the defendant to do a thing and "preventive" when it requires the defendant to do a thing and "preventive" when it requires the defendant to refrain from doing it. Mandatory injunction thus would appear to be resembling Mandamus because they both command the respondent to do a thing but actually there is a difference between the two.

5. **Certiorari.** Certiorari literally means to be certified or to be made certain. The writ of Certiorari means the direction

of a superior court to an inferior court for transferring the records of proceedings of a case pending with it for the purpose of determining the legality of proceedings and for giving more satisfactory effect to them than could be done in the inferior court concerned. The writ of Certiorari resembles the writ of Prohibition as both are meant to supervise the work of the judicial authority, but Certiorari is something more than the writ of Prohibition. Prohibition is only preventive and curative. Prohibition prevents an inferior court from proceeding with a trial but Certiorari enables the superior court to sent for record of the proceedings and other of the inferior court, to enquire into its legality and to quash the order if found beyond its jurisdiction.

6. **Quo-Warranto.** Quo-Warranto literally means 'What warrant or authority.' The writ of Quo-warranto is issued by the court to enquire into the legality of the claim which a party asserts to an office or franchise and to oust him from its enjoyment if the claim be not will-founded or to have the same declared forfeited. The conditions necessary for the issue of the writ are that the office under dispute must have been created by the Constitution or by a statute and should be public and not a private one. Secondly, the tenure of the office must be permanent i.e., it should not be terminable at pleasure. Thirdly, the persons proceeded against must have been in actual possession and user of the office. The purpose of this writ is thus to try a claim to a public office. The burden of proof to prove his title is on the respondent.

The Supreme Court in India has been empowered under the new Constitution "to issue directions, orders or writs in the nature of Habeas Corpus. Mandamus. Quo-Warranto and Certiorari for the enforcement of fundamental rights of the Indian citizens and the High Courts have been empowered within their jurisdiction "to issue to any person or authority directions, order or writs for the enforcement of fundamental rights and for any other purpose."

LIMITATIONS OF JUDICIAL CONTROL

The judicial remedies mentioned above under the "Rule of Law' system provide an effective control against official excesses or abuse of power and in protecting and liberties and rights of the citizens. But judicial control has certain limitations. In the first place all administrative actions are not subject to judicial control. There are many kinds of administrative actions which according to the Constitution cannot be reviewed by the law courts. Then there is a tendency on the part of the Legislature also to exclude by the law certain administrative acts from the jurisdiction of the judiciary. For example, in India and Administration of Evacuce Property Act. 1950 vests final judicial powers in the Custodians and Custodian General of Evacuee Property and the law courts have no jurisdiction to interfere in the decision made under this Act.

Secondly, eve in those administrative actions which are within its jurisdiction, the judiciary cannot be itself take cognizance of excesses on the part of officials. It can intervene only on the request of somebody who has been affected or is likely to be affected by an official action. Human nature being what it is legalism is the last sphere in which it would like to enter.

Thirdly, the judicial process is very slow and cumbersome. The courts follow certain set technical pattern of procedure beyond the comprehension of a layman and then the procedure is so lengthy that it cannot be knwon as to when the final judgement shall be given. There have been instances when cases have been pending with the courts for years together. Sometimes the decision of the court comes when the damage has been done beyond repair : "Justice delayed is justice denied". An aggrieved person cannot wait indefinitely to avail himself of the judicial remedy. The dilatory judicial procedure will not in any way console the sufferer or reconcile his affected mind.

Fourthly, the government may deprive the person of the remedy granted to him by the court by chaning the law or rules thereof. In a case of High Court ordered that the petitioners be promoted to the senior posts of Professors and that direct selection for these posts contravenes the provisions of the States Reorganisation Act in as much it changes the conditions of service of the petitioners to their disadvantages.

Fifthly, Judicial action in incredibly expensive and cannot therefore be taken advantage of by many people. Filling a suit means paying the court fee, fee of the lawyer engaged and cost of producing withnesses and undergoing all inconveniences which only those who can afford can bear. This keeps many people away from the court who prefer to suffer.

Lastly, The highly technical nature of most of the administrative actions saps the force of judicial review. The judges are only legal experts and they may have little knowledge of the technicalities and complexities of administrative problems. Their legal bent of mind may hinder them in arriving at a right decision. They have to follow the prescribed procedures and observe some formalities. W.A. Robson writes, "The liability of the individual official for wrong doing committed in the course of his duty is essentially a relic from past centuries when government was in the hands of a few prominent independent and substantial persons so called Public Officers, who were in no way responsible to ministers or elected legislatures or councils. "Such a doctrine is utterly unsuited to the Twentieth Century State, in which the Public Officer has been superseded by armies of anonymous and obseure civil servants acting directly under the orders of their superiors who are ultimately responsible to an elected body.

THE COMMUNITY'S CONTROL OVER ADMINISTRATION

Every popular government is ultimately responsible to the people "Public Administration is, in fact, a creation of public opinion, unlikely to transcend its creator in depath of vision and insight except on marginal matters." Though the people generally do not bother about the governmental machinery as they are busy in their daily pursuits with little time to think of the governmental machinery, yet the fact remains that it is they who set the whole mechanism of democratic government in motion. They elect the head of the State and the members of legislature directly or indirectly. In some countries they even elect the officials. Public administration is meant to serve the people and it is they who suffer at the hands of irresponsible administration.

The formal methods of community's control over administration are the following:

(1) Election. The head of the State is usually elected by the people directly and indirectly. The Prime Minister in a parliamentary system is the leader of the party returned in majority by the people. The Ministers are the members of the legislature and are elected by the people. The top administrative officials are responsible to these elected representatives of the people.

(2) Recall. The system of recall is the logical corollaryof the election of officials. Under this system the electors can call for the dismissal of an official before the expiry of his term. The system of recall makes the official continuously subject to popular whims and understanding and thus neglectful of the correct practices of his profession.

(3) Pressure Groups. "Pressure Group is an American term for a section of the public organised and active in the pursuits of some special interests which its members join to promote". Usually a pressure group is a vested group. It is a group of industrialist and traders with organised commercial interests. These pressure groups bring pressure both upon the legislature through 'lobbying' and upon the administration through liaison officers. It is difficult to exactly assess the extent of influence exerted by pressure groups upon administration, as no factual study has so far been made. However, in the United States they are quite active.

The activities of pressure groups are sometimes useful to the administration. They may convey to the administration the reactions of the 'interests' to administrative decisions in time and may thus enable it to adjust its policy and activities so that there may be no opposition from those particular interests. But sometimes these groups employ illegitimate means to secure an official favour.

(4) Advisory Committees. A direct link between members of administration and the public has during the recent years appeared in the advisory field. The advisory committees a councils or boards are appointed at different levels of administration from the top to the lower levels. These councils or committees consist of important citizens and of representatives of the special interests. The government departments providing social services have a specail need of such councils. Stressing the need of these bodies in administration the Haldane Committee observed "so long as advisory bodies are not permitted to impair the full responsibility. Ministers of Parliament, we think that the more they are regarded an integral part of the normal organization of a department, the more will Ministers be enabled to command the confidence of Parliament and the public in their administration of the services which seem likely in the increasing degree to affect the lives of large sections of the community." Sir Arthur Salter has said, "The proper use of advisory bodies is the right answer of representative democracy to the challenge of corporate states as they are an invaluable instrument for breaking administrative meausre on to the back of the public." Thought the function of these bodies is merely advisory, but they render a highly positive service to Public Administration. They functions as a liaison agency between the public and the officials. They interpret the feeligns and interests of the people of officials and the aims and purposes of the official activities to the public.

DIVISIONAL COMMISSIONER IN STATE

Below the State level and above the District level, in India we have regions or divisions. Each state is divided into regions and is looked after by a Regional or Divisional Commissioner.

Divisional Commission. He is incharage of a Division and represents the Division in it. Whether there should or should not be the post of a Divisional Commissioner is matter of controversy. Several Committees setup after the independence have recommended the abolition of this post. But today, it is gradually being appreciated that a Division Commissioner is a useful link in the running of state administration.

Functions of Divisional Commissioner. Divisional Commissioner is required to perform the following important functions:

1. He decides appeals against District Collectors in revenue matters.
2. He co-ordinates revenue and public administration activities in the State.
3. He settles inter-departmental disputes at the divisional level.
4. He supervises the work of muncipal and Panchayati Raj institutions.
5. He examines police administrative reports.
6. He tooks after relief operation work.
7. He takes steps for promoting faith of the public in democratic institutions.
8. He ensures that public servants behave properly with the public.
9. He discharges O & M responsibilities.
10. He ensures integrity of public servants.

Case Against Divisional Commissioner. After independence there was a cry for the abolition of the post of Divisional Commissioner, in the words of V.K.N. Menmon, "Divisional Commissioners have been a some what controversial matter in India. Their abolition as, more or less a fifth wheel of the administrative coach was one of the early political demands in India and some states have experimented with their abolition in recent years." Bengal Administration Enquiry Committee (Rowland Committee) recommended the abolition of Divisional Commissioner on the ground that the office is very expensive as compared with the work handled by him.

Case for Divisional Commissioner. But today trend is in favour of retention of the post of Divisional Commissioner. The reason put forth for the retention of this office are under as under:

1. It is necessary to retain this post for giving guidance to young and junior District Collectors. In the words of A.D. Gorewala, "At a time when District officials are so often young and inexperienced, there is much to be said for having a body of senior officials who cannot only guide them on occasions but be a strong barrier between them and the stocks that sone both from above and below."
2. By the abolition of his post there will be centralisation of work and authority, as against decentralisation which has been accepted as useful system of administration in India.
3. Today he supervises both police and revenue administration. It is very difficult to find out an officer, who will perform supervisory functions in his absence. It is more so because officers at the lower level doing this work are already over-burdened with work. Assigning them more responsibility will result in delays and inefficiency.
4. The abolition of the post will bring the people to the contact of the state governments who are at present dealt with the disposed of by the Divisional Commissioner. In this way the work of state Government will considerably increased.
5. A Divisional Commissioner today act as a buffer between the government and the administration. He is a very useful buffer and abolition of his post is likely to create many complication and administrative problems.

In the regional administration, the importance of Divisional Commissioner is being increasingly realised. A.D. Gorewala has rather appropriately said, "His supervision of other departments may be informal but none the less effective. A good many injustices can be prevented and a great deal of corruption stopped if it is known that the Commissioner of the Division is prepared to take considerable trouble personally to find out the exact facts and try to have action taken accordingly."

POWERS AND FUNCTIONS OF SUPREME COURT

The Supreme Court is the highest body in our judicial system. Under the new constitution it is the highest court and no appeals can be taken to any other authority or court against its decisions. Of course, the President can grant pardons, reprieves remissions of punishments etc. if he so likes, to a person declared criminal by the court of law.

Appointments of Judges. The Chief Justice and other Judges of the Supreme Court are appointed by the President. In their appointment the President may consult such other judges as he thinks necessary but he is not found by the advice given to him by any body in this regard. However in the appointment of the judges of the Supreme Court the President must consult the Chief Justice of the Supreme Court. When the office of Chief Justice of India falls vacant or when he is, by reason of absence or otherwise, unable to perform the duties of his office these shall be performed by one of the other Judges of his court as the President may appoint for the purpose.

The Constitution lays down that there will be a Chief Justice and not more than seventeen other Judges of the Supreme Court. The Parliament has a right to increase the number of Judges in the Supreme Court. The constitution is silent about the minimum number of Judges, but strength could not possibly be less than five. This is so because the quorum of Judges in constitutional matters is five.

Tenure of Office and Removal. The Judges of the Supreme Court continue in office till they attain sixty-five years of age but can resign earlier as well. The Judge can be removed from office for incapacity or corrupt behaviour. If the two Houses of Parliament present an address to the President recommending the removal of a Judge from office on the ground of proved misbehaviour or incapacity, the president, shall remove that judge from his office. However, that address of the Parliament, which recommends the removal of a Judge, has to be supported by a majority of the total membership of each House and not less than two-thirds of the each House, present and voting.

After retirement, no Judge of the Supreme Court shall plead or act in any court or before any authority within India. He also can not accept any other assignment in or India abroad without prior approved of the government.

POWERS OF THE SUPREME COURT

(1) Original Jurisdictions. The Supreme Court has vast original jurisdictions. While exercising powers the Supreme Court acts as a balancing agency between the centre and the states. Those disputes which can be sent straight to the Supreme Court are:

(a) Disputes arising between the centre and the states;
(b) Disputes between states themselves; and
(c) Disputes betwen the central government and one or more states on the one hand, and one or more states on the other.

These disputes arise either on a question of power or jurisdiction or on a constitutional matter. It can be a dispute on the interpretation of Constitution or jurisdiction over the subjects mentioned in one of the lists.

However, there are certain such disputes which cannot be decided even by the Supreme Court, e.g. those relating to treaties and agreements concluded with the erstwhile Indian princely states before the commencement of the Constitution leading to their merger in the Indian Union etc.

(2) Appellate Jurisdictions. Besides original jurisdictions, the Supreme Court has appellate jurisdictions as well. Appeals are against the judgements of the High Courts or other courts. The Supreme Court is the highest court of appeal in India. The judgements and decisions of the Supreme Court are final.

(a) Appeals in Civil Matters. In civil matters an appeal can be taken to the Supreme Court if the High Court gives a certificate that *(a)* the amount involved in the particular case is not less than twenty thousand rupees or *(b)* even though the amount or property involved in the case is not worth that amount the High Court feels that it is a fit case for appeal to the Supreme Court. Besides, the Supreme Court may grant special leave to appeal against any judgement of lower court.

(b) Appeals in Criminal Matters. Appeal can be taken to the Supreme Court in criminal cases when:

(i) the High Court has reversed the judgement of lower court and changed the acquittal into death sentence; or

(ii) Converted capital punishment into acquittal; or

(iii) the High Court has requistioned a case from a lower court and has given death sentence; or

(iv) the High Court gives a certificate that the case is fit to be sent for appeal to the Supreme Court.

(c) Appeals in Constitutional Matters. To interpret the Constitution in its real spirit is the man function of the Supreme Court. Appeals in all civil. criminal and other matters are entertained in the Supreme Court on the recommendations of the High Court or otherwise. If the the Supreme Court is satisfied that clearification of law or interpretation of the Constitution is involved in a case.

Advisory Functions. India has parliamentary form of Government with a federal set-up. In it disputes are bound to arise on the interpretation of the Constitutions and over jurisdictions for legislation. Law-making process is very complex and complicated as well as time-consuming. In order to save the nation from disputes and to enable the President to discharge his constitutional responsibilities, the President has been empowered to seek advice from the Supreme Court on any matter of constitutional importance and the Court is bound to advice him.

Othcr Functions. Supreme Court is the Highest court of law and as such its decisions shall be binding on the all courts within the territory of union India. The Supreme Court is the guardian of the Constitution. It protects the Constitution and interprets its various Articles. Any Act which is against the spirit of the Constitution will be declared *ultra vires*.

(a) Judicial Review. A very important function of the court is commonly known as that of Judicial review. If any Act passed by the Union or State Legislature is found to be contrary to the spirit of the Constitution, the Supreme Court can declare that Act *ultra vires* or null and void, provided an appeal to this effect is made to the court by the citizens.

(b) ***Protection of Fundamental Rights.*** Besides, performing the functions that have been mentioned so far, the Supreme Court also undertakes the responsibility of safeguarding people's Fundamental Rights. A person whose fundamental rights have been violated by any person, body or the institution, can move the Supreme Court to get justice.

Court of Record. The Supreme Court is a court of record as well. All the decisions of the Supreme Court are recroded and these form precedents for other cases of similar nature. If any person, body or institution of the country shows any disrespects to the decision of the Supreme Court or shows contempt for the court the Supreme Court any institute 'Contempt of Court' proceedings against that person, body or institution.

Impartially of Judiciary. Our constitution makers made very sincere efforts to ensure that our judiciary remains independent and impartial. The salaries of the Supreme Court Judges are charged on the 'Consolidated Fund of India'. The result is that the Parliament has no right to vote on them. The salary and other allowance gives to the Judges of the Supreme Court cannot be reduced during the term of their office. To avoid the possibility of showing special favours, while in service to their would be clients, the Judges are not allowed to plead in any court after retirement. All these provisions are calculated to give the Judges a free hand to act impartially.

Critically Evaluation of Impartiality of Judiciary. These days it is said by the critics that the impartiality of judiciary is in danger because of several reasons. First of all it is said that the government has been promoting even the junior judges to the position of Chief Justice overlooking the claims of senior ones. It is felt that this is indirectly an indication to the judges that they to the government line, otherwise, they will be superseded.

But inspite of all this the judges in India have worked and decided cases with atmost impartially and the courts are maintaing impartiality.

❑

3
Rights and Duties

Just as a citizen enjoyes certain rights, he also has to discharge certain duties towards 'Right' and 'Duty' are used as if they are opposed to each other and would exclude each other. The impression is quite wrong because rights and duties are closely connected with each other and they always go together. There are two ways of proving this. Whenever a right is given to one citizen, say 'A', then it becomes the duty of all other citizens 'B', 'C' and so on to respect that right, to allow citizen 'A' to enjoy that right and not to do anything to destroy it. When I am given the right to property, it is the duty of all other citizens not to take away my property, and to allow me to use my property in any way I would like to use it. But is should be remembered that the same rights are given to all citizens and can be enjoyed only if each allows all others to enjoy the same. The right to property is given not only to me but to all other citizens and just as it is their duty to allow me the right of enjoying any property, it is my duty to allow others to enjoy the same right to property. this would mean that I can enjoy my right to property only it I accept at the same time my duty to respect if for other. This rights and duties are so closely related with each other that one cannot exist without the other.

Rights are the claims or privileges enjoyed by a citizen recognized by the State. It is the duty of the State to protect your rights, otherwise rights are meaningless. Your right imposes a two-fold duty on you. You have a duty to see that you do not interfere in any way with the enjoyment of similar rights of others. As you have a right, so have others. It is your duty not to take any action likely to interfere with their rights. Secondly, rights cannot be enjoyed for nothing. You are gvien certain rights so that you can perform certain duties as a citizen. These rights are necessary to enable you to exercise your civic duties. The State by guaranteeing these rights, imposes on you the duty to act as a responsibile citizen of the community. It will be your duty to develop your abilities and to try your utmost to further the common good of the country.

Rights and duties are related in the following way:

1. One's Right is Another's Duty. A right belonging to one person imposes a corresponding duty on the others to respect his right. His right is, therefore, their duty. For instanec, an individual's right to property implies that it is the duty of others not to take away or steal his property without his consent or to interefere with his enjoyment of it. In this sense, rights and duties are the two sides of the same coin. From the stand point of man who enjoys, it is a right and from the point of view of others who must allow him to enjoy, it is a duty. But it is necessary that every right should carry a corresponding duty with it. For instance, a landlord has only right over his tenants and no duties towards them and that the tenants have only duties and no rights. In fact, in such a case, no right or duty is involved and it is a case of exploitation, not a right or duty. The landlord really has no right over the tenants but only a power backed by the wealth and influence. A right can trully be called a right only if it does not hinder the general welfare of other people.

2. One's Right is One's Duty Also. A right is at the same time a duty. If an individual enjoys a right, it must be remembered that the same right belongs to all other individuals. Therefore, it is his duty not to interefere in the enjoyment of other's rights. For instance, if 'A' has the right to express his opinions freely it is also his duty not to deny the same right to 'B'. Further may right to use public road also implies my duy to admit the fact that others too possess the same right. This right implies one more duty also. If I enjoy liberty of speech, it is my duty not to misuse this right by preaching anything that is against law or that disturbs peace or spreads hatred among different communities.

3. One's Right is One' Duty to Use it in a Right Way. It is the duty of an individual to make proper use of this rights. The improper use of rights proves harmful for others and society can never tolerate it. If an individual is given the freedom of speech and expression, he should not misuse this right by spreading hatred among different communities. He should not instigate the people against the government. He should not spread rumours. Misuse of rights by the citizens of a State leads to disorder and anarchy. I leads to settting up wrong precedents. Public welfare is ignored if people do things of thier own accord.

4. Duties Towards the State. Rights of an individual imply certain duties towards the State. The State gives us rights and they are also safeguarded by the State. State creates such an atomosphere as is necessary for making full use of rights. Rights have no meaning without the State and hence it is the duty of every individual to respect the laws of the State.

5. One's Right is One's Duty to Use it for Social Good. A right is not only the means for furthering self-interest but it is also a means for promoting the general interests of society. An individual enjoys right only so long as he contributes his best instructed judgement to the common good of the people. In case an individual misuse his rights, and his activities prove harmful to the welfare of the community, his rights are forfeited and he becomes liable to punishment. For example, if an individual uses his right to freedom of speech to spread bitterness between different sections of the community or to preach violence or anarchy, he becomes a hindrance in the way of social development.

HUMAN RIGHTS

There are certain rights of the individuals which are inherent in his personality. Such rights are called as Natural Rights. Man is moral and rational being and this very state entitles him to the enjoyment of certain, rights, which are called as Human Rights. These rights are derived from the inherent dignity of the human person and they should be available to man every where and at all times. These rigths are necessary condition for the development of human personality and without them man would really not be man. The ideal of human rights and fundamental freedoms is universally accepted and this problem never received so much attention as to day. The Declartion of the Rights of Man following the American and French Revolutions contained fundamental human rights. The Declaration of American Independence, 1776 stated: "We hold these truths to be self-evident, that all men are created equal, that they are endowed by their Creator with certain inalienable rights, that among these are life, liberty and pursuit of happiness." The French Declaration of the Rights of Man, 1789 emphasised the concepts of "liberty, equality and fraternity." In 1941 in his message to American Congress, President Roosevelt laid stress on 'Four Freedoms, of Man and said, "We look forward to a world founded upon four essential freedoms—freedom of speech and expression, freedom of worship, freedom from want and freedom from fear." Right from the Atlantic Charter till the end of the Second World War in their wartime conferences the Allied Powers laid particular stress upon the human rights and fundamental freedoms. In the Declaration of the United Nations of 1942, the United Nations put on record that 'complete victory over enemies is essential to defend life, liberty, independence and religions freedom and to preserve human rights and justice in their own lands', But unfortunately, while it is accepted in principle, it seems to be ignored in practice. There are very few states where the human rights and fundamental freedoms are avialable, otherwise in most of the states people are deprived of it. They are the cases of racial and religious discrimination in general and the problem of apartheid in particular. Again, there is economic and political exploitation. In totalitarian regimes and dictatorships people are deprived of their political rights and freedoms. In 1971 inhuman and barbaric cruelties, and genocide committed on the people of Bangladesh moved the very conscience of manking. The policy of apartheid pursued in South Africa has been condemmned by all. The General Assembly has repeatedly condemned this policy as a 'crime against humanity.'

THE UNITED NATIONS AND HUMAN RIGHTS

Even before the end of Second World War the Allied Powers expressed the hope that after the victory in the war, efferts would be made for the protection of human rigths in every state. In Dumbarton Oaks Conference of 1944 the emphasis was laid on the promotion of human rights and fundamental freedoms.

The representatives gathered at the San Francisco Conference demanded that the declaration of human rights should be included in the U.N. Charter itself. Though a separate declartion of human rights does not find place in the Charter but the specific mention of the human rights has been made in the Charter at various places.

The pearnble to the United Nations Charter refer to the determaination of the United Nation's 'to affirm faith in fundamental human rights, in the dignity and worth of the human person, in the equal rigths of men and women.'

Under Atricle 1, one of the purposes of the United Nations is to achieve international co-operation 'in promoting and encouraging respect for human rigths and for fundamental freedoms for all without distinction as to race, sex, language or religion.'

Under Article 13 it is the duty of they General Assembly to assist 'in the realisation of human rights and fundamental freedoms for all without distinction as to race, sex language or religion.'

Under Article 55 it is provided that the United Nations shall promote 'universal respect for, and observance of, human rights and fundamental freedoms for all without distinction as to race, sex language or religion.'

Under Ariticle 62 it is the duty of the Economic and Social Council 'to make recommendations for purpose of promoting respect for, and observance of human rights fundamental freedoms for all.'

According to Article 68 the Economic and Social Council is required to set up commissions for the promotion of human rights.

It is for the first time that the provision in regard to the protection of human rights and fundamental freedom has been made in the U.N. Charter. Under the Charter the United Nations is empowered only to encourage the promotion of human rights and fundamental freedom, but has no power to take any binding measure in this regard. The Charter deals with the human rights and the fundamental freedoms but it does not give any precise definition of there rights or a clear acknowledgement of the principle of their observance. In fact, the Charter aims at the voluntary co-operation of the states in achieving this objective. There is no duoubt that the provisions of the Charter in regard to human rights have absolutely no binding authority but at the same time the protection of human rights has ceased to be the exclusive jurisdiction of states and has become the concern of the United Nations. According to Oppenheim, 'It cannot of the that the provisions of the Charter on the subject signify a full and effective guarantee of the inalienable rights of man on the part of international society. In particular, these are absent from the Charter Clauses embodying either a more precise definition of these rights or a clear acknowledgment of the principle of their observance... Whatever these may be, the observance of fundamental human rights in so far it is the subject-matter of local obligations, ceases to be one of exclusive domestic jurisdiction of states and has become a matter of legitimate concern for the United Nations and its members.'

UNIVERSAL DECLARATIONS OF HUMAN RIGHTS

The United Nations Commission on Human Rights was asked to prepare a draft on the general principles governing the human rights. Afters two and half years of painstaking labour the Commission on Human Rights prepard a draft of the 'Universal Declaration of Human Rights,' as a common standard of achievement for all peoples and all nations. This declaration, the first of its kind in history, was approved by the General Assembly on December 10, 1948. This declaration is the first international deffinition of the rights of man, It is, therefore , 10th December, is commemorated every years as Human Rights day.

The Declaration of Human Rights contains 30 Articles including the preamble. The Preamble stresses the 'dignity and worth of the human person.'

Article 1. All human beings are born free and equal in dignity and rights.

Article 2. Every one without any distinction is entitled to all the rights and freedoms set forth in this Declaration.

Article 3. Every one has the right to life, liberty and the security of person.

Article 4. No one shall be held in slavery or servitude; slavery and slave-trade shall be prohibited in all their forms.

Article 5. No one shall be subjected to torture or to cruel, inhuman or degrading treatment or punishment.

Article 6. Every one has the right to recognition everywhere as a person before the law.

Article 7. All are equal before the law and are emitted to equal protection of the law.

Article 8. Every one has the right to an effective remedy by the competent national tribunals for acts violative of the fundamental rights granted to him by the constitution or by law.

Article 9. No one shall be subjected to arbitrary arrest, detention or exile.

Article 10. Every one is entitled in full equality to a fair and public hearng by an independent and impartial tribunal.

Article 11. Every one charged with a penal offence has the right to be presumed innocent until proved guilty according to law in a public trial. No one shall be held guilty of any penal offence which did not constitute a penal offence at the time when it was committted.

Article 12. No one shall be subjected to arbitrary interference with its privacy, family, home or correspondence, nor to attacks upon his honour and reputaion.

Article 13. Every one has the right to freedom of movement and residence within the borders of each state.

Article 14. Every one has the right to seek in other countries asylum from persecution.

Article 15. Every one has right to nationality. No one shall be arbitrarily deprived of his nationality nor denied the right to change his nationalty.

Article 16. Men and Women of age, without any limitation due to race nationality ro religion, have the right to marry and to found a family.

Article 17. Every one has the right to own property and no one shall be arbitrarily deprived of his property.

Article 18. Every one has the right to freedom of thoght, conscience and religion.

Article 19. Every one has the right to freedom of opinion and expression.

Article 20. Every one has the right to freedom of peaceful assembly and association.

Article 21. Every one has the right to take part in the goernment of his country with equal access in public service.

Article 22. Every one has the right to social security and is entitled to realization of the economic, social and cultrual rights indispensable for his dignity and the free development of his personality.

Article 23. Every one has the right to work, to free chice of empolyment, to just and favourable conditions of work and to protection against unemployment. Every one has the right to equal pay for equal work. Every one who works ans the right to just and favourable remuneration.

Article 24. Every one has the right to rest and leisure, including reasonable limitaton of working hours and periodic holidays with pay.

Article 25. Every one has the right to adequate, standard of living, including housing, medical care and security in the servent of sickness, widowhood and old age.

Article 26. Every one has the right to education.

Article 27. Every one has the right to take part in the cultural life of the community and to share in the scientific advancements and its benefits.

Article 28. Every one isentitted to social and international order in which the rights and freedoms set forth in this Declaration can be fully realized.

Article 29. Every one has duties to the community in which alone the free and full development of his personality is possible. In the exercise of his rights and freedoms, every one shall be subjected to due recognition and respect for the rights and freedoms of others and just requirements of morlity, public order and general welfare.

Article 30. Nothing in this Declaration may be interpreted as implying for any state, group, or person any right to engage in any activity or to perform any act aimed at the distruction of any of the rights and freedoms set forth above.

The Universal Declaration of Human Rights is a historic event of great importance for the mankind. It is an international. 'Magna Carta' of all men everywhere. According to Dr. Charles Malik of Lebanon, this Declaration was not simply a resolution but the part of U.N. Charter itself. About the Declaration, American representative in the United Nations observed: "In giving our approval to the declaration to-day, it is of primary importance that we keep clearly in mind the basic character of the document. It is not a treaty ; it is not an international agreement. It does not purport to be a statement of law or of legal obligation. It is a declaration of specific principles of human rights and freedoms, to be stamped with the approval of the General Assembly by a formal vote of its members and to serve as a common standard of achievement for all peoples of all nations." According to Palmer and Perkins, "The declaration is merely a statement of principles, not a legally binding instrument; but it has become one of the best konwn of international documents, and it has often been referred to in resolution of the U.N., the specialized agencies, regional arrangements and other international orgainsations, and in national constitutions, legislations, and court decisions. It is a beacon light for all mankind, even though it has been honoured more often in the breach than in the observance."

However, it must not he forgotten that no machinery has been provided to enforce the provisions of this Declaration. The states cannot be compelled to enforce this Declaration. Oppenheim remarks. 'The Declaration is not an instrument which is legally binding either directly or indirectly" In 1948, the Commission on Human Rights tried to make this Declaration binding on the states but this could not be possible as it would have provided an opportunity to the majority states in the U.N. to interfere in the internal affairs of the other states.

Although the Declaration is only in the form of a recommendation to the states, yet the U.N. General Assmbly has condemned the states which have violated the declaration. The General Assembly has a number of times condemned South Africa for its policies of apartheid. Lacking in binding and legal force the Declaration, nevertheless, presents a moral ideal before the states in very clear terms. The states can hardly afford to ignore the world orgnisation and the world public opinion.

International Covenants on Human Rights. The United Nations not only made a Declaration of human rights but it also took steps in the direction that they are effectively implemented by the states. With this view the General Assembly in 1951, requested The Commission on Human Rights to prepare draft of two covenants, one on 'Civil and Political Rights' and the other on 'Ecconomic, Social and Cultural Rights.' The purpose of these covenants is to give more precise definition of the human rights and make necessary provision for their observance. These covenants, after being approved by the General Assmbly, were to be submitted to the U.N. members as treaty, and it would be binding upon all states that ratified it. On 16th December, 1966, the General Assembly adopted and opened for signature, ratification and accession three International Covenants on Human Rights—*(a)* International Covenant on Civil and Political Rights; *(b)* International Covenant on Economic, Cultural and Social Rights; and *(c)* The Optional Protocol to the International Covenant on Civil and Political Rights.

The principles proclaimed in the Declaration of Human Rights have been embodied in a number of International Conventions, binding upon the states which ratify them ; and in some cases the international machinery necessary to ensure the application of the Conventions has been established. The important conventions adopted by the General Assembly are—Convention on Genocide (1948), Conventaion on the Political Rights Political Rights of Women (1952), Convention on Slavery (1956) and Convention on the Elimination of Racial Discrimination (1965). On 20th November, 1959 the General Assembly unanimously approved the 'Declaration of the Rights of the Child.' This Declaration contains a number of human rights and fundamental freedoms that are provided in the Universal Declaration of Human Rights of 1948.

The U.N. has been able to do lot for the promotion of human rights and fundamental freedoms. The General Assembly has repeatedly declared that the policies of apartheid pursued by the Government of South Africa are a negation of the U.N. Character and constitule a crime against humanity. From 1952 to 1960, the General Assembly made repeated appeals to the South African Government to revise its policy on this question in accordance with the principles of the U.N. Charter In its resolutions adopted in 1963 and 1964, the Security Council called on all states to implement an arms embargo against South Africa. In 1965 the General Assembly appealed to all states to stop their economic collaboration with South Africa. In 1970, the General Assembly made a General appeal for contributing moral, political and material assistance to the people of South Africa in their legitimate struggle against apartheild. The General Assembly established the United Nations Trust Fund for South Africa to provide legal assistance, relief and education to the oppressed people of South Africa, March 21, is celebrated as "International Day for the Elimination of Racial Discrimination." The Genreal Assembly designated 1968 as the "International year for Human Rights." and 1971 as the "International year for Action to combat Racism and Racial Discrimination."

In spite of whatever has been done by the United National for the protection and promotion of human rights. It has not yet become a reality with regard to its universal obseravance. There is no U.N. machhinery to provide any assistance in case there is any violation of human rights. The interperation and very implemenation of these have been left to the concerned states. Owing to the differences in the values and attitudes of the states, it appears difficult to achieve a uniform standard of human rights.

The Universal observance of human rights would promote the ideals of freedom, justics and peace in the world. It would also help in the advancement of international co-operation and good-will. But this has given a great set back to anti-democratic, imperialist and colonialist forces. It is hoped that the states would be more and more inclined to fulfil their obligations under the Charter to promote respect for, and observance of human rights and freedoms in deference to the world public opinion.

Strictly speaking, human rights are concerned with the individual states and it is their concern to make provision of fundamental rights and freedoms for their citizens. Every sovereign states by it own laws provides for the relationship between the state and its citizens, It is the domestic juriscdiction of every state and the same is determined by its municipal law. The United Nations cannot compel the states in regard to the fundamental rights and freedom as it wourld be an interference in the domestic affairs of the states. Though the states which have ratified the international covenants on human rights are bound by it, but the question of interpretion and the very implementation of these rights rest with the individual States. In the prevailing international system it is a most question whether the scheme of fundamental rights will really be implemented by the sovereign states. Human rights constitute a universal ideal and it is suggested, that this can realised only by the establishment of a world government. For universal enforcement of human rights, perhaps, it appears necessary to exercise binding authourity upon the states and to impose some limitation on their sovereignty. Since this does not seem feasible, the only course available is to rely upon the force fo moral pressure and the constant reminder of the rights embodied in the Universal Declaration of Human Rights and the obligations under the charter in this regard. However; the world organisation is not completely unconcerned about this question as the protection of human rights has ceased to be exclusive jurisdiction of states and has become the legitimate concern of the United Nations and its members.

CHARACTERISTICS OF RIGHTS

The citizen has to seek 'the good life' not only for his own sake but also for the community. If he has to live up to his ideals, he needs certain conditions. He can justly claim them. He has right to them for the fulfilment of the common good. Rights are those conditions and guarantees which the state should provide to every citizen in order that he may attain his best self in society. Man develop all his mental physical and spirtual qualities only if he is given certain rights and privileges by the State. Each State gives certain rights to the citizens which are essential for the development of the personality of the individuals.

What is a Right? Different scholars have defined Rights in different ways. Some important definitions of Rights are given below:

According to Holland, "Right is one man's capacity of influencing the acts of another by means not of his own strength but of the opinion or the force of society".

According to Bosanquet, "A Right is a claim recognised by society and enforced by the State."

According to Wilde, "A Right is a reasonable claim to freedom in the exercise of certain activities".

According to H.J. Laski, "Rights are those conditions of social life without which no man can seek to be himself at his best."

On the basis of the definitions given above we can say that Rights are those conditions of social life without which human personality cannot develop. Rights are useful both for the individual as well as for the State. The rights are recognized by the State.

Difference between Rights and Claims. Rights is a claim of the individual for doing things independently. The individual claims his rights from the society. But all claims are not to be reagrded as rights because rights are only those claims which are recognised as such by society and enforced by the State. The claim of the individual takes the form of a right only when it is recognised by the society. Without such a recognition rights are empty claims. An individual is a part of the society and individual cannot have any right apart form what the society concedes.

VARIOUS CHARACTERISTICS OF RIGHTS

On the basis of the definitions of rights given above we can say that the following are the essential features of rights:

1. **Rights are Available Only in the Society.** Rights can be possible only in the society. The rights cannot be possible outside the society. Whenever an individual lives in society

he is to seek the help of others for various purposes. Outside the soecity every individual is absolutely free and he makes use of force for achieving his end.

2. **Right is a Claim of the Individual.** Right is a claim of the individual for doing things independently. The individual claims his rights from the society. In other words, rights means demand for certain facilities.
3. **Right is Reasonable and Moral.** The society recognizes only that claim of the individual which is reasonable and moral. The society recognizes only that claim which concerns the welfare of the individual. A claim which is harmful to society cannot be accepted.
4. **Rights and Duties Go Together.** Rights is always accompanied by duties. Rights and duties go side by side. A's right is B's duty and B's right is A's duty. Rights cannot be granted without the performance of certain duties.
5. **Rights can be Used for Public Good.** A right can be used only for social good and not against the interest of the society. Rights can be had in society and are recognized by the society. Therefore, it is but natural that they should be exercised in the best interests of society.
6. **Rights are Recognized by Society.** Rights are those claims of the individual which are recognized by the society. The claim of the individual takes the form of a right only when it is recognized by society.
7. **Rights are Universal.** Rights are given equally to all the people in society. Right is not the claim of a particular individual but it is a claim of all the individuals. A right which is enjoyed by one individaul is also enjoyed by other individuals.
8. **Rights are Enforced by the State.** Another important feature of right is that it is enforced by the State. The rights are also protected by the State. The State grants through laws and those who violate the law are punished by the

State. The State is the guardian of the rights of the individuals.

9. **Rights Change with the Time.** Rights are not static. Rights change with the changed social, economic and political conditions. For example, in the early phase of industrial expansion, the right to unfettered use of one's property was recognised. But in the mid-twentieth century the right to property has been considerably curtailed in almost every country. Hence, no permanent and unchanging catalogue of right can be compiled.

KINDS OF RIGHTS

Mainly the rights are of three types:

1. Natural Rights. Natural rights are those rights which have been given to man by nature. Some people are of the view that Nature conferred certain rights on man even before the birth of society. Locke also champoined the cause of these rights. Rights to life, liberty and property cannot be ended by anyone. Some people people interpret the meaning of natural rights in a different way. They say that there are certain things to which man has an inherent rights. They are natural because they are essential and inherent in the eminent worth of human personality.

2. Moral Rights. A moral right is a right which is based on the ethical rules prevailing among the people. It is upheld by the moral opinion of the community, but not by the powers of the State. If there is a breath of these rights, the State will not punish the individual or individuals concerned.

3. Legal Rights. A legal right is one which is recognized and enforced by the State. If any individual interferes with such a right of another person, he will be punished by the State.

Legal rights can further be classified into Fundamental Rights, Civil Rights, Political Rights and Economic Rights.

(i) ***Fundamental Rights.*** Legal rights mentioned in the Constitution are called Fundmental Rights. In India, Japan, the U.S.A., France, Switzerland etc. citizens enjoy

Fundamental Rights. Part III of the Indian Constitution embodies Fundamental Rights.

(ii) ***Civil Rights.*** Civil rights are those which enable an individual to lead a decent civic life. They are the indispensable conditions of civilized existence. For example, the right to life, the right to private property, the right to freedom of thought and expression, the right to freedom of association, the right to move about freely and the right to make contract are civil rights.

(iii) ***Political Rights.*** Political rights are those privileges recognised and guaranteed by the law of the State, which enable the citizen to participate in the political affairs and governance of the country. According to Laski," A democratic system is one in which the will of the average citizen has channels of direct access to the sources of authority. There is, therefore, a right to political power." For example, in India the right to vote, the right to contest election, the right to occupy a public post and the right to criticise the government are political rights.

(iv) ***Economic Rights.*** Economic rights are those which are essential for the economic development of an individual. In communist countries, economic rights are the part of legal rights. For example, in China, the right to work, the right to wages, the right to social security etc. are economic rights.

CIVIL RIGHT OF AN INDIVIDUAL

In the modern democratic state, the citizens are granted the following civil rights.

1. Right to Life. Each State grants its citizens the right to life. Aristotle was of the opinion that the State came into existence for the sake of life and countinues to exist for the sake of good life. This right is important both for the State and the individual. The individual personality can develop to the fullest degree only if he is granted the right to life.

The State Protects the Life of the Individual. The individual is given the right to self-defence. An individual cannot be allowed to commit suicide.

The State can award death sentence to an individual is dangerous to the lives of others or if an individual works against the interests of the State, the can be awarded death penalty. The modern view is against awarding death punishment.

2. Right to Personal Liberty. The citizen is also given the right to personal liberty for the development of his personality. The Government cannot arrest anybody arbitrarily. Nobody can be deprived of his life, liberty and property without his having broken a law established in an ordinary court of law. A person can be arrested only when he violates the laws of the State and he can be punished only when the charge against him is established in a court of law. The policy cannot keep anybody in its custody for more than 24 hours without the permission of the judge. Besides this the accused is given complete liberty to defend himself against the charge.

3. Right to Family Life. Every citizen has the right to maintain a privacy of life in the family without any outside inerference. The children possess the right of inheritance in their family property and also have got the right to get full support from their parents up to the age of maturity. Parents have the full rights over their children so long as they remain minors. Every person possesses the full right to marriage in any way he likes but the sanctity of marriage must be maintained in the society.

4. Right to Freedom of Religion. Rights to freedom of religion is most essential for the development of the personality of the individual. Every citizen should be free to profess and practice any religious faith he likes. In ancient times this right was not recognized by the State but modern States generally recognise this rights.

5. Right to Education. Citizenship has been defined as the contribution of one's instructed judgement to the public good. The citizen has the right to such education as will fit him for the task of citizenship. Every citizen should have that education which would enable him to weight, judge, choose and decided for himself. The State grants the right to education to all its citizens. The individuals should have the right of receiving education according to their sweet will. the State should provide all facilities regarding education to its citizens. Now eadays the State opens shcools and colleges for the spread of education. The State nowadays opens adult education centres, reading rooms, libraries and research centres. It opens colleges and universities.

6. Right to Freedom of Movement. A citizen has the right to freedom of movement and settlement in any part of the country. He cannot be restricted by any exercise of power. This way every citizen can settle at a place which he likes and where he can have his business. Nobody can be compelled to leave a certain place.

7. Right to Contract. The right to contract enables the citizen to enter into contract freely with others. Though every State gives the individual this important civil right, it makes the necessary laws to regulate contracts and to prevent the making of contracts which are injurious to the interests of society.

8. Right to Freedom of Thought and Expression. Freedom of speech is a valuable right. In all free countries citizens have the right to speak out honestly what view they may hold. Freedom of press is included in this right of free expression of opinion. It is merely the right to publish in print what a man can lawfully speak. Citizens can criticise government measures even severely. This freedom is no doubt subject to the law of libel and sedition. Men who are prevented from thinking freely will soon cease to think at all. Freedom of speech and of expression helps to create an enlightened public opinion. It is a powerful weapon against official tyranny as it is one of the most powerful means for the redress of public grievances.

9. Rights to Equality. In the civilized State the citizens are also given the right to equality. Equality is the basis of democracy. All the citizens are considered equal in all aspects of life. Equility does not mean that the income of all the individuals should be equal or all of them should have the same status in life. Equality means that all the individuals should enjoy equal opportunities and nobody should be discriminated against on the basis of sex, caste, creed, colour, blood and religion. Everybody should be equal in the eys of law. Nobdoy should enjoy special privileges.

10. Right to Freedom of Press. In the modern age, the

freedom of press is given great importance. People enjoy to speech and the same time they are given the right to expression. They can get their views published. The newspapers are given freedom and they publish news of their own sweet accord. Articles are published in the newspapers. They newspapers provide every sort of knowledge to the people. The newspapers formulate and express public opinion. They appreciate good actions and condemn bad actions of the government. They protect the rights and liberties of the people. The newspapers are nowadays called the watch-dog of the rights and liberties of the people. If the government imposes restrictions on the newspapers and journals, then it results in the death of democracy.

11. Right to Freedom in Domestic Affairs. The citizens should be given freedom in their domestic affaris. The State should not interefere in the personal life of theiIndividuals. The citizens, should be free to use dress and food of their own choice. The State cannot prescribe a particular dress for the people. The State cannot lay down the rules for fashion. The individuals should be left free in their domestic affairs.

RIGHTS OF CITIZENS

Political rights are of great importance. It is with the help of these rights that an individual gets the opportunity to participate in the affairs of the State. In the absense of these rights deomocracy cannot be real. Political rights are given only to the citizens and not to the foriegners. Generally the political rights mentioned below are given to the citizens.

1. Right to Vote. Right to vote is the most important political right. It is through the exercise of this right that citizens in a democracy take part in the government of the country. Criminals, bankrupts, lunatics and alines are not given the right to vote. In most of the modern States every adult person, man or woman, is given the right to vote. The State does not take into consideration the caste, creed colour and religion while extending the right to vote to its citizens. In India, every citizen of the age of 18 years is given the right to vote and in the U.S.A. also every citizen of the age of 18 years is given the right to vote. By getting the righ to vote the people govern over themselves.

2. Right to Contest Elections. Every voter is normally given the right to be elected to the local boards and State or Central Legislatures. Certain States sometimes impose certain restrictions regarding age, education, etc. for being elected to the legisalture bodies. The poorest citizen is as eligible for contesting an elections as the richest. This right is given equally to all the citizens of the State. Nobody is deprived of this right on the basis of caste, religion, creed and colour. Some qualifications for contesting the election can, of course, be laid down. In India no citizen who is below 25 years of age can contest elections. If all the people are given the right to contest election, then democracy cannot be well established. The elected representatives of the people enjoy the right to frame laws and to run the administration.

3. Right to Hold Public Officers. All the citizens are eligible to hold public officers. It does not mean that anybody may assume any office, it simply implies that all citizens in the State should be equally eligible for appointment to offices for which they are qualified by virtue of education, judgement, training and experience. Merit should be then main rather the sole criterion for all public appointments. Every public office—executive, legislative and judicial—in equally open for all citizens if they are otherwise duly qualified to hold that office. There is no bar on the ground of social status, wealth, colour, caste or any other such cause.

4. Rights to Criticise the Government. Every citizen has the right to criticise the government and express his views about any action or policy of he government if it goes against he welfare of the people. In democracy, the administration is run by the representatives of the people. If the right to criticise the government is denied to the people then the goverenment will behave arbitrarily. Every citizen can express his opinion on the policy of the government. Let this criticism be constructive and with the best of motives.

5. Right to Petition. Every citizen is given the right to address petitions or complaints to the competent authorities. This right may be exercised by individuals or by several persons together. The right is important in the sense that the people can get their grievances redressed by the government by addressing their petitions.

6. Right to Form Political Parties. In democratic countries, citizens enjoy the right to form political parties. Political parties are inevitable in a democratic states. For example, in India citizens enjoy their important political rights.

LEGAL DUTIES

The citizens are to perform so many duties towards the State. The duties which are prescribed by law are called legal duties. The citizens are to perform the following legal duties:

1. Allegiance. Every citizen has allegiance to the State to which he belongs. He must defined the State against all enemies and dangers and he has a duty to assist the State in the suppression of crimes and revolution. The State can call upon him or even require him to take up arms in its defence. It can precribe a period of compulsory military training for the citizen. The citizen should be pepared, if necessary, even to lay down his life in defending the State and to discharge the duties involved in his allegiance to the State.

2. Obedience. Every citizen has the supreme duty of obeying the law. Good citizenship consists more in obedience to law than in any other thing. Law are enacted for the welfare of the community, so the man who has a regard for law, has the good of the community, at heart. Respect for the laws and the institution of the State makes one a good citizen.

There may be occasions when public opinion has to be organised to repeal laws which are anti-social in character.

Disobedience of law may, in exceptional circumstances, the morally justified but even in such cases it ought to be carefully considered whether the object underlying such disobedience could not be better attained by other means.

Respect of law, once undermined, may shake the very foundations of our social order.

3. Payment of Taxes. It is the duty of the citizen to pay taxes which are legally imposed on him. The administration of the government cannot be run without public funds. There is no other source for the government except to collect money from the citizens in the form of taxes. All these taxes are utilized for the payment of salaries to the public servants and other State has the right to tax its citizens who should pay all these taxes without any hesitation because the money thus collected will be spent for their welfare.

4. Co-operation with Government. Every citizen should extend fullest degree of co-operation to the government. It is his duty to help the government officials in the proper discharge of their duties. He shold help the police, the army and other officials in maintaining law and order in the country. The citizen should not give shelter to or defend criminals.

5. Protection of Public Property. It is the duty of the citizens to protect public property.

DEMANDS OF STATES: RECENT TRENDS

The demands of the states when analysed reveal following trends about state autonomy:

(a) India is not a nation state and so it should be divided into various semi-independent states. Though at the moment this trend is very insignificant, it has advocates among certain intellectuals. However, it is felt that the rise of regionalism is not something which should unnecessarily worry the centre because it is inevitable result of the 'rising consciousness of the developed and developing nationalities, one should not therefore impute motives to adherence to this school of thought.'

(b) It is also revealed that 'the states should get greater autonomy in almost every sphere. The exreme view in this trend advocates that excepting three subject including defence, foreign affairs, and currency all other subjects should be transferred to the states. There also exists other shades of opinion in this trend.'

(c) It is revealed that the dominant position of the Centre in our federal system should continue to prevail and adjustment should be made within the existing framework of the constitution.'

DEMANDS FOR MORE STATE AUTONOMY

The demand for greater state autonomy is one of the most debated issues of the Indian Federal System. It because more intense in the general election of 1967, non-Congress governments came into existence in many states. The then DMK Government in Tamil Nadu was most staunch among them. In recent past the lead in this arena has come from the Marxist government of West Bengal which has 'adopted a 2,500 words memorandum suggesting the change in the constitution.'

Time and again Communist Party of India (Marxist) government led by Jyoti Basu are attempting on more radical scale, "What Mr. Annudurai and his DMK Govt. did in 1969. In that year DMK and his Govt. appointed Rajamannar Committee to examine Centre-State relations and to suggest suitable amendments to the constitution so as to secure to the states more autonomy. The committee's recommandations being most comprehensive, reveal a desire to maintain an essential framework of the constitution and not jeopardising the integrity of the country. The intention of the committee thus was not to grasp this sorry things of entirely and to shatter it to the bits and then removed it nearer to the heart's desire but to effectuate such change as to make the constitution more federal."

It was emphasised in the memorandum adopted by West Bengal Government that although it wants the states to be stronger on no account does it want the Centre to be weak, Shri Basu of course claims that he and his party do not want a 'Weak Centre' and the cocnept of strong states in not necessarily in contradiction to that of a strong Centre, provided their respective sphere of authority are clearly marked out. But the total sum the recommendations of the West Bengal memorandum give a contemporary impression. If the constitution originally frammed tilts in the favour of the Centre, the memorandum aiming completely in favour of the states, leaving to the Centre's care only defence, foreign affairs, foreign trade, currency, communication and economic coordination. Most of the recommendations of the memorandum appear to have been modelled on the recommendations of the Rajamnanar Committee, it view on Article 80 (Composition of Rajya Sabha) 200, 201 (President's power to give assent to state Bills), 248 (resideury powers of legislation) 302 (Parliament's power to legislate for inter-state elations) 356, 357 (President's rule in the states), 360 (declaration of financial emerency) financial devolution between the centre and states and the statute of the planning commission, are identical with total of the recommendations of Rajamannar Committee."

Under State Relations and Rajamannar Committee' constitutional provision mentioned above, relating to one party rule at the centre and the states, to financial dependence of the states on the Centre and to the role of the development Council and the planning commission. Form this view point it may be said that the West Bengal memorandum is very close to the Rajamannar Committee.

"It has been further alleged by the memorandum that, all the manners of pressures have been used sometimes for merely through the powers of the Centre. Sometimes indirectly by denying financial and other resources etc to non-Congress governments and by applying pressuress on the Chief Ministers of the Congress party, through the organsiation and leadership. During the last few years the Centre's tentacles have further spread to the states even in the sphere of law and order, which is formerly a state subject, through the creation of the Central Reserve Police, Border Security Force and the Industrial Security Force etc. By 42nd amendment to the constitution education which was state subject, was transferred to the concurrent list.

Some of these charges contain substance, but the solution does not lie in fundamental change in the constitution of India; but in making suitable adjustments, in the light of past experience, in the constitutional provisions. As far as West Bengal is concerned, it desparately looks for the favourable change in favour of the states. If these demands for more autonomy to the states are granted it would lead to a steady weakening of the Union of India.

The four Chief Ministers of the Southern States meet on March, 24, 1983 and wanted that fiscal commission to ensure more funds for the states. They also demaded that the legislature should be given the powers to enact laws in the state on the Concurrent list of the Seventh Schedule of the Constitution without prior permosion of President. Further more the High Court Judges should know the language of the states in which they are posted.' These demands seem to be reasonable. The states of Andra Pradesh and Karnataka are not asking for the Kashmir type of autonomy. However, the Akali Dal and CP (M) want Kashmir type autonomy, through some sections of sikh militants are persisting for a sikh state-Khalistan others talk of autonomous sikh. State within framework of the constitution and in like manner, the AIADMK and the DMK will appreciate autonomy of the Kashmir pattern. Now the southern states along with CP (M) in West in West Bengal and the Akalis in Punjab should realise that the type of autonomy granted to Jammu and Kashmir is not possible in Indian federal system.

GRIEVANCES OF STATES AGAINST THE UNION

Particular Grievances of States. The states have particular as well as general grievances against the union. One of the Specific grievances of Kerala was that the Centre was not supplying it adequate foodgrains to the state. Then Chief Minister, E.M.S. Nambodiripad (CPI Marxist) even went ahead on 18th May, 1967, and threatened that if the centre failed to fulfil its commitment to the state he would proceed to make arrangement from China. He sought a share of Kaerala's foreign exchange earnings from the Union Governement. In 1969 relations between the Union government and United Front Ministry of 'West Bengal led by Ajay Mukherjee became strained, while addressing the two house jointly on 6th March 1969 the Governor omitted two paragraphs of the speech prepared by the Cabinet led by Mukherjee which described the dismissal of his United Front Ministry in November 1967 by him premptory and unconsitutional.' The constituents of the United Front expressed great resentment and the CPM demanded the immediate recall of governor Dharamvira because no normal relations can be established between him and the United From Minister. Chief Minister also stressed should be consulted.

The Chief Minister of Punjab Gurnam Singh on 28th June, 1969 alleged that the centre had exhibited political dishonesty in respect of determination of Panjabi suba and decision of the future of Chadigarh. In the similar way the Chief Minister of Karnataka. Mr. Veerendra Patil complained on Nov. 1970 that the Chief Ministers not belonging to the other parties were humilitated by the Centre. He also alleged that these Chief Ministers will not be taken confidence in respect of central policies etc., He accused the Union Ministers visiting the state capital alluring the MLAs to defect to their party with the intention to topple his government. According to him it was very difficult for the state Ministers to get interviews with the Union Ministers in the national capital. In Bihar, under the Chief Ministership of a Mahamaya Prasad Sinha new dimension of frustration was experenced. Mr. Sinha, appealed to the Soviet union to come to his state's help to save the people from famine situation there. In U.P. the Chief Ministers, C.B. Gupta and Mrs. Sucheta Kriplani complained that the Centre had neglected the needs of their state. They wanted that the plan allocations should be porportionate to the population of a state. The Chief Minister of Orissa. Mr. R.N. Singh Deo sought the establishment of a second steel plant in his state. The Chief Minister was critical of centre for its alleged attitude towards Orissa as intransigent, indifferent and discriminator. The attitude of Union Govt. towards Rajasthan was described as most apathetic. In Delhi, its executive Councillor V.K. Malhotra, leading Jan Sangh (now BJP) government argued that the centre was assuming an anti-Delhi posture and stiffling, the welfare plans of Delhi.

Akali Dals always nursed a grouse that centre has shown a step motherly treatment to their demands. The sikh psyche felt hurt at 'blue star action' resulting in descretion of golden temple. This action has given rise to military and eventually impetus to the demand of separate sikh state for the sikhs.

GENERAL GRIEVANCES OF STATES AGAINST CENTRE

1. Deployment of Paramilitary Force. In addition to specific grievances of states against the Centre there have been some general complaints against the Centre. The first is in relation to the use of para-military forces including Cenrtral Reserve Police and Border Security Force. It was stressed by union government that, the CRPF units in particular were deployed in almost every state and Union Territories because they 'were a versatile force trained and equipped to deal with armed hostilities as well as anti-social elements.'

According to the contention of Union Home Minister these units were pressed into action in the wake of a danger to Central Govt. undertakings and the State Govt's inability to ensure sufficient protection to the central property. Before Mrs. Gandhi's Prime Ministership the Central governments expenditure on its Para-military force was less than 50 Crores. After eleven years this expenditure reached to the level of a total of little less than 300 Crores of rupees a year. The state alleged that BSF according to its Charter was the force to be called by the Union for ensuring the security of Indian Borders.

The states also argue that under the constiution, the maintenance of law and order is a state subject and the state government wanted that BSF units should be used by the centre within its own administrators. On 19th September 1968 a serious trouble emerged between the Centre and Kerala Government over this issue, when the Central Government employees all over the country were on strike and the situation in some palces had become even violent and without consulting or even informing the Kerala Govt. The then Union Home Minister Y.B. Chavan sent a battalion of CRP into that state. The state Chief Minister Namboodripad protested against this action and on 18th December, state cabinet decided to take back, all cases related with the strike. This decision of the state was taken seriously by the union Government and it warned the state government that the latter's action was illegal and unconstitutional.'

In West Bengal, on 8 April, 1969 the Defence Security Personnel at the Gun and Steel Factory, Cossipore (West Bengal) resorted to firing to disperse violent mob thereby killing five persons. As a result of this, The Rastriya Sangram Samiti, called 24 hours Bengal Bandh which was a complete success. The union Home Minister Y.B. Chavan decalred that the centre would set up a single member commission of inquiry to go into the facts and circumstances relating to firing. But this move was strongly objected to by the Deputy Chief Minister Joyti Basu (CPI-M) on the ground that it was done without consulting the State Government. In Public the Chief Minister Gurnam Singh too resented the deployment of CRP units in Punjab and emphasised that these units have no right to act without authority from the State Government.

The deployment of Army in the Punjab and Union Territory Chandigarh is being resented and denounced by Akali Dals and the militant organiations. Even the Commmunists have not appreciated this step. They are suggesting immediate withdrawal of these forces whereas centre is keen to restore normaly for conducting long delayed elections in the state. The latters action is justified in the national interests.

2. Control of the Union Government on Industries. The State complain for the monopolised control of Centre over the industries, trade and commerce and production and disribution of goods. It was also argued by the states that these were the subject of the state Legislature list viz. industries in entry 24 trade and commerce in entry 26 and production supply and distribution of goods in entry 27, but the advantage of Parliament to regulate them in national interest used by the Centre had brought even these under its own control. The Industries (Development and Regulations) Act specified those industries which had to be controlled by the centre in national interest'.

3. Encroachment upon State Assembly by the Union. One of the grievances of states against the union government is the latter's encroachments of autonomy even in respoect of subjects included in the State Legislature List with the view to check the increasing inclination the State legislature inclination towards centralization, the State leaders started demanding more powers, Chief Minister, M. Karunanidhi of Tamil Nadu sought an amendment of the Constitutional for the purpose and Namboodripad said, on 19 April 1971, "that unless the States were given maximum autonomy there was, every likelihood of Bangladesh being repeated in India."

4. Inadequate Funds from Union. States complain that the Union Government had not shared taxes with them in the spirit of the Constitution, and under the existing procudure of allocation of funds the rich State got more and poor States less. Apprehending lest the Central assistance to the State should be made selectively and on political considerations, the framers of the Constitution had provided for an independent agency, a Finance Commission, under Article 280; The Finance Commission has control over a small amount of Statutory grants, whereas, the bulk of the funds by the union to the states were the discretionary grants being assigned on the recommendation of Planning Commission.

5. Arbitrary Use of Article 356 by the Union. One of the general grievances of states against the Centre was the promulgation of Presidential rule under Article 356 of the Constitution, in the states barring a few exceptions where the imposition of Central Rule was appreciated even by the State Govt. and the leaders of the opposition parties. Post fourth general election period witnessed this promulgation very often united front government were formed in six states, but none of these governments could last for its full term of five years. During the period states were placed under Presidential Rule and in almost in all cases the States accused the centre of acting at the behest of Mrs. Gandhi's Government at the Centre. Mrs. Gandhi was accused for toppling these government for her own party interest.

❐

4

National Integration

The social world of India harboured different races evolved different philosophies accepted different religious, introduced different customs and followed different traditions. The solution of such a disparity, or divergence was found in the harmonious functioning of caste. So the foundation of caste institution was laid on sanctimonious principle. No one had the right to question. Human interference was entirely ruled out. The group customs, conventions and laws were recognised by caste as the basis of social life. It permitted each group to follow its life pattern. The rights of each group were recognised. Each group was free to follow its tradition and conventions. Thus in ancient India, social life was the core of caste. Gradually the harmonious functioning of the caste institution was disrupted. The values of equality, compassion and tolerance faded into the hazy background. Various practices which had authority neither in Hinduism nor in tradition came to be regarded as fundamental. Indian society was devided into an inchoate mass of small units.

After Independence. When India became free, it had to function as a democracy emphasising secularism and equal opportunity for all. The constitution offers that the State shall not discriminate against any citizen on grounds of religion, caste, sex, place of birth or any of them. Nevertheless the vasted interests under the cover of politics, language, religion and caste undermined the unity of India.

In view of these destructive tendencies it was thought that positive steps should be taken for national unity and integration. Therefore, from time to time the government emphasised national intergration throught such programmes as national youth camp, national tours by students and national programmes over All India

Radio. Nevertheless positive steps are needed to strengthen the national or emotional integration.

Meaning of National or Emotional Integration. When we try to study the problem of National integration our attention is drawn towards its nature and definition. Chiefly social integration refers to that sentiment which binds the people of a country together. In other words, by social integration we mean emotion and sentiment which are in paramount in the life of the members of a nation.

The report of the committee on Emotional Integration (1962) contains the analysis to the questionnaire issued by it and on its basis it has given the following definitions of social integration:

(1) "Emotional Integration is a strong feeling of brotherhood and nationhood that inspires a people in all spheres of its thought and activity and helps it to sink and ignore all real differences individual, parochial linguistic or religious."

(2) "Emotional integration means the common mental bond that would find all men and women of our land, irrespective of their religions and faith, for one common ideal *i.e.*, the true progress of their country, aesthetically spiritually and materially."

(3) "Emotional integration means creating mental outlook which will prompt and inspire every person to place loyalty to the country above group loyalties and the welfare of the country above narrower sectarian interests."

(4) "Emotional integration implies a feeling of oneness, as distinct from thinking. When all people irrespective of their religion, caste, language etc. are emotionally drawn together on all vital national problems, they may be described as a nationally integrated community."

(5) "Emotional integration means the welding of the diverse elements of society into a very compact harmonious and homogeneous mass with common ideals and objectives, which may guide the people to make unflinching sacrifice of the highest order for a just and proper cause. Emotional integration is the denial of separatism".

FACTORS HINDERING NATIONAL INTEGRATION

There are several factors of disintegration in the country which are jeopardising national unity. These factors are as follows:

(1) Casteism and communalism.
(2) Regionalism.
(3) Linguism.
(4) Party politics and exploitation by political parties.
(5) Illiteracy and lack of proper education.
(6) Lack of patriotism.
(7) Corruption and narrow-mindedness.
(8) Religious bigotry and intolerance.
(9) Lack of common goal.
(10) Reorganisation of states on linguistic basis.
(11) Social and economic factors.

The above factors are well-known as such need no explanation. Nevertheless there is a need for a definite state policy which may bring about social and economic justice and equality. The problem of poverty is also a great factor of disintegration. India is being industrialised and due to rapid industrialization several social and economic problems have arisen. One of them is that rich are becoming richer and the poor, poorer. The slogan of socialization has to made meaningful for the masses. Only then conditions for social integration will be created.

SOME SUGGESTIONS FOR NATIONAL INTEGRATION

(1) Eradication of Untouchability. The existence of untouchability is one of the main factors of social disintegration. In the caste hierarchy the untouchables are placed at the lowest level. They suffer the various social and religious disabilites. After independence, untouchability has been declared unconstitutional but the fact cannot be denied that this step could only remove the constitutional disability of the exterior castes. If all the basis of untouchability are not destroyed, a simple provision for its legal status will bear scanty fruits. Due to disabilities, the members of the untouchable class feel themselves aloof from other castes.

(2) Elimination of Casteism. Casteism splits the Hindu brotherbood into innumerable groups of different interests. In this way caste has been dragged into political arena such as 'Brahmanvad and Kayasthavad' etc. It is nothing but a blind and narrow group loyalty. Thus casteism is inconsistent wih social integration. If India has to attain social integration, the casteism shall have to be removed.

(3) Encouragement to Inter-Caste Marriage. Endogamy or marriages within the caste has been very much responsible for encouraging tendencies of separation. Inter-caste marriages would break the psychological barrier between different castes and groups. This would also create an atmosphere favouring the group integration or social integration.

(4) Development of New Attitudes. The consciousness about caste, religion and province is developed among the children at the age of 4 or 5 Education should have to be so arranged that it discourages this type of consciousness and opposes casteism, regionalism and communalism. It is the education that is responsible for forming and moulding the attitudes of young boys and girls. Apart from it a sense of cultural unity among people of different castes and regions should be encouraged.

(5) Propaganda Against the Fissiparous Tendencies. The fissiparous tendencies are cutting at the roots of nationalism and democracy. Therefore strong propaganda is needed to propagate the cause of social integration. Through newspapers, films, radio and other agencies, the attitudes favouring casteism, linguism and regionalism should be discouraged.

(6) Development of Nationalism. For social integraiton, development of nationalism is very essential. National integration is not possible without patriotism. It implies love for the nation. If a person is patriotic, he would ignore his communal and regional interests.

NATIONALITY NORMS

Till recently, the terms nationality and nation were used interchangeably. Now they are used as two distinct terms, but even those have distinguished between them, have by no means been in agreement as to the difference. This is obviously due to the fact that both nation and nationality have to share the same adjectival from 'national' and they have the same root *natu* which connotes the idea of birth or race. But nation has now definitely become political in meaning as a consequence of the universal acceptance of the principle of 'one nation, one State.' It means a political unity. a body of people distinct from others having their own distinct and separate political identity. Nationality has no reference to political unity. It serves to indicate the totality of the natural qualities that characterise the nation, without the idea of legal status which is connected with the term nation. Nationality emphasises its root meaning of common birth, real or fictitious. It is in this context that James Bryce defines nationality. He says, "A nationality is a population held together by certain ties, as for example, language and literature, ideas, customs and traditions, in such a way as to feel itself a coherent unity distinct from other populations similarly held together by like ties of their own." Whereas a nation is a nationality "which has organised itself into a political body either independent or desiring to be independent." John Stuart Mill's conception of nationality is materially similar to that of James Bryce.

Nationality, thus, indicates a common spiritual or psychological sentiment among the people having some common affinities or a "socio-cultural complex," as MacIver puts it. Barnes says that nationality "is the collective name given to that complex of psychological and cultural factors which furnish the cohesive principle uniting a nation." It is, like religion, a matter of feelings thinking and living a pursuit of such a conviction. If any group of people begin to think themselves distinct from others, which distinction they are keen to maintain, they constitute a nationality.

The feelings of nationality are subjective and there is no measurable factor universal in application to which it can be traced. It is a sentiment of unity, a common mass consciousness that may be the result of many factors, like common race and language, common history of victories won and sufferings endured, common traditions and customs giving birth to a common culture and common political aspirations. When all or some of these elements are present among the peoples, there is a feeling of kinship and their uniqueness that distinguishes them from others. All these factors have considerably contributed, at one stage or another, to the development of that sense of unity which marks off those who share it from the rest of mankind.

Community of Race. Racial unity is one of the stronger bonds of cohesion. Writers, like Zimmern, put emphasis on racial purity and consider it as a vital factor helping in the formation and strengthening the idea of nationality. But racial unity is not a necessary element of nationality, for no race can claim its purity. Anthropology and history have shown that there is no pure race any where on earth. From the historic and prehistoric processes of development and amalgamation mankind found themselves split into a number of board divisions mainly on geographical lines. Almost every section "hedged itself with pride and prejudice" and believed itself a pure and superior race.

By the community of race we may then mean a belief in a common origin, fictitious or legendary. Every nationality, as a matter of fact, has legendary tales of its non-historic origin which make the people to forget the diversity of their origins. Whenever a body of people believe that they belong to one race, they become a group of common consciousness and interests. One of the subtle ways of satisfying this group consciousness is to judge one's own group by its best specimens and others by their worst.

Community of Language. No less is the influence of language in binding the people together and developing in term the sentiment of like-mindedness. It is very often assumed that language and race go hand in hand because the colour and quality of language determine the colour and quality of those who use it. The racialist theories of the Germans are largely based upon these fallacious assumptions. It cannot, however, be denied that there is nothing more which readily gives unity to people conscious of their divergent origins as the unity of the tongue. Language is the medium through which people express themselves, maintain mutual intercourse, share common thoughts and participate in their weal and woe in the same idioms. Common language helps the growth of feelings and traditions, at first through folk songs and folk tales and later through a written or printed literature. "There is nothing," says Ramsay Muir, "that will give unity to divergent races as the use of a common tongue, and in very many cases unity of language and community ideas which it brings, have proved the main binding force in a nation." Bohen explains that the concept of a mother-tongue has made language the source from which springs all intellectual and spiritual existence. Earnest Barker finds the closest affinities between nationality and language. "Each word is charged with associations that touch feelings and evoke thoughts. You cannot share their feelings and thoughts unless you can unlock their associations by having the key of language. You cannot enter the heart nor the mind of nation unless you know its speech. Conversely, once you have learned the speech you find that with it and by it you imbibe a deep and pervasive spiritual force."

The general view is that diversity in language greatly weakens national sentiments. The most recent example is the revolt of Bengalis in the erstwhile Eastern Wing of Pakistan and their secession from its Western Wing to form the sovereign State of Bangladesh. But if diversity of language weakens the national spirit, linguistic unity does not always bring national unity. It has not united the Irish with the British, nor the Austrians with the Germans. Spanish Americans show no disposition to join the Spaniards or even to consolidate in South America. The Swiss are a nation, though they are divided linguistically and four languages and a number of local dialects are far more generally spoken than the official languages. Paradoxical as it may seem, nothing whatever is done officially or privately, to lesson the linguistic differences. Nevertheless, language is important, not exclusive, as a factor in welding the people together in common ties.

Community of Religion. Religion had been at all stages of mankind's development played an important role in binding the people in oneness of purpose and community of interests. If religion and kinship welded the ancients, it is a potential joining and separating force even today. There were several reasons for Belgium to break away in 1830 from the imposed union with Holland, but not the least was the diversity of religion. The partition of India in 1947, into two separate States, India and Pakistan, was essentially the result of

Mohammed Ali Jinnah's two-nation theory based upon religious differences, between the Hindus and the Muslims.

Religion, no doubt, was and is a great cementing force, but now writers are little inclined to lay stress on religion as a contemporary factor: "Sameness of religion" says Burgess, "was once a most potent factor in national development, but the modern principle of religious freedom has greatly modified its influence." If Burgess should have combined with the modern principle of religious freedom the modern decline in the religious faith, his explanation would have been more apt. In developed countries religion has since long been separated from politics and the cases are at least as numerous in which deep-rooted religious differences have formed no obstacle to national unification. Apart from religion there are other factors which are a strong incentive to cohesion. The rise of fundamentalism accompanied by terrorism during recent years is, however, alarming.

Garner appropriately sums up the importance of religion as a factor in the development of nationality. He says, "While community of religion has in some cases been a powerful factor in the development of nationality and in the strengthening of the bond of national unity, and while in other cases the absence of it has contributed to the disruption of the State, it is no longer, thanks to the modern spirit of toleration, an essential or important element of determining nationality." Freedom of religious belief and the spirit of toleration at least take away the sting the fanaticism and create a sense of amity and neighbourly relations in societies containing diverse religious groups.

Geographic Unity. Geographic unity is another factor that fosters sentiments of unity. It is desirable that people constituting a nationality should occupy a fixed territory, the parts of which are contiguous, which they may proudly call their own, sweet home-country. A fixed and contiguous territory produces a community of interests and feelings of co-operation and sympathy. People living in contiguous areas form their own distinct habits, customs, traditions, culture, common experiences and interests that distinguish them from others. It develops national character of the people and affects their institutions.

Common Historical Traditions. Common historical traditions are regarded by Ramsay Muir as an "indispensable factor" in cementing the bonds of nationality. John Sturat Mill has given them the first place of precedence and Hayes places them second only to language. Such traditions, Ramsay Muir says, involve a memory of sufferings endured and victories won in common, expressed in song and legend, in the dear name of great personalities that seem to embody in themselves the character and ideals of the nation, in the names of the sacred places wherein the national memory is enshrined. "Here is the source of that paradox of nationality, that it is only intensified by sufferings, and, like the giant Antueus in the Greek fable, rises with redoubled strength every time it is beaten down into the bosom of its mother earth. Heroic achievements, agonies heroically endured, these are the sublime food by which the spirit of nationhood is nourished; from these are born the sacred and imperishable traditions that make the soul of nations."

Common Interests. Common interests, like economic and defensive, act as a fillip in strengthening the ties of unity. Economic and defensive problems are vital in the formation of federations. Economic interests reconciled Scotland to a union with England. The Zollverein bringing Germans with a customs union laid the foundation of the confederation in 1867. No one will, at the same time, deny that economic interests may intensify national consciousness.

Common Government. A people, howsoever, heterogeneous in their outlook and sentiments develop national feelings of oneness if they live for long under the same government. The process of unity is accelerated if the government is alien. People become unified in their resolve to free themselves from the shackles of foreign domination and exploitation. Two hostile classes come into existence; those struggling against the oppression and exploitation of the alien rulers and those who make all out efforts to perpetuate their hold and suppress the aspirations of the subject people. Misgovernment is a prolific source of national awakening as the malcontents of today are the revolutionaries of tomorrow.

There is other side of the same problem also. When diverse people live for a long time under one government and the government is tolerant in its policy towards all such diverse elements, with the passage of time they merge into a single unified nationality. Their children become political half-castes, and the third and fourth generations lose their parental prejudices. The peoples of the original thirteen Colonies, which comprised the United States of America after the Declaration of Independence were in their first generation either Englishmen, Germans, Poles or Czechs. Their political aspirations to get rid of foreign domination welded them in bonds of unity and all the different nationalities were fused together in one American nation. Common government is the instrumentality through which much of the common historical heritage of a people takes form.

NATIONALISM AND SELF DETERMINATION

Self-government and nationalism are twin-born. The French Revolution was primarily responsible for national sentiment. Cohesion in the society was sought on the basis of kinship and sentiment of oneness aided by the natural boundaries that helped the formation and strengthening of such feelings. Since the cardinal principles of the Rights of Man were equality, and popular sovereignty joining them with nationality, loyalty and allegiance of the people were to rest with the nation alone and for that matter with the State integrity of which they were committed to preserve. This is the second stage in the development of the nation-State. Hans Kohn, accordingly, maintained that the French Revolution inherited and continued the centralising tendencies of the kings, but at the same time it filled the central organisation with a new spirit and gave it a power of cohesion unknown before. Nationalism was unthinkable before the emergence of the modern State in the period from the sixteenth to the eighteenth century.

Thenceforward Nationalism became a dogma and dominated the human mind over a large part of the globe. Enthused with this new spirit and attitude of mind and a pattern of attention and desires, poets, historians, journalists and politicians roused the sentiments of nationalism in Central Europe and in the Balkans. Elsewhere in the Near East and far away in India, China and Japan "it began to cast a spell by promising relief from actual or threatened domination."

Meanwhile, the Industrial Revolution was made a means to promote national purposes and interests rather than to gain benefits for all communities and States. The Revolution had a national content and national purposes as its home was a national State and it spread chiefly to national States imbued with the traditions of mercantalism. "Even the enormous transit of ideas and news" Hayes says, "which the Industrial Revolution made possible; assumed for linguistic reasons, a complexion predominantly national."

Nationalism came into its own in the early nineteenth century. Since then it has gradually spread throughout the world. Within the last seven decades it flared up to new heights of militancy in Nazi Germany. It transformed an international movement in Soviet Russia into a strongly nationalistic movement. It even changed the complexion of the movement in China. It stirred passions to fever pitch in the Middle East, leading nations to take actions contrary to their economic interests, as in the case of Iran and probably Egypt, and it sparked powerful desire for self-government in majority of the colonial areas of the world. Once these colonies attained independence, it was attuned to the extreme type of nationalism in order to retain their newly won independence, placed as they were in the midst of power-hungry nations, and, at the same time, to accelerate the pace of economic growth to usher an era of just and happy life for the people hitherto trodden under the heels of the alien rulers.

Nationalism is almost one idea for which masses of men live and die. It combines love of country and suspiciousness of foreigners. Love of country comes from shared values, and suspiciousness of foreigners comes from the belief that foreigners do not share such values in the same strength. "The first shared value is the love of familiar places. the neighbourhood, the land, the homes, the valleys, and the mountains, all of the surroundings that one loves because they have been a part of oneself from infancy." This is the logical corollary of the eternal truth of man's nature that he is a social animal and his instinct of living together and co-operting with others among whom he lives-creates perpetual bounds of affinity and good-will and a love for the land-home country-which provides them with the wherewithal of life. But nationalism, as it emerged with the nation-

State, assumed the form of ancient group principle pride in one's group and resentment of injury to a member of one's group as it was an attack on the solidarity and the honour of the whole. Pride in one's group usually led to an imaginative abasement of all others. "Pain economy," says Beni Prasad "set a high value on group solidarity and encouraged an exclusiveness which inspite of some contrary influences of a political and ethical character, sanctified group prejudices."

A Nationalist wants his people and his country to command all the respect and deference from others, his people to have all the power, all the wealth, and all the well-being. He tends to claim all the rectitude and virtue for it, as well as all enlightenment and skill; and he gives it a monopoly of his affection. In sum, he totally identifies himself with his nation. Devotion to the nation transcends all his loyalities, like the family, the village, the caste, religion and other associational loyalities. Hans Kohn defines nationalism in this context and says; it "is a state of mind permeating the large majority of the people and claiming to permeate all its members; it recognises the nation-State as the ideal form of political organisation and the nationality as the source of all creative cultural energy and economic well-being. The supreme loyalty of man is therefore due to his nationality, as his own life is supposedly rooted in and made possible by its welfare."

RIGHT OF SELF-DETERMINATION

The modern theory is that each nationality should form a separate State and each State should comprise a single nation. The principle of mono-national State has lent support to the revolt of nations hitherto held in subjugation and the right of every nationality to become a nation. It stands for President Woodrow Wilson's right of self-determination of nations and nationalities enunciated by him in January 1918 and embodied in his famous Fourteen Points. He declared that an evident principle runs through all the programmes "I have outlined. It is the principle of justice to all peoples and nationalities and their right to live on equal terms of liberty and safety with one another, whether they may be strong or weak." In an address to the United States Congress, he elaborted the point and said, "Peoples and provinces are not to be bartered about from sovereignty to sovereighty as if they were mere chattels and pawns in the game. Peoples may now be dominated and governed only by their own consent. Self-determination is not a mere phrase. It is an imperative principle of action, which statesmen will henceforth ignore at their peril."

President Franklin Roosevelt and Prime Minister Winston Churchill in a meeting on August 14, 1941 somewhere on the Atlantic, issued an Eight Point Joint Declaration (popularly known the Atlantic Charter) embodying the objectives for which the Allies were fighting against Germany and explained the principles that would serve as the basis of the future peace of the world. The United States and Britain solemnly pledged themselves not only to uphold the Rights of Man within their own territorial limits, but to enforce the same throughout the world. It was explicitly stated that neither the United States nor Britain sought territorial or other aggrandisement anywhere in the world and that both the countries would respect the rights of the people to choose their own forms of government.

The principle of self-determination had earlier been advocated by some eminent thinkers and statesmen. John Stuart Mill maintained that "wherever the sentiment of nationality exists in any force, there is a prima facie case for uniting all the members of the nationality under the same government, and a government to themselves apart." He regarded it as only a logical application of the right of self-determination and expressed the opinion that free institutions are next to impossible in a country made up of different nationalities. He explained that it is in general "necessary condition of free institutions that the boundaries of government should coincide in the main with those of nationalities."

Appraisal of the Doctrine. The advocates of a mono-national State, who are numerous, claim that a single-nation State is the monument of common history and culture, traditions and customs and common symbols and myths and such a homogeneity of the people fosters fellowship, co-operation, mutual trust and internal harmony. A cohesive society ensures promotion and preservation of social heritage, rapid material advancement and growth of civilisation. Hegal expounded the idea of the State as containing all the worth which the human being possessed. It was the guardian of the whole moral world, because organised moral life was to be found only within the State. To Bosanquet, who as-profoundly influenced by Hegal, the State appeared as a complete idea of the realisation of the human capacity. Such a State could only be a mono-national State; the epitome of moral self-sufficiency. It is claimed. History provides innumerable examples of small independent States that have preciously contributed to the advancement of civilisation. The Greek City-State developed to the stage of a conscious effort directed to the realization of liberty and equal laws. It was a great experiment not only in the art of self-government, but also in quest of virtue.

A mono-national State, is a homogeneous and viable State and the possibilities of "Cracking and splitting," a normal feature of a multi-national State, are remote, if not non-existent. There is a common centre of loyalty and allegiance and that is the nation. The mass consciousness of oneness divides the people on economic and political issues and not both horizontally and vertically. A single unified party or a group of parties, agreeing on basic fundamentals, man the government and pursue its policies in programme vigorously with the electoral mandate at their back. But if the population, as Mill argued, is composed of various nationalities, the government may resort to the policy of 'divide and rule', an old maxim of statecraft to ensure its stability and the handy weapon to carry out its policies and programmes. If one single nationality happens to command a brute majority it may even be ruthless in its policies and attitude towards nationalities in minority.

The right of self determination and to decide about one's own political future has a democratic basis, international recognition, and collective commitment of nations. It sparked the national-consciousness of the people yoked to the shackles of the foreign-rules. From the time of the declaration of Woodrow Wilson's Fourteen Points there had been an upsurge first in Europe and then in Asia, Africa and Latin America resulting into the ultimate liquidation on the Colonial Empires. Within the last five decades the British Empire has become a Commonwealth of Nations. Most of the rich Dutch Colonial Empire was lost when Indonesia became independent and a republic. The events in Africa proved a last phase in the history of the Colonial Empires. Today, there are just a few stray colonies that exist and the fate of their rulers is as precarious as it was of their predecessors or sin in the network of the defunct Colonial Empire.

The critics of the right of self-determination, though not many, are equally articulate and their criticism is rather trenchant. They assert that it is historically unsound and sociological untenable. There are even now many States in which the population is composite and in all such States there is maximum freedom for all and all nationalities are equal participants in the United States of America, Switzerland and India. The Swiss people are not a homogeneous whole. They sharply differ in race, language, religion and even to a certain extent in civilisation. Yet in this diversity is to be found unity in the Swiss nation and Switzerland presents to the world the most striking example of not only a united people, but one of the most united, and certainly the most patriotic among the peoples of Europe.

Nor is it entirely true that liberty and free institutions can exist and flourish in a mono-national State alone. To cite, again, the example of Switzerland one feels inclined to agree with Hans Kohn that Switzerland has "developed a democratic nationalism, similar to the one know in England and the United States, a nationalism made secure and strong by its insistence on individual liberty and on respect for diversity" Switzerland was the first country in the world to establish republican institutions, and the only one State in Europe which has always been a republic. When the United States of America was born as an independent nation, Switzerland had behind it a republican tradition of some five hundred years.

The United States of America itself originally consisted of thirteen Colonies of immigrants drawn from nearly all countries of Europe. By the gradual process of intermingling of different culture, a new culutre, a blend of English and Continental characteristics, conditioned by the environments of the New World, was produced. Together the new Americans fought their War of Independence and in a Declaration of Independence adopted on July 4, 1776 announced the birth of a new nation. There were in the words of Bluntschli, the conjunction of various peoples who gave to the new State of Americans "breadth and variety" that served "as an alloy to give strength and currency to the nobler metal". The delegates of the thirteen original States, assembled at Philadelphia Convention in May 1787, to revise the Constitution of the Confederation, adopted entirely a new Constitution, which, according to Gladstone, was "the most wonderful work ever struck off at a given time by the brain and purpose of man." The new American system of government was based, as James Madison said, "on that honourable determination which animates every votary of freedom to rest our political experiments on the capacity of mankind for self-government." A publication of the United States Information Service, gives a matter of fact summing-up: "The United States is a country of great diversity...Geographically, there is a variety too...And at the core of this varied land are the poeple. the most varied of all, for they stem from countries and social levels throughout the world. But in spite of many differences, certain traditions—freedom, equality, individual rights are common to all and are taught in the home, in the church, and in the schools."

Lord Acton was a relentless critics of the mono-national State and the right of self-determination. He believed that a multinational State embodied the genius of all the nationalists and consequently it is the amalgam of vigour, promise and advancement. "The combination of different nations in one State," he argued, "is as necessary a condition of civilised life as the combination of men in society. Inferior races are raised by living in political union with races intellectually superior. Exhausted and decaying nations are revived by the contact of a younger vitality... This fertilising and regenerating process can only be obtained by living under one government. It is in the cauldron of the State that the fusion takes place by which the vigour, knowledge and the capacity of one portion of mankind may be communicated to another."

Presence of too many nation-States add to international complications and help to mount mutual rivalries and conflicts ultimately into a conflagration involving in it even the major States. Lord Curzon remarked at the Lausanne Conference that the right of self-determination "is like a two edged sword and can be admitted only with reservations." The right of self determination fragmented many existing States, immediately after World War I, redrawing the political map of Europe, and gave a fillip to the struggle for freedom in subject countries in Asia and Africa. During the last four decades, it became a powerful instrument as well as an argument for liberation from their colonial masters.

Disintegration of Soviet Russia in 1991, brought into existence fifteen independent and Sovereign states based on ethnicity and it is the most recent connotation of the right of self-determination. But the United States of America and many other countries including India, are against the division of multi-ethnic states in the name of the right of self-determination and minority rights. Addressing a 53-nation commission on Human Rights in Geneva in February 1993, Morris Abraham, the United States Ambassador, explained that self-determination "should not be confused with ethnic isolationism." But ironically in today's World "Self-determination has become the world cry of groups which for ethnic or religious reasons, are bent on dividing nations." Self-determination, he added, was intended for colonial people as self-determination meant the right to be free from imperialist power, often ruling from across an ocean. "In today's version, self-determination often is asserted against a neighbours within the same territory". The controversy boils down to this fundamental question of what defines a nation and he himself answered. "If it is common culture, a common language and historical claims to territory, there could be thousands of nations instead of less than two hundred." The right of self-determination, "in the sense of right to break away from one's own nation does not necessarily attach to a group simply because its individual members share ethnic, religious or cultural history", he emphasised.

But the birth of so many sovereign States have created an international disequilibrium. Most of these newly-born States are not viable units to firmly stand on their own legs in order to ensure a political and an economic poise. With their jittering' political stability and precarious economic resources they have to perforce lean heavily on some big power, neighbouring or distant, who can come to their rescue and steer them through their predicaments. This has two results. In the first place, it disturbs the balance of power in the international sphere, and secondly, it creates an atmosphere of suspicion and distrust with the logicial implication of a mad race for armaments. Every State, big or small, old or new, pursues a vigorous policy of arming itself against any future contingency and, thus, begins the hysteria of war-preparedness. That had been the course of history since the Treaty of Versaillers. Laski has correctly said that nation-States enter into "a competition in the armament of power which acts so as to jeopardise the maintenance of peace, to provoke an atmosphere of nervous hostility, and to induce the smaller States into alliance with powerful neighbours that may win security by that multiplied strength.

Two other disquieting legacies of the right of self-determination are: the hunger for new markets and the craze for economic self-sufficiency, especially with the newly-born States. Economic self-sufficiency is an alias for economic nationalism and it has more dangerous effects than political nationalism, though in the final analysis they are the two sides of the same coin. Economic self-sufficiency suffocates the normal channels of trade and commerce and worst of all is unethical restrictións on immigration and fanning of race-hatred. This tug-of-war between the nation-States is another major addition to the already existing vicious circle of international distrust and intrigue.

NATIONALISM AND INTERNATIONALISM

The emergence of the nation-State was hailed as a landmark in the evolution of the State as it provided a structure for the emotionally integrated people to live together in a cohesive society with shared values of commmon interests and purposes and the psychological satisfaction of common feeling which make them a community of patriotic sentiments. Many regarded the nation-State as "the ultimate unit in human organisation." But the nation-State soon after the start of its career degenerated and landed itself in the narrow alley of nationalism which excessively favoured an attitude of separatism, arrogance, and economic aggrandizement.

Fichte was responsible for a scheme of an international league to enforce peace, and nationhood was to him "a manifestation of the primordial, the divine, the eternal. the absolute." Yet he felt that a nation could not dispense with arrogance. Even Mazzini attacked the cosmopolitans on the ground that it was impossible to love all without distinction of nationality. Some statesmen bluntly stated the extreme implications of nationlism. While defending his Polish Policy, Von Bulow declared that "in the struggle between nationalities, one nation is the hammer and other the anvil; one is the victor and the other the vanquished. It is a law of life and development that when two civilizations meet they fight for supremacy." When the nation is glorified and the State idolized, the characteristic of such a, State is vigour and force. Tensions and conflicts mount and disputes between States, real or imaginary, are decided by the arbitrament of war. There had been a regular succession of wars, major and minor, since the birth of the nation-State and there seems no end to such wars. In fact, makind is scared by past wars and is scared of new ones. In the nuclear age of our times, no country can afford to wait for defence to ward off the probablities of war and to win it, if it actually comes.

The nation-State is an exclusive State and it has two aspects. In the first place it means race superiority and its supremacy. The race problems becomes aggravated in proportion to the conjecture of physiological and cultural differences with econmic conditions and political clash. On the economic side, the ideal of economic self-suficiency, combines with the exigencies of modern industry. its ever present needs of raw supplies and markets and sometimes cheap labour. to prompt the annexation or control of territories inhabited by weaker peoples. There is an old maxim that flag follows the trade and economic nationalism has its counterpart in economic imperialism. Big industry and high finance manipulate the patriotic sentiments and enthusiasms and equate nationalism with imperialism.

The eighteenth and nineteenth centuries saw many wars between the imperial powers. It was estimated that about half the population of the world spread over more than half the surface of the earth had been under the suzerainty of the imperial powers. This phase in the history of the Colonial powers is more or less over now, but colonialism has taken a new form. There is a regular race between the "big" powers to establish and extend their spheres of influence and the obvious victims are the under developed and strategically important States. The most recent example of this political manoeuvring are Afghanistan and Kuwait.

Internationalism. The rationable of the nation-State was democratic as it joined nationality with the twin principles of self-government and equality. But nationality became, in the words of Tagore, "one of the most powerful anaesthetics" that the ingenuity of man has ever invented. Education often inulcates the type of patriotism which sanctifies an attitude of "my nation, right or wrong." The feelings of patriotism so drummed into us from the earliest childhood that it is "only by a considerable intellectual effort that any of us can liberate themselves from these forms of thought, to which we have been moulded." Such a patriotic fervour to which nationals of all States had been taught and trained did not us her an era of peace, cordiality, mutual trust, goodwill and co-operation in the family of nations. On the other hand, the nation-State system is a dismal chronicle of national arrogance, aggression, chauvinism expansionism and all the worst that human nature can display. Hayes, accordingly, comes to the conclusion that it is highly doubtful if 'the recasting of political geography on national lines has actually promoted either humanity or justice and whether nationalism is a reliable harbinger of a quieter and better world in the immediate future."

But the old ideas in the relations of races and nations have become anachronistic and the former notions of nationalism are breaking down in the atmosphere of contemporary civilisation. Laski says that "the scale of modern civilisation has made the national and sovereign State an institutional expedient of which the political unwisdom and moral danger are both manifest." He categorically affirms that the notion of a sovereign independent State, on the international side is "fatal to the well-being of humanity. The way in which the State should live in relation to other States is clearly not a matter to which the State is entitled to be the sole judge. The common life of States is a matter of common agreement between States."

It is not implied that the tangles of centuries can be resolved so immediately. It is not given to any generation of men to write on a clean slate. The logic of history rules out the sudden dawn of internationalism. But much leeway has been made during the past seven decades or so. The rapid technological advancement in every country and the consequent economic growth and economy of plenty have removed the root causes of the conflict which made nations so exclusive in spirit and aim. The new means of transport and communication, the new industry and the new commerce have made the world a single economic unit and produced new economic homogenety in the economic interests of all the nations. In the seventeenth century an English writer vigorously propounded the doctrine that commercially a country could progress only at the expense of another. That is no longer true and with general economic improvement it "will become the exact anti-thesis of the truth."

Internationalism is a way of life and pattern of behaviour and its prerequisite is to master the art of living together. Its rationale is the well-known dictum of Kant; "So act as to treat humanity whether in your person or that of another, in any case as an end, and never merely as a means." If nations follow the voice of reason and eschew emotions, parochial loyalties and narrow considerations ipso facto disappear and an atmosphere of fellow-feelings prevails that knows no territorial limits. The brotherhood of man is the basis of internationalism. It rouses no passions and does not blur man's vision to distort his notions. Reason is the just steward of man's mind. Internationalism presupposses the existence of sovereign national States and the voice of reason enjoins to reconcile national interests with the larger interests of makind with a just mind in an atmosphere of mutual trust and goodwill. Interdependence is the natural necessity of nations and all are integral parts of one single human society and their weal and woe is inseparably interwined. Laski has succinctly said that there are "no longer lotus-fields where men may linger careless of life about them.

The method of this unity and international solidarity is reflected in a vast network of inter-governmental bodies and in a series of international organisations and voluntary international organisations that have been established during the course of the Present Century. Any problem which affects or is likely to affect the peace, security and well-being of mankind is a matter of common concern and it is obligatory on all States to accept the decisions arrived at in the inter-governmental bodies and international conferences. The scope and subject mater that the international conferences and agencies deal with have expttanded so tremendously that there is virtually no topic excluded from international treatment. For example, discussions on values of national currencies are frequent and a matter of vital common concern as the rise or fall in the value of the currency of one State has an impact on the economy of other States, if not to the same extent at least to a disturbing level of disequilibrium.

A sovereign nation-State, however, remain the basic foundation of all interantional activity. Laski and many other eminent thinkers have assailed the moral validity of the doctrine that attributes sovereignty to the State and emphatically maintain that it "will pass, as the divine right of the kings had its day." But it seems highly doubtful to happen in the foreseeable future. Sovereignty remains sovereignty and no State is prepared to surrender it, not even the communist countries whose ideological base is a stateless society. Even the subejct matter of International Law are the sovereign States and membership of the United Nations Organisation is open for them alone. It is, accordingly, within the framework of the national State that sovereignty is to be interpreted restrictively in order to broaden the scope and obligatory nature of the decisions arrived at the international conferences.

The modern nation-State, to sum up, is a sovereign State and it is within the four walls of this framework that nationalism is to be reconciled to internationalism. A revision of present day political arrangements is the sine qua non of the emergence of nationalism free from the taints of intolerance and aggression. It has two dimensions. Nationalism and internationalism are not antagonistic and exclusive, provided Nationalism, as Laski says, is equated with right. The right of every nation to be equal to others, to preserve and promote its individuality and ensure is security with the corresponding obligation of recognising the same right of other nations and States. Thus, harmonising and balancing of diverse national interests in a spirit of mutual trust, co-operation and goodwill. Secondly, the spirit of exlusiveness and aggradizement, which has long characterised human relationships and which the educational machinery in every nation-State has been used to inculcate, is out of tune wth the present trends. It must give way to that of political equality and co-operation among all the peoples of the world.

NATIONAL INTEGRATIONS AND ETHNICITY

The centrifugal forces and parochial tendencies that were operating all over the country in the form of communalism, casteism, regionalism and linguism caused serious concern in Central Government circles. It was felt that the sovereignty and integrity of India would be seriously jeopardised if these forces were not checked in time. With this object, two Bills designed to suppress communal propaganda were intorduced in the Lok Sabha on 10 August 1961. This first Bill, adopted on 31 August, made it an offence punishable with imprisonment for up to three years to promote 'enmity or hatred between different religious, racial or language groups or castes or communities.' The second Bill, passed on 4 September, laid down a similar penalty for attempts to appeal to religious, racial, communal caste or linguistic sentiments for electioneering purposes and disqualified those convicted of this offence from voting or from membership of Parliament or State Legislatures.

NATIONAL INTEGRATION CONFERENCE, 1961

Shortly after the introduction of these Bills in Parliament, the Central Government convened in New Delhi, from 28 September to 1 October, a conference to discuss and examine what it called 'the problem of national integration'. The Prime Minister, Cabinet Ministers, Chief Ministers of States, leaders of political parties and prominent educationists, writers and scientists attended the conference. It was inaugurated by Vice-President Radhakrishnan, a philosopher statesmen. In the course of his speech he said: "... Though caste is today ceasing to be very much of social evil, it has become a political and administrative evil. We are utilizing caste loyalities for the purpose of winning elections or getting more people into jobs." Speaking on the language question he said that the reorganisation of states on a linguistic basis, however necessary and desirable, had made people more conscious of their own languages. He suggested that "...we must get back to the time when these things did not play an important part."

The main theme at the conference was unity in diversity, National integration, as then defined, was concerned with education and psychological process involving the development of a feeling of unity, cohesion, solidarity and loyalty for the country in the hearts of the people. The conference took note of the fact that politicians and political parties played a considerable role in fomenting communalism, regionalism and linguism to serve their own ends and, therefore, it evolved a code of conduct for them. Some of the norms of behaviour and conduct agreed upon were as follows:

(1) No political party should indulge in any activity which aggravated existing differences, created mutual hatred, or caused tension between different castes and communities religious or linguistic groups.

(2) The government, while taking measures to maintain law and order, should take care not to impose undue restrictions on civil liberties, and should not employ such measures as interfered with the normal functioning political parties.

(3) Political parties should not resort to agitation (for seeking redress against any grievances relating to communal caste, regional or linguistic issues) which was likely to disturb peace, create bitterness or increase tension between the different sections of the public.

(4) Political parties should desist from creating obstructions to or breaking up meetings, processions, etc., organized by other parties.

The conference noted that education played an important role in promoting national integration. Views were expressed that in the interests of greater uniformity and cohesion of educational policy, education should be made a subject of the Concurrent Legislative List.

The conference set up a National integration Council (NIC) consisting of the Prime Minister, Union Home Minister, Chief Minister of states, seven leaders of political parties, the chairman of the University Grants Commission, two educationists, the Commissioner for Scheduled Castes and Scheduled Tribes, and seven other persons nominated by the Prime Minister. The NIC was asked to draw code of conduct for general public, the students, and the Press.

Prime Minister Nehru directed the NIC to examine the problem of national integration in all its aspects and make necessary recommendations of deal with it.

NATIONAL INTEGRATION CONFERENCE, 1968

The code of conduct devised by the conference was followed by the political parties, including the Congress, and the government at the Centre and in the states did not make serious and concerted efforts to implement the recommendations of the National Integration Council. During 1966 and 1967 more serious and widespread communal riots, regional disorders and disturbances over the language question occurred in U.P., Bihar, Andhra Pradesh, Maharashtra and Jammu and Kashmir. It appeared as if the country was going to disintegrate and tear into pieces.

The Union Government revived the National Integration Council (NIC). Its size as increased from 39 to 55 members, and representatives of industry, business and trade unions were included in it. The council met at Srinagar from 20 to 22 June 1968, and adopted a declaration condemning all tendencies that "strike at the root of national solidarity."

COMMUNAL RIOTS AT AHMEDABAD NIC CALLS FOR MASS CAMPAIGN

During the months following the Srinagar conference, the Union Government implemented, as claimed by Home Minister Chavan, all its decisions. But the communal riots and regional outbursts remained unchecked. A very serious communal flare-up took place in Ahmedabad and the conscience of the nation was stirred. On 16 October 1969, the standing committee of the NIC called for a joint mass campaign and education by all political parties to foster communal unity. This committee decried the campaign of Balraj Madhok, leader of one faction of the Jan Sangh, that the Muslims should be "Indianised' and characterised his demand for exchange of population with Pakistan being a solution of the Hindu-Muslim problem as 'totally inconsistent with secularism and nationalism, besides being harmful to the country's unity and security.'

COMMUNAL RIOTS AT BHIWANDI. AICC DEMANDS BAN ON COMMUNAL PARTIES

In May 1970, there was a serious communal riot at Bhiwandi in Maharashtra. The NIC chalked out a programme for a mass campaign to end communalism. In June, the All-India Congress Committe adopted the following resolution: "Para-Military communal organisations like the RSS and Jammat-i-Islami have no place in our secular society. The Government should seriously consider whether such organisations should be allowed to continuously poison our society with communal violence and hatred."

FORMATION OF INSANI BIRADARI

In August 1970, a non-official organisation, by the name Insani Biradari (human brotherhood), came into existence. The idea of this grew out of Khan Abdul Ghaffar Khan's visit to India. Jayaprakash Narayan, the Sarvodaya leader, became its President and Sheikh Mohammed Abdullah, the Vice-President. The membership of the Insani Biradari was opened to all irrespective of caste, creed, religion and politics. It was based upon three key words. tolerance, understanding and appreciation, and was designed to combat the forces of communalism and national disunity.

The Khudai Khidmatgars. Modelled on the Khan's famous "Red Shirt" band during the struggle for India's freedom. became is voluntary, non-violent "combat" wing. They were to prevent communal violence and do rehabilitation work if and when it occurred.

FORMATION OF ALL-INDIA SAMPRADAYIKTA VIRODHI COMMITTEE

In view of the unabated fury of communal riots, Mrs. Subhadra Joshi, a Congress leader, set up another non-official organisation by the name, All-India Sampradayikta Virodhi Committee (an organisation to oppose communalism). From 11 to 13 December 1970, it held a convention and adopted resolutions relating to the problem of communalism. One of the resolutions stated that communal riots have been "engineered by organised forces of communalism, mainly symbolised by the RSS. Jan Sangh whose purpose was to disrupt the secular democratic character of our polity and to replace it by communal fascist forces."

Other resolutions were in the form of recommendations to the Union Government asking the latter that communal parties like the Jan Sangh should be excluded from the NIC, that "para-military organisations" should be legally banned, that a 'special task force composed of men and officers firmly committed to secularism and democracy' should be formed, and that the educational system should be made secular.

COMMUNAL AND REGIONAL VIOLENCE AGAIN. NIC REITERATES DEMAND TO BAN COMMUNAL PARTIES

During 1971 and 1972, more violence of a communal and regional nature took place in some states, such as Uttar Pradesh, Maharashtra and Karnataka, and the advocates of communal amity and national solidarity again became active. In the second week of January 1974, the National Integration Council convened in New Delhi a convention and adopted a resolution, strongly reiterating the demand for banning the RSS, the Shiv Sena, the Jammat-e-Islami and Ananda Marg. The resolution asked the All-India Sampradayikta Virodhi Committee to launch a multi-directional attack on the evil and ensure that the recommendations of the National Integration Council for curbing communalism, particularly in regard to communal riots, were implemented in letter and spirit. The commission of the NIC dealing with education and communalism recommended that it was imperative that reading material used in educational institutions ought to be free from communalism and anti-democratic overtones. The commission on communalism and trade upon movement opined that concerted efforts by the Sampradayikta Virodhi Committee and other secular forces were necessary to expose and foil the efforts of the communalists to disrupt and mislead the working class.

SEVEN-POINT ACTION PLAN FOR NATIONAL INTEGRATION

In the last week of November 1976, a working group of the National Integration Council recommended a series of measures aimed at promoting communal and regional harmony, curbing violence and providing greater opportunities for education and employment for minorities. It suggested ending the hold of obscurantist and extremist elements over sections of the population; the growth of positive elements of modernity in all spheres of life; ending of the suspicions and prejudices about the minority communities; free mixing of children belonging to various professions and faiths, and highlighting through mass media of the forces which brought different faiths closer to each other.

The recommendations of the working group to tackle other threats to national integration included the following:

(1) The Prime Minster's 20-point programme should be vigorously implemented; legitimate demands of students should be looked into well in time; and political parties should be asked to keep their hands off students.

(2) Joint councils and steps to prevent avoidable lay-offs, lockouts and strikes have already created a favourable climate. The idea of one union in one industry should be pursued as an objective in the interest increased production, workers and management.

(3) Greater emphasis should be laid on modern education as opposed to traditional education especially on science and technical subjects. Students belonging to minorities should be given opportunities to get themselves admitted to reputed and progressive educational institutions. Voluntary organisations of minority communities could advise young men and women to register themselves with employment exchanges and to apply for jobs in reply to UPSC advertisements. Registration at employment exchanges should be encouraged. There should be opportunities for greater mixing of Muslim and non-Muslim students through well thought-out programmes in schools and colleges.

(4) An eight-point action programme was recommended. It envisaged Preventive steps, prompt investigation of particular cases, effective prosecution to secure punishment of the guilty, imposition of punitive fines, provision of legal aid to weaker sections; relief and rehabilitation assistance to victims, prompt supply of factual statistical information to the Central Government and provision of special arrangements in the states to look into complaints of atrocities and to undertake periodic review of the situation.

(5) The working group endorsed the broad strategy evolved under the current plan for promoting tribal development. It aimed at total development of each region, so that no critical element was left out of consideration. Elimination of exploitation got the highest priority.

(6) The problem should be viewed from three standpoints. economic, in relation to regional and linguistic tensions and emotional. While the economic aspect had been sought to be taken care of the fifth Plan by special weightage to Central assistance to backward states the working group suggested that the concerned state government as well as the Planning Commission should examine the cause for regional imbalances. The administrative machinery should be revamped. The Department of Personnel Land Administrative Reforms in the Union Home Ministry should study the weakness in the organisational structure of the concerned states and suggested measures. The Planning Commission should evolve and prescribe clear-cut norms for uniform applicability.

The Union Home Minister, K. Brahmanand Reddy, expressed, on 28 November 1976, the hope that the above recommendations would lead to a "purposeful national endeavour," and the difficulties that hindered national integration would be overcome successfully.

In 1977, the Janata Party Government also constituted a committee under the chairmanship of Jagjivan Ram to review the problem of national integration and to examine whether it was necessary to revive the NIC. But this Government became involved in internal squabbles and even though communal, regional and caste violence increased immensely it could do little in that regard.

NIC SETS UP WATCH-DOG COMMITTEE. EIGHT-POINT ACTION PLAN TO CURB COMMUNALISM

The Government of Mrs. Gandhi constituted in January 1980 was confronted with the acute problem of regional, communal and caste tensions. Commencing from Moradabad (in Uttar Pradesh) on 13 August 1980, the Hindu-Muslim riots assumed a serious form, and commencing from the north-eastern region the problem of regionalism became tremendously grave. The NIC was revived, and it held its first meeting on 12 November 1980. Addressing the participants the Prime Minister made an appeal for the involvement of everyone in the task of bringing about national integration which, she said, was not a mere phrase but "an awareness of the burden and task that history has placed on our shoulder." The council set up a standing committee to keep a "constant watch" on the activities of communal and other divisive forces posing a threat to the country's unity. It also drew up a 8-point plan of action to put down the canker of communalism. The plan stipulated that the governments of Uttar Pradesh, Bihar, Andhra Pradesh and Maharashtra should examine the problem of communalism from educational, historical, economic and social angles and should draw up a time-bound programme of implementation, that due place should be provided to minorities in state police forces, that the problem of communalisms should be examined by a Home Ministry cell on a continuing basis, that the victims of communalism should be speedily rehabilitated and that control room in communally-sensitive areas should be set up as an aid to controlling disturbances.

Even with all these plans and proposals the canker of communalism continued to eat into the vitals of Indian polity. During May-June 1984, serious Hindu-Muslims riots occurred in Bombay and Bhiwandi, and in late July, the capital city of Andhra Pradesh and Hyderabad witnessed a very grave communal outburst resulting in killings and destruction of public and private property. During 1985 and the first few months of 1986, the terrorists and extremists in Punjab whipped up their drive to work up the Hindu-Sikh hatred and to attain their political objectives, and the violent activities there immensely escalated. The National Integration Council met on 7th April 1986, and it recognised terrorism in Punjab as an attack on the unity, integrity and secular ideals of the country. A 21-member committee under the chairmanship of Jagjivan Ram was set up to devise suitable strategies to face the menace of terrorism and to unite for peace and stability inside the country.

❐

5

Centre-State Relations

What should be centre-state relationships is a very serious problem in India. India is a political democracy and as expected chances have been when the same political party has not remained in power both in the Centre as well as in the states. This happened for the first time after the General Elections of 1967. In that year whereas Congress party came to power in the Centre, anti-Congress governments were in power in the States. D.M.K. came to power in Tamil Nadu and Jansangh in Union Territory of Delhi. Similarly many coalition governments popularly Union as Samyukta Vidhayak Governments were formed in the States. This resulted in serious centre-state relationship in all the fields namely: *(a)* Administrative field *(b)* Legislative field and *(c)* Financial field. Though the strains relaxed after 1971 elections, 'yet the problem exists since then. In 1977 when elections were held in the country Janata government come to power at the center but in Southern States non Janata Parties were in power. Similarly when elections were again held after 1980 many non-Congress (I) governments came of power in the states though in that year Congress (I) came back to power at the centre.

Administrative Relationship between the Centre and the States. According to constitution the subject for the purposes of legislation have been divided into *(a)* Central List *(b)* State List and (c) Concurrent List. It has been provided that ordinarily the Centre will enact on the subjects enumerated in the Central List whereas the States will act on the subjects mentioned in the State list. Both the Center and States can enact on the subjects mentioned in the concurrent list but in case of a clash it is central law which will prevail over the state law. The residuary powers have also been left to the Centre.

Under the existing arrangements matters connected with subjects like Customs, Income Tax, Railways, Post Offices, Defence, External Affairs, Currency, Civil Aviation etc, are the responsibility of the Centre and that is required to administer them. The State have practically no initiative in their administration.

It has also been provided that the State will so formulate their policies that the execution of central law is neither hampered nor delayed. Under Articles 256 and 257 of the Constitution the Centre can give directions to the states for the execution of a law.

One also finds that it is practically the responsibility of the central government to conduct elections in the States. The President is empowered to appoint a Governor in every State and the later will report to the former about the administrative efficiency of the State in which he is posted. The judges of High Court are posted and transferred by the President of India. Comptroller and Auditor General of India, who is appointed by the President of India, gives directions to the state governments about the maintenance of accounts and getting these audited.

The Central government has special responsibility about development and advancement of scheduled castes and scheduled tribes and can issue directions to the States to administer their affairs in a particular manner and fashion.

The State governments are required to work under the directions of Central government about matters connected with the construction and maintenance of such means of communication which have been declared either of national or of military importance. It is the responsibility of the state governments to protect and save railways in their jurisdictions.

The Parliament is empowered to adjudicate and settle interstate disputes regarding control of waters of inter-state river valley projects. The President is empowered to appoint inter-state council to advise on disputes between States and also investigate subjects of common interest. Such a council may also suggest measures for better co-ordination of policy between Union and the States.

In the administrative field, the Central government has a hand in the running of State administration by providing All India Administrative and All India Police Service personnel. The parliament can also create new All India Service and members of these services are recruited by the Union Government under the rules and regulations framed by it. The personnel of these services hold key posts.

The centre-state relations in the administrative field are also influenced by the absence of economic self-sufficiency of the States. The Centre can give financial assistance to a State provided the administration of such a project is run in a particular direction.

Administrative Relations During Emergencies. Under the constitution if a state government fails to carry out the administration of the State in accordance with the provisions of constitution or if the State fails to run state administration according to constitutional directions of the central government, the President is empowered to declare failure of constitutional machinery in the State. If such a declaration is made and emergency declared, the central government takes over the administration of the State. It will appoint an adviser or team of advisers which will help the central government to run State administration in the desired manner. Administratively the federal structure, for that particular State becomes unitary.

CENTRE-STATE POWERS

The Constitution of India, as stated already, has established a federal form of Government characterised by a high degree of centralisation. The essence of a federal system is the division of powers between the Federal and State Governments by the Constitution. However, the scheme of distribution differs from country to country and embodies its peculiar needs. Hitherto the farmers of a federal Constitution have divided the governmental powers in either of the two ways: the specific powers of the Centre are enumerated and the residuary powers are left to the units; or the powers of the units are specified and the balance is left for the Centre. The former scheme has been adopted in the Untied States of America and Australia, while the latter in Canada. Surprisingly the word, 'Federation' is not found any where in the Constitution.

Three Lists. The Indian Constitution, following the precedent set under the Government of India Act of 1935, divides the governmental powers into three lists—the Union List, the State List and the Concurrent List. The distribution is remarkably elaborated and detailed and attempt has been made to cover the whole field of all possible governmental activity as far as the human mind can visualise at present. If still some powers are left unspecified, they are vested in the Centre. The Union List contains those matters on which the Union Parliament has exclusive right to frame the laws. The State Legislatures have the exclusive powers of making laws with respect to matters enumerated in the State List. As regards the Concurrent List, both the Union Parliament and State Legislature have concurrent powers with the provision that, in case of a conflict, the Central law must, to the extent of repugnancy, prevail over the State law.

The Union List contains 97 subjects including such subjects as defence; atomic energy; citizenship; railways; posts and telegraphs; foreign affairs; shipping; airways; banking and insurance; currency and coinage; mines and minerals; fisheries, opium, war, peace and treaties; etc. The State List contains 66 subjects and includes public order; police; jails; local government; education; agriculture and forests; public health and sanitation; roads, bridges, ferries, municipal tram ways and traffic therein; ponds and the prevention of cattle trespass; irrigation and canals; courts of wards; industries: weights and measures except establishment of standards; in as and inn-keepers: betting and gambling: state public services; etc. The concurrent list contains 47 matters and includes such subjects as criminal law: criminal procedure: civil procedure: marriage: divorce: contracts: adulteration of foodstuffs: trade unions: labour welfare: price control; factories; electricity; newspapers; legal, medical and other professions; charities and charitable institutions; stamp duties other than judicial stamps etc.

From a perusal of the three lists it is quite clear that the Central government has been given very many powers. The total number of subjects specified in the Union List is as much as 97 as compared with 66 that are enumerated in the State List. Besides, the Union Parliament has powers to make laws in respect of 47 items included in the Concurrent List, but as told already in case of an inconsistency between the State Law and Union, the latter supersedes the former. It would not be an exaggeration to say that whenever the Union so desires the Concurrent matters can for all practical purposes turn into Union matters.

ASPECTS OF CENTRE-STATE FRICTION

A Change in the Pattern of Centre-State Relations. The pattern of Centre-state relations began to change after the General Elections of 1967. For the first time political parties other than the Congress came to power in as many as nine states. The Congress strength in the Parliament was also reduced. In such a situation the position of the states *vis-a-vis* the Union was strengthened. The most serious confrontation between the Centre and the States arose with the formation of the United Front government in West Bengal in 1967. The different non-Congress governments in the states began to claim autonomous powers for the state governments. The DMK raised the demand for a separate flag for Tamil Nadu, and Shiv Sena wanted its own flag for Maharashtra. But the landslide victory of the Congress party in the mid-term elections to the Lok Sabha in 1971 resulted in an apparent political relegation of the claims of the regional forces.

Centre Preponderant Again. Pursuing a vigorous policy of poverty alleviation, land reforms, Constitutional amendments aiming at social justice and tiding over the Bangladesh crisis, the Congress was riding high in public esteem. The factor changed the grid of state power in such a manner as to make the Centre preponderant again. The political and bureaucratic weight of the regime was overweighed in favour of the Centre. Even when the Janata Party came to power at the Centre in 1977 no qualitative change occurred in the working of the federal polity. The Janata Party also went the same way as the Congress and dismissed Congress ministries in nine states due to political considerations. Morarji Desai, the Janata Prime Minister, rejected the demand of a number of states for a greater share in the national resources.

Demand for Greater Autonomy to States and Appointment of Sarkaria Commission. With the return of the Congress (I) to power at the Centre in 1980 and non-Congress ministries in some states, the debate for greater autonomy to states began to rage afresh. Centralisaiton had increased manifold due to many factors, such as, wars with Pakistan and China, Charismatic leadership of Nehru and Indira Gandhi one-party dominance of the Congress for long period of time, planning for economic development, and rapid industrializaiton, India's growing role in the Third World and socialist orientation of public policy. The Parliamentary systme itself was reinforcing centralising and unitarian tendencies. Simultaneously, regional forces were also growing. The Punjab issue, the sliding of Congress control from the Southern States like Andhra Pradesh and Karnataka, disturbances in the north eastern regions, growing demands for Gorkhaland, Jharkhand, Uttarakhand etc. were challenging the central leadership. Many regional political parties came to power in the states in the Assembly elections in 1984. Not only the regional political parties, but even some national political parties joined hands in demanding drastic changes in the existing federal structure. All this led the Central government to appoint the Sarkaria Commission in 1983 to enquire into the Centre-State relations and suggest.

Despite the fact that there is a division of powers between the Centre and the States, the States are dissatisfied because they feel that the balance of power is heavily in favour of the Centre.

The Partisan Role of the Governor. Apart from the Constitutional rights of interference in the affairs of the states, the Union has a considerable grisp on the state governor. A convention has developed that the governors are generally not appointed to a state from among persons from that state. The result is that very often they are not even able to speak the language of the state to which they are appointed and cannot judge the problems of that state by themselves. Being agents of the Centre, they are used to distabilise government at the state level. They play a partisan role in appointing and dismissing the state ministries. The Governor reserves a large number of bills for the consideration of the President.

Imposition of President's Rule. The Constitution provides that if the 'President on receipt of the report from the Governor of a state or otherwise, is satisfied that a situation has arisen in which the government of the state cannot be carried on within the Provisions of the Constitution, the can declare the failure of the Constitutional machinery. Failure of constitutional machinery can also be declared when the state fails to comply with or to give effect to, any direciotn given in the exercise of the executive power of the Union. These two provisions given wide powers to the Centre to intervene in the affairs of the state. And given the partisan role of the Governors, these powers are apt to be abused. In all, till September, 1984, President's rule was imposed seventy times. Many times state governments were dismissed while they were in majority and were prepared to prove it on the flour of the House.

Differences on Finance and Planning. Financially the states are in a very tight position because the distribution of taxes between the Centre and the states has been so done that most of the flexible sources of revenue have been assigned to the Centre. The states have to depend heaivly upon central grants and assistance. There has been a general complaint on the part of the states that the Union government has been discriminatory in allocating financial resources in general, and loan and grants in particular. Even in plan allocation of funds and central projects, discrimination is made. Besides, the distribution of tax as well as the actual sharing of tax and other governmental receipts are heavily tilted in favour of the Centre.

Law and Order Problem in the States and the Role of Centre. Law and order issue is another gorund of friction between the Centre and the states. Constitutionally, whenever any internal disturbance arises or is likely to arise in a state, it is the duty of the union to extent proteciton to the State. It is not necessary for the Union government to consult the state government to extending help through deployment of Central Reserve Police Force, Industrial Security Force, Border Security Force etc. Besides, the union government can deploy such forces for the protection of Central offices and properties in States. The use of these forces in states at times has been resented by them.

Misuse of Bureaucratic and Mass Media Apparatus by the Centre. Control over bureaucracy is another issue of friction between the Centre and the States. The States criticise the Centre for its partisan use of the All India Services. The state governments do not have adequate control over these services as for as their developmental responsibilities are concerned. Members of these services look to the Centre for protection to the detriment of state's political authority. Manning strategic and powerful positions in the state administration, the officers of all-India Services from an elite corps.

Implementation of Central Laws. Articles 256 to 257 empower the Centre to direct the State governments to act in accordance with the laws passed by the Parliament, and also about the use of executive authority of the State. Directions in this regard can also be given for the welfare of the Scheduled Tribes. Such Central directions have in some cases not been accepted by the State governments and have become issues of tension in the Centre State relations.

All India Services. We have seen above that the Central government sets up All India Services. Members of these services are recruited and controlled by the Central agencies like Union Public Service Commission and the Ministry of Home Affairs of Government of India with increasing number of activities of the State, the number of such services have increased. But many of the officers of such services are placed under the state governments and they perform important functions. The Indian Administrative Service and the Indian Police Service are two examples of such services. These officers work udner the day-to-day supervision of State governments. This creates anomalous situations at times, because the officers are recruited and controlled by central agencies but work under the supervision of State governments.

Miscellaneous Issues. There have been certain other poitns on which the states have raised issues of central bias. Revision of state boundaries and creation of states have often been resented by the State governments. For examples, the demand for Jharkhand State in Bihar, is a matter of controversy between the Centre and the Janata Dal Government in Bihar. There have been disputes between states regarding their boundaries. For example, Maharashtra-Karnataka dispute on Belgium, Karnataka-Kerala dispute on Karagod. There have been similar disputes between Haryana and Punjab, Assam and

Nagaland. The states have also complained about the Industrial Policy formulated by the Central Government. Sharing of river water has been another contentions issue among states. For example, Ravi Beas and Sutlej water dispute between Haryana and Punjab, their Dani dispute about sharing of water from Ravi River.

Besides these issues, there are other minor matters on which difference crop up between the Centre and the States. These could be the postponement of Assembly by elections on partisan ground, appointment of Inquiry Commissions against Chief Ministers not amenable to Central Government, visit of Prime Minsiter or Ministers to the States for partisan end, etc.

ADMINISTRATIVE RELATIONS

Administrative Relations. The administrative relations between the Union and the States as envisaged under the Constitution, largely follow the pattern laid down by the government of India Act, 1935. The arrangement is designed to serve a two-fold purpose: first, to ensure effective federal executive control of matters falling within the legislative jurisdiction of the Union Parliament and second, to minimise the possibilities of conflict between the Union and State administrative machineries.

The general rule is that the executive power in respect of all those matters on which the Union Parliament can legislate, belongs to the Union Government, while the executive power inrespect of the matters specified in the State List belongs to the State Government. Now, the existing arrangement is that some of the matters like customs, income-tax, railways, post offices, defence are directly administered by the officers of the Central Government, while the administration of the rest, and the execution of the union laws generally is entrusted to the State authorities. This is particularly evident in the judicial sphere. All the courts, with the exception of the Supreme Court, are State courtrs. In this respect there is a striking contrast between the American and Indian federal system. In the United States there is a complete set of federal executive and judicial officers for the executive and interpretation of federal laws. In India it is unlikely that a complete system of Union officers and courts to take exclusive charge of the Union laws will ever be established.

Therefore, the Union government depends largely on State authorities for the execution of its laws. However, this administrative coordination between the Union and the States is a two—way traffic. If certain federal matters are administered by State authorities, officers of Union Government occupy higher positions in State administration.

Union Direction of and Control of State Administration. The Union state administrative relations are so organised in India as to enable the Union Government to exercise considerable control over the administrative machinery of the State. Thus it is clearly provided that the executive power of every State shall be so exercised as to ensure compliance with the laws made by Parliament, and that the executive power of the Union shall extend to the giving of such directions to a State as may appear to the Government of India to be necessary for that purpose—(Articles 256, 257). If the State Government fails to carry out the directions of the Union Government, the President acting under Article 365 may proclaim a breakdown of the constitutional machinery of the State and place all the powers of State Government in the hands of the Union Government. Apart from this drastic action, that can be taken against a State Government the Union Government exercises general powers of direction and control in several other matters which concern the Union as well as the States. Thus, the superintendence, direction and control of all elections, whether to Union Parliament or to the State Legislatures are vested in the Election Commission appointed by the President. The judges of the High Courts are appointed and can be transferred by the President. The financial accounts of all States are under the supervision and control of the Comptroller and Auditor-General of India. The President has been given special powers in respect of the welfare of scheduled tribes and backward classes.

Besides, the Union Government may give directions to a State as to the construction and maintenance of the means of communications declared to be of national and military importance and measures to be taken for the protection of the railways in the States. Under Article 253 the President may, with the consent of the State Government, entrust to it functions in relation to any matter to which the executive power of the Union extends.

Mention may also be made of Article 355 which imposes a duty on the Union to protect every State against external aggression and internal disturbance and to ensure that the Government of every state is carried on in accordance with the provisions of the Constitution.

Inter-State Council. Though the federating units are autonomous within their own territorial limits, yet the Constitution of India empowers the Parliament to provide for the adjudication of any dispute or complaint with respect to the use, distribution, or control of the waters of, or in, any inter. State river or river valley. Parliament may by law also provide that neither the Supreme Court nor any other court shall exercise any jurisdiction in respect of any such dispute or complaint. Provision has also been made for the creation of inter-State Councils charged with the duty of *(i)* inquiring into and advising upon disputes between States; *(ii)* investigating and discussing subjects of common interest to some or all States; and *(iii)* making recommendations on any subject and, in particular, recommendations for the better co-ordination of policy and action with respect to that subject. Parliament also possesses the power to impose restrictions upon inter-State trade and establish such authority as it considers appropriate for enforcing the provisions of the Constitution with regard to such trade and commerce.

In addition to these powers which the Parliament may exercise in regard to the States in normal time, the Constitution vests general powers of direction and control over the States in times of national emergencies. Thus when a Proclamation of Emergency has been issued by the President and is in operation, the Union Government can give directions to any State as to the manner in which the State's executive power should be exercised; during such periods Parliament is also empowered to make laws conferring powers and imposing duties upon the Union or its officers regarding matters which are not enumerated in the Union List. As stated earlier the consequence of the various emergency provisions will be to suspend the legislative and the executive authority of the State even in respect of matters which have been specifically allotted to them by the Constitution. For all practical purposes all the governmental powers will be concentrated in the hands of the Union and the federal government will be transformed into a unitary government for the time being.

LEGISLATIVE RELATIONS

While the Constitution confers exclusive jurisdiction upon the State Legislatures to make laws with respect to matters specified in the State List, there are certain Articles in the Constitution which empower the Union Parliament to make laws on matters contained in the State List. The Parliament can make laws on State matters in the following cases:

(i) If the Council of States has declared by resolution supported by not less than two thirds of the members present and voting that it is necessary or expedient in the national interest that Parliament should make laws with respect to any matter specified in the State list specified in the resolution. Such a resolution remains in force for one year at a time, but it may be renewed any number of times by the Council of States and during the period of its operation, the Union Parliament can legislate on State subjects specified in it.

(ii) While a Proclamation of Emergency is in operation the Parliament has the power to make laws with respect to any of the matters specified in the State List. Such a law ceases to be in force after six months of the expiry of the operative period of the proclamation to the extent of the Parliament's competency in respect of the making them (Article 250).

(iii) In case of failure of the Constitutional machinery in State, the President may be proclamation authorize the Union Parliament to legislate for the State in respect of State matters. (Art. 356)

(iv) If two or more States pass a resolution to the effect that it is desirable that any of the matters in the State List should be regulated in such States by Parliament by law, it is lawful for Parliament to pass an Act for regulating that matter accordingly and any Act so passed shall apply to such States and to any other State by which it is adopted afterwards by resolution passed in that behalf by the legislature of that state. (Art. 253)

(v) In concurrent matters both the centre and the states make laws. However if simultaneously both make laws on a concurrent subject the will of the centre will prevail.

If any provision of a law made by the legislature of a State is repugnant to any provision of law made by Parliament which Parliament is competent to enact or to any provision of an existing law with respect to one of the matters enumerated in the Concurrent List, then the law made by the Parliament shall prevail and the State law shall to the extent of repugnancy be void. But when a law made by a State legislature with respect to any one of the matters specified in the Concurrent List contains any provision repugnant to the provisions of an earlier law made by Parliament or an existing legislature of such State shall, if it has been reserved for the consideration of the President and has received his assent, prevail in that State.

The effect of these provisions authorising the Union Parliament to legislate on State subjects is to overcome one of the defects of federations, namely, the weakness of the Central Government in the management of the internal and external affairs of the State on account of division of powers. On the other hand it has reduced the state to mere glorified municipalities.

FINANCIAL RELATIONS

Turning to the financial relations it may be first noted that the Constitution does not enumerate separately the heads of taxation. The power to tax is included in the power to legislate. Thus the subjects which are numerated in the Union List are in the purview of Central Government for purposes of taxation and similarly the State Governments have the power of taxation in respect of subjects enumerated in the State List. The three lists of powers given in the Seventh Schedule divide the sources of revenue between the Union and the States as follows:

(A) The Union Sources

(a) Taxes on income other than agricultural income.

(b) Custom duties including export duties.

(c) Duties of Excise on tobacco and other goods manufactured or produced in India except alcoholic liquors for human consumption and opium, Indian hemp and other narcotic drugs and narcotics.

(d) Taxes other than stamp duties on transactions in stock exchanges and future markets.

(e) Corporation tax.

(f) Taxes on capital value of assets, exclusive of agricultural land of individuals and companies; taxes on capitals of companies.

(g) Rates of stamp duty in respect of bills of exchange, cheques, promissory notes, bills of lading, letters of credit, insurance policies, transfers of shares, debentures, proxies and receipts.

(h) Estate duty in respect of property except agricultural land.

(i) Terminal taxes on goods or passengers carried by sea, air or railway.

(j) Fees in respect of any of the matters in the Union List except fees taken in any court.

(k) Taxes on sale or purchase of newspapers and on advertisements published therein.

(B) The State Sources

(a) Land revenue.

(b) Taxes on agricultural income.

(c) Duties on succession to agricultural land.

(d) Taxes on consumption or sale of electricity.

(e) Taxes on sale or purchase of goods other than newspapers.

(f) Estate duty in respect of agricultural land.

(g) Taxes on land and buildings.

(h) Taxes on advertisements other than those published in the newspapers.

(i) Taxes on mineral lights subject to limitations imposed by law.

(j) Excise duties on alocoholic liquors for human consumption and opium, hemp and other narcotic drugs.

(k) Taxes on the entry of goods into a local area for consumption, use or sale therein.

(l) Taxes on goods and passengers carried by road or in land water-ways.

(m) Fees in respect of any of the matters in the State List.

(n) Taxes on animals, and boats.

(o) Tolls.

(p) Taxes on vehicles for use on road's.

(q) Taxes on luxuries, entertainments, betting and gambling.

(r) Rates on stamp duty on documents other than those subject to Union stamp duty.

(s) Taxes on professions, trades, callings and employments.

(t) Capitation taxes.

The Concurrent List does not contain any subject in respect of which taxation may be levied.

The division of the resources as given above does not mean that the party to which a tax is assigned is the sole authority to determine it and is entitled to all the proceeds of that tax. So far as the taxes in the State List are concerned, they go entirely to the States but it is different with the Union taxes, the proceeds of many of which are assigned to or shared with the States. The Constitution distinguishes for categories of Union taxes which are available, whole or in part, to the States:

(i) Duties levied by the Union but collected and wholly appropriated by the State: Stamp duties in respect of bills of exchange, cheques, promissory notes, bills of lading, letters of credit, policies of insurance, transfer of shares, debentures, proxies and receipts and excise on medicines and toilet preparations containing alcohol.

(ii) Taxes levied and collected by the Union but wholly assigned to the States: duties in respect of succession to property other than agricultural land; terminal taxes on goods and passengers carried by rail, sea or air; taxes on railway fares and freights; taxes on the sale or purchase of newspapers and advertisements published therein.

(iii) Taxes which are levied and collected by the Union but whose proceeds may be distributed between the Union and the States if Parliament by law so provide. Union duties of excise other than such duties of excise on medical and toilet preparations fall under this category.

(iv) Taxes levied and collected by the Union but whose proceeds are shared between the Union and the States. The tax which comes under this category is income tax.

Grants-in-Aid. The Constitution also provides for Grants-in-aid to the States. Thus Assam, Bihar, Orissa and West Bengal receive grants-in-aid in lieu of export duty on jute and jute products. Apart form the Union Government's constitutional obligation to provide grants-in-aid to the States for financing approved schemes for the welfare of the Scheduled Tribes and for improving the standard of administration in Tribal areas, Article 275 of the Constitution makes a general provisions for Union grants in aid to the States. It is for the Union Government to fix the extent of these grants and lay down the conditions under which they are to be administered. It need not be stated that grants-in-aid are potent instrument, for the extension of Central control and direction on the States.

Financial Emergency. During the Proclamation of Financial Emergency the President may empower the Union to give directions controlling State's financial activities and require State Money bills to be reserved for his consideration. Besides salaries of state employees also can be slashed to meet the situation.

Borrowing Powers. The Constitution also makes certain provisions in respect of the borrowing powers of the States. A State can borrow only within India and it cannot raise a new loan without the consent of the Union Government if there is outstanding any part of a provisions loan and guaranteed by the Union or owed to it. The Government of India may, subject to such conditions as may be laid down by or under any law made by Parliament, make loans to any State provided that the limits set by parliament to Union loans are not exceeded.

It will be clear from the above description of Union-State relations that every effort has been made to make the union Government much stronger than what central governments are usually found to be in other federations. The emphasis is more on the authority of the Centre than on the autonomy of the State. As a matter of fact interference and dictation by the Centre is not only so prohibited, but authorized as a normal procedure of the functioning of the Constitution. The absence of equal representation to the States in the Council of States; the power given to that chamber to declare by a two—thirds majority any subject to be of national importance, and then to enable the Union to give directions to make a law thereupon; the power of the Union to give directions to the State Governments; and the power given to the President practically to suspend the State Constitution in times of emergency—are some of the exceptional features of the Indian Federation which have led the critics to describe the Indian Federation as being only a quasi-federation or as a unitary federation. Hence some states like Assam, Punjab and Kashmir are in open revolt against the centre. They seek fully autonomous status. The Sarkaria Commission made 247 recommendations to improve centre state relations besides suggesting 12 amendments to the Constitution and 20 new legislations. But the past experience reveals that states demands carried weight when centre was on a weak wicket and they were ignored the moment the centre became powerful. The Sarkaria Commission was the outcome of the states' demands for more powers but when the ruling party at the centre got a massive mandate it was forgotten. Now again the issue has been raked up perhaps because Narasimha Rao's government is in minority & many states are ruled by the non congress governments. A committee has been set up to review the Gadgil formula under the chairmanship of Pranab Mukerhji. It has also been decided to revive inter state council. The Home Minister has assured that the centre will be consulting states in matters other than those in concurrent list. It appears the present govt. has been the writings on the wall.

ROLE OF CASTE IN STATE POLITICS

State politics in India has been particularly the hot bed of political casteism. Andre Beteille very candidly observes: "Caste enters much more directly into the composition of political elites at the state level... Thus, the Mysore cabinet is dominated by Lingayats and Okkaligas, the Maharashtra cabinet by Marathas and some have referred to the Madras cabinet as a federation of dominant castes." Michael Brecher remarks: "Caste plays a major role in state and local politics but it is marginal at the all-India level. Tinker observes: "...State politics will be caste politics throughout most of India for many years to come."

BIHAR

Politics in Bihar has been mostly organised on the basis of caste. All those parties which happen to have a multi-caste membership have powerful functions. This was true of the undivided Congress as much as it is nature of Congress (I), the Bhartiya Janata Party, and other major parties. The caste orientation of parties and groups does not mean that they are motivated only by caste interests of their members or that person from other castes are completely barred entry or that the parties or groups actually serve any special or general interests of the caste. These are not service organisations for their castes but power machines which use caste labels for building loyalty around some personalities. In other words, the caste gets politicised and becomes a means in the elite politics of securing or retaining power.

The single case of Bihar is adequate to prove the thesis that caste considerations are vital in political matter. Almost all the top leaders of Bihar Congress Party have been connected with their respective caste associations. Rajendra Prasad, who held office as President of India, was for three decades connected with the All-India Kayastha Conference and had presided over its Jaunpur Session in 1925. A.N. Sinha, another prominent leader, was connected with the all-India Kashtriya Mahasabha. S.K. Sinha's association with the Bhumihar Brahmin Mahasabha, and his use of it to put political pressures, are also well known.

Initially, there were six groups in the Bihar Congress, viz., the Bhumihar group led by S.K. Sinha, the Rajput group led by A.N. Singh, the two factions of Brahmins, one led by L.N. Mishra and the other by Binodanand Jha, the Kayastha group led by K.B. Sahay and the backward castes led by R.L.S. Yadav. These groups were not altogether at peace among themselves. For instance, while the L.N. Mishra faction of Brahmins was supporting the powerful Bhumihar group. Pandit Binodanand Jha was supporting the Rajput faction. K. B. Sahay, the Kayastha leader was supporting the Bhumihars till 1957, but after that he defected to the Rajput group. The backward castes leaders R.L.S. Yadav was the political disciple of Sahay and his loyalty used to change with Sahay's. After the death of S.K. Sinha, Binodanand Jha became Chief Minister. In the meantime A.N. Singh had died too, and the leadership of the Rajput faction was conferred on his son S.N. Singh, In the same manner, M.P. Sinha inherited the leadership of the Bhumihars from his father. While the rajputs supported the 'Brahmin Raj' led by Jha, the Bhumihars, the L.N. Mishra faction of Brahmins, the Kayasthas and the backward castes opposed it. The Jha Ministery could not face such a strong opposition and the Chief Minister had to resign under the Kamaraj Plan. 'Kayastha Raj' followed with K.B. Sahay as head. He successfully won over the Rajputs and the new power equation thus was: Kayastha, backward castes, a faction of Brahmins, Rajputs vs. Bhumihars and the Binodanand Jha faction of Brahmins.

Non-Congress parties have by no means had a clear, non-caste basis. In fact till 1967, under Congress domination, their attitude towards the ruling party depended on who, representing which caste, was in power. For instance, when Bhumihar S.L. Singh was Chief Minister, the than leader of the PSP Legislative Wing, Ramanand Tewari was very critical yet when Binodanand Jha came to power, Tewari's attitude softened–even as Besawan Singh another PSP leader, became more critical. Tewari is a Brahmin and Singh a Bhumihar. Thakur Prasad, the Jana Sangh chief, used to maintain a lukewarm attitude towards the government headed by K.B. Sahay, both were Kayasthas. At the time of the Congress split, too, the so-called ideological discussion inside each political party was actually guided by caste considerations. While the Brahmins and the backward castes of most of the opposition parties fell for 'progressive ideas of Indira Gandhi, the Bhumihars, Rajputs and Kayasthas, supported the old Congress.

Bihar, in fact, represents the scene of a clash among four castes, *viz.,* Rajputs, Brahmins, Kayasthas and Adivasis. The adivasis or the backward tribal people of Bihar-Orissa border organised themselves into Jharkhand Party which in the elections of 1957 had been able to capture most of the seats reserved for tribal and backward sections of the society and with its increased strength intensified the demand for a separate tribal state (Jharkhand) comprising all tribal areas of Bihar, Orissa and Madhya Pradesh. It afforded a potential challenge to the Congress Party. In order to face this situation, the Congress High command deputed a Christian lady, Raj Kumari Amrit Kaur, to go to the tribal areas in order to wean away many tribesmen (particularly those converted into christianity) from the influence of this new organisation. The Congress succeeded in depleting the ranks of this party which in a truncated form is now known as the Hul-Jharkhand.

The influence wielded by the Raja of Ramgarh—a Rajput by caste—over his area and in Bihar politics as a whole despite all his acts of corruption, misappropriation, etc., has been most extraordinary. The Raja and his family interests for a decade have been the cancer of Bihar politics. In the post-1967 period, his group acquired a balancing position in as much as its support or denial thereof could make or unmake many of the coalition governments.

Cases of Kayasthas (Sinha) struggling for power against the Brahmins (Jha) have also come to light particularly at the time of Ministry-making or selecting the leader of the legislature party.

The articulation of the sentiments of the backward castes during the tenure of Chief Minister K.B. Sahay and, more especially, since the time of the distribution of the Congress tickets for the general election of 1967 helped mobilize the lower-middle farmer castes of the state. It was not a mere co-incidence, therefore, that of the nine governments formed in five years between the two elections as many as seven were led by leaders belonging to backward or Harijan castes. The fact that most Chief Ministers since 1967 did not belong to the 'forward castes' came to operate by 1970 as an important parameter of state politics in Bihar. The Lok Sabha elections of 1971 only sharpened the crystallization of the 'backward' sentiment and further deepened the process of mobilization of the backward classes, especially of the Yadavs, Kurmis and Koiris, Politics in Bihar has, thus, come to be articulated in terms of the backward *vs.* the forward.

In Bihar, instead of trying to attend to the pressing problems of the people, the Janata Chief Minister, Karpoori Thakur, chose in early 1978 to introduce a controversial measure for reservation of government jobs for the backward castes. It was a highly emotive issue at a time of widespread unemployment among the educated youth. There were demonstrations and counter-demonstrations and caste riots on a mass scale. The real reason behind the reservation issue was precisely a desire to creat riots and caste conflicts so that there should be a polarisation between the so-called backward and forward castes. In this way, Karpoori Thakur thought he could become the leader of the backward castes and could find a solid base of support among them. Thus, the caste riots were viewd with profound satisfaction in circles close to Thakur. They hoped that the deeper the caste cleavage, the more permanent will be their influence among certain castes.

KERALA

In Kerala also caste considerations have played an important role in state politics. According to the 1971 Census, the Hindus number 59.4 per cent and the two minorities, the Muslims and the Christians, account for 19.5 and 21.1 per cent respectively. It is generally held that four major groups are contending for a dominant place in the political life of the state: Nairs, Ezhavas, Christians and Muslims. Numerically Ezhavas lead with 26.4 per cent, followed by Christians with 21.17 per cent, Muslims with 19.5 per cent and Nairs with 12.5 per cent .

The Hindus account for 59.4 per cent of Kerala's population and caste ranking places the Namboodiri Brahmins at the peak of the Hindu hierarchy. Numbering less than 5 per cent of the population, the Namboodiris remain primarily a land-owning community. But despite the number of political leaders from this caste, such as the Left Communist E.M.S. Namboodiripad the Communists have had little political power. A far more potent political force is the Nair community—the traditional warrior of Kerala. As a land-owning and mercantile community today, the Nairs, numbering 17 per cent of the population, are a pivotal force in Kerala politics. They have traditionally held the balance, making or breaking a government by shifting sides. Economically subservient to the Nairs are the Ezhava or Tiyyar as they are called in Malabar. With 25 per cent of the population, however, the economically depressed Ezhava are perhaps the single most powerful community in Kerala. In addition to the mutually antagonistic Nairs and Ezhavas, the Christian community ranks as a major political power in Kerala. The Christians account for 19.5 per cent of the population, divided among the Syrians, the Protestants and the Roman Catholics. It is the Catholic community that numerically dominates and holds the locus of political power, largely through the organisation of the Church. The Muslims, with 18 per cent of the population and represented by the Muslim League, are a major factor politically, particularly in the Malabar region of northern Kerala where muslims are the dominant community.

Just as the Muslims are concentrated in certain areas of Malabar, each of the other communities dominate a particular region of Kerala. The Christians are concentrated primarily in Ernakulam and Kottayam districts. The Nairs form the dominant community in the area of Trivandrum district, and the Ezhavas are particularly strong in Palghat. Each political party in Kerala must, therefore, seriously consider the dominant community, or as the communists prefer to call it 'the social base' in the selection of its candidates. That each party tends to choose its candidates from the dominant community, however, does not cancel out community as a factor. Although there are elements of each community in all parties (except for the Muslim League), the parties in Kerala have come to be associated with particular communities, and within each party, factionalism expresses the divisions of religion and caste. Indeed, the politics of caste form a fundamental reality of political life in Kerala.

The Nairs and even the Namboodiri Brahmins, soon followed in the creation of caste associations; the first of these being the Nair service society, followed by the Uthana Kerala Nayar Samajam in Malabar and Namboodiri's Yogakshema Sabha. Caste quickly became politicised when political parties began to form. In Malabar, the lower castes (like the Ezhavas) opposed the Congress as being Nair dominated. After Independence, the Congress became increasingly a party of christian domination, just as the Praja Socialist Party was regarded as a virtual Nair preserve. The Muslim League commands allegiance from most Muslims in Kerala, and the Communist party has drawn its strength primarily from the Ezhava and untouchable communities. The district in which the communists have maintained their strongest hold, winning more than 40 per cent of the vote in each election since 1957, is Palghat, the only district in Kerala with an Ezhava majority.

In Kerala, the elaboration of caste ranking and the generally common economic position shared by members of a caste, together with the high correlation between caste rank and economic position, have given rise to a political situation in which the most significant actors are castes and communities. While these communities are by no means wholly united, there is nevertheless a tendency toward an alignment of major communities with different parties. These socio-political constellations, reflecting a superimposition of ritual rank, social status, and economic position, represent essentially a class orientation. This is particularly evident in the social base of the Communist parties in Kerala. The Communists draw support from the poorer classes of each community—Nairs, Christians and Muslims. While the majority of the depressed Ezhavas may support of the party, the middle classes and the SNDP itself, have leaned towards Congress–especially during the period of Sankar's leadership in the early 1960s. The 1965 election campaign, for example, was in large part fought by the Congress and the Communists to secure the affection of the Ezhavas. The failure of any party to secure a majority, however, only emphasised the fact that while the politics of Kerala may be caste-bound no party can rule with the support of one community alone.

ANDHRA PRADESH

Caste politics in Andhra Pradesh seems like a game of cock-fighting between the Kammas and Reddys. The important castes in the state are the Brahmins, the Reddys, the Kammas, the Harijans, the

Velamas, the Rajus and the Kapus. Politically, the Reddys and the Kammas are regarded as the dominant castes for they are numerically the strongest in the village or local area and economically and politically exercise a preponderant influence. The most important source of their power is their control over land. As the major landholders and occupants of important positions in the villages, they control the village political life. The two castes cultivated feelings of jealousy and rivalry as a result of which while the Reddys joined the Congress party, the Kammas lent their support to the Communists. It is owing to this that Andhra Communists struggled heavily to stage Telengana rebellion in 1948. Support of the Kammas to the local communist leaders in the first general elections became alarmingly noticeable and the Congress had to take note of this fact on the eve of second general elections of 1957 when the official High Command nominee, S.K. Patil tactfully requisitioned the support of Kamma leader N.G. Ranga and "matched caste with caste in the choice of candidates."

In Andhra Pradesh, the landed castes and particularly the Reddy rural gentry constituted the backbone of the Congress party. The Communist rebellion in Telengana, and later, a Communist bid to form the Ministry soon after Andhra state was formed in 1953, frightened the dominant castes so much that they gave extensive support to the Congress. Both the national and the state leadership of the Congress party tried to reach the voters not directly but through local influentials belonging to the dominant castes. This arrangement worked extremely well given the social status and economic power of the dominant castes and the low political consciousness of the other castes. The composition of the cabinet has reflected the same phenomenon. The Reddys, the Velmas and the Kammas held between them 45 to 58 per cent of the seats in the state cabinet, with the Reddys being the single largest group (28 to 38 per cent) till 1971. During the same period the representation of the backward classes and scheduled castes in the cabinet remained below 25 per cent.

After the 1969 Congress split an attempt was made to restructure the support base of the Congress party. The upper middle class, landlord and peasant caste support structure of the party was considered to be a hindrance to bringing about socio-economic changes, which the new Congress, in a radical mood, was talking about. With P.V. Narsimha Rao as the Chief Minister changes, started. Though a Brahmin, but not from a landed caste, Narsimha Rao initiated the policy of giving greater representation to the backward classes and weaker sections in the legislature and the Council of Ministers. In the 1972 Assembly elections, a large number of tickets were given to backward classes and minorities. The 26-member Ministry formed under his Chief Ministership had the largest number of persons belonging to the weaker sections (4 Harijans, 6 from the backward classes, 1 Girijan, 2 from the minorities—total 13). The upper castes had for the first time a markedly lower representation with only 4 Reddys, 2 Kammas and 3 Brahmins (total 9).

After the formation of the Janata party, the bulk of the prosperous agriculturists drawn from different peasant castes were attracted towards it. Its support came overwhelmingly from the Reddy community.

If caste politics in the states of the Indian Union is examined from a comparative standpoint, it appears that Andhra Pradesh occupies the most conspicuous place. Harrison comments: "As an example of Hindu caste discipline in political motion, the post-war decade in Andhra merits special attention. Caste has played so fundamental a role during this period that this examination becomes in effect a case history in the impact of caste on India's representative institutions." A very notable feature of caste politics in Andhra Pradesh finds place in its blending with the forces of regional politics. It has added much height to the politics of the Telengana agitation. The people of a particular caste living predominantly in a particular region have given a caste-cum-regional complexion to an issue in question. Obviously, this kind of relationship between a caste and a region is widespread in Andhra Pradesh as a result of which regional claims "are often only a disguise for caste claims."

HARYANA

Next to Bihar, caste exercises the single most important influence on politics in Haryana. Some of the classes and castes have a more or less set pattern of political behaviour. In a population of a little over about 10 million in the state of Haryana, Hindus are 89 per cent, Muslims less than 4 per cent and Sikhs 6.5 per cent, the four major caste groups among the Hindus are: Brahmins 12 per cent, Jats 23 per cent, Ahirs 8 per cent and scheduled castes 22 per cent; others are Gujars 8 per cent, Rajputs 5 per cent, and Banias 8 per cent. Castewise, the Jats are the toughest and constitute the single largest group with the Scheduled castes coming next. The latter are sharply sub-divided between the Chamars, the weavers and the sweepers. Of these, the Chamars are the more numerous (18 per cent) and the more privileged in as much as they always obtained a greater shares of political spoils. Among the higher castes, the Brahmins, for reasons of traditional caste superiority and higher level of literary exercised a tremendous influence and occupied many positions of power quite disproportionate to their numbers.

Besides being the most numerous caste group, the Jats are the land-owning class, they also supply the largest number of recruits to the army. They are traditionally imbued with the ambition of love of power and they have been basically anti-Congress, particularly because of the influence of the Union is Party. But now there is a slight change in their voting behaviour. They vote not for a political party but for a candidate and in this respect the sub-caste become more important than caste considerations. An Ahir in the Gurgaon-Mahendragarh areas, for example, would not easily vote for any party unless its candidate happens to be an Ahir. The same holds good for other caste groups in other parts of the state. There is a very telling local slogan heard during the elections which says: "Jat ki beti Jat ka, Jat ko vote Jat ko." In other words, just as a Jat's daughter should be married only to a Jat, a Jat's vote should go only to a Jat. The Ahirs and Brahmins, by and large (exceptions apart) are pro-Congress or anti-Congress according to the directives of Rao Birendra Singh and Pandit Bhagwat Dayal. The refugees, by and large, were with the Jana Sangh but like the Jats, they also vote for the candidate. If the contest is between a refugee and non-refugee candidates, they will, by and large, vote for a refugee candidate, whatever may be his party. If the contest is between the non-refugee candidates, then they prefer a Bhartiya Janata Party candidate. The caste influence is not confined to Hindus alone. The Meo-Muslims have their owen 'gotras' and they also prefer to vote for the candidate of their own gotras unless a Meo has to be supported against a non-Meo.

Jats as a community had been a political force in Haryana. They constitute about 23 per cent of the total population of the state and have a commanding position. As a community, the Brahmins have tried to challenge their leadership. About Brahmins, it should be noted that their representation in the legislature is not very large but at the same time in the elections they have a substantial influence because in the first instance they are found practically in every village and as such they can exercise some influence. This is all the more because as a community they are more united than others and vote more or less *en bloc.* They also try to organise other non-agricultural communities at the village level and in every constituency. About the Jats, it should be noted that as a dominant community, they do no mind the leadership of other agricultural communities coming up except that of Brahmins. One of the reasons why they are not prepared to tolerate Brahmin leadership is that there is a basic conflict between these two communities at the village level. In the Jat majority areas, the Brahmins try to organise the other communities against them in the elections which neither the Jats nor other agricultural communities would like them to do.

CASTE IN OTHER STATES

In the case of Karnataka, the tug of war is between two dominant castes—the Lingayats and Okkligas—and this mutual rivarly is colouring every matter, whether it be appointment to government posts or reservation of seats in colleges or election to local bodies and legislatures. In Maharashtra, also there are three main castes *viz.,* Marathas, Brahmins and Mahars (untouchables), which have played an important role in the politics of the state. In Punjab, the conflict is not between castes but between two systems of castes—the Hindus and Sikhs. The Hindu-Sikh conflict took on the guise of a linguistic conflict.

6

Regionalism and Politics

Regionalism means love of a particular region or state in preference to the country as a whole. Whereas communalism means the love of the community in preference to the nation, regionalism means the love of a particular region in preference to the country and in certain cases, in preference to the state of which the region was a part This feeling may arise either due to the continuous neglect of a particular area or region by the ruling authorities, or it may spring as a result of increasing political awareness of the henceforth backward people that they have been discriminated against.

"A region is a defined territorial unit including particular language or languages, jatis, ethnic groups or tribes, particular social setting and cultural pattern, folk dance, music, folk arts, etc." A 'region' is a profound sociological fact reflected in its being treated as the nucleus of a social aggregation for multiple purposes. in the vocabulary of a sovereign state, it generally denotes a territory which is smaller than itself but is larger than its single constituent units, variously called states, provinces, cantons, etc. What precise factors must pre-exist before a tract of territory could be called a region, is neither as yet fully known, nor can be firmly predicted. What is known is that several variables must be simultaneous inter-play in varying degrees over a considerable period of time which, then, set a particular territory apart from other areas. geography, topography, religion, customs and mores, political and economic stage of development, way of living, commonly shared historical experience, etc. The world 'et-Cetra' is significant, says Shriram Maheshwari, Regionalism, to be sure, needs all these ingredients, but the concept is much more inclusive-when all is said and done, it remains at least partially elusive. The essential fact is that a region is characterised, more than anything else, by a widely shared sentiment of 'togetherness' in the people, internalised from a wide variety of sources, which might even include common prosperity, comraderie developed in a common struggle, etc., and what is more 'separateness' from others. At the centre of regionalism is a more or less intense sense of identity having both positive and negative dimensions which is no less real to the people than the feeling of belonging to a particular state or nation or to a language group.

Why Regionalism Grew. One of the most significant aspects of the Indian polity is that it is an aggregation of regions and sub-regions. These regions and sub-regions have a distinct socio-cultural personality within the framework of the seven natural regions of India.

Parochialism and regionalism is a conspicuous phenomenon of India's political life. The mushroom growth of private political armies in the form of Gopal Sena in Kerala, Lachit Sena in Assam, Subhash Sena in West Bengal and, above all, of the Shiv Sena in Maharashtra, in addition to many other similar organisations, big or small, operating in different states of the Indian Union reflected 'parochialism' run mad.

Why did regionalism grow? It grew largely due to four factors. First and foremost among these was the problem of economic and social development of Indian society. After independence, India lacked a balanced economic growth of all parts and regions. Instead of caring for the interests of the country as a whole, political leadership became narrow minded and began to clamour for the progress of their own state or region.

Four states, two in the north and two in the west, are placed at the top of the scale of the per capita income. Punjab (Rs. 2,250), Maharashtra (Rs.1,670) and Gujarat (Rs.1,590), cover a population of 126 million (about 18 per cent of India's total of 684 million indicated by the 1981 census).

Next in order follow the middle income group consisting of West Bengal (Rs.1,247), Himachal Pradesh (Rs.1,230), Karnataka (Rs.1,202), Tamil Nadu (Rs.1,165), Kerala (Rs.1,162), Rajasthan

(Rs.1,127), Jammu Kashmir (Rs.1,100) and Andhra Pradesh (Rs.1,006).

The low income states falling in the third category are. Assam (Rs.960), Orissa (Rs.918), Madhya Pradesh (Rs.895), Uttar Pradesh (Rs.870) and Bihar (Rs.755).

The people living in the second and third categories of states are approximately equal in numbers. The extent of disparity is indicated by Punjab's per capita income which is three times that of Bihar.

Closely connected was the increasing awareness of the people in the more backward parts of India that they were being neglected in the matter of education and job opportunities, in the setting up of plants and factories, in the construction of dams and bridges, and above all, in the allocation of Central funds and grants.

The third factor that gave rise to regional and parochial tendencies in the country was the personal and selfish ends of the politicians. The weakening of the Central authority and in some cases, of the state authority, was considered by the regional and state leaders of all parties as vital to enhancing their own authority and power, and they did not hesitate from propagating regionalism among the people. Moreover, the creation of more and more states meant more Governors, more Chief Ministers, more Ministers and more MLAs, and these were what the politicians in India cared for.

The fourth factor was the creation of linguistic states which reinforced regionalism and stirred demands for increased state autonomy. Very often the sub nationalism sentiment which is initially based on linguistic, religious or ethnic groupings gains strength with a blend of economic issues such as those relating to land, water and regional backwardess. One of the most significant developments has been the rise of linguistic chauvinism, re-arrangement of the boundaries of the states on linguistic basis, imposition of the language of the majority in a state on the minorities and disregard of the special provision relating to language spoken by a section of the population of a state, resulting in fissiparous tension.

Discussing the question of 'linguistic regionalism' which had even sparked off a wave of riots in recent times. K.C. Pande maintained that while these riots and inter-regional rivalries were ostensibly motivated by linguistic loyalties, the real forces operating behind such movements as Shiv Sena, etc., stemmed from economic frustration of the people in one area being deprived of employment opportunities or being unable to compete with outsiders in this sphere. Language, Pande remarks, in such cases only provided a convenient cloak for the deep-seated economic malacides and added that he same held good for religion also because most of the so-called 'communal riots' were also rooted in economic maladjustment as in the case of recent riots in working class areas, viz., Ranchi and Ahmedabad where economic tensions and not religious differentials trigger communal violence.

FORMS OF EXPRESSION OF REGIONALISM

Regionalism is a country-wide phenomenon, and often, it took the form of well-conceived and well-organised agitations and campaigns. Almost every state has spawned a militant native movement directed against outsiders. The fundamental issue has been employment for local people, and many state governments, either officially or unofficially have supported the protection of jobs for the 'sons of the soil'. Of the movements, the most virulent has been the Shiv Sena, founded in 1966 in Bombay. Exploiting Maharashtrian grievances and economic frustration, the Shiv Sena, under the banner of 'Maharashtra of the Maharashtrians' has directed its attack, both verbal and physical, primarily at South Indian immigrants.

Regionalism in India has assumed various forms and found expression in more than one way. It assumed four forms in the political field. *(i)* secession from the Indian union; *(ii)* demand for separate statehood; *(iii)* demand for full-fledged statehood; and *(iv)* inter-state disputes.

Regionalism and Secession from the Indian Union

It is in its extreme form of regionalism that a region demands that it wants to break away from the Indian union. The DMK in Tamil Nadu, the Akali Dal in Punjab and the Mizos and Nagas in North-East India, and more recently the supporters of Khalistan movements have been demanding secession from India.

Demand for Dravida Nadu. As early as 1960 the DMK and the Nan Tamil (We Tamils) organised a joint campaign throughout Madras state demanding its secession from India and for making it an independent sovereign state to Tamiland. In 1961, another organisation by the name of Tamil Arasu Kazhagam launched an agitation for the renaming of Madras state as 'Tamil Nadu'. A little later, the DMK proposed that the states of Madras, Andhra Pradesh, Kerala and Mysore should secede from the Indian Union and form an independent 'Republic of Dravida Nadu'. In 1962, C.N. Annadurai maintained that the people of South India were of different stock from that of the north. He alleged that the South had been ignored and neglected by the Union Government in plans for India's industrial development.

In view of the disintegrating trends in the country, the Parliament in early October, 1963, adopted the Constitution (Sixteenth Amendment) Bill which enabled it to make laws providing penalties for any person questioning the sovereignty and integrity of the Indian Union. As a result, the DMK dropped from its programme the demand for a sovereign independent Dravidian federation and its secession from the Indian Union. Instead, the party's objectives, thereafter, were declared to be the formation of a 'Dravida Union' of Madras, Mysore, Andhra and Kerala within the framework of the sovereignty and integrity of India. The agitation went on unabated. In September, 1970, the DMK convened a 'state autonomy conference' in Madras. In April, 1971, Chief Minister Karunanidhi threatened that separation of Tamil Nadu from the Indian Union would become 'unavoidable' if the demand for state autonomy continued to be neglected for long. At one stage, he even demanded a separate flag for Tamil Nadu. Being a regional party, the DMK always sought to focus on local issues to work up people's passions in order to stay on in power.

Demands of Sikhistan. In Punjab there was a demand for Sikhistan. As early as 1949 the Sikhs under Master Tara Singh declared that the Hindus of Punjab had become highly communal and that the Sikhs could not hope to get any justice from them. Tara Singh demanded a 'Sikh State' consisting of the Gurgaon district of Punjab and Patiala and the East Punjab States Union (PEPSU). This demand grew stronger after the reorganisation of the states on linguistic basis in 1956, when the demands of Punjab for its reorganisation on unlingual basis was not conceded. The Sikhs under the Akali Dal put a demand for a separate Punjabi speaking state. When the Sikhs were demanding bifurcation of Punjab, some political and religious bodies like the Jana Sangh and Arya Samaj were demanding that composite Punjab should be created, which should include not only the present Punjab, but also Himachal Pradesh and PEPSU. The demand for a separate Punjabi speaking state assumed serious dimensions after the Akali dal leader Sant Fateh Singh announced his plan to burn himself alive if the demand of Punjab suba was not conceded by 25 September, 1966. In view of the serious repercussion of this threat being implemented, the Government of India conceded the demand for a Punjabi speaking state.

The creation of separate Punjabi Suba did not satisfy all Punjabi leaders. Certain Sikh leaders continued the agitation for the establishment of a 'Socialist Democratic Sikh State'; Dr. Jagjit Singh, former a\General Secretary of the Akali Dal, undertook a tour of a number of foreign countries to mobilise world opinion in favour of this demand. During this tour he tried to enlist the support of the members of the Sikh community living abroad for this purpose. He also prepared a plan for the setting up of a 'Rebel Sikh Government', at Nankana Sahib, the birth place of Guru Nanak, in West Pakistan.

The Akali Dal leadership is well aware that it is not possible to have Sikhistan, as a separate independent state outside the Indian Union. They, therefore, started demanding, like the DMK in Tamil Nadu, that the state should be given more powers and autonomy today, the Akali Dal stands for more powers for the state and there is no demand for Sikhistan.

Demand for Khalistan. Since April, 1981, the Akali extremists have been taking a hard-line approach for establishing a new all-Sikh nation called Khalistan, a demand originally voiced, by a former member of the Akali Dal, Jagjit Singh in June. This was taken up in various milder forms by officially reorganised and influential bodies such as the Sikh Gurudwara Prabandhak Committee (SGPC). Even a purely educational organisation known as the Chief Khalsa Diwan, at its 54th Sikh Education Conference in Chandigarh in march, 1981, passed a resolution demanding Khalistan and seeking associate membership of the United Nations. Later, moderate members of the community withdrew its demand for UN membership but stood by the Sikh nation theory. The chief political organ, the Akali Dal, clearly split over the issue, with the extremist group headed by Jagdev Singh Talwandi demanding a separate nation, and middle-of-the-road Akali leadership led by Sant Harchand Singh Longowal, President of the Akali Dal, bemoaning the "pariah status of the Sikhs." Sikh demands of as similar nature have their precedent since Indian independence when a resolution passed by Hindi Sikh members of the Punjab Assembly stated that "in the divided Indian punjab special constitutional measures are imperative to meet the just aspirations and rights of the Sikhs."

The Dal Khalsa an extremist and militant Sikh youth organisation whose members hijacked the plane to Lahore, was started on 6th August, 1978, with the avowed objective of attaining an 'Independent Sovereign Sikh Nation'. According to intelligence sources, the Dal's active membership is now around 600 and it has three units in Chandigarh, Gurdaspur and Mohali. As a part of their strategy to expand their bases in Punjab, the Dal started actively participating in the political activities of all the Akali factions. For example, Dal Khalsa activists were vocal and conspicuous during the month-long agitation launched by the Akali Dal in May 1981 demanding holy city status for Amritsar. Subsequently on 26th July, 1981 Gajinder Singh and his followers distributed pro-Khalistan literature during the World Sikh Convention held in Amritsar. Less than a month later while the rest of the nation was celebrating independence on 15th August, 1981, over a dozen Khalsa volunteers gathered in a Gurudwara and saluted their flag which had the map of the proposed Khalistan state inscribed in the centre. On 27th August, Dal Khalsa members raised pro-Khalistan slogans from the gallery of the Punjab Assembly. According to Home Ministry sources, the Dal has been getting donations from prosperous Sikhs both in India and abroad and its monthly expenditure is estimated to be over Rs. 50,000 since April, 1981.

The Mizo Demands in Assam. The hill districts of Assam have also displayed great regional feeling and demanded the formation of an independent Mizos state. They demanded a separate state of Mizoram outside the Union of India and in order to press their demand they organised themselves in a political front known as the Mizo National Front (MNF). The Union Government, naturally, turned down this demand and sought to suppress the movement. The Mizos organised armed agitation and commenced guerrilla warfare. In the wake of the Chinese aggression, the MNF was banned. It is believed that the Mizos got active support from China and Pakistan in men, money and material. Their activities continued and spread to the Cachar Hills of Assam and the Union Territory of Tripura.

It was early in 1971 that a three-member delegation of the National Mizo Front headed by its President, Chunga, met Prime Minister Indira Gandhi and explained the background of their agitation. They demanded a referendum over the question of statehood for Mizoram. The government, keeping their aspirations in view decided to make Mizo Hill area a Union Territory; which was inaugurated by the Prime Minister herself on 21st January, 1972. It was named Mizoram.

There were, however, many extremists and hard core Mizos headed by Laldenga who were not yet satisfied with the arrangement. They felt that only a separate Mizo state outside the Union of India could satisfy them. They, therefore, continued their guerrilla activities. The talks between the rebel Mizos and the government of India held both in 1973 and 1974 failed. In 1975, the rebels killed the Inspector and Deputy Inspector General of Police and operations commenced in a big way to suppress the rebels. In July, 1976, an agreement was signed between the government of India and Laldenga by which it was decided that all disputes and problems between Mizo and the Central Government would be solved without the use of violent means. But in March 1977, this agreement was violated when Laldenga launched a massive drive to enroll his followers and again began to follow violent means. Recently, however, Laldenga has again agreed to give up violence and solve every problem by constitutional means.

Demand for Nagaland. Another tribe that fomented secessions from the Indian Union and agitated for an independent state was the Nagas of Assam. The Nagas formed the Naga National Council under Z Phizo to carry on an agitation for the grant of independent status. In February, 1950, Phizo held a plebiscite on the issue of Naga independence and 99 per cent of the Nagas were said to be in favour of a sovereign independent state. in 1952, he organised a boycott of the general election and this was a great success. The Naga National Council even proposed to take issue of Naga independence to the United Nations. To pressurise the government to concede their demand, the Nagas resorted to large-scale violence and soon the conditions deteriorated so much that the Indian government had to despatch an army to deal with the situation.

Meanwhile, there were some Naga leaders who did not follow Phizo's line of action. They met the Prime Minister in 1956 and demanded that the Nagas should be untied and brought under one single administration. Prime Minister Nehru was willing to comply with such a demand provided the Nagas restored peace and agreed to settle every problem with the framework of the constitution. In 1957, a convention of loyal Nagas was convened in Kohima, which adopted a resolution and the demand for an independent Naga state was dropped. The convention also appealed to the rebel Nagas to give up violence and co-operate with the Government of India. In 1960, the Government of India signed an agreement with the Naga People's Convention about the settlement of the problem of the Nagas. In 1962, the Constitution Thirteenth Amendment Act, was passed and Nagaland was given full-fledged statehood, as the sixteenth state of the Indian Union.

In November, 1975, an agreement was reached between the Government of India and hostile Nagas whereby the former agreed to release all detained Nagas. The Nagas agreed to give up their violent activities and to surrender all arms and ammunition and to find a solution to every problem within the Indian constitution by peaceful means. The agreement also stipulated that underground Nagas would formulate proposals for resolving other problem of Nagaland. But unfortunately this accord did not last long, as many under-ground Nagas started violating that.

In June, 1977, Prime Minister of India Morarji Desai had a meeting with Phizo in London in a bid to find a solution to the Nagaland problem, but nothing concrete emerged. The rebels continued to be on the war path, although a vast majority of the Nagas has, however, now come within the peace movement and have agreed and reconciled themselves to the idea that all efforts to create a separate independent state of Nagaland outside the Indian Union will be a futile attempt and of no avail.

GROWTH OF REGIONALISM

State autonomy does not mean the independence of sovereignty of the states. It indicates non-interference of the Centre in the prescribed domain of the states. The rights of the states to work independently in the prescribed area is called autonomy.

Demand for More State Autonomy. Frustrated with slow economic progress and the dominant Congress Party rule, the leaders of the regional parties in the states have consistently clamoured for more and more autonomy for the States. In fact, the problems and the areas of friction between the Centre and the states have been the basis of persisting demands of greater autonomy for states. The DMK leaders of Tamil Nadu almost consistently agitated for more and more autonomy for the states. The West Bengal Government demanded a thorough revision of the Centre-State relations and also called for the revision of Centre-State relations in order to secure greater State autonomy. The Akali leadership in Punjab also voiced the same sentiment in the past. Sheikh Abdullah and now his son, have long been a vocal and outspoken supporter of the demand for more decentralistion of power. No less than the ex-President of India, Mr. Sanjiva Reddy, also called for a national debate and consensus on the issue. With the growth of so many strong regional parties in almost all the states and the coalition government at the Centre of these parties, the demand has grown further and it seems more realistic now than ever before. In short, the growing self-consciousness and self-assertiveness of the regional government, has made the demand for autonomy stronger.

Growth of Regionalism After 1967. In fact, ever since the commencement of the Constitution conflicts and tensions have persisted between the Centre and the states. However, during the years 1950-1967, the relations between the Centre and the States were not characterized by that open conflict and tension because the same political party (Congress) was in power both at the Centre as well as in the States. But after the Fourth General Elections in 1967 with the formation of non-Congress governments in nine states. viz., Haryana, Punjab, Uttar Pradesh, Bihar, West Bengal, Orissa, Madhya Pradesh, Tamil Nadu and Kerala, these non-Congress governments challenged the dominant role of the Central Government. They tried to show greater independence of action. The weakening of the Congress following its split in 1969 gone further encouragement to states like Tamil Nadu under DMK and Punjab under the Akalis to assert independence against central control. However, the trend did not last long. In 1971 Congress succeeded in re-establishing its hegemony all over the country (with the exception of Tamil Nadu and Goa). The Emergency of 1975-77) further strengthened the hold of the Centre over the states and the spirit of cooperative bargaining which characterised the relations between the Centre and the states was replaced by central bossism. After the end of emergency in 1977 the era of co-operative bargaining was revived. During their short span of Janata Government's rule the Centre-State relations operated in a true federal mould. With the exception of dissolution of governments of nine states (in 1977) where Congress was still in Power, the Janata Government by and large refrained from unduly interfering in the affairs of the states.

Main Grievances of the States. Thus the states which have been most vocal in criticizing the growing power of the Centre and have put forward demand for greater autonomy including West Bengal, Jammu and Kashmir, punjab, Maharashtra, Kerala, etc. Later on Andhra Pradesh and Karnataka also joined this category. These states demanded an overall review of the Centre-state relations as well as greater financial autonomy for the states. The main grievances of these states against the Centre are as follows:

Firstly, they are challenged the basic assumption of the framers of the Constitution that a strong Centre implies the existence of weak and dependent states. The states, particularly West Bengal, have argued that strong Centre and strong states can co-exist side by side and there is no contradiction between the two Jyoti basu, the Chief Minister of West Bengal in his memorandum to the Centre Government asserted that the concept of strong state was not necessarily in contradiction to that of a strong Centre, provided that their spheres of authority were clearly marked.

Secondly, states the Kerala and Tamil Nadu have expressed dissatisfication over the assumption of more and more powers by the Central Government. They have alleged that the Central Government was trying to control even those subjects which were not within the sphere of the Central Government. For example, they have not approved of the Centre undertaking functions like public health, education, etc. which actually belong to the State.

Thirdly, it has been alleged that the Centre is interfering in the field of law and order, which exclusively belong to the States. They have objected to the use of the Boarder Security Force, the Central Reserve Police and the Industrial Security Force, which were maintained by the Central Government without the concurrence of the States for the Protection Railways, Post Office and other Industrial establishments. As already noted, in 1968 when the government employees decided to go on strike the Central Government sent Central Reserve Police to Kerala without consulting the State Government. Similarly in 1969 these forces were used in Bengal to deal with the situation in the Gun and Shell Factory at Cossipur. both these states insisted that the Central Government should not have the right to see BSF or CRP to the States without the consent of the State Governments. This as not acceptable to the Central Government and naturally produced strain in the Centre-State relations. The Central Government was so adamant that it effected a change in the constitution (42nd Amendment) whereby the Centre was empowered to send armed forces to a state if the situation so demanded. However, the provision did not stay on the statue book for long and was revoked by the Forty-forth Amendment.

Fourthly, the states have pleaded that they are not getting their due share in the national finances. The Constitution has placed more financial resources at the disposal of the Centre even though more vital functions involving greater expenses has been assigned to the states, who do not possess sufficient financial resources. Further, the financial resources of the Centre are lightly elastic, while those of the states highly inelastic. As a result, the states have become increasingly dependent on the Centre.

Fifthly, the states have charged the Centre of avoiding taxation under Article 299 whose proceeds were meant for the states. On the other hand the Centre was imposing excise duties on a number of items which were previously taxed by the state. They have also criticised the Centre for this refusal to share the corporations tax with the states even though the latter had made significant contribution to the development of corporate sector. The abolition of the Railway Passenger Tax, whose proceeds were to go to the states, and substitution of a fixed grant in lieu thereof is also considered too inadequate by the states. The raising of the taxable income and imposition of surcharge on income tax which was not to be shared with the states further reduced the share of the states in income tax, without affecting the Centre. Even the proposals of the Central Government to abolish sales tax, which accounts for 60 per cent of the revenue of the states has not bound approval with the states because they see in it a serious threat to their economic autonomy. These states have insisted that the Central Government must either consult the State Governments before increasing the D.A. of the Central Government employees because this gave rise to a similar demand from the state government employees.

Sixthly, States like Kerala have complained about the regional imbalances in industrial development. They have alleged that the Central Government failed to adopt an integrated approach to the development of the backward regions, or location of Central Sector Projects, which has results in regional disparities.

Seventhly, the cultural minorities of the country, in order to preserve their independent entity, have also demanded greater authority for their regions so that they may not be absorbed by the majority culture. For the preservation of their cultural identity they have tried to capture economic and political power.

Arguments for and Against State Autonomy. The state autonomy concept is supported on the following grounds. First, autonomy, is not independence of the states and the autonomy is demanded under the Indian federal structure and therefore there is no danger for disintegration. Secondly, the functions of the states as such are increasing day-by-day. It is not proper to make them financially dependent on the Centre while they are performing the functions of rural development and implementation of five years plan. If they are assigned separate resources of finance then it will be convenient for them to perform developmental functions speedily. Thirdly, state autonomy is essential for the establishment of a true and genuine federal policy. At present the status of the states as such is like municipalities and they are always afraid from Central intervention. The Centre controls the states by issuing directives and even exercises control over the exclusively state spheres like education and health. Fourthly, the autonomy will inculcate the responsibilities among the states. They will seek additional revenue resources and will not depend on the Centre. The concept of a federal policy could materialise on our country only by allowing full freedom of development to every linguistic cultural state.

The ruling party at the Centre has opposed the demand for autonomy. The Union Government at the Centre felt convinced that the strength of the country as a whole is the best guarantee of the autonomy of the states, and that if somehow that strength was shattered, there would be neither sovereignty of the Union nor the autonomy of the state.

Looking at the argument for State autonomy, we are convinced that some reforms are required and right code of conducts and conventions should be followed. But there should be a limit of such reforms. In this connection we should follow Sarkaria Commission's concern for better Centre-state relations.

According to Commission's concern, there were widespread dissatisfaction with the existing state of Centre-State relations. The Commission made 247 recommendations to improve Centre-state relations, besides suggesting 12 Amendments to the Constitution and 20 new legislations. The Commission recommends. *(i)* Before issue directions to a state under Articles 256 and 257; *(ii)* the Union should explore the possibilities of setting points of conflict by all other available means; *(iii)* The Governor of a state should be appointed with the concurrence of the Chief Minister; *(iv)* Article 356 should be used very sparingly, in extreme cases, as a measure of last resort; *(v)* Before deploying Union armed and other forces in a state in aid of the civil power, it is desirable that the State Government should be consulted; *(vi)* By an appropriate amendment of the Constitution, the net proceeds of Corporation Tax may be made permissibly shareable with the states.

The Sarkaria Commission was the outcome of the States demand for more power, but when the ruling party at the Centre get a massive majority, it was forgotten.

IMPACT OF REGIONALISM

Regionalism, like Communalism refers to love for something in preference to the Nation; as Communalism stood for love for a community in preference to the nation similarly Regionalism refers to the love for a particular region in preference to the State of which the region is a part. But like Communalism, Regionalism is a nation-wide phenomena spreading from north to south and east to west. Regionalism has assumed following four forms in our country:

I. Demand for secession from the Indian Union;

II. Demand for separate Statehood;

III. Demand for full-fledged Statehood;

IV. Inter-State difference and disputes.

A complete study of the impact of Regionalism can be understood by analysing the above four aspects.

I. DEMAND FOR SECESSION FROM THE INDIAN UNION

The Dravida Munnetra Kazgham (DMK) in Tamil Nadu. The ugly head of Regionalism was seen emerging for the first time in the formation of Dravida Munnetra Kazgham (DMK) on 5 June, 1960, in the State of Madras. Nam Tamil ('We Tamils') staged a campaign jointly with DMK demanding secession of Madras State form the Union of India and in rampant, they publicly burnt the map of India excluding "Tamil Nadu". On January 30, 1961, another organisation Tamil Arasu Kazhagam started agitating for renaming the State of Madras as 'Tamil Nadu'. Later on 9 April, 1961, several members left the DMK and formed a National Tamil Party under the leadership of an M.P. E.V.K. Sampath. This party demanded a change in the Constitution introducing more decentralisation schemes in which the States have the 'right to secede'.

DMK continued with its programme of demanding secession and it won 50 seats in the Assembly during the Third General Election, on this ground. In 1957, it won 7 seats of Lok Sabha. On 1st May, 1962 DMK leader C.N. Annadurai alleged that the South is being 'neglected' by the Union Government. Pandit Nehru rejected this idea by calling it as "manifestly outrageous."

Parliament enacted the Constitution (15th Amendment) Bill in 1963, empowering Parliament to make laws to penalise any one challenging the sovereignty of the country. DMK withdrew its demand of secession from Indian Union and recoined its demand of forming 'Dravida Union' of Madras, Mysore, Andhra Pradesh and Kerala.

Continuing with their agitation in September, 1970 DMK convened "State Autonomy Conference". In April 1971 the Chief Minister Karunanidhi threatened to secede from the Union of India if their demand was continuously overlooked. He repeated his threat to launch an agitation for State autonomy on 19 September, 1975. On 5 March, 1975, he expressed to undergo imprisonment like Sheikh Abdulla for achieving the autonomy of the State. Later he accused the Central Government of "insulting and humiliating" the Government headed by DMK in the State, He reacted sharply that under present circumstances the States are pitiably dependent on the Centre for the alms. He argued that for rapid growth, the State must be awarded more autonomy.

DMK having regional influence organised itself to drive Malyali speaking people. In May, 1974. Tamizhar Pudukappu Peravai (Tamil Protection Organisation) took out "drive out Malayalis" procession in Madras and agitated to 'give employment to Tamilians alone" and debar any non-Tamilian from heading any undertaking and organisation in the State. During the procession two Cinema Halls screening Malayali pictures were ransacked and badly damaged. The next day Chief Minister Karunanidhi declared that Government was keen to reserve 80 per cent of jobs for the local aspirants.

On 9 December, 1974, the founder of DMK, E.V. Ramaswamy Naicker threatened secession of Tamil Nadu if Centre did not abolish the caste system before January 26, 1975 and he further emphasised that if Centre failed to abolish the system of dividing Brahmins from Non-Brahmins "We will proclaim that we are not the citizens of this country".

The Akali Dal and Prokhalistanis in Punjab. Master Tara Singh, the staunch Sikh leader, paraded during the struggle for freedom for a separate State to be called 'Khalistan for India. On 2 November, 1949, he demanded "Sikh Province" and declared that the Hindus of East Punjab had become "narrow minded communalists", and it was not possible for Sikhs "to get a fair deal at their hands". The agitation was kept continued during 1950-1960 and their demand for Punjabi Suba was conceded by the Centre on November 1, 1966.

Even this gift from Centre did not pacify their emotional attachment to separatism and they started demanding 'Sikh Homeland' so that they could establish a "socialist democratic Sikh homeland in North India". The General Secretary of this group Dr. Jagjit Singh went to foreign countries to propagate for their demand and even planned to establish a "rebel government" Sikhistan at Nankana Sahib. But he was expelled from the Akali Dal by Sant Fateh Singh in the wake of the Sixteenth Constitutional Amendment Act.

Having realised the impossibility of a Sikh State, the President of SGPC, Gurbachan Singh Tohra MP, demanded on 9 March, 1975 that the States should be given more powers and alleged that Centre was discriminatory in its acts. The Secretary of SGPC threatened to launch a mass agitation for securing a Sikh Homeland and he pleaded the non-Congress leaders to help his faction.

Time passed and even those who had never believed in the demand for separate statehood, felt that the interests of the Sikhs were "not safe in the hands of the so called secular and national government", and demanded that Sikhs should be allotted 'a Sikh homeland within the Indian Union". When in 1983 the Congress Ministry was installed, the Akalis declared that the problems before the Centre were created by its "false promises and administrative mismanagement", and the solution rested only in the awarding of more autonomy to the States.

Dal Khalsa was organised as a militant counter attack against the security means of the Government and fight for the separate Sikh Homeland. Sant Bhindrawale supported the separatist movement. One of the supporters of separate Sikhland is Ganga Singh Dhillon who had been busy in mustering the outside support in U.S.A. was said to an intimate friend to ex-President Zia of Pakistan.

Recently he had denied having favoured any kind of partition. Dhillon's cardinal tenet taken from the Granth Sahib is . Jo ji Saave so raji Jaave (there is no compulsion; and go freely), feels that "whenever the sikh's asserted their right of distinct cultural identity and autonomy, the mass media controlled by majority screamed 'Partition'. If one cries "wolf" too often it is likely to pay a visit. Those who raise the spectre of partition over every Sikh demand are the one who are unwittingly doing the greatest harm to the very cause they claim to espouse. If the majority persists in using these crude tools, India's balakanisation would be their responsibility. The issue of the Sikh nation cannot be wished away or washed away. We are not asking for the moon but only a place under the sun where we can lead a life of dignity worthy of the khalsa Panth and in our own little cultural republic". Indicating the Indian leaders and reacting sharply to the attitude of the Government he said, "The Government of India has never talked to the real Sikh leaderships. Zail Singh and Darbara Singh are puppet creations of the Congress. Darbara Singh merely exploits the Khalistan issue. He holds powers by telling Mrs. Gandhi he can keep the radicals down. Sant Bhindrawala's arrest like a common crook was a shame. Can you imagine-Punjab was made into a B.S.F. chavini just to arrest one man? So long as these tools are used nothing will be achieved. Mrs. Gandhi can pacify Badal or Balwant Singh. Now they are using Longowal.

The separatist and extremists were dealt with a heavy hand by the centre when on 26 June, 1984 in the operation Blue Star' it sent army in side the temple at Amritsar to rush out the extremists. Besides many others, Bhindrawala was also killed in this operation.

Reacting to it two sikh guards gunned down the Prime Minister Indira Gandhi in New Delhi on the morning of October 31, 1984.

Rajiv Gandhi succeeded his mother and emerged victorious in the Eighth General Elections, he signed an accord with the movement leader sant Harchand Singh Longowal.

Election in Punjab were declared but Sant Longowal fell to the bullets of the extremists. 'Rajiv Gandhi's settlement covered eleven points. Many of them referred to an attempt which took place after Operation Blue Star-the mutinies, the anti-Sikh violence and the security force drive against terrorists. The three major issue which remained unsolved in June, 1984 were Chandigarh, the river waters and the Anandpur Sahib Resolution. Rajiv Gandhi gave Chandigarh to Punjab and set up commission to give a ruling on the border disputes. The commissions terms made it virtually impossible for Abohar and Fazilka to go to Haryana. That infact had been Mrs. Gandhi's final offer, but by then it was too late to reach a settlement because Bhindrawale was insisting that Anand Pur Sahib Resolution should be implemented in full. Rajiv Gandhi only agreed to send the resolution to the one man commission on centre state relations set up by his mother. The Akalis would have accepted that if Mrs. Gandhi had conceded their demands on Chandigarh and the river waters. The river water issue was also resolved on terms the Akali's had accepted under Mrs. Gandhi. Punjab retained its share of water until a commission presided over by a judge decided on a permanent allocation. So in the end it all came down to the one issue-Chandigarh.

The centre decided to handover Chandigarh on June 21.1.86 but till *status quo* is being maintained.

The National Front Government headed by Mr. V.P. Singh called an all-party meeting on Punjab, in Chandigarh but the Akali Dal headed by Mann could not be present to take part in the consultation on the ground that Congress-I was also invited to attend the Meeting.

Chandra Sheikhar who take over a s Prime Minister after V.P. Singh to restore normacy and hold elections for long. New election were held in May, 1991. Rajiv Gandhi was assassinated. P.V. Narasimha Rao leader of the Congress (I) the largest majority party in the Lok Sabha formed the Government. He has announced election in the Punjab in February, 1992. All parties conference on Punjab was convinced by him and his desire to hold election was communicated. The Akalis hold varying views. The militants are opposed to elections and are not prepared to negotiate till Khalistan is on the agenda of the Meeting.

The Mizos in Assam. Assam is yet another Indian State to suffer from the holocast of fictional demands for autonomy. The natives of Mizo Hill districts covering an area of 8,200 square miles and numbering about 200,000 demanded their secession from Assam as well as from the Union of India. They wanted "independent Mizo State" and for campaigning; they formed Mizo National Front (MNF) Centre took repressive measures and the Mizo turned hostile and engrossed themselves in guerrilla warfare. In the wake of Chinese Aggression in 1962, MNF was banned under Defence of India Rules (DIR), but Mizos continued with their agitation which resulted into the collapse of the civil administration.

It was on May 2, 1968, that the Union Government alleged that the Pakistan Government was inciting the Mizos though it was stated "totally false" by a declaration from Rawalpindi. In January, 1971 three-member delegation headed by their President Chunga met the Union Leaders in the Capital and a memorandum was submitted to the Prime Minister Mrs. Indira Gandhi.

They shifted from their idea of secession and in 1971, demanded a referendum to decide the necessity of the Mizo State. Union Government, in its bid to pacify the turmoil, declared Mizoram as an Union Territory and was inaugurated by Mrs. Indira Gandhi on 21 January, 1972.

Later on, the Mizos became more haughty and on December 1, 1974 Mizo National Army promulgated a notice to the effect that, 'all Indian Nationals now in Mizoram are hereby ordered to leave Mizoram before January 1, 1975. The responsibility for violation of this order shall lie upon the defaulters." But they enacted a ghastly crime on January 13, 1975 when the two gunmen wearing police uniforms entered the Conference room of IG Police of Aizwal and killed IG, the DIG and the SP on the spot. This led to army operation by the Union Government against the rebel Mizos. It was well known that China and Pakistan were in collusion to help these rebels with money and arms. In May, 1975 MISA rules were tightened and the underground leader of Mizos Laldenga surrendered on 11 July, 1976. Secret discussions were held between Laldenga and the Union Government in which the former accepted that Mizoram was an integral part of the Union of India.

But Laldenga again acted cunningly, incited his followers to strengthen again and for this the Mizo National Front in March-April, 1977, staged on extensive campaign to enroll more and more volunteers. Thus the secessionists are still at-large, and demand for a separate Statehood has not died completely.

Nagas in Assam. Nagas of Assam are another tribals that have agitated for secession from the Union of India. They resided in Naga Hill district and in the Tuengsang division situated on the 'Indo-Burmese Frontier', comprising a population of early 400,000 Zapo Pihgo was the leader 1950, a plebiscite was conducted by Naga National Council headed by Phizo and it was proclaimed that 99 per cent of the Nagas were in favour of a separate Independent State for Nagas. In 1952, they staged a boycott of the General Elections. In 1952, serious acts of violence were organised by the Naga National Council resulting into the death of 300 Nagas and consequently the area where such incidents occurred was declared a "disturbed area."

As many as six Naga leaders, in 1956 met Prime Minister Nehru and condemned the secessionist movement carried on by Zapo Phizo. Nehru assured them and the Government of Assam declared a reward of 5,000 for the arrest of Phizo and his thirty-seven followers. A meeting of Royal Naga leaders was convened and the "conventions adopted unanimously a resolution demanding the integration of Naga areas as a single administrative unit under the Indian External Affairs Ministry to be administered by the Governor of Assam on behalf of the President of India."

On January 24, 1961, the President of India Dr. S Radhakrishnan declared the formation of the Nagaland. (Transitional Provision) Regulations, thereby making provisions for the administration of this region before the award of the full statehood.

It was only on 21 August, 1962, that the State of Nagaland Bill and the Constitution (Thirteenth Amendment) Bill was introduced and on September 4, 1962, Nagaland became the Sixteenth State of Indian Union.

But the story started was not to end here. Nearly, 1,500 Nagas regrouped and started there abonxious attempt of "Hit and run". They were provided by foreign powers with arms and ammunition. The Nagas hostility increased day by day and even their Chief Minister Hokishe Sema narrowly escaped on August 7, 1972 from a guerrilla operation committed by the rebels.Late the "Prime Minister" of Naga Revolutionary Government, Scato Wasu and former "General" Zuharto surrendered and pledged to cooperate with the Government of India.

On September 2, 1974, the Unlawful Activities (Prevention) Act was extended to two more years and all the activities and organisations of rebel Nagas were banned and declared unlawful. Various attempts made by the Government failed to bring the things in order and the seccesionist leader Zapo Phizo now operating from London is still busy in planning secession from the Indian Union.

II. DEMANDS FOR SEPARATE STATEHOOD

The framers of Constitution have abolished the contemporary names of constituent provinces and have renamed them as different States. The States were classified into the three categories, in the manner given below:

Category A. This category included in Governor's Provinces. These were. Assam, Bihar, Bombay, Madhya Pradesh, Madras, Orissa, Punjab, Uttar Pradesh and West Bengal.

Category B. This included formerly Princely States. There were. Hyderabad, Jammu and Kashmir, Madhya Bharat, Mysore, Patiala, and East Punjab States' Union, Rajasthan, Saurasstra and Travancore Cochin.

Category C. This included the Chief Commissioner's Provinces. These were Ajmer, Bhopal, Bilaspur, Coorg, Himachal Pradesh, Kutch, Manipur, Tripura and Vindhya Pradesh.

When it was realsied that the reorganisation of States was the call of the time Government constituted the State Reorganisation Commission (S.R.C.) in 1953. About the territories mentioned under Category D; the S.R.C. observed that, "Democracy in these areas should take the form of the People being associated with the administration in an advisory rather than a directive capacity."

The distinction between States of category A and category B was abolished. In 1961, Goa, Daman and Diu came under the rule of India. In 1962 the Goa, Daman and Diu (Administration) Bill, declared it a Union Territory. Punjab was reorganised in 1966, creating the State of Haryana and Chandigarh was declared a Union Territory. At a late stage Goa was delinked from Daman and Diu. It became a full fledged state, Daman and Diu were left as Union Territories.

III. DEMAND FOR FURTHER REORGANIZATION OF STATES

The reorganisation on States of the basis of language did not pacify the demands but made the situation more grave and gave new impetus for the aspirants of separate Statehood.

(a) Bifurcation of Bombay. Bombay become the issue of battle between the Gujarati speaking and Marathi speaking communities. The recommendation of the State Reorganisation Commission (S.R.C.) was not acceptable to either of these communities. The Samyakta Maharashtra Samiti was formed to demand a separate Maratha State with bombay as its capital. On the other hand Mahagujarat Janata Parishad was formed to advocate the demand for separate Gujarat State with Bombay as its capital.

In 1959, the Congress Working Committee decided to bifurcate the State of Bombay into two States, and "It was mutually agreed that Bombay would become the capital of the Maharashtra State and she would contribute towards the cost of building a new capital for Gujarat". On March 8, 1960, the Bombay Reorganisation Bill was introduced and on April 25, 1960, it got the Presidential assent.

(b) Demand for Separate State of Vidarbha. When the case of bifurcation of Bombay was being discussed certain MLAs from Nagpur strongly demanded for a separate Vidarbha State. Many Congessmen opposed it and on December 4, 1959, Congress Working Committee condemned the demand. but favoured that separate arrangements be made to safeguard the interest of Vidarbha.

On March 14, 1960, the State Government gave some assurances for giving importance to Nagpur, but it did not satisfy the agitators. The people of Vidarbha region formed Nag Vidarbha Andolan Samiti and on March 30, 1961, serious riots occurred in when the police had to resort to firing leading to death of several people.

(c) Reorganisation of Assam. Non-Assamese tribals formed All Party Hill Leader Conference (APHLC) and demanded a separate Hill State. The Union Government agreed to recognize the Assam on the federal basis, but Assam Congress Committee objected to its raising several issues. In December 1967, the APHLC declared that its members would resign from Legislative Assembly if the Government did not order for reorganisation of Assam before the budget session of Parliament and this was not done, consequently members belonging to APHLC resigned and the situation became tense.

(d) Bifurcation of Punjab. Under the leadership of Akali Dal, Punjab speaking people demanded a separate State for Punjabis, whereas the Hindus under the leadership of Jana Sangh, Hindu Mahasabha, demanded for creation of a Union of Punjab. M.P., Patiala, East Punjab States Union into 'greater Punjab.' 'Violence', 'threats and fasts unto death' were common feature and the situation in Punjab become grave. Looking into all the aspects of the situation, Centre decided on November, 1, 1966, to divide Punjab on the basis of language, in which Punjabi speaking region was named as Punjab whereas the Hindu speaking areas was named the Haryana State.

(e) Demand for Bifurcation of Andhra Pradesh. It was recommended by the State Reorganisation Commission that multi lingual State of Hyderabad should be divided whereby the Kannada speaking region should be merged with the Mysore and Marathi speaking areas with the Bombay. However, the Commission suggested for the State of Telengana for the Tillage speaking people.

The Union Government did not accept the separate State for the Telegu speaking people and decided to unite Telengana with Andhra. An accord was reached between the Congress leaders of Telengana and Andhra in 1956 and on the basis of this accord the State of Andhra Pradesh was reformed on November 1, 1956. But the people of Telengana were not satisfied with this arrangement. In spite of the efforts of the State Government, Telengana Praja Samiti (TPS) was formed and it was supported by many Ex-Congress Ministers. On April 11, the TPS was assured of better place, and for this Prime Minister announced an eight-point programme. But TPS being dissatisfied launched a non-violent movement on May 26, 1969.

On June 28, 1969, eight Ministers in Brahmanand Reddy's Government, belonging to Telengana resigned, pleading that they would work among the people "in order to create a psychological climate conductive to achieving full integration of the two regions of the Andhra Pradesh." Hereafter Chief Minister also resigned Union Home Minister Y.B. Chavan reiterated Government's intimation of not allowing any split of Andhra Pradesh and soon after this, Chief Minister withdrew his resignation. TPS fought Lok Sabha Election in 1970 and won ten seats. Then started negotiations between TPS leader Chenna Reddy and Prime Minister and a 'Six point' agreement was reached. Many TPS dissidents formed a rival TPS on January 10, 1971.

This Bill was strongly opposed leading to the resignation of the then Chief Minister P.V. Narasimha Rao and President Rule was imposed. But after eleven months, on December 10, 1973, a new Ministry was installed under the Chief Minsitership of J. Vengal Rao.

The six-point formula launched earlier was given constitutional validity when Lok Sabha passed Constitution (Thirty-third Amendment) Act by 31 votes to 8 with 9 absententions on December 16, 1973.

Though the demand of separate Telengana State never saw its materilisation, yet dissatisfaction continued for the times to come.

(f) Bifurcation of West Bengal and the Demand for the Gorkha Land. The history of Gorkha movement that has reached to a point to demand a separate state, is as old as 1907 when hill leaders of Darjeeling region had submitted a memorandum to the British Government for a separate administrative unit comprising Darjeeling districts from sub-division-Siliguri Kurseong, Kalimpong and Darjeeling, outside Bengal.

"The All India Gorkha League (AIGL) has been on the forefront of the movement since long, as asserted by its general secretary J.D. Rai," to demand a separate state within India or to seek a separate administrative set up for this region, outside of West Bengal but within the Indian Constitution is not a secessionist movement."

'The Hill People's Association-precursor of the All India Gorkha League-had in 1907 and 1919 sought from the British a separate administrative set up. In 1907 Darjeeling district was attached to Bhagalpur Presidency.

The Gorkha League in 1943 sent a member to the Bengal Provincial Assembly at Calcutta. The political demand at that time was Uttrakhand in North Bengal. In 1946, the demand evolved into "Gorakhasthan". There was support from the Communist Party of India (then undivided) for this political aspiration of the Nepalis inhibiting the region.

During the reorganisation of the states in 1955, a lot of hue and cry was raised for a separate administrative set up for Darjeeling. But the movement for regional autonomy actually gathered strength after 1956. The Gorkha League joined the Leftists in the West Bengal Assembly and became a partner in government in 1969.

Mr. Deo Prakash Rai, a leading luminary of the Gorkha League was an MLA from 1957 to 1980. He was thrice a member of the West Bengal Cabinet. On March 12, 1980, Mr. Deo Prakash Rai is on record as having said, 'if Darjeeling is treated in this way, a time will come when it may not remain in West Bengal. If the hill area is burden to you or a burden to West Bengal, let me know. If it is so, then in some other way we can manage it. Let the present Chief Minister declare that it is a deficit area. We do not want to be a burden to you."

In June, 1980 the Gorkha League district committee passed a resolution for a separate State, Gyani Zail Singh as Home Minister visited Darjeeling on April 13, 1981. The Gorkha League submitted a memorandum to him, recalling the report of the State Reorganisation Commission of 1955, that the wishes of the majority of the people of this region was the important consideration, besides the linguistic principle.'

AIGL General Secretary J.D.S.Rai observes that the influx of "other people" (Bangladeshis and Biharis) into North Bengal was severely upsetting the demographic pattern in the Dooars, towns and the terai regions of Darjeeling district.

He recalls that in 1952 when the first elections took place following the enforcement of the Constitution, the Gorkha League won all four assembly sectors-Darjeeling Kalimpong, Kurseong and Siliguri.

The influx of Bangladeshis in 1970-71 and the ouster of "foreigners" during the six year long agitation in Assam, substantially changed the population composition in North Bengal and the Gorkha League did not any longer expect to win in the Siliguri legislative sector.

In 1973 when the Congress-I was in power in West Bengal and Mr. Siddartha Shankar Ray was the Chief Minister, the Gorkha League prepared a blue-print for an autonomous administrative set-up. On February 21, 1974, Darjeeling district observed a "bandh" on the joint call by the Gorkha League and the Communist Party (Marxist). The Congress-I opposed it.

Lok Sabha member from Darjeeling, Mr. Ananda Pathak (CPM) brought a Private Member's Bill in Parliament in late February 1986 seeking autonomy for Darjeeling district and inclusion of Nepali language in the eighth schedule of the Constitution. This the Gorkha League considers "a deviation from the joint blue-point of November 1973".

On May 29, 1979, Mr. Morarji Desai as Prime Minister visited Darjeeling. He was greeted with black flags and shouts of "Morarji Desai go back" by volunteers of the All India Nepali Bhasa Samiti.

Almost all of Darjeeling town appeared deserted when Mr. Desai arrived.

Vehicles were off the road. The "bandh" called to press the demand for the inclusion of Nepali in the eighth schedule of the Constitution, was peaceful-and total. Tele-communication links with the rest of the country were snapped for the day.

The Gorkha League boycotted the June 1981 election to the West Bengal Legislature (by hindsight it considers it to have been a grave mistake) as it felt let down on the autonomy issue.

On March 20, 1986 there was a bandh" organised in Darjeeling district to evince resentment over the expulsion of about 1,000 Nepali colliery workers from Meghalaya by a students' movement against aliens.

Another 5,000 Nepalis and their families saw the writing on the wall and left on their own. They all went to Assam, where they were quickly isolated and transported to North Bengal. From there many went back to Nepal, for they were nationals of Nepal by their own admission.

The Gorkha League at a meeting on March 26, 1986, protested against eviction of Nepalis from Meghalaya and Assam and deletion of their names from the voters' list. A new youth wing of the Gorkha League was formed on May 15, 1986, to give impetus to the twin objectives of the organisation.

However an agreement reached between the state government and the Gorkha land chief Subhash Gheising brought peace in the State.

On August 22, 1988 a tripartite pact was signed in Calcutta by Subhash Gheising on behalf of the Gorkha National Liberation Front Rathin Sengupta on behalf of West Bengal Government and C.G. Somaiah on behalf of the Union Government in the presence of Union Home Minister and the Chief Minister of West Bengal. The Memorandum of settlement lays down, "In the over-all national interest and in response to Prime Ministers' call the GNF agrees to drop the demand for a separate Gorkhaland." However in the same document provision has been made for setting up Darjeeling Gorkha

Hill Council for the social economic and cultural advancement of the people residing in the hill areas of Darjeeling District. It has solved the identity problem of the Nepali people living in the hill areas as they will no longer as treated as foreigners. The Hill Council will exercise general power of supervision over municipalities and panchayats falling within its jurisdiction. The chairman of the council-the Chief Executive Councillor would enjoy the states and the privileges of a Minister in the State Council of Ministers. Disciplinary action against government servants were withdrawn. The agitationists except those who were charged with murder were excused.

The critics however fear that the accord might eventually lead to a separate state of Gorkhaland. They quote the example of Meghalaya-formerly created as sub-state within the state of Assam became a full fledged state. The tendency to appease secessionist forces is not desirable.

SITUATION IN OTHER PARTS OF INDIA

Demands for separate statehood were not confined to the above narrated parts of the country and the following narrations in brief throw more light on the politics of regionalism in our country:

(1) Assam plain Tribals met through their leaders with the Prime Minister, on 20 December 1973, that they were being suppressed by the State Government and demanded for separate State.

(2) The people living in former princely State of Mysore demanded for the separation from the Karanataka district.

(3) In U.P., the people living in the hilly region of Kumaon and Tehri Garhwal, demanded a separate State for themselves.

(4) The tribal people representing the Dangs and Dubhas in tribal region of Gujarat demanded a state of their own.

(5) A demand for Jharkhand State was raised by the tribals living in 15 tribal districts of Bihar; Orissa, West Bengal and Madhya Pradesh. In March 1973, the Jharkhand Party submitted its Memorandum to the Prime Minister. 1. The Hindustan times; New Delhi(City edition) 1 June 1986.

(6) Many clamoured for a separate State of Chhatisgarh.

(7) Demand of Delhi politicians to award full-fledged Statehood to the Union Territory of Delhi. Recently through 74th constitutional Amendment Bill passed by the Lok Sabha and Rajya Sabha on December 20, 1991, Delhi has been allowed an assembly of 70 members and also a Council of Ministers but it will remain Union Territory termed as 'Capital Territory of Delhi.'

Besides, there are numerous issue of regionalism involved in the inter-State disputes. Some of these are given below:

(a) Dispute between Maharashtra and Mysore relating to the boundary.

(b) Dispute between Punjab and Harayana over Chandigarh.

(c) Inter-State disputes on River Water:

(i) However, the Cauvery accord was reached in December 1981. Again it has caused a conflict. This matter is subjudice. The Prime Ministers' intervention is being sought.

(ii) Dispute on the distribution of waters of Krishna river between the State of Maharashtra, Karanataka and Andhra Pradesh.

(iii) Controversy among the States of Punjab, Jammu, and Kashmir, Haryana, Rajasthan and Himachal Pradesh over the construction and ownership of dams for the generation of electricity.

REGIONAL POLITICS

Regionalism and Demands for Separate Statehood. Another form in which regionalism has found an expression in India is that some of the areas have been demanding separate statehood, where the people of the area could develop their language and culture. This demand is mainly raised with a view to attain a distinct political entity for the people of a particular region. This type of regionalism gained momentum after the reorganisation of the states on a linguistic basic. The States Reorganisation Commission had made certain recommendations about the reorganisation of states on linguistic basis, but these recommendations created several serious problems and those regions which were not satisfied with its reports became violent and in many parts of the country there were violent demonstrations and some people demanded the creation of separate states for their linguistic areas.

Bifurcation of Bombay State. The States Reorganisation Commission had recommended that Bombay should remain a bilingual state, but also suggested the creation of a separate state of Vidharbha, by adding some areas of Madhya Pradesh. There was violence in the state and two separate organisations, viz., the Samyukta Maharashtra Samiti and the Maha Gujarat Janata Parishad, were founded. They sought the creation of two separate states of Gujarat and Maharashtra. Both these organisations got sufficient support from the masses and in May, 1960, these states came into being.

Bifurcation of Punjab. The Punjabi speaking people of Punjab, mainly Sikhs, demanded a separate Punjabi speaking state. They resorted to agitation, violence, strikes and fasts, sometimes 'fasts unto death'. Sant Fateh Singh held out a threat that if the demand for a Punjabi speaking Suba was not conceded he would burn himself to death. Apprehending danger, the Centre decided to divide Punjab on linguistic lines and two separate states of Punjab and Haryana were created in November, 1966.

Reorganisation of Assam State. The demand for a separate state of Meghalaya was raised by the people living in the hilly areas of Garo, Khasi, Jainta and North Cachar. They formed the All Party Hill Leaders Conference (APHLC) and demanded the creation of a separate hill state. in December, 1969, the Assam Reorganisation Bill was passed by the Parliament and the Hill state of Meghalaya was created as an autonomous unit with Assam. According to the arrangements envisaged in the Act the State of Meghalaya was provided with its own Legislature and a Council of Ministers. However, this did not fully meet the aspirations of the people of the area and the Meghalaya Assembly unanimously passed a resolution on 30th September, 1970 requesting the Government of India to accord them the status of a full-fledged state, a demand which was conceded by the Government in January, 1972. With the conversion of Meghalaya into a full-fledged state the strength of the Indian states rose to eighteen.

Demand for Separate Vidharbha State. When in 1960 a proposal for the bifurcation of Bombay was under consideration that demand for the creation of a separate state of Vidharbha was revived. Some Congress MLAs from the Nagpur area strongly demanded the formation of Vidharbha. In order to forcefully and effectively press their demand, the people of the region organised Nav Vidharbha Andolan Samiti, which also organised violent demonstrations near Nagpur city. That the Vidharbha area would be given special representation and finance for its development, did not satisfy them.

Demand for Telengana. The States Reorganisation Commission recommended that Telengana should be a separate state, but that a provision should be made for its union with Andhra Pradesh after the third general election "if a two-third majority of the legislature of Telengana expressed itself in favour." But the government decided to unite Telengana with Andhra on the ground that the resultant uncertainty would retard Telengana's economic development. As a condition for union the Congress leaders of Andhra and Telengana concluded in 1956 the following accord. *(a)* All members of the State Assembly from Telengana would form a Regional Committee to deal with matters relating to that region; *(b)* The entire revenue from Telengana would be spent on the development of the region, of course after meeting its proportionate share of the common expenditure of the State; *(c)* The recruitment to government posts in Telengana carrying a salary of upto Rs. 500 a month would be made for five years only from among the persons who had lived in Telengana for at least fifteen years; *(d)* When the Chief Minister of the state came from Andhra the Deputy Chief Minister would be drawn from Telengana and *vice versa*.

On the basis of this agreement, the state of Andhra Pradesh was reconstituted on 1st November, 1956. But the agreement did not work well, and the people of Telengana began to express their dissatisfaction and resentment. Voices were raised throughout the 1960s that they should be separated from Andhra Pradesh. In early January, 1969, they commenced an agitation, which was at first generally peaceful, but later it turned violent. The agitation was essentially a by-product of an acute economic problem. It has brought to light the regional imbalances and discontent of the people living in backward, undeveloped and neglected conditions.

The main cause for the outbreak of the Andhra agitation in 1973 was the Supreme Court's decision of 3rd October, 1972 on the Mulki Rules. It has reversed the earlier High Court ruling and found that the Mulki Rules were 'laws in force' which had remained valid and operative even after the formation of Andhra Pradesh. This ruling of the Supreme Court was disadvantageous to the Andhra Personnel with regard to employment opportunities and educational facilities in the Telengana region which included the capital of the state, Hyderabad. In Andhra, the students reacted to the Supreme Court judgment by organising strikes and urging that the Mulki rules be scrapped to preserve the integrity of the state. There was a counter-demand from the Telengana students and the President of the Federation of Telengana Employees Association for the implementation of the judgment. The students delegations went to Delhi and diametrically opposite views were placed before the Central government. The verdict of the Supreme Court seemed to have made the Andhras feel that they were treated as second class citizens in their home state. They demanded that Andhra should be made a separate state. Andhra Congress legislators demanded the shifting of the state capital from Hyderabad to any other place in the Andhra region. The situation became very grave and the Army had to be called in to assist the civil authorities in maintaining order. President's Rule was promulgated in the state in a bid to prevent bifurcation of the state and to restore law and order. Congress leaders of Andhra decided to resign from the party, and declared that if by 5th February, 1973, a separate Andhra state was not formed 'revolution unprecedented in history' would take place. On the same day, the Congress leaders of Telengana formed the Congress Forum for Separate Telengana to work for immediate separation from Andhra. The agitation in both the regions became widespread and violent.

According to this formula, the Telengana Regional Committee would cease to exist and the Mulki Rules would be abolished. In all matters of recruitment to the lower posts, local candidates would be given preference. In order to look into the grievances of civil servants a high powered tribunal was to be set up and a state level Planning Board with sub-committees for different backward areas were to be established. It was also provided that a central University would be set up at Hyderabad. In order to give effect to these decisions, the Constitution Thirty-third Amendment Act was passed in December, 1973. But this formula did not work and a new committee known as the Telengana Rights Protection Committee was formed in 1974. The aim of the Committee was to launch an agitation for the creation of a separate state of Telengana.

Demand for Jharkhand. In Bihar, but also in West Bengal, Orissa and Madhya Pradesh, tribals have demanded a separate Jharkhand State since the 1940's The States Reorganisation Commission (1956) rejected the demand on the ground that the "tribal population is only a little more than one-third of the total population and is divided into several language groups." Since then tribals have continued their campaign for a Jharkhand State. Under the leadership of Jaipal Singh, Adivasi Mahasabha, founded in 1938, was transformed into the Jharkhand Party in 1950, which declared the formation of a separate state for the Jharkhandis as its main objective. The Jharkhand movement can be justified on the basis of administrative viability and unity, geographical contiguity of the proposed districts from Bihar, West Bengal, Orissa and Madhya Pradesh, ethnic and cultural homogeneity of a large segment of the population in the region and exploitation of the local people by outsiders.

While the Government of India are holding discussions at the level of Union Home Minister and Home Secretary, the movement has revived its agitation. Bandhs and blockades are being organised and there is large scale violence. The state government is taking measures to contain the agitation.

Demand for Gorkhaland. The Gorkha National Liberation Front (GNLF) under the leadership of Subhash Ghishing has steered a demand for separate Gorkhaland. It spearcheaded a violent agitation for 28 months in the Darjeeling hills. They have also demanded the status of official language for Nepalese in their area.

Demand for Bodoland. The Bodo agitation is led by the Assam Bodo Students Union (ABSU), which is demanding a separate state and has resorted to widescale violence and a series of crippling bandhs to pursue their demand. The Bodos are the largest single tribal community in the North-east. The rulers of Assam are extremely worried if they give into Bodo demands—they are not thinking of a separate state but greater autonomy at the local level—then the scores of tribes and sub-tribes spread across the state will start demanding similar facilities. Where will it all end?

Separate Statehood Demands in other Parts. Demands for separate statehood were made in several other parts of the country. The hill areas of U.P. have been demanding a separate state to be carved out of the present state of U.P. In Haryana there was and continues a demand, for the creation of a 'vishal Haryana' which it is claimed should be include some districts of Western U.P. and Rajasthan in addition to the present state of Haryana. The people of the former Princely State of Mysore demanded separation from Karnataka. The tribal people in South Gujarat asked for a tribal state as a home for the Dangs and the Dublas. There was a clamour for a separate state of Chhattisgarh. The Buddhists of Ladakh had an agitation for grant of Union Territory status to the Ladakh region. Ladakh has for years complained of neglect and of inadequate grants for the region's development. All these were nothing but manifestations of regionalism.

REGIONALISM AND DEMAND FOR FULL-FLEDGED STATEHOOD

After the passing of the States Reorganisation Act, there were two categories of units in the country, *viz.*, the states and Union Territories. Regionalism found its expression in the latter also when Union Territories demanded that they should be given the status of a full-fledged State. The agitation in these Union Territories became so intense that with the passage of time the Union Territories of Himachal Pradesh, Manipur, Tripura and Goa, Mizoram and Arunachal Pradesh got full statehood. The Union Territory of Delhi also raised a cry that in view of its large population and financial viability, it should also be made a full-fledged state. But the Union Government turned down their demand, mainly on the ground that Delhi was the country's capital and separate statehood for it would not be in the national interest. The 69th Constitution Amendment paves the way for the establishment of a Legislative Assembly in Delhi with a 7 members Council of Ministers. Now the Union Territory of Delhi is known as "National Capital Territory of Delhi."

REGIONALISM AND INTER-STATE DISPUTES

Another form of regionalism in India has found expression in the form of inter-state disputes. There is a dispute over Chandigarh between Punjab and Haryana. There are boundary disputes, for example, between Maharashtra and Karnataka on Belgaum, where the Marathi speaking population is surrounded by Kannada speaking people, between Karnataka and Kerala on Kasargod and several other border areas, between Assam and Nagaland on Rengma reserved forests in Rampagani area, between Assam and Meghalaya on several hill areas and between Assam and Arunachal Pradesh on Pasighat sub-division.

The first important dispute regarding use of water resources was over the use of water resources of three rivers namely Narmada, Krishna and Cauvery, in which the states of Madhya Pradesh, Rajasthan, Gujarat and Maharashtra were involved. Another dispute arose among the states of Maharashtra, Karnataka and Andhra Pradesh over the use and distribution of waters of the Krishna river. Disputes also arose over the use of Cauvery waters among the states of Tamil Nadu, Kerala and Karnataka. In Punjab there was dispute over the use of waters of Ravi river where even the construction of dam was delayed. The disputing states in this case being Punjab, Jammu and Kashmir, Rajasthan and Himachal Pradesh. There were many other disputes involving the distribution of the waters of other rivers, but these were of minor importance.

In all these cases the state Chief Ministers behaved like spokesmen of independent nation and endeavoured to obtain the maximum for the own state. It appeared as if India was a multi-national country.

REGIONALISM AND THE PROBLEM OF LINGUISTIC MINORITIES

Regionalism in the Indian context is related with the continuation of linguistic and religious minorities within the states. On an average about 18 per cent of a state population has as its mother tongue a language other than the official state language (the figure varying from 5 per cent in Kerala to 35 per cent in Karnataka, with the exception of Assam where the non-Assamese speaking people constitute as much as 44 per cent of the state population). The problem has not caused much trouble except in areas where the 'outsiders' occupy important administrative or industrial position and are perceived as 'exploiters' as in the case of Gujaratis and South Indians in Maharashtra, Bengalis in Assam and Orissa, and Marwaris in West Bengal. Militant movements of the 'sons of the soil' against these outsiders have emerged in the urban areas of those states notably Shiv Sena in Maharashtra and the Lachit Sena in Assam. The sentiment against the Marwaris in West Bengal, and in part, Tamil Nadu is also getting vociferous. As some of these movements such as the Shiv Sena, are led by highly obscuratist elements and employ the symbolism of extremist chauvinism and a para-military appeal, they pose a source of great danger.

ROOTS OF MARATHI REGIONALISM (THE CASE OF THE SHIV SENA)

The Shiv Sena in Maharashtra is a parochinal organisation built on the theory of the welfare of the 'sons of the soil'. In the city of Bombay, in mid-sixties the nation watched a sudden tide of the regionalis movement of Shiv Sena which eventually gathered momentum and exploded into violent riots in February, 1968. Bal Thackre touched a very vulnerable note when he raised the non-Maharashtrian bogey and the slogans 'sons of the soil'. He took up the plea that no Maharashtrians should be turned out of Bombay. The study of Shiv Sena in terms of its ideological position leaves a strong impression of its being a parochial organisation, dedicated to the economic and social welfare of the Marathi people. It stresses that Maharashtrians *(i)* should not visit udipi hotels, they should make it a point to visit only Maharashtrian establishments; *(ii)* they should buy or sell a house only among themselves; *(iii)* Maharashtrian businessmen should employ only Maharashtrians; and *(iv)* that an adequate percentage of employment should be reserved for the local population in private as well as the public sector.

The stress on economic grievances of Maharashtrians in their own state, particularly after the bifurcation of the unlingual Bombay state, is the sheet anchor of the ideology of Shiv Sena. It follows that its objects is to secure a rightful and honourable place for the Maharashtrians in their own state. It has demanded 80 per cent jobs for the Maharashtrians on the basis of precedence as in, West Bengal when late Chief Minister B.C. Roy had laid down an unwritten rule that every business establishment should have 75 to 80 per cent Bengali employees. The struggle for the redressal of the economic grievances naturally took the shape of a struggle against the South Indian people whose vast numerical strength was regarded as the main cause of economic injustice to the 'sons of the soil'. The economic crisis provided a congenial atmosphere for Shiv Sena's growth, particularly because the grievances of the Maharashtrian people highlighted by it were not altogether imaginary. As a result, the Shiv Sena took no time in promoting itself from the status of a pressure group to a political party. It captured its first target Thana municipality—curiously in a battle of the ballot box in 1967. It was definitely a great day for the Shiv Sena when it registered an impressive performance in the civil elections of Bombay Municipal Corporation held in March 1968 by capturing 53 seats.

GROWING INFLUENCE OF REGIONAL PARTIES

Since independence till 1967 the Congress Party had dominated the Indian political scene to such an extent that India was often described as a one dominant party system. This typology was a commonly accepted one but even at the height of Congress dominance, it was only partially accurate. It suggested an even greater imbalance in the party system than in fact existed. While even after the 1969 mid-term elections in five states, the Congress had an over-whelming preponderance in the Lok Sabha, it never won a majority of the popular votes in any national election. The numerous opposition parties, while weak in the number of candidates elected to the Lok Sabha and Vidhan Sabha, reflected many facets of Indian political life that were not always embodied in the Congress and exercised an influence out of proportion to their electoral successes.

One Party Domination Invalid. In the states the description of one party dominance was even more misleading, and after the 1967 general elections and the 1969 mid-term elections in four key states and Nagaland, it was obviously invalid. Hence, it spite of the frequent use of the terms 'one dominant party system' by some of the most astute students of Indian politics including Professors W.H. Morris Jones and Rajni Kothari, such a nomenclature should, in fact, be used cautiously and with qualifications even for the period prior to 1967. After 1967 one can no longer so characterize the political situation in many states and is of limited utility even with reference to the Centre. "India".

Case of Congress Party Domination. Sternly Kochneck in his study of the Congress Party, referred to some basic objections to the concept of one-party dominance. He stated, "To classify India as a dominant one-party system during the first two decades of independence tells very little about the nature of the dominant party or about the Indian political systems."

Unhappy Experience. India's experience with political parties has not been an altogether happy one. Nevertheless parties have been and continue to the prominent features of Indian political life. Parties in India, imperfectly but discernibly, have played an important role in political aggregation, articulation, socialization and participation. Thus, they have been important components of the Indian political system. It may be preferable, however, as Rajni Kothari suggests, to "look at the party system in India not so much in terms of discrete organisational entities known as parties in the fashion of the interest aggregation theory, but rather as part of an interacting process of governmental penetration, performance at various levels and society's response to such penetration and performance."

Typologies of Parties. Various typologies of political parties in India could be suggested, but basically they consist of the Congress Party and all the rest Another possible division between national and regional, state or local parties. Norman D. Palmer points out. "Most parties are really local or at most regional groupings, often hardly more than the followers of some leader. Such groupings spring up, put up their candidates in a general election, and disappear quickly, or merge with similar groups or move in and out of electoral arrangements, sometimes of a weird character."

Important State Parties. The most important of the State parties are the Dravida Munnetra Kazhagam(DMK), AIDMK Telugu Desham, Asom Gana Parishad, Akali Dal and National Conference. Some of these are of great significance in their localities, and can give the Congress stiff competition in these areas. They usually are built around a few leading personalities and emphasize communal, caste or sectional interests and loyalties.

Victories of Local Parties. In their own localities, a number of local parties or groupings have scored impressive victories. Notable among these were the Gantanatra Parishad and Utkal Congress in Orissa, the Dravida Munnetra Kazhagam in Madras, the Jharkhand Party in Bihar, Samyukta Maharashtra Samiti and the Maha Gujarat Janata Parishad in the Maharashtra and Gujarat sections of Bombay State, Shiv Sena in Maharashtra, Bharatiya Kranti Dal in U.P., Akali Dal in Punjab, Anna-DMK in Tamil Nadu, National Conference in Jammu and Kashmir, the Muslim League in Kerala and SP-BSP in Uttar Pradesh.

Powerful Forces. The Akali Dal in Punjab, the National Conference in Jammu and Kashmir, and the AIDMK and DMK in Tamil Nadu have become a powerful political force in their respective states. Barely, six months after coming into existence, Telugu Desam successfully stormed the Congress stronghold in Andhra Pradesh. The Asom Gana Parishad was formed in the fall of 1985, and was swept to power by the year end. In 1986, Laldenga signed an accord with the Union Government, abjured insurgency and led his Mizo National Front to power in Aizawal. For some years now, Congress has had an informal alliance with the AIDMK in Tamil Nadu and it joined Farooq Abdullah's coalition government as a junior partner in Jammu and Kashmir. The All Party Hill Leader's Conference (APHLC), which was mainly responsible for the creation in 1970 of an 'autonomous' tribal state of Meghalaya within the State of Assam and the Nagaland Nationalist Organization, which had been continuously in power since the State of Nagaland was formed in 1963, are parties of regional outlook. In West Bengal, the Bangla Congress, Forward Bloc and Socialist Unity Centre, and the role of Kerala Congress, KTP and KSP in Kerala are wholly governed by regional pressures. The Bangla Congress in West Bengal, the Kerala Congress in Kerala and Tamil Manila Congress (TMC) in Tamil Nadu were outstanding examples of political groups that were formed almost exclusively by dissident Congressmen. Each was confined to one state but some groupings of Congress dissidents cut across stateliness.

Political Realignment. When the Gowda Ministry was sown in on June 1st, 1996, it was the culmination of the most turbulent and the most tortuous process of political realignment the nation had ever witnessed. Apart from the Janata Dal, four of the most prominent regional parties that comprise the 13 party front—the TDP, DMK, TMC and the Samajwadi Party—were represented. And with the AGP following suit, it paved the way for a genuinely federal government for India.

What is a Regional Political Party? It is suggested that a regional political party must satisfy three specific criteria. The first criterion must, naturally be the territorial differential. By its very nature, a regional party restricts its area of action to a single region which, in the prevailing Indian situation, means a state. The second criterion of a regional political party is that, topically, it articulates and seeks to defend a regionally-based ethnic or religion-cultural identity. Thus DMK and ADMK act as the voice and champions of Tamil cultural nationalism against the inroads of what is perceived as the Aryan imperialism, of the north. In the third place, it is in the very nature of a regional party to be "primarily concerned with exploiting local sources of discontent on pressing a variety of primordial demands based on language, caste, community or religion."

Regional Political Parties: The Rationale. The emergence of regional parties in India has a geo-political rationale. Indian is a continental polity with a wide range of socio-cultural and ethnic diversities. Under conditions of democratic culture, these diversities are bound to and indeed did aspire for political autonomy. One way of expression of political autonomy in a federation is the formation of regional parties and groups in order to bargain with the Centre for a better for regional development.

Negligence of State Units. Experience has shown that almost all national parties had neglected to give adequate importance to their regional and state units. Because Congress has been the major all-India party. Its lapses has been more known than those of other parties. In the first two decades of independence, the Congress Party remained in power in the Centre, and in most of the state. In a way its continuous hegemony in the Centre, led to the neglect of the sentiments of the states. The Congress Party increasingly treated its state units, not as autonomous units, but as subordinate branches of the Central Congress Party. This led to a simmering discontent not only within the ranks of the state units of the Congress, but also in their support base and among the people of the state at large. The control of state affairs by the central leadership—for instance in matters of distribution of tickets at election time, formation of ministries, selection of Chief Minister, state planning priorities, location of industries etc.—and their style of working and public behaviour towards state leaders, were often arbitrary and not quite democratic. It offended sensitivities of state leaders and rank and file. They complained that their 'pride' and 'dignity' was burnt.

Suppressed Feeling. In South India, where an early initiative for separate parties was taken, there was also a long suppressed feeling among the leaders and the people that North India, historically, had tried and often dominated the South. The North was portrayed as expansionist, hegemonic, even colonial and imperialist in its design. This in-built animosity between the North and South, was further accentuated by identifying the northern leadership as Aryan, Brahmanical and Kshatriya, trying to dominate the Dravidian, non-Brahmin low and middle caste groups imbued with a democratic ambition to play a free and equal role in new India.

Major Regional Parties. There have been three types of regional parties in India. For years the Congress dissidents, off and on, formed several regional parties and groups, mostly short lived and often for ad-hoc purpose as a bargaining counter. Examples of this have been the Bangla Congress, the Kerala Congress, the Utkal Congress, the Telengana Praja Samiti and Tamil Manila Congress. The second type are tribal parties as focal points of building a tribal political identity and a platform for obtaining more concessions from the Centre. They had often talked even of secession from India and demanded complete independence. Examples of this trend have been the militant movements like the Naga National Council (NNC), the Mizo National Front (MNF) and the APHLC. The third type of regional parties are larger political formations in ethnically, culturally and linguistically defined regions like Tamil Nadu, Andhra Pradesh, Punjab, Jammu & Kashmir and Assam. DMK, AIADMK, Akali Dal, National Conference, Shiv Sena, Asom Gana Parishad (AGP), All India Muslim League, Bahujan Samaj Party, Samajwadi Party are some of the examples of such regional parties.

ROLE AND CONSEQUENCES OF COMMUNALISM

Because of being instinctive, religion plays a very important role in society. James G. Frazer regards it as a belief in "Powers superior to man which are believed to direct and control the cause of nature and human life." According to MacIver and Page, "Religion implies relationship not merely between man and man but also between men and some higher power." The concept of religion is as old human consciousness. It appears religion is permanently embedded in human psychology. It not only soothes the man in grief, but also serves as the ultimate source of social cohesion by advocating social values such as love, non-violence and respect of the elders.

Dis-service of Religion. Religion also serves to perpetuate dogmatism and blind faith with the result that people lack courage to break through traditions and customs. The followers of one religion hate the followers of another religion, resulting in tension and even violence. Human history is full of religious crusades. It breeds exclusiveness and segregation. Moreover, religion also propagates fatalism.

ABSENCE OF COMMUNALISM IN INDIA BEFORE BRITISH RULE

The muslims who came as raiders in India found the Hindus with quite a different religion and social system. They did indulge in religious conversion which often led to waves of repression, religious bigotry and hatred on both sides. But Akbar was among them a great supporter of Hindu-Muslim unity. The great Indian concept of tolerance, of "many roads to the same truth," helped mutual adjustments and mutual influences which made them live like good neighbours. Rajput generals and outstanding Hindu ministers got high ranks in the Mughal courts. The Bhakti movement that cut across all religions of India and the distinction of birth, status and sex created an atmosphere of cultural and political integration. "India was not yet a nation," says Rajni Kothari, "but it certainly was a society and a civilisation, and there was widespread consciousness of being one." This was achieved all due to the great Indian tradition of assimilation and eclecticism in as much as the Hindu society is pluralistic in nature. Prior to the British regime, there is no record of Hindu Muslim tension affecting the masses of the people. Wars were there no doubt, but between Hindu and Muslim rulers only. Attempts were made no doubt to persecute persons belonging to certain religious faith but this fell essentially in the category of oppression by the rulers against a section of the subject. Never did it take the shape of religious enmity between the Hindu and Muslim masses. Even the Simon Commission bore a testimony to this fact when they said. "In British India a generation ago, communal tension as a threat to communal peace was at a minimum. But the coming of the reforms and the anticipation of what may follow them have new point to Hindu-Muslim competition."

Beginning of Communalism. There is no denying the fact that the British rulers played the game of 'divide and rule'. They patronised the Muslim community and thus gave rise to Hindu-Muslim antagonism. They found in Sir Syed Ahmad Khan a Muslim who could serve their purpose. He had, pleaded that not Muslims but "irresponsible members of the whole Indian community were to blame for the mutiny." The British had on the other hand, blamed the Muslims because the Maulvis had issued a 'fatwa' supporting the rebellion. They had also proclaimed Bahadur Shah as the emperor of Delhi Sir Syed acclaimed that God had made the British their rulers.

Consequently, British favour began to pour in and he began to be recognised officially. On his visit to England in 1869-70, he was accorded on official reception. On return, he brought out a paper 'Tahzibul Ikhlaq' in which he induced Muslims to turn to Western sciences. He hinted at starting a Muslim institution of learning where Muslims could also go in for English studies. Sir John Strachy got allotted the present site of the Aligarh University while Lord North Brook donated the first big sum of Rs. 10,000 for the College, significantly named as Mohammedan Anglo-Oriental College. Beck, the principal of the college, played an important role in moulding Sir Syed Ahmed Khan against the Hindus. He performed such a glorious job that his services were praised by 'The Times'. London in an obituary in 1899, in these words. "An Englishman who was engaged in Empire building activities in a far off land has passed away. He died like a soldier at the post of his duty. The Muslim, are a suspicious people. They opposed Mr. Beck (because Sir Syed was not favourably inclined towards him) in the beginning suspecting him to be a British spy, but his sincerity and selflessness soon succeeded in his gaining their confidence."

Sir Syed once appealed to the Hindu and Muslims to "become one heart and soul and act in unison." He said the at "the words of Hindu and Muslims are meant merely for religious distinction otherwise all persons. Hindus, Muslims and Christian who live in this country are all in this particular respect belonging the one and the same nation." Under the British instigation and patronage, he came to bread enmity against the Indian National Congress as a Hindu organisation. He even went to the extent of posing civil war among the Hindus and Muslims. He once said, 'I consider the experiment which the Indian National Congress wants to make fraught with dangers and sufferings for all the nationalities of India especially the Muslims. The Muslims are in a minority, but they are highly united minority.

Muslims Deputation of 1906 and Separate Electorate. Sir Syed in this way left a good legacy for the Muslim League and organised in 1887 the Muslim Educational Conference which began to hold its sessions like the Congress every year. This was all due to the influence of Mr. Beck who misled Sir Syed into 'believing that while an Anglo-Muslim alliance would ameliorate the condition of the Muslim community, joining the rationalist agitation would lead them once again to sweat, toil and tear." In their policy of 'divide and rule' the British Government tried to derive a wedge between the two communities through the Partition of Bengal in 1905.

While correspondence was going on between Mr. Morley and Lord Minto on the subject of political reforms and on the necessity of "having a deal" with the Congress, the Secretary of State in collusion with the British bureaucracy in India was busy planning to destroy from within political progress by introducing communalism in Indian Politics. This he was doing by making separate communal electorate part of projected political reforms. It is certainly most surprising that Lord Morely was not only consulted but appears to have been deliberately kept in the dark about the mischieveous move. In 1906, Lord Minto formed a committee to consider the necessity of further reforms for India. This immediately led to a deputation of Muslims, headed by His Highness the Agha Khan, who met Lord Minto at Simla on October 1, 1906.

Formation of Muslim League. Some time after the formation of the Muslims Educational Conference, the Patriotic Association, and the Upper India Defence Association, the educated Muslims began to discuss the desirability of starting some political association on the lines of the Congress. Sir Mohd. Shafi had advocated the formation of Indian Muslim League in 1901 but nothing tangible came out of it. On December 30, 1906, exactly ninety days after the Simla deputation, the Muslim League was formed at Dacca. The objects of the League were defined as follows:

(a) To promote among the Mussalmans of India feeling of loyalty to the British Government and to remove any misconception that may arise as to the intention of the Government with regard to any of its measures.

(b) To prevent the rise among the Mussalmans of India of any feelings of hostility towards other communities without prejudice to afore-mentioned objects of the League.

(c) To protect and advance the political rights and interests of the Mussalmans of India and to respectfully represent their needs and aspirations to the government.

Congress-League Honeymoon Period. The Muslim League had no doubt been formed in 1906, but this implied only a sort of political consciousness among the Mussalmans. It was in no way directed at the division of the country. Their avowed aim was no doubt that of promoting "among the Mussalmans of India a feeling of loyalty to the British Government," but the leadership in a league soon realsied that the League should take a full part in the struggle for national freedom Under the able leadership of M.A. Jinnah and the Ali Brothers (Maulana Mohd Ali and Shaukat Ali), the League adopted in 1913 the objective of attainment of self-government under the British, the promotion of a national unity, co-operation with other communities for "the said purpose".

The matter did not end here. Gandhiji supported the Khilafat Movement, a movement in support of the Sultan of Turkey. The integrity of his empire and his Caliphate. This he did with a view to uniting Hindus and Muslims in India. The immediate result was the attainment of the support of the Muslims but it misfired Gandhiji called off the agitation at the height of the movement as it had grown violent. It was evidenced by the mob-attack on 22 police men in Chauri Chaura in U.P. Gandhiji's decision aroused resentment and bitterness and communal violence between the Hindus and the Muslims at many places. But the Muslim League even at the times of the arrival of the Simon Commission in 1928 was divided into two factions. One faction was led by Jinnah advocating joint electorate and which boycotted the Commission along with the Congress.

Alienation of Jinnah. Jinnah, the ambassador of third Muslim unity, could get no place and no accommodation in the Congress. "Gandhiji's overwhelming personality and his intrasigence on 'moral means' and the use of traditional symbols (often based on Hindu religious ideals) alienated the more rational among the Muslim leadership. The dilemma was that whereas the traditionalists among the Muslims were basically anti-secular, the modernists like Jinnah had no sympathy for Gandhi's political style and no patience for the larger goals of social regeneration that Gandhi so strenuously sought to achieve. The result was a perfect stalemate." This stalemate made Jinnah a changed man though he never wanted to change even until the late 1930's. On the question of accommodating the Muslim in the provincial governments formed by the Congress after the 1937 elections Jinnah got a point blank refusal from the Congress.

Pakistan Resolution. "The concept of a separate State for Muslims in place of demands for special protection," says Rajni Kothari "was the result of a radical re-appraisal of the political situation on the part of the League leaders and altered the whole context of Hindu-Muslim relations in India. There is little doubt that the League's frustration with democratic politics contributed to the new militancy and extremism. Henceforth, Jinnah became the fervent supporter of the 'two nation theory' and the exponent of India's partition into two." At its Lahore Session in 1940, under Jinnah, the Muslim League adopted the Pakistan Resolution.

There is no denying the fact that the British rules played the game of 'divide and rule' by patronising the Muslim community and created Hindu-Muslim antagonism. The fact can at the same time never be lost sight of that national leadership during the struggle against the British rule since the beginning of the twentieth century, committed Himalayan blunders which instead of turning national unity fostered communalism. This resulted not only in tension but in communal riots at different times in different places. In spite of the fact that the Cabinet Mission Plan could see no reason for the creation of Pakistan as late as 1946, the Muslim leadership in India had been obliged to declare for their separate homeland in 1940. The refusal of the Cabinet Mission to concede the demand for the formation of Pakistan led to direct action on the part of the Muslim league that plunged the whole of India particularly Bengal and Punjab, into the flames of riots.

Communalism in Independent India. Consequently, partition of the country came in August, 1947, as a result of which the population of the Muslim dwindled to 9.93 per cent and that of the Hindus rose of 89.94 per cent. Nevertheless, the Hindu-Muslim antagonism continues as a deep-rooted legacy although in a changed character. It is deep-rooted in the sense that according to the Tribune of June 12, 1979 nearly 9500 communal clashes have occurred in India since 1947, Out of the total, 410 have occurred between March, 1977 and January, 1979. The character is changed in the sense that in the period before partition it was Muslim communalism that spearheaded riots while in the free India, it is alleged, it is Hindu communalism which has become aggressive. It may be true in the sense that responsibility for maintaining communal amity lies on the shoulders of the Hindu community being the larger majority but not in the sense that it is always the Hindus that evoke riots.

Hindu Communalism. This is not to absolve the Hindus of the communalism which they profess on in certain organisations like the Rashtriya Swayam Sewak Sangh. The late Guru Golwalkar, chief of the R.S.S., in a speech on January 15, 1961 at Nagpur said, "In our oblivion of past history and our own national entity we have put the aggressors (Muslims and Christians) on par with the sons of the motherland, the Hindus." The 'Organiser' in its issue of 27th February, 1961 virtually incited the Hindus to attack the Muslims as it said. "That Jabalpur should have reacted-strongly to the rape of an innocent girl showed that our people are basically in good health... It is only healthy bodies that reach. It is really reassuring to find that the people are quite awake, Panditji's anesthetics notwithstanding."

The role of Hindu communalism is really surprising in a land which is known for association and electicism. Their role should be a positive one in welding together the disgruntled elements in the Muslim Community because not all Muslims are anti-national.

Muslim Communalism. The Muslims, says Morris Jones "Dazed and subdued by partition and the disappearance of their main leaders...seemed to accept as inevitable a loss of political dentity. Separate electoral rolls disappeared and the leading political party of the community, the Muslim League, died a natural death except in the south." But sad it is that even after partition. Muslim League has been allowed to flourish in India. Not only they are allowed to exist, they were patronised by the Indian National Congress in Kerala and otherwise on the pretext that they are not communal in the modern context. "The cause of Muslim integration," according to Kulkarni, "could not be advanced by the action of the Congress in promoting an electoral alliance with the Muslim League in Kerala. Nehru, a great secularist, failed to ponder over the serious implications of such cynical opportunism. His daughter went a step further. During the mid-term elections in Kerala in September, 1970, she acclaimed the Muslim League as a non-communal organisation-a certificate that was politically rejected by none other than the party's own 'national' President."

The Commission that enquired into the riots in the Bihar towns of Ranchi and Hatia in 1967, found that Muslim predilections for Pakistan played no small part in the inflammation of communal feelings there. It said 'what used to be more local affair between Hindus and Muslims before the partition in 1947, now tended to become a matter of international importance. This feeling of distrust which appears to be natural consequence of the position of the country and the creation of Pakistan and its future attitude towards the Muslim in this country is not diminished by the conduct of certain people among the Muslims on occasions, when they happen to shout 'Pakistan Zindabad' indicating their sympathy with Pakistan."

Role of Religion in Indian Politics. "A person born and brought up in this atmosphere," writes Ghous, "develops communal bias at a very early age." It has become so deep-rooted a fact of Indian life that certain organisations like the R.S.S., Muslim League, Jamat-e-Islam etc., talk always in term of particular religion. The R.S.S. has projected a concept of Hindu Rashtra.

Not only that some organisations but even certain political parties that have vested interest, exploit the religious feeling of the Indian people. All political parties like the Indian National Congress have been to a very great extent responsible for creating a bogey of communalisms in India. It has always projected itself as the only saviour of Muslims in India. It has always given out that the Muslims should vote for the Congress if they want their interests projected. Consequently, the Muslims have voted for the Congress except, for the first time, in March, 1977 election when they voted for the Janata Party. The propaganda of the Congress has worked in the sense that Muslims who did not want to vote for the Congress have kept away from politics. They feel estranged and alienated. They have not joined any other political party. Naturally, their participation in politics has gone to the minimum. They have been cut off form the national mainstream of politics. They have started feeling aliens in their own homes. There is no discrimination on the basis of religion but still they feel themselves as second rate citizens. They have developed such a psychological attitude. They do not feel encouraged to enlist themselves even in services.

Some people have alleged that "The Muslim minority is often discriminated against in matters of employment, the grants of licences, permits, control etc., in matters of admission to institutes and in other ways." The constitution no doubt guarantees equal right but practice is something real than theoretical observations. They should be persuaded to come in numbers to man the high administrative posts. But this should not mean that they should be patronised in a way to keep them off the national mainstream. Their secularisation should be assured and not communalisation.

CAUSES OF COMMUNALISM

There are various causes responsible for the spread of communalism in Indian. These are:

1. Existence of Fanatic Religious Organisations. Certain fanatic religious organisation such as Rashtriya Swayam Sewak Sangh, Jamait-e-Islam etc., exist in Independent India. They preach openly against the other community. There activities are mainly directed towards creating communal tension Mrs. Indra Gandhi, speaking in Parliament on the Bhiwani riots, said. "It was coincidence, if at all it was a coincidence, that wherever the Jana Sangh and the Rashtriya Swayam Sewak Sangh went, there was communal disturbances."

2. Vested Interest of Parties in Communalism. Almost all political parties in India have some vested interest in communalism. They want to gain prominence on this account. They not only tolerate but help it. Even Communist Party of India and the Congress are not exceptions. They had a truck with the Muslim League in Kerala. The Congress has never been shy of entering into electoral alliances with parties which it had earlier dabbed as regional communal reactionary, and even secessionist.

There have been appointed seven enquiring Commissions so far on communal riots. Each one of them has criticised political parties in one way or another. The Raghubir Dayal Commission (Ranchi-1969) said. "The political parties should change there attitudes in approaching the people for their gain, especially at election time. They should not exploit communal or caste feelings for their purposes. No political, economic or cultural issues should be discussed or agitated from a purely communal angle. Communal harmony should be taken to be too sacred to be tampered with for-political gain.

The Jaganmohan Reddy Commission (Gujarat-1969) said. "All political parties and religious organisations should have an unwritten convention not to say or for anything which will aggravate the situation, particularly when a commission of enquiry is to be appointed to enquire into all aspects of the matter..."

The Datta Commission (Chaibasa-1970) said. "The political parties should make no attempt to secure votes by appealing to the religious sentiments of any of the communities as this is bound to create further cleavage and mistrust between different communities."

The Madon Commission (Maharashtra-1970) said. "There are political parties and other organisations which do not restrict their membership only to persons of a particular community. Nonetheless their activities are communal and oriented to members of one community only. As a facade, however, they take a few persons of other communities as members and very often as office-bearers."

The Joseph Commission (1971) said. "...It has to be said that communalism has infiltrated into the rank and file of the secular democratic parties also. This is an unwholesome tendency which should be checked by the parties concerned."

3. Muslim Tendency to Keep Aloof from the National Mainstream. Perhaps the greatest, or rather the only cause of communalism in India is that Muslims keep aloof from the national mainstream. They do not as yet join the political, administrative and other arenas of national life. They feel shy of it. Sheikh Abdullah has also exhorted the Indian Muslims to join the national mainstream by partaking in every activity otherwise they will lag behind. It cannot be denied that the Congress had made them feel that their future is safe only in the hands of Congress. They naturally felt about their future as to what will happen if some day Congress was no longer there. This is the only cause in the sense that if the Muslims join national stream, all other causes recede into the background.

For any minority, it would be good to spread themselves in all parties so that they need depend on no single party-and no party can exploit them. It would be good for the Muslims and Indian if they become leaders in the Socialist, Communist, Congress, Janta and the Bhartiya Janta Party instead of depending upon any one party.

4. Encouragement by Pakistan. Pakistan spares no stone unturned in encouraging communalism in India. Whenever there were communal riots between the Hindus and the Muslims in India the Pak leaders accused the Government of India of connivance in the crime. At the time of riots at Aligarh Muslim University, President Ayub Khan said the riots, "could not have happened without the connivance of the Indian Administration.." The High Commissioner of Pakistan at Delhi, Agha Hilaly, described it as "organised killing" of Muslims by "militant Hindu communalists." When there were riots in Kashmir in the wake of the theft of the holy relic, Zulfikar Ali Bhutto alleged that the theft had been "permitted" by the Indian occupation authorities and their puppets as a part of India's plan to reduce the Muslim majority in Jammu and Kashmir to minority.

5. Indo Pak Wars. The wars between India and Pakistan also caused communal tensions. These wars are considered by certain people as war between the Hindus and the Muslims. A witness told the Commission that enquired into the riots in Bihar towns of Ranchi etc., in 1967 that during the Indo-Pak War of 1965 "very few Muslims were noticed hailing Indian victories."

6. Failure of Government in Taking Firm Action. It can also not be denied that the concerned governments in India failed in taking firm action against the instigators. Such things need iron hand which was lacking. The failure of the government has been on the side of law enforcement machinery and the intelligence agencies. At the recent 1979 riots at Jamshedpur and Aligarh the preparations made by the anti-social and misguided people is pilling up of fire arms, bombs and the like did not come to the notice of the authorities until it was too late. There has been much idle talk but sheer incompetence in tackling communal riots.

MEANS OF ERADICATING COMMUNALISM

Various efforts are being made by the Central government to deal effectively with the menace of communalism. Even the Minority Commission appointed by the Janta Government has been entrusted with the job of recommending means for the solution of communalism. Various bodies and individuals have suggested means. Even the Jamat-e-Ulemai Hind has suggested nine means for the eradication of communalism. The most important of the means recommended by various bodies so far as detailed as under:

1. Accountability of Administrative and Intelligence Authorities. It has been suggested, and rightly too, that the administrative and intelligence authorities of the district in which the communal riots take place should be held responsible for the outbreak of these riots. It is alleged that the lapses on the part of the law enforcing machinery are generally responsible for such episodes. It is reported that the preparations made by the antisocial elements in piling up of fire-arms, bowls etc., at Jamshedpur and Aligarh riots in 1979 remained unreported to the 'authorities until it was too late. If they are made accountable, they will always be alert and take effective measures.

2. Adequate Representation to Muslims in Law Enforcing Agencies. It has also been suggested that adequate representation should be speedily given to the Muslims in law enforcing agencies and the civil services. To secure this end, it is necessary that a large number of young Muslims to appear in competitive examinations. A recent study discloses that the representation of Muslims in the police force and in the Civil Services as a whole is totally disproportionate to their population.

3. Exemplary Punishment to Communal Rioters. It is also suggested that the communal rioters should be given exemplary punishment. Only this will create a sense of confidence among the Muslims.

4. Special Courts for Communal Offenses. It has also been suggested that special courts should be established for dealing with communal offence. Administration of justice is very much delayed in the ordinary courts due to rush of work etc. Justice delayed is justice denied. Delay has a demoralising effect upon the aggrieved party. Speedy administration of justice on communal offences will go a long way in suppressing this evil.

Role of Minority Commission

It was the Janata Government which for the first time in India established Minority Commission to look after the interests of the minority communities as promised in the Janata election manifesto. The Janata government also brought forward 46th amendment bill to give independent statutory status to it so that it could effectively play its part in curbing communal feelings. However, this amendment fell through in the Lok Sabha as the Janata Party failed to get special majority in the Lok Sabha.

The Minority Commission in its preliminary study about the communal riots during the past two years has revealed that these riots had taken place because of dispute over cow-slaughter, playing of music in front of mosques, desecration of religious places, land disputes, sprinkling of Holi water on Muslims and misbehaviour with women. The report made it clear that R.S.S. had no hand in these riots, directly or indirectly. It was also revealed that in these riots more Hindus were killed than the Muslims. In Jamshedpur, riots broke out because the Muslims wanted to throw out Harijans from a piece of land and construct a market there.

REGIONAL PARTIES

Haryana Vikas Party. The Haryana Vikas Party was launched by Bansi Lal who served Haryana as Chief Minister twice from 1968 to 1975 and June 1986 to June 1987. In 1996, elections Haryana Vikas Party with an alliance with BJP fought Assembly as well as Lok Sabha polls. The HVP manifesto contained following promises:

(i) Making provision of electricity for 24 hours within two months of coming to power in the State.

(ii) Providing more water for drinking and irrigation facilities.

(iii) Bringing an end to inter-state water dispute.

(iv) Removing Caste bias.

(v) Introducing compulsory prohibition.

(vi) Bringing cleanliness in State politics.

(vii) Appointing Lok Pal for checking corruption.

(viii) Utilising flood waters of Yamuna.

(ix) Constructing Agra canal.

(x) Restoring law and order situation.

(xi) Constructing canals including early construction of SYL canal, Haridwar-Karnal Canal.

(xii) Introducing Crop insurance for farmers.

(xiii) Granting of easy loans to farmers.

(xiv) Charging of electricity rates from the farmers at low rates.

Decline of the Party. Haryana Vikas Party and BJP alliance came into powers in the State. But it could not prolong for a full term. In the recent development H.V.P. was split. Many party members of Legislative Assembly left the party, complaining against the high handedness and nepotism of the Party Supremo Bansi Lal. His traditional political rival, Tau Devilal along with his son Om Prakash Chautala emerged victorious with their Indian National Lok Dal. B.J.P. found it more convenient to betray Bansi Lal Government did one remarkable reform regarding total prohibition of liquor in the State. However, the ethical enterprise proved to be a boomerang. The total failure in implementing the policy, along with loss of revenue made Bansi Lal to withdraw the Act. H.V.P. is now in doldrums-almost a fading phenomenon.

Assam Gana Parishad. The Assam Gana Parishad (AGP) was the outcome of a gradual but vigorous students movement in the north-eastern state of Assam, in the late 1970s. The entire movement revolved around the issue of 'foreign nationals' in Assam. Therefore, a unique feature of the movement was that it functioned outside the existing framework of the Party system in Assam. Initially, it was led by the All Assam Students Union (AASU) and its political wing, the All Assam Gana Sangram Parishad (AAGSP) which had gathered mass political support on a very large scale. The question of foreign nationals arose out of the 'illegal migration' mainly of Bengali speaking migrants from what is now Bangladesh, which began during the partition of India in 1947 and continued thereafter. Apart from them, there have been migrants from Nepal, and Bihar, who had all come to Assam in search of jobs and better livelihood. In course of time, the immigrants settled down on a permanent basis and legitimized their position by entering into electoral voters list. By 1979, these immigrants were in absolute majority in seven out of Assam's thirteen districts. On the one hand, the Assamese developed fear of bearing swamped in their own land by 'foreign' migrants. On the other, the national political parties which were interested in the migrants as vote banks raised the legacy of harassment to whom they called Indian citizens to prevent the detection of their genuineness.

Causes of Assamese People. Thus, it was left to the AASU and AAGSP to step forward and take up the cause of the Assamese people. Moreover, for the growing and aspiring Assamese educated professional middle classes, there was little scope for upward mobility given the Bengali domination in the bureaucracy (a legacy of the British) and the Marwari domination in business. Therefore, the students' movement can be seen as a culmination of the Assamese antagonism towards the non-Assamese and the then Central Government (or the Congress Party) and the feeling of injustice, aggravated further by the penetration of immigrants.

Not Separatist Movement. However, it would be wrong to call it a separatist movement because its demands were based on the recognition of the legitimate rights, thereby seeking to have its rightful place as a strong and equal partner in the Indian Republic.

These objectives, became the essence of the draft programme of the movement, which held two national conventions in January and November 1984. The Assam Gana Parishad (AGP) was formed in December 1985, two months before the Assam Assembly elections in 1986. Meanwhile in August 1985, the Central Government signed the famous AssamAccord with the AAGSP leadership which stated the "Constitutions, legislative and administrative safeguards, as may be appropriate, shall be provided to protect, preserve and promote the cultural, social, linguistic identity and heritage of the Assamese people." But by the time this accord could be implemented, the stage was set for the Assembly Elections (in 1986) which the AGP under the leadership of P.K. Mohanta (who became the Chief Minister) and Bhrigu Phukan, won by an absolute majority. Surprisingly its candidates also won from migrant dominated regions.

Decline. However, in 1991 State Assembly elections, the party witnessed a humiliating defeat with only 19 seats. It was stated that the voters of Assam had punished the AGP and its President cum Chief Minister P.K. Mohanta because the AGP Government could not control the rampaging United Liberation Front of Asom (ULFA). The defeat of AGP was followed by the formation of Congress Government under Hiteswar Saikia. The debacle of AGP was also due to the vertical split in the AGP and a new party Nutan Asom Gana Parishad (NAGP) came into existence. In1996, again the luck favoured AGP when it won 59 seats in the State Assembly out of 122 seats for which elections were held. Its allies captured 11 seats and thus AGP along with its allies formed the coalition Government in Assam under Prafulla Kumar Mohanta. The AGP was also a partner in the Untied Front Government at the Centre. However, in the 1998 Lok Sabha elections, AGP could not win even a single seat.

The AGP is committed to identifying the illegal migrants from Bangladesh and their deportation. It also demands more autonomy to the states.

The Jharkhand Party. The existence of a political movement and its transformation into a tribal party in the mineral rich region of mainly BIhar and the adjoining areas of West Bengal, Orissa and Madhya Pradesh, marks the culmination of the ongoing struggle of the tribal people of India to emancipate themselves from the centuries old exploitation, the essential nature of which has not changed in the post-independence era.

Origin. The origins of the Jharkhand party can be traced to the Adivasi Mahasabha of the pre-independence decades which was dominated by educated Christian tribals and which had mainly two streams—*(i)* the pro-British, anti-Congress one and *(ii)* another, which favoured Gandhian Satyagraha method of struggle. Renamed as the Jharkhand party in 1952, it contested the 1952 and 1957 Bihar Assembly elections with spectacular success. This was the time when it came forward with its demand for a separate Jharkhand state. But in 1963 it merged with the Congress party, though this merger was never complete as the rank and file of the party began to design of elites to share the spoils of the ruling class. Against this backdrop, a major split occurred in 1968 when the Santhals separated themselves from the Chhotanagpur tribals to form the Bihar Prant Hul (revolutionary) Jharkhand Party (BPHJP). Again in 1972, even this split into two with the 'HUL' group advocating radical methods to achieve the tribals' goals. In course of time, there emerged more than one party claiming to represent the demands and interests of Jharkhand is who are actually multi-lingual and multi-ethnic. However, the Jharkhand party, in whatever form it existed, has appealed to the Primordial sentiments of the tribal people promising to press upon the central and the State government to solve their economic problems and also these arising out of their distinct culture and social set-up.

JMM. Despite fragmentation, the aspirations of the tribal people have been too strong to die down. Today, the Jharkhand Mukti Morcha (JMM) is their leading voice. Under the leadership of Shibu Soren and in alliance with the Congress in the 1980 general elections, however, the JMM was rejected by the voters, quite in line with rejection of other regional parties at that time. Under the plea for improving the lot of the tribals and also by acquiring an ideology to legitimize its agrarian, social and cultural demands the JMM regrouped with the Jharkhand Party in 1986 to renew its struggle for the creation of a separate Jharkhand state. In the 1989 General elections, it won three seats from Bihar's tribal belt.

National Conference. The all J&K National Conference (N.C.) like the other regional parties in India had its origins coloured in the politics of a particular religion and a community's aspirations. Political consciousness in the predominantly Muslim Jammu and Kashmir State started growing the mid 1930s. When it was ruled by a Hindu Maharaja in whose regime it was said that there was discrimination against the majority community, that they were inadequately represented in the services, denied religious freedom and that there was lack of freedom of the press and political organisation.

In all started with the formation of a society known as 'Anjuman-e-Islamia' in 1921, to look after social and educational welfare of the Muslims. By 1931, this type of an effort was transformed into a holy war (Jehad) against the oppressive rule of the Maharaja and the All Jammu and Kashmir Muslim Conference was formed. But at a later date, the gates of the party were thrown open to a like minded Hindus and Sikhs who felt the need for bringing about a change in the Maharaja's rule. Thus, in 1938, the party issued a national demand stating that its ultimate goal was to change the social and political outlook of the people and to achieve a responsible government under the aegis of the Maharaja. In June 1938, the Muslim Conference met at Srinagar and after a prolong discussion, decided to transform itself into an All J&K National Conference.

Beginning. The first session of N.C. was held in 1939 which reiterated the implementation of the national demand, which compelled the Maharaja to appoint some N.C. members as ministers in his court. The N.C. however regarded such reforms as half-hearted and continued its demand for representative government and an end to autocracy. During this time, Sheikh Mohammed Abdullah emerged as the most important leader of the Party, which resisted the Tribal-Pakistani invasion of Kashmir in 1946-47 and at the same time, was responsible for the state's accession to India in 1948 the year when a popular government was installed in Kashmir.

Deeds. In first major deed was to transfer the land to the tiller under the Big Landed Estates Abolition Act. Next, through a forceful struggle, N.C. was instrumental in compelling the Centre to include Article 370 in the Constitution of India, which gives the state a distinct Constitutional personality and 'quasi' autonomous position within the Indian polity. In 1965, the N.C. and the Congress were merged, but the former was revived in 1975 by Sheikh Abdullah, after his release from imprisonment of 1953 under Indira-Sheikh accord (1975). In the 1977 Assembly elections, the N.C. won an absolute majority. Stress was now laid on organizing the party in a better way and on revival of its original policies.

New Kashmir Concept. But the concept of 'new Kashmir' remains the declared objective of this party, which is actually a blue-print for rebuidling the state on democratic lines and for the economic upliftment of the Kashmiri people on a socialistic pattern.Nevertheless, intra-party factionalism as the case of the other political parties, has not spread N.C. once again, it is the personality and ego clashes, rather than significant issues that have been the prominent causes. Way back in 1949, Ghulam M. Kar left the party to organize a new party (Kashmir Conference) as he could not find a berth in the Seikh's first cabinet. After Sheikh Abdullah's arrest in 1953, the N.C. split into pro-Sheikh faction led by M.A. Beg and the other led by G.M. Bakshi which maintained dominance in the party in 1953 when Sheikh Abdullah was put behind the bars because of his anti-national activities and his deputy Bakshi Ghuylam Mohammed was appointed as the Prime Minister (as the Chief Minister of Jammu and Kashmir was then called) of the State. Under the leadership of Bakshi Ghulam Mohammed, the National Conference got the ratification of the accession to India by the Constituent Assembly of Jammu and Kashmir. However, Plebiscite Front of Mirza Afzal Beg demanded plebiscite to settle the issue of State's accession to India and posed a serious challenge to the National Conference Government. But a firm hand of Bakshi Ghulam Mohammed tackled the challenge successfully. He also implemented a number of progressive and welfare measures to improve the lot of the people of Jammu and Kashmir. In 1957 State Assembly elections, it secured 68 seats, while remaining six seats went to Harijan Mandal (1) and Praja Parishad (5). In 1957, there was a split in National Conference and another paryt called Democratic National Conference was launched. However, this new party subsequently merged with the parent body.

Bahujan Samaj Party (BSP). BSP banks on dalit votes. In UP in 1993 polls, it had an alliance with the Samajwadi Party led by Mulayam Singh Yadav but later on BSP withdrew its support. The Mulayam Singh Government fell. BSP formed the Government with the BJP support in June, 1995 and Mayawati, the General Secretary of BSP was sworn as Chief Minister of UP. She was the first dalit Chief of the State. But in October 17, 1995, BJP withdrew its unconditional support and Mayawati resigned and President's Rule was imposed. In 1996 Lok Sabha election the BJP had 11 members. It polls percentage went up substantially to about 18 per cent. It has sold dalit votes plus a chunk of lower caste Muslims and OBCs support.

The BJP's support comes from UP where it has substantial following. It also has pockets of influence in M.P. HP and Punjab.

AIADMK. Factionalism in general proved to be the major reason for the birth of regional parties and it is specifically so in the case of the AIADMK. In fact the emergence of AIADMK is the outcome of factional quarrels within the DMK when intra-party conflicts, rigidity and factions began to appear. The DMK faced factional problems even before the emergence of AIADMK, one when C.N. Annadurai was alive and another after his death. The former factionalism was led by E.V.K. Sampath in 1961 and later by V.R. Nedunchezhian in 1969. But these two did not affect the parent party. When the factional problems arose in 1972, between M. Karunanidhi as the prisoner of the factional politics inside the DMK and M.G. Ramachandran as the monument of strength derived from the film world and kingmaking in the succession struggle of 1969, the latter rocked the organisation to its very core.

Alliance Win Congress. The Congress-AIADMK alliance, which bagged 37 of the 39 seats in 1984 poll repeated its performance in 1989. The AIADMK captured 11 seats.

In June 1977, elections to the Tamil Nadu Assembly were held. Of the 234 seats in the Assembly, AIADMK opted to contest 200 and won 126. The AIADMK formed its first ministry on June 30, 1977 with MGR as the Chief Minister. The AIADMK Ministry and the

Tamil Nadu Assembly were dismissed in February, 1980 and fresh elections were held for the seventh Assembly in May 1980. But surprisingly the people of Tamil Nadu opted for the rule of the AIADMK. The AIADMK which obtained the absolute majority, formed the ministry under the Chief Minsitership of MGR on June 9, 1980. In the eighth general elections of Tamil Nadu Assembly in 1984, the AIADMK contested only 153 seats and won 132. The AIADMK for the third time, has been enthroned in Tamil Nadu, returning with its highest ever election majority.

Defeat. The AIADMK lost 1989 Assembly elections because it was a divided house. The AIADMK factions (Jayalalitha faction and Janki faction) and the Congress I-the three of them had fought together in 1984 and won 205 seats with 53.6 per cent of the votes. But the 2 per cent swing away from them cost them 1'46 seats. Theorists argue that if the Congress (I) and Jayalalitha had joined hands, they would have been catapulted to power because together they polled more votes than the DMK in about 146 Constituencies. In all AIADMK (JL) won 27 seats and 21.7% of votes while AIADMK (JR) won 1 seat with 9.1% of votes. The 1991 Tamil Nadu Assembly elections were a personal victory of Jayalalitha and AIADMK swept 163 seats of the 232 seats for which elections were held. The AIADMK is polled 1.67 per cent votes in the Tenth Lok Sabha elections (1991) and won 11 seats. Faced with corruption and authoritarian style of functioning in 1996 Jayalalitha led AIADMK lost election to Karunanidhi led DMK. The verdict was virtually unprecedented from holding an impressive 164 of the 234 seats in the last Assembly, the ruling AIADMK plummeted to just 4 seats even as all its ministers lost their seats and some even their deposits.

Pledge. In fact, AIADMK pledged first to uphold the basic theme of the Indian constitution and styled itself to function as centrist party in order to balance and educate conflicting social interests. Since federalism in India has been handed down by the British as an institutional mechanism and as an administrative convenience, the AIADMK feels that there is much of centralisation in the constitutional and extra-constitutional processes leading to regional imbalances in India. At the same time the party understands that the political relations are the denominator for harmonious Centre-State relations. Therefore, the party has shunned conflictual tactics and has willingly accepted the co-operative strategy as the basis for all federal relations. This strategy of the AIADMK proved to be successful with the Janata Government as well as with the Congress (I) Government at the Centre. However, Jayalalitha could not pull up with the BJP led alliance till long. Currently she is in the dock, facing many trials in, one of which she is sentenced to one year rigorous imprisonment.

Shiv Sena. In Maharashtra Shiv Sena is a powerful regional party. It was named after the famous national hero, Shivaji who fought against Aurangzeb, the Mughal emperor. The Sena is highly critical of big industrialists and want to provide justice to the people of Maharashtra. For this purpose Shiv Sena also renders social service.

Shiv Sena has been a militant organisation. It is also a pro-Hindu group. When not in power, it has been resorting to demonstrations, bandhs and strikes. There have been allegations that it has been behind communal riots and killings. It is also alleged that Shiv Sena had a role in the demolition of disputed structure at Ayodhya.

SALIENT FEATURES OF REGIONAL PARTIES

The regional parties are more concerned with the interests of certain groups than with the general welfare of the nation. They are limited in their aggregative potential by being identified with the interests of an particular ethnic, linguistic or religious groups. Parochial or regional parties have grown considerably in India since Independence. Many of these differences were, of course, submerged in the national movement. Frequently middle class politicians exploited parochial sentiments to propel themselves into position of prominence. Sometimes caste and other traditional loyalties may be overlaid by political or ideological statement.

Caste Parties. In India pure caste parties are relatively few. However, the areas of influence of those parties which campaign for greater autonomy of a region or for linguistic rights of a community is mostly confined to the area where certain castes and tribes have nevertheless acquired some of their characteristics. The Jharkhand Party, for instance, aims at achieving a Jharkhand State for its million primitive tribals who live in the high plateau of Chhota Nagpur(Bihar). Similarly, the Nag Vidarbha Andolan Samiti agitates for a Vidarbha State.

After Linguistic Reorganisation. The Third General Election clarified that after the linguistic reorganisation of the States the parties which had played up language patriotism had lost their emotional appeal. But the political situation in Assam apparently proves that the linguistic diversity of the Indian Union encourages parties to take up linguistic matters from time to time. Thus, in protest against the Assam State Language Act of 1960, the All Party Hill Leaders Conference (APHLC) was formed to spearhead the demand for a separate Hill State. The tribal leaders succeeded in their objectives. On 11th September, 1968 the Government of India announced a plan for creating an autonomous state to be known as Meghalaya. The tiny sub-state embraced three major tribes, the Khasis, the Jaintias and the Garos.

Linguistic Minorities. Linguistic minorities living in various states are also fighting for the protection of their language. Their area of political influence is very marginal, but that does not prevent them from representing their demands with vehemence. Sometimes they take shelter behind the slogans of more autonomy or administrative reorganisation. The Lok Sevak Sangh (West Bengal), the Karnataka Prantheekarana Samiti (Kerala), and the Maharashtra Ekikaron Samiti may be mentioned as examples of linguistic oriented minority parties.

Participation Explosion. The emergence of increasingly vigorous regional parties in electoral competition with the Congress has been a significant catalyst of the 'participation explosions. The possibilities for victory at state level, dramatized in the 1967 elections and enhanced by the economic crisis and politi caldisillusionment that supplanted the 'Indira wave' of the early 1970's have accelerated party efforts to mobilize new base of support and to aggregate a range of various interests.

Growing Presence. The growing presence and salience of regional parties is, undoubtedly, the most outstanding aspect of political development in India over the past few years. They have catalysed a realignment of political process and their impact on the structure and process of politics have been multi-directional and far-reaching. At least three distinct dimensions of what have been described as regionalisation of politics in India can be briefly indicated here.

Personality Cult. Thus the regional parties are organised on the personality cult. In the beginning, they start as parties of pressure. They played the role that pressure groups play in a political system. They stand for separate statehood, state autonomy and regional language. Sometimes they are communal in outlook and plead the cause of certain communities. As political mobilization increases, the role of local parties and independents as well as regionalisation of 'national' parties may increase rather than diminish.

Regional Parties and the Political System. The changing political landscape has brought into focus the new emerging role of regional parties. Mr. P. Chidambaram recently highlighted this fact before a distinguished group of international business leaders by observing that the regional parties are "close to the people and impatient to develop India." Not only this, the Chief Ministers, who represent the regional parties, and aspirations, are "actively involved in deciding national affairs."

Political Clout. In the first-place, the political clout they have acquired poses the hitherto most powerful challenge to India's 'one-party dominance' or 'one party plus' system. In the challenge to Congress dominance at the Centre that is now building up, regional parties have a critically important role. They form a sizeable block in parliament. It is not surprising, therefore, that it is also a front runner in the chase after a 'national' alternative to Congress(I).

Extensive Participation. Lastly, regional parties can be said to have made politics more competitive and popular participation in the political process more extensive at the grassroots. So long as the Congress held a virtually undisputed saw in the political arena, the party's 'Vote bank' strategy rested on the mediation of local caste and community leaders who could deliver the rural vote at the h. Regional parties have inducted in the districts a new breed of rural-elites who have risen from the soil, speak in an idiom the people understand and have as a result, narrowed the mass-elite communication and culture gap.

However, it is essential to demystify the reality of regional parties and politics for properly understanding the real challenges of emerging regionalism in India.

Inter-State Disputes. Every single state in the southern, eastern, north-eastern, northern and north-western regions is involved in either inter-state boundary or river water disputes. Since every regional party is co-terminus with its state boundaries, these parties cannot negotiate with their neighbours because of the fear of alienation of local state sentiment on the basis of which these parties come to power.

Mr. Chandrababu Naidu of Andhra Pradesh, Mr. Karunanidhi of Tamil Nadu or Mr. Mohanta of Assam may be experiencing new freedom in the context of regionalisation of Indian politics, but these Chief Ministers have not been able to find any solution on their own to either inter-state river water disputes like Cauvery or Almatti or inter-tribal or intra-tribal fracticidal wars in North-east India. Regional parties are nurtured and nourished by local sentiments and it is impossible for them to resolve inter-state disputes without a powerful arbiter i.e., an effective Central Government.

Local Interests. The regional parties represent local caste and class interests and these interests come into conflict with either the neighbouring states or with larger social goals of development of India. The Akali Dal of Punjab represents caste, community and class interests of the Jat-Sikh capitalist farmer and Mr. Badal emerged as a lobbyist of his social constituency by raising the issue of the minimum support price for wheat. Further he has issued a warning to the whole country that if the support price for wheat is not enhanced to Rs. 550 or Rs. 650 per quintal, the official procurement agencies will not be able to induce the farmer to sell this products to them and the modified Public Distribution System will not succeed in the absence of new ineentives to the producers of wheat.

Parochialism and Fanaticism. Not only this, many regional parties have intensified the feeling of parochialism and language fanaticism. Punjab and Haryana have given a warning that wheat is not available except on the terms and conditions laid down by Mr. Badal and Mr. Bansi Lal. The ULFA or ASSU-AGP in Assam may follow Mr. Badal and Mr. Bansi Lal and stop the flow of oil to the country.

The upshot of the above arguments is that it is wrong to romanticize the regional parties. The powerful regional leaders of U.P. and Bihar like Mr. Mulayam Singh Yadav, Ms. Mayawati and Mr. Laloo Prasad Yadav have not shown any capacity to pull out U.P. and Bihar from backwardness.

T.D.P. The Telugu Desam is a comparatively new political phenomenon that in 1982 gained dominance in Andhra Pradesh's politics under the chrismatic leadership of N.T. Rama Rao, a marine idol. The party originated in reaction to Indira Gandhi's frequent imposition of unpopular Congress Party Chief Ministers of the people of Andhra Pradesh. Most of these Chief Ministers did not last very long and the faction-ridden state Congress party failed to deliver on its promises.

Regional Themes. NTR emphasized regional themes of Telugu nationalism. He stressed the Congress' corrupt political culture and argued that repeated intervention from Delhi had destroyed the Telugu people's capacity for, and pride in self-government. These themes probably appealed to many amongst Andhra's urban middle class. NTR also promised special new government programmes to help women and youth secure better educational facilities and jobs 'Reservations', and thus better job and education opportunities for the backward classes, was another major plank of the campaign platform. Plans to sell subsidized rice and to provide free launch for all school children were announced.

Symbols and Idiom. The political symbols and the idiom that NTR used to transmit his message were as important as the substance of his campaign promises. Clad in his saffron robe—the traditional garb of India's holly men—and riding around in a convertible transformed to look like a chariot, NTR might have been a figure from the Mahabharata, reincarnated to protect the dispossessed from worldly evils. NTR succeeded, in part, because all his populist promises were made not as an aspect of socialism a La. Congress, but "through home grown imageries and idioms available in the backward of the nation."

Anti-New Delhi Domination. The Telugu Desam denounced the New Delhi domination of the state politics and in 1983 won an impressive majority in the state election, defeating the Congress Party. The Telugu Desam secured 198 seats while its ally the Sanjay Vichar Manch won 4 seats. Since its formation, the Telugu Desam has faced various challenges from the Congress Party. In both the 1984 parliamentary election and the 1985 state election, however, it routed the Congress (I) at the polls. For the Lok Sabha it won 28 out of 49 seats and in the March 1985 state elections it won 202 out of 287 seats. In fact in the Lok-Sabha, it emerged as the single largest Opposition Party in 1984, with more members than the other all-India parties.

NTR Voted Out. However, in November, 1989 poll, the people of Andhra Pradesh gave a decisive vote against NTR's rule. N.T.R. and his Telugu Desam party were rejected by the electorate, not because of ideology or as a result of any wave but for sheer lack of performance and failure to implement the promises he had made to the electorate. The party secured only one of the 22 Lok Sabha seats it contested and won only 74 Assembly seats. The Party in 1991 Lok Sabha elections polled 3.02 per cent votes to win 13 seats. In 1991 parliamentary elections it regained some of its lost ground and in 1994 once again won the Andhra Assembly elections.

NTR, who came to power with such a massive mandate in December, 1994, winning 220 out of 294 seats for his 'Telugu Desam, bowed out of the office of Chief Minister on August 31, 1995 and paved the way for his son-in-law Mr. Chandrababu Naidu, to succeed him.

Chandrababu Naidu. Mr. Chandrababu Naidu had revolved against NTR in a "family coup" and was duly sworn in on September, 1995 as new Chief Minister. In 1996 parliamentary elections the TDP won 16 seats and joined the Deve Gowda and I.K. Gujral governments at the Centre as coalition partner. As the convenor of the Steering Committee of the United Front, the TDP leader Mr. Chandrababu Naidu has emerged as the kingmaker. He and his party are strong advocates of greater state autonomy. Though, Chandrababu's image is a moderniser and a sybre-chief minister, has installed him on national scene, he has to abandon many of NTR's social welfare schemes like cheap rice, saris, old age pension, etc. The rice supply scheme, which alone cost the exchequer Rs. 200 crore annually, helped nearly 40 millions poor. The benefit of old age pension went to about 6 lakh peoples. The TDP loyalists had a reason to claim that NTR Government was seen by the masses as benevolent, spreading prosperity and stability in the state.

❒

7

Linguistic Reorganisation

ROLE OF LANGUAGE

Language has played a vital role in Indian Politics right from the very beginning. Pro-Hindi and Aniti-Hindi movements have achieved the status of beging a national issue. Regional Language have also been in this fray.

'The dynamics of influences caused by the language factor in Indian Politics can be studied under following headlines:

1. Reorganisation of State on Linguistic Basis. The States Reorganisation Commission was set up to recommend the grounds on which the State should be reorganised. The State Reorganisation Commission, along with stressing the unity of India and emphasizing the need of national integration, recommended that States should be reorganised on the basis of language *i.e.*, the regions speaking the same language should be put together.

Parliament passed the States Reorganisation Act 1956, and States were reorganised on the basis of language to which C. Rajagopalachari reacted that it was a 'blunder' and his reaction proved to the fact that in later periods, demands to reorganise States or bifurcate particular State on the basis of language persisted.

2. Language Commission and Non-Hindi Speaking States. The recommendations of the Language Commission was thought as chauvinistic rather than nationalistic goals. They felt the development and promotion of their own language can bring more benefits than the promotion of Hindi. The recommendation of the Language Commission was opposed by the Congressmen as well as non-Congressmen belonging to such States and nearly 50 MLAs submitted a memoradum on 3 September 1957, that the replacement of English by Hindi in 1965, "would cause grave injury to the administrative machinery" and proposed that this replacement should be postponed until 1990.

The Statewise reaction was a follows:

(i) West Bengal Assembly on 26 March 1958, resolved that they would not replace English by Hindi as the official language.

(ii) Assam Assembly rejected both Hindi as English and official language and created Assamese as the official language of the State.

(iii) Akali Dal in Punjab refused to accept Hindi language on 16 November 1960. The Punjab State Assembly enacted the official Language Bill, which provided that Punjabi in Gurumukhi Script and Hindi in Devnagari Script would be the official language of Punjabi speaking and Hindi speaking areas respectively. Punjabi University was opened in Patiala on June 24, 1962 by the President of India. Dr. S. Radha Krishnan.

Pandit Nehru and Hindi. The report of the Commission was tremendously opposed by the Non-Hindi speaking States as well as people. Pandit Nehru on August 7 and again on September 4, 1959 declared in the Parliament that English would remain "as an alternative language as long as people require it".

Presidential Order. Looking into the merits of the situation on April 17, 1960, the President of India Dr. Rajendra Prasad issue an order under Article 344(6) of the Indian Constitution, "making teaching and training of Hindi for employees of the Central Government obligatory".

Three Language Formula. The National Integration Conference recommended three language formula to pacify every language speaking community. The conference comprising eminent educationists, scientists, politicians and writers was called on in the wake of the communal riots that started on October 3, 1961 and spread to most of the States. The Conference was held from September 28, 1961 to October 1, 1961.

The Conference recommended a 'Three Language Formula' as follows:

(a) **For the Non-Hindi Speaking States.** Compulsory teaching of English, Hindi and the regional language.

(b) **For Hindi-Speaking States.** Compulsory teaching of Hindi, English and one of the Modern Indian Languages (MIL).

The conference also recommended that the regional language should be adopted as the medium of instruction in the place of English in the universities as over country.

The Official Language Bill. The Union Government in order to solve the confrontation in April 1963, introduced a Bill in Lok Sabha titled as the Official Language Bill. This Bill attracted long and heated discussion in both the Houses of Parliament and finally Lok Sabha passed this Bill on April 27, 1963 whereas Rajya Sabha passed it on May 7, 1963.

Anti-Hindi Agitation. Official Language Bill drew a wide-spread agitation from the Non-Hindi speaking State. Some of the highlights of this anti-Hindi agitation are as follows:

(1) On June 10, 1963, DMK threatened to launch a direct action programme against the Official Langauge Bill, in order to "smash conspiracy to relegate the people of the South to the position of second class citizens. The agitation was briskly launched in November in which copies of Part XVII of the Constitution, dealing with the Official Language was publicly put to flames.

(2) On June 6, 1964, Andhra Pradesh Assembly adopted a Bill declaring to continue English as the official language after January 25, 1965.

(3) The State of Kerala, Mysore and the Union Territory of Pondicherry, also voiced against the Official Language Bill.

(4) West Bengal Government also declared to contine with English as their official language.

Modification of the Official Language Bill. Prime Minister Shri Lal Bahadur Shastri, reaffirmed what Nehru had said and the

Official Language Bill was modified. Getting the assurance, the Anti-Hindi Agitation initiated by DMK and Tamilanadu Students, Anti Hindi Agitation Council suspended their further programmes of agitation. In December 1967, a Bill to amend the Official Language Bill (1963) was enacted.

Recommendations of Kothari Commission. The Union Education Minister Shri M.C. Chagla, on March 12, 1964 appointed a Commission under the Charimanship of Dr. S. Kothari, Chairman of UGC to look into each and every aspect of education in India and to make recommendations. The Report of the Kothari Commission was published in June 1966 seeking modification in the three language formula. It recommended that besides the regional language either Hindi or English or another MIL or European Language should be taught. All India Educational Institutions should keep up with English as the Medium of instruction.

Three Language Formula Again. The Union Government not being affected by the disturbances and opposition reverted to the 'Three Language Formula'. In November 1970, the Education Minister Dr. V.K.R.V. Rao declared that government will not make any departure from the "Three Language Formula". However, during the period of transition, English will continue to be used as Official Language.

Suggestions of the National Integration Panel. In 1973, NCERT set up a panel under the chairmanship of S. Gopal. The panel made following suggestions:

(i) The Central Government must decide to teach Hindi in Non-Hindi States and another MIL in Hindi speaking States.

(ii) State Government should do their best to distribute text-books at a reasonable price to all the linguistic minorities within the State.

(iii) Government should implement the three language formula with more emphasis.

Inspite of steps by the Government, it would be misapprehension of the problem to think that the Linguistic Currents are no more in the flow of the country's political mainstream. It is a fact that the language issue still eludes solution and only time will bring the answer.

Observation on Language Problem. If we analyse the language problem in the politics of our country we came to certain concrete conclusions as follow:

(i) Despite linguistic heterogenity the problem of national language is not beyond solution. India stands for unity in diversity. Hence Hindi as well as other regional languages deserve a place of however-English a foreign language is a language of the elite and not of the masses. It should be treated as optional to be chosen by the students opting for study of scientific and technical subjects and enabling them to come in contact with the foreign countries. Thus Hindi in Devnagri script be the 'lingua franca' whereas regional language be an associate language.

(ii) National integration has suffered an eclipse due to language as the base for political reorganisation of the country. It has fomented linguistic chauvinism which is not only inimical to the Federal Centre but impairs national unity.

(iii) The solution of this complicated problem first in Constituent Assembly and there in the parliament in 1963 and 1967 indicates the politics of decision making in our country. Non Hindi speaking states how so far an upperhand. It may be hoped that at no distant future some amicable solution to the satisfaction of all will emerge out and in single community will be able to overwheming the rest.

(iv) The politics of language is the creation of the Communalists. The perpetuation of distinction betwen Hindi, Urdu and Hindustani languages is the outcome of their vicious minds. In the words of Shiva Rao, "It is the community of self seeking politicians who try to create linguistic hysteria for the sake of repeating certain dividends." In fact both the regionalists and the communalists find a convenient scapegoat in linguism.

(v) There is a constructive aspect of language politics as well. It has initiated a huge number of people into organisational modes of political participation. It has politicized the people. J.D. Gupta opines that most of the people, "have been trained to love their regional community but in the process of working for their demands may have been increasingly socialised into the values of the wider political community."

LANGUAGE POLITICS

Language has been, in India, the major factor in influencing politics. Among the many factors which have gone against national integration and democracy the politics of language, has assumed, since independence, serious political dimensions leading to disturbances in the social, economic and political framework of India. Protests against Hindi imperialism in Tamil Nadu, tension over language and script in Punjab, North *versus* South, all have their roots in linguistic chauvinism. The question naturally arises as to why the people of different parts of India have chosen language as the basis of their identity. Religion and caste have played a secondary role. This is because of the fact that identity on religious grounds gained notoriety after the partition of India on religious grounds. Language became handy as a sophisticated plank to arouse feelings. This is not to suggest that religious appeal has had no response. We find communal cots increasing everyday. But the fact remains, as witnessed only recently in January 1983 elections, that the Telegu speaking people have asserted their distinctive identity. The religious issue did not come to the force even though a substantial minority of the Muslims, particularly in Telengana, are largely Urdu speaking. Similarly, the prolonged struggle in Tamil Nadu for clear linguistic identity did not cause active resistance of the non-Tamil speaking communities.

POLITICS OF LANGUAGE

The politics of language is mainly concerned with these basic and interrelated issues:

(i) Official or link language.

(ii) Language as medium of instruction.

(i) Politics of Official or Link Language. Our national leaders wanted India to get freedom from English language also. It was because English had been not only symbol of alien rule but also a symbol of those Indians through whom the British had maintained their rule in India. English in fact perpetuated the division between the ruling elite and the ruled masses.

During the course of the last 30 years efforts have been made to replace English by Hindi as the official or link language but nothing has come out of it. The things have been spoiled instead. Hindi is spoken by a large majority of people in majority of states and regions. It was on this account adopted by the Constituent Assembly as the official language of the Union. Hindi is considered as a symbol of revivalism and its imposition resisted by non-Hindi states. The constitution also provides for the promotion and development of regional languages. So, the non-Hindi states have started using their regional languages alongwith English for official purposes. This has retarted not only growth of Hindi but also stood in the way of national integration.

(ii) Politics of Language as Medium of Instruction. Another aspect of politics of language has appeared in the shape of medium of instruction in education. Most of the states have made regional languages as the medium of instruction in education up to the under graduate level while English also continues. This has also led to the retardation of the growth of Hindi.

RELATED ISSUES OF POLITICS OF LANGUAGE

This politics of language in India has resulted in linguistic nationalism and regionalism.

Language has been a very convenient cloak to hide the real intentions of the selfish regional leaders. The selfish regional leaders who wanted to grind their own axe in opposition to the national interest, took refuse under language. The D.M.K. in Tamil Nadu made anti-Hindu attitude its great plank. The Akali Dal in Punjab changed its demand from Khalistan to Punjabi Suba purely to cover the real content under the name of language. The Shiv Sena in Maharashtra also took advantage of Hindi cause to project its own regional interest.

The various regional parties took upon themselves the task of advocating or criticising a particular language. The politics of regional parties are based mainly on advocacy or opposition to a particular language.

The politics of various regional parties or movements that took shelter behind language are discussed as under:

1. Dravida Munnetra Kazhagam. The popularity of D.M.K. in Tamil Nadu depends mainly in its opposition to Hindi. They came to power only on raising the bogey of Hindi imperialism. They opposed strongly the imposition of Hindi. They launched campaign against Hindi being made as the official language of India in 1965. They burnt down the copies of the Constitution of India. They demonstrated rather violently.

The D.M.K. party originated from the Justice Party in Madras. The Justice Party stood for the rights of non Brahmins against the monopolistic hold of Brahmins on the administrative and political positions. The more militant among the members of the Justice Party formed Dravida Kazhagam (DK) which called upon the Dravidian people of South India "to guard against a transfer of power from the British to the Aryans." It demanded a separate South Indian state, Dravidistan. E.V. Ramaswamy Neicker, who led the movements, interpreted the Hindu scriptures as non-Dravidian and the sole-fabrication of the Brahmins. Under his leadership, the South Indians burnt copies of the Ramayana as being the story of a conflict between the North represented by the Aryans, and the South by the Dravidians. It pleaded for the eradication of Sanskrit words from the South Indian languages.

By 1954, however, political power shifted from the Brahmins to a distinctly indigenous 'Tamilized' and non-Brahmin leadership under the new Chief Minister, Kamraj Nadar. The DK threw its support to the Congress ministry. This divided the DK and the splinter organisation named itself as Dravida Munnetra Kazhagam (DMK) which pledged again for the attainment of Dravidistan. In June 1960 the DMK and the 'Now Tamil' organised a joint campaign for the secession of Madras from India and for making it an independent sovereign state of Tamil Nadu. They burnt the maps of India. Then they proposed that the State of Madras, Andhra Pradesh, Kerala and Mysore should secede from the Indian Union and form an independent "Republic of Dravida Nad".

In April 1961, several leading members of the DMK resigned and formed the Tamil National Party under the leadership of E.V.K. Sampath, a member of Parliament. It rejected the DMK proposal and instead advocated a radical amendment to the Constitution so that India should become a highly decentralised federation of autonomous linguistic States, each of which could "have the right to secede." Several DMK members of the State Assembly and of Madras Corporation, including the Mayor of Madras, joined the new party.

The DMK made heavy gains in the Third General Elections in 1962. It, therefore, intensified its agitation for an independent Dravidian State. During a debate in the Rajya Sabha on May 1, 1962, C.N. Annadurai, its leader asserted that the people of Southern India were of different stock from those of the North. He alleged that the South had been "ignored" by the Union Government.

In view of the disintegrating forces in the country, the Parliament adopted in October 1963 the sixteenth Amendment to the Constitution, which, *(i)* enabled Parliament to make laws providing penalties for any person questioning the sovereignty and integrity of the Indian Union and *(ii)* laid down that a candidate for election to Parliament or a State Legislature would have to undertake by oath or affirmation to have true faith and allegiance to the Indian Constitution and to uphold country's sovereignty and integrity. Consequently, the DMK in November 1963 dropped from its programme the demand for a sovereign independent Dravidian Federation and its secession from the Indian Union. Instead, it declared the formation of a 'Dravida Union' of the four States mentioned above "with as large powers as possible within the framework of the sovereignty and integrity of India and of the Constitution."

Its posture against Hindi as the official language continues unabated. The opposition to Hindi came not from the East but only from the South, particularly from Madras, now Tamil Nadu. On the question of introduction of Hindi, violent outburst in large parts of Madras State took place. The result was a precipitous crisis that took the turn of an unprecedented act of self-immolation by two DMK leaders in Madras city.

The agitation for autonomy within the Indian Union continues . In mid-September, 1970, the DMK convened in Madras city a "State Autonomy Conference" and its leader, V.B. Raju, M.P., criticised "Delhi attitude" in trying to administer States subjects, holding the states as its "debtors" and using its financial strings" to control them. Various other regional parties, including the Akali Dal were invited to attend the Conference. The Conference did not make much headway in that autonomy was desired but the extent of autonomy could not be defined. The attitude of the DMK was most far-reaching which others could not endorse.

Whatever it was, the DMK remained in power until 1967 purely on the basis of its opposition to Hindi. It has aroused so anti-Hindi feeling among the people of Tamil Nadu that All India Anna DMK which has come to power in July 1977 is also deadly opposed to Hindi.

2. Shiv Sena. Like the DMK in South India, the Shiv Sena in Maharashtra offered a posture of regionalism through a gesture of linguism. Though opposed diametrically to each other, they pose the same problem to the unity and integration of India. "The former is... an anti Brahminic anti-Hindi and thus anti-North movement," says Shiv Lal. "While the latter is an expression of Maratha cult posing as a saviour of 'Aryavarta' (India) and Hindi, following the footsteps of Shivaji."

Founded by Bal Thakeray, the Shiv Sena is the creation of Sampooran Maharashtra Samiti, a union of Maharashtrians belonging to all political parties. It has come to stay as the worst kind of Maratha Chauvinism. It is opposed to all non-Maharashtrian people as a result of which the Gujaratis with their commercial and industrial undertakings have started fleeing from Bombay. Their major target has, however, been the South Indians. Accordingly a couple of M.P.'s from the DMK's Tamil Nadu submitted a memorandum to the then Prime Minister Indira Gandhi bringing to her notice that the Shiv Sena is a pure military organisation with more than two lac volunteers, comparable to the Razakar movement of Hyderabad. The Shiv Sena has a ten point pledge to be taken by its members. The points included in the pledge are that every Maharashtrian has to support his 'Maharashtrian brothers' in trade and commerce, and to sell his property only to one of his 'brethren.'

The Government of Mysore in its pamphlet "Cruse of the case on the Maharashtra and Mysore Border Dispute" also mentions similar Maharashtra aspirations in these words. Their first effort was to get the inclusion into their state of the Vidarbha Districts which were proposed to form a separate state. They next managed to see that Bombay city was not carved into a separate city state. Then even after the reorganisation, they succeeded in pushing out Gujarat from the bilingual State. There still remains two more ambitions to be achieved. one is the claim against Mysore and the other is the merger of Goa into Maharashtra, to secure each of these objectives they have a distinct type of claim to make."

But it is a pity that the Congress leaders for their temporary election gains joined hands with the Shiv Sena in the Fourth General Elections held in 1967 in a contest for a parliamentary seat between a South Indian, Krishna Menon and a Maharashtrian Barve. The Shiv Sena once again got the funds and political boost at the hands of the Congress in another bye-election between Krishna Menon and Barve's sister's election that was occasioned after Barve's death. The Shiv Sena won for the Congress the coveted seat in Parliament: thus gaining prestige for itself also. In an editorial published on March 28, 1968, the Times of India commented. "Apart from the local sentiment its (Shiv Sena's) success can be ascribed partly to the clandestine encouragement it received from the Congress during the last general election."

3. Creation of Andhra Pradesh. It was as early as 1917 that the Telugu speaking delegates of the Madras Provincial Congress Committee resolved to form a separate unit of Andhra. The movement for Telugu speaking unit was given momentum due to the policy of the Indian National Congress that encouraged recognisation of State on linguistic basis.. However, the Congress realised its mistake after coming into power. The Das Commission rejected the proposal of the recognisation of the country on linguistic basis as it would create chaos and national disintegration. The politics of language dominated as a result of which the J.V.P. Committee consisting of Nehru, Patel and Pattabhi was created to look at this problem from the political angle. The report of J.V.P. Committee went in general against the formation of linguistic states. However, it made an exception in the case of Andhra for which a strong case exited. It, therefore, pleaded that it would be better to have an open mind with regard to the creation of that state.

The J.V.P. report strengthened the hands of the separatist elements. A momenting sentiment for Andhra soon led to a situation difficult to control. The demand grew in dimension to the extent that the Congress Working Committee was obliged to endorse the demand. It recommended in 1949 for the creation of Andhra. The Central Government was, however, reluctant lest the creation of Andhra should encourage demands from other linguistic groups in the various multi-lingual states and promote linguistic nationalism. The statement resulted in the split of the Congress opinion. Various opposition parties joined the Congress dissenters in the demand. Sriromulu undertook a fast unto death on this issue and died. Eventually, a separate state for the Telugu speaking people was created in October, 1953.

Having succeeded in getting Andhra Pradesh carved out as the first State in India on linguistic basis, the leaders there felt complacent about their achievement. This helped the Congress to remain in power untill January, 1983, when under the leadership of N.T. Rama Rao, Telegu Desam, a party formed only in May, 1982, won Assembly elections by a two-thirds majority.

4. Telengana Agitation. The State Reorganisation Commission had recommended the split up of the multi lingual State of Nizam of Hyderabad. It added that the Kannada-speaking areas should be merged with Mysore while the Marathi speaking areas with Bombay. The Commission observed that there were strong arguments in favour of the Union of the Telugu speaking areas of Hyderabad known as Telengana merging with Andhra in a single Telugu-speaking state. But it did not suggest this step immediately because of a feeling existing among the people of Telengana that they might be "swamped and exploited" by the more highly educated people of Andhra. The Commission, therefore, recommended Telengana as a separate State but with a provision for its union with Andhra after the third General Elections "if a two-thirds majority of the state legislature expressed itself in favour."

The Union Government, on the other hand, decided to unite Telengana with Andhra on the plea that uncertainty about the future of Telengana as a distinctive state would hamper its economic progress. Consequently, the Congress leaders of Andhra and Telengana concluded the following accord:–

1. All members of the State Assembly from Telengana would form a Regional Committee to deal with matters relating to that region.
2. The entire revenue from Telengana would be spent on the development of that region, of course, after meeting its proportionate share of the common expenditure of the state.
3. When the Chief Minister of the State comes from Andhra, the Deputy Chief Minister would be drawn from Telengana and vice versa.
4. The recruitment to government posts in the region carrying a salary of up to Rs. 500 a month would be made for five years only from among persons who had lived in Telengana at least for fifteen years.

The aggrement paved the way for the merger of Telengana area into Andhra Pradesh but this system did not work any longer. The people of Telengana began to express their dissatisfaction and resentment. They began to demand the formation of a separate Telengana State. The fears got so much accentuated that in January. 1969 the Telengana students of the Osmania University, on the fear that they would not be able to compete successfully with Andhra students and their future employment opportunities would suffer, started an agitation for the implementation of the 1956 agreement "fully and sincerely". The agitation was launched with peaceful intentions but turned violent as usual. Consequently, Chief Minister Brahmananda Reddy along with 44 other members of the Assembly announced that all Andhras appointed on posts reserved for Telengana would be immediately transferred to Andhra region, and all the vacancies would be filled by qualified candidates from Telengana. The revenue surplus from Telengana would also be fully utilised for the development of the region. On this announcement, the agitation was called off.

Then the formula was used to replace the Mulki Rules with certain other safeguards and convert the Telengana Regional Committee into a Development Board. The abolition of the Mulki Rules is meant to remove misgivings in the minds of the people of Andhra Region. The people of Telengana have been assured of preference for recruitment to non-gazetted posts, corresponding posts under local bodies and the posts of Tehsildars, junior engineers and Civil Assistant Surgeon. The safeguards and the spirit of the Mulki Rules have thus been retained.

Secondly, the formula envisages the constitution of a State Planning Board as well as sub-committee for different backward areas to ensure their uniform and speedy development. Legislators from both the regions are to be associated with the development body and the subcommittee.

Thirdly, there is a proposal for the constitution of a high power tribunal to deal with service grievances, and uniform arrangements for giving preferences to local candidates in admission to educational institutions.

Fourthly, a new Central University will be established at Hyderabad to augment existing educational facilities. This should satisfy the Andhra people who have been feeling that they were being treated as foreigners in their own State.

Fifthly, a high power administrative tribunal will be set up to deal with the grievances about admissions, security and promotions to safeguard the interests of government employees in both the regions.

Lastly, the constitution will be amended to the extent necessary for implementing the above five points.

The Formula thus aimed at maintaining the integrity of the State of Andhra Pradesh. The Telengana Praja Samiti (TPS) decided to merge itself into the Congress. It was decided that a person from Telengana be made as the Chief Minister. Accordingly, Brahmanand Reddy resigned and P.V. Narsimha Rao occupied this office.

This agreement led to a division in the TPS with the result that a rival TPS under Satyanarayan Reddy of the Samyukta Socialist Party, was born. The former TPS came to terms but the latter TPS continued its fight, though on a low key. It was lent support by the Congress (O), the SSP, the Swatantra Party and the Republican Party. On the eve of the Fifth General Election, the rival TPS passed a resolution that nothing short of separate statehood or Telengana would satisfy the people of Telengana. However, there is no progress.

5. Akali Dal. Master Tara Singh as the leader of Akali Dal in Punjab raised the question of the formation of Khalistan as early as 1946 when the Cabinet Mission visited India. But he met disappointment on securing no special recognition. Migration from newly formed Pakistan further added bitterness to the community's sufferings and retaliations. Then he demanded a "Sikh State" consisting of the Gurgaon district of Punjab and, PEPSU. On November 2, 1949, he demanded a "Sikh Province" in East Punjab, declaring that the Hindus had become "narrow-minded communalists" and the Sikhs could not "hope to get a fair deal at their hands". This demand was then given the name of Punjabi Suba in the early fifties and agitation for its attainment continued.

The agitation turned violent at times but made no impact on the government or the State Reorganisation Commission. The Commission reported that the demarcation between the languages, as they were spoken, was "more theoretical than real." The Commission further pointed out that demand for further partition of Punjab was confined to "communal elements in the Sikh Community." "The leadership of Master Tara Singh seemed," says Morris Jones, "as so often in the past, to be alone firy and uncertain reflecting perhaps community's own divisions and its inability to agree on whether intransigence or conciliation would secure most." The prominent leaders agreed in 1957 Elections to back the Congress though Master Tara Singh attempted a last minute reversal. As a result, compromise formulae known as the 'Regional Formula' and "Sachar Formula" on language policy in the state were adopted.

Then Master Tara Singh charged that the Sikhs were being discriminated against. A commission consisting of S.R. Das (retired Chief Justice of India), M.C. Chagla (retired Chief Justice of Bombay High Court), and the late Shri C.P. Ramaswami Aiyer (a distinguished lawyer) was appointed to go into the complaint. The Commission reported that the community had been receiving the most generous and honourable treatment in the country.

The agitation for the attainment of Punjabi Suba continued, though haltingly. Having made no impact on the government, the ardent supporters of Punjabi Suba pressed Master Tara Singh to go unto a fast to death. On this Morris Jones writes that "The government remained firm and Tara Singh lost much face by abandoning the fast in return merely for a promise to have a commission to enquire into Sikh grievances; the newspaper photos showed him engaged in the menial task of shoe cleaning a penance for his unwillingness to die." With this, the leadership of Akali Dal passed into the hands of Sant Fateh Singh. After the death of Nehru, the agitation was again revived and Sant Fateh Singh threatened to burn himself within the precincts of the Golden Temple at Amritsar if their aspirations were not fulfilled. He was dissuaded from this by the appointment of a Parliamentary Committee which went into the question. It recommended in March 1966 for the creation of Punjabi Suba which came into being on 1st November, 1966.

Punjabi Suba was conceded but Chandigarh was made Union Territory. In this the government adopted the middle course as the Commission had recommended the transfer of Chandigarh to Haryana. This agitated the minds of the fathers of new Punjab and therefore, Sant Fateh Singh, in the following month, began another fast to burn himself to death. Mrs Gandhi refused to concede any demand under such threat. The pyre was being prepared when the Sant was persuaded to break the fast on the PM's agreeing to arbitrate. "Not until 1970," says Morris Jones, "by which time Fateh Singh had begun another fast and the government was presumably convinced after two elections and several changes of state government that the issue was not going to die away, was the decision finally taken to give Chandigarh to Punjab and various compensations to Haryana."

Chandigarh continues to stand even today as a Union Territory. Whosoever wants to exploit the linguistic sentiments of some of the Punjabis, raises the question of the merger of Chandigarh with Punjab. Mahant Sewa Dass has so often threatened and undertaken fast unto death for the merger of Chandigarh into Punjab. The Akali leadership has started an agitation for the inclusion of Chandigarh and some other Punjabi speaking areas into Punjab.

Whatever causes have given support to a feeling of regionalism, should be tackled and suppressed in the right manner. Nehru had realised that concession to linguistic bigots would lead to the balkanisation of the country, and declared that linguistic provinces "produced more conflict and trouble than any kind of peaceful solution to the problem." Sardar Patel was even more forthright and denounced the champions of linguistic reorganisation as the "assasins of nationalism".

LINGUISTIC REORGANISATION OF STATES

Language is the medium of communication among the people. Further, in modern times it is also a means of getting employment. Both the factors make the language a political issue in Indian politics. Particularly in 1950's and 1960's, it rocked the Indian political scene creating a great danger to the national unity and integration. However, with the passage of time and the flexibility of the political leadership towards the language issue, much of the crisis has subsided and one can say with confidence that language issue no longer remains a major problem towards national integration.

Indian Diversity. The Indian diversity is best characterised by the existence of too many languages and dialects. The 1961 census recorded as many as 1018 different languages. However, still one can find a sort of unification among these diverse languages and dialects as they fall under four broad language families. i.e. Indo-Aryan,

Dravidian, Tibeto-Chinese and Austro-Asiastic. Out of this, the first two families of Indo-Aryan and Dravidian dominate the Indian linguistic scenario and there has been a constant borrowing from each other. As per the 1961 census, 73.3 per cent of Indian population spoke Indo-Aryan while 24.5 per cent belonged to he Dravidan family. 1.5 and 0.7 per cents people belonged to the Austro-Asiatic and Tibeto-Chinese languages families respectively. Therefore, the Indian Constitution listed fourteen languages of India i.e. Assamese, Bengali, Gajarati, Hindi, Kannada, Kashmiri, Malayalam, Marathi, Oriya, Punjabi, Sanskrit, Tamil, Telugu and Urdu. As per the 1961 censuss 87 per cent of the people gave these fourteen languages as their mother tongue. Later on Sindhi, Kokani, Manipuri and Nepali were also in this list, making the number of 18. Another aspect of linguistic scenario has been the fact that there always has been a link language understood in the entire country. Firslty, it was Sanskrit followed by Persian and Urdu.

During Freedom Movement. During the freedom movement, the Indian National Congress felt the need of linguisatic reorganisation of states but after the independence, the Congress leadership was against it. Gandhi feared the danger of linguistic balkanisation of India. The Dar Commission appointed in 1948 also opined that "the formation of provinces on exclusively or even mainly linguistic considerations is not in the larger interest of the Indian nation...In the formation of new provinces, whenever such a work is taken in hand, oneness of languages may be one of the factors to be taken into consideration along with others; but it should not be the decisive or even the main factor. If India does not survive, nothing will be gained by solving her linguistic provinces problems alone". The Congress Committee of Jawaharlal Nehru, Sardar Patel and Pattabhi Sitaramayya also rejected the reorganisation of states on linguistic basis stating that language was not only a binding but also a separating force, and the primary consideration was the security, unity and economic properiety of India for which every separatist and disruptive tendency should be rigorously discouraged. However, this was not accepted to many. Even the Congress Working Committee headed by P.D. Tandon demanded the immediate formation of linguistic states in 1951. In

South, a very strong movement for the formation of Andhra Pradesh for the Telugu speaking people developed which also became violent which led to the creation of Andhra Pradesh in 1953. This encouraged the demand for the formation of linguistic states in other areas and as a result in 1956, the political map of India was remade on the basis of linguistic factor. 14 states were created, *i.e.* Andhra Pradesh, Assam, Bihar, Bombay, Jammu and Kashmir, Kerala, Madhya Pradesh, Madras, Mysore, Orissa, Punjab, Rajasthan, Uttar Pradesh and West Bengal. Besides, there were six Union Territories also which were to be governed by the Central Government. In 1960, Bombay state was divided into Maharashtra and Gujarat after much of violence and agitation.

Problems. The reorganisation of States on the basis of language created many problems. Firslty, it created the problems of linguistic minorities in almost every state who were considered as outsiders after the linguistic reorganisation and there have been allegations of discrimination against them. In some states 'son of the soil' theory was advocated and the outsiders were asked to leave the State. For instance, Shiv Sena raised the banner of Maharashtra for Maharashtrians and the South Indians were attacked and humiliated so that they leave the state. Similarly, Lachit Sena was organised in Assam to oust Bengalese. In West Bengal, Marwaris became the victim of the son the soil theory. Particularly in Assam, the Assamese people think that they are a national minority. Thought in majority, they fear of becoming a minority within the state itself due to influx of Bengalese the problem has further aggravated because of illegal migrants from Bangladesh. In Guwahati and several towns of Assam, the Assamese are in minority. In Bangalore, the Tamils outnumber the Kannada speaking people. In all these places the son of soil theory finds a fertile place to developes. Secondly, the linguistic reorganisation of states encouraged regionalism. As the States were formed only on the basis of languages, they also got developed as well as underdeveloped areas. The movements for separate statehood in Telengana in Andhra Pradesh, Vidarbha in Maharashtra, Saurasthra in Gujarat Jhakhand areas in Bihar, Uttarkhand and Budelkhand in Uttar Pradesh, Gorakhaland in West Bengal and Chattisgarh and Mahakosal in Madhya Pradesh are some of such examples. Thirdly, the linguistic state reorganisation also encouraged the demand for state autonomy; Particularly, the DMK in Tamil Nadu and Akali Dal in Punjab demanded a review of constitutional division of power between States and the Centre for more autonomy to states. Fourthly, it also led to boundary disputes between the states. We have boundary disputes between Arunachal Pradesh and Assam, Punjab and Haryana, Maharastra and Karnataka, Karnataka and Kerala etc. however, it is also clear that the linguistic reorganisation of states has consolidated the national unity contrary to the apprehensions of Gandhi, Nehru and other leaders.

Official Language Problem. Another aspect of language problem was the question of official language in India. After much controversies and discussion, the Constituent Assembly of India opted for Hindi as the official language of Indian Union. However, for a period of fifteen years from the commencement of the Constitution, English was to continue to be used for all the official purposes of the Union. After the expiry of the said fifteen years, the Parliament was authorised to provide for the use of English language for such purposes as many be specified in the law. It was also provided that the President might also, during the said priod of fifteen years, authoriser the use of Hindi in addition to English for any of the official purposes of the Union.

Recommendations. The Commission was to make recommendations to the President on:

(a) the progressive use of the Hindi language for the official purposes of the Union;

(b) the language to be used for all or any of the purposes mentioned in Article 348;

(c) restrictions on the use of the English language for all or any of the official purposes of the Union;

(d) the form of numercially to be used for any one of more specified purposes of the Union; and

(e) any other matter referred to the Commission by the President as regards the official language of the Union and the language for communication between the Union and a

State or between one state and another and their use. The recommendations of this Commission were to be examined by a Committee cosnsisting of twenty members of the Lok Sabha and ten members of the Rajya Sabha to be elected by the system of proportional representation by means of the single transferable vote. The President after cosnsidering the report of such committee would issue directions in accordance with the whole or any part of that report. However, in making such recommendations, the Commission is required to give due regard to the industrial, cultural and scientific advancement of India and the jsut claims and interests of persons belonging to the non-Hindi speaking areas in regard to the public services. Thus, while the Constitutions declared Hindi to be official language of India, it also adopted a pragmatic and cautious approach keeping in view the fact that English was dominating the scene and immediate switchover was not posible due to many reasons including the underdeveloped status of Hindi language and the apprehension of non-Hindi speaking people. Article 351 contained the directive to the Central Government for development of Hindi language. It says, "It shall be the duty of the Union to promote the spread of the Hindi language to develop it so that it may serve as a medium of expression for all the elements of the composite culture of India and to secure its enrichment by assimilating without interfering with its genius, the forms, style and expressions used in Hindustan and in the other languages of India specified in the Eighth Schedule, and by drawing, wherever necessary as desirable, for is vocabulary, primarily on Sanskrit and secondarily, on other languages." Article 348 also made it clear that all the proceedings in the Supreme Court and High Court, the authoritative texts of bills to be inttroduced or amendments in legislatures or acts passed by them and all orders, rules, regulations and bye-laws shall be in the English languages. However, as per the Article 348(2), the Governor of a state may, with the previous consent of the President, authorise the use of the

Hindi language, or any other language used for any official purpose of the state, in proceedings in the High Court having its principal seat in the state provided that nothing in this clause shall apply to any judgement, decree or order passed or made by such High Court. But where the legislature of the state has prescribed any language other than English for the introduction of Bills, passing of Acts, issuing of ordinances or making of rules, regulations and bye-laws, they will be translated in English and published in the official Gazette under the authority of the Governor and will be considered as the authoritative texts in English.

Constitutional Provisions. The framers of the Constitution gave due regard to the regional languages. The Constitution provides that:

(i) The Legislature of the State may be law adopt any one or morc of the language in use in the State or Hindi as the official language or languages to be used for all or any of the official purposes of the State. Unit the State Legislature provides, otherwise by law, English shall continue to be used for those official purposes for which it was being used immediately before the commencement of this Constitution.

(ii) If the substantial proportion of the population of a State requests the President that a language spoken by them should be recognised as the official language of the State for certain purposes, and if the President is satisfied about the genuineness of their demand, he may direct that such language should be officially recognised throughout that State or a port thereof for the purposes, he may specify.

(iii) For innter-state communication and for communication between the Union and the State, the official language of the Union shall be used for official purposes. However, if two or more states agree to use Hindi for communication between and among them, they can do so.

Special Directives. Further, there are special directives which *(i)* entitles every person to submit a representation for the redress of any grievance to any officer or authority of the Union or a state in any of the languages used in the Union or in the states, as the case may be (Article 350); *(ii)* provides the state with a duty to endeavour to provide adequate facilities for instruction in the mother-tongue at the primary stage of education to children belonging to linguistic minority groups; and the President may issue such directions to any state as he considers necessary or proper for securing the provision of such facilities (Article 350-A); *(iii)* empowers the President to appoint a special officer for linguistic minorities who shall investigate and report to him whether the constitutional safeguards provided for the linguistic minorities under the Constitution are being observed and the President shall cause all such reports to be laid before each House of Parliament and send them to the government of the States concerned (Article 305-B) and *(iv)* vests with the union to a duty to spread of Hindi language (Article 351).

Diverse Elements Dissatisfied. The detailed provision regarding the language show the genuis and wisdom of the framers of the Constitution. However, they could not satisfy the diverse elements of India. On the one hand, the Hindi protagonists became chauvinistic and wanted Hindi even to be imposed on the non-Hindi speaking people. Some of them argued for a highly Sanskritised Hindi which was even difficult for a layman Hindi speaker to be understood. On the other hand, the non-Hindi speakers decried and violently opposed the imposition of Hindi on them. This resulted in anti-English riots in Hindi speaking areas and anti-Hindi riots in non-Hindi speaking areas in which anything written in the other language was removed or defeated and many precious lives were lost in agitations. The use of Hindi language was resisted in South, especially in Tamil Nadu violently. It was also resisted in West Bengal, Punjab and Assam where they insisted for the use of the local regional language. The Central Government's efforts to promote the Hindi language was not liked by the non-Hindi states. The aggressive anti-Hindi stance of non-Hindi states compelled the then Prime Minister Jawahar Lal Nehru to assure time and again the non-Hindi states that Hindi would not be imposed and that the English language would be continued to be used 'as long as people required it.' In 1963, the Official Language Act was passed which provided that *(i)* despite the Constitution provision of replacing English by Hindi after 26 January 1965, English would continue to be used for all official purposes of the Union in addition to Hindi *(ii)* whee a state legislature had prescribed any language other than Hindi for use in Acts of the legislature, a Hindi as well an English translation might be published, *(iii)* whereas the Constitution require all high Cours judgements to be in English language, the Governor with the prior consent of the President may authorise after 1965, the use of Hindi or of the official language of the state for the judgements, orders or decrees of the state High Court, provided that an English translation would also be issued. The Act evoked a strong protest in Southern States, espically in Tamil Nadu and Andhra Pradesh. Ultimately, the Prime Minister Lal Bahadur Shastri had to report the Nehru's assurance that English would continue as an alternative language till the people require it. Accordingly, the Official Language Act of 1963 was amended in 1967.

Three-language Formula. In 1961 the National Integration Council recommendation the adoption of three-language formula for secondary education all over the country. According to this formula the schools would teach three language—English, Hindi and any one modern Indian language. The other recommendation were *(i)* the replacement of English by the regional language as the medium of instruction in universities and *(ii)* the need to have a link-language to be used in universities throughout India which was to be English at present but ultimately to be replaced by Hindi. The formula was half-heartedly implemented and subsequently given a good-bye.

Resistance by Southern States. The Southern States have always resisted any move to impose Hindi on them and time and again various Prime Ministers have assured then that Hindi would not be imposed on them. Thus the problem remained. However, now we find that the lingusitic problem no longer remains a big issue in Indian politics. Many reasons can be cited for this change. Firstly, the voice of Hindi chauvinism is no longer there. The Hindi protagonists no longer talk of Hindi imposition on non-Hindi people or firecely advocate the cause. Secondly Hindi has been spreading in the entrie country. It is due to the Hindi films and the spread of elecronic media. Infact, instead of Hindi or English, it is English (a curious and even ridiculous mixutre of English and Hindi) which is being promoted by the electronic media and public personalities. Thirdly, the English language is also spreading. It remains a valid visa for the entrance to science and computers and jobs in the flourishing private sector and multi-national companies. Finally, the regional language are also developing at a face pace. On the whole, these developments have satisfied the various literary segments in India and the language issues has gone to the margin for good.

HINDI-ENGLISH CONTROVERSY

In the case of language policy-making, the official language of the Union has been laid down by the constitution of India (Article 343), which has also identified, in its Eighth Schedule, the various languages of the country to be used for purposes specified in Article 345 of the constitution. Further, the constitution has put all authority in the hands of the Central Government, both for formulating and implementing the language policy. For example, it is the responsibility of the Centre to safeguard the cultural interests of the minorities and to see that they have adequate facilities for receiving at least primary education through their mother tongue (Article 350A). It is also the special responsibility of the Centre to develop and spread the official language (Hindi) of the Union (Article 351). The state governments, however, are left free to adopt either a regional language or the official language of the Union for the official purposes of the state (Article 345).

According to the Indian constitution, education for long has been (now it is a concurrent subject) a state subject (Article 246). From the strictly legal point of view the Government of India has had no authority to make any policy decisions in the field of primary and secondary education. Policy statements made by the Centre, therefore, like the National Policy on Education (1968) have served only as guidelines for the states. With regard to the tertiary level of education, however, the Centre is required to coordinate and maintain standards in higher education. With the adoption of the technique of Five Year Plans and the creation of the Planning Commission, there has been a trend towards centralisation in educational policy-making. The Planning Commission lays down broad policies with the help of various

Central and State authorities. Proposals regarding educational planning are submitted to it at the state level by the education departments and Universities at the national level by the Ministry of Education and the University Grants Commission. Responsibility for implementation lies in the case of the states with the education authorities of each state and in case of the Centre with the Ministry of Education.

The Chief Ministers of the various states are also important participants in national policy-making through the Conference of all the Chief Ministers. In the particular field of policy making-concerned with the official language, the role of the Chief Minister's conference held in August 1961 accepted the Government's proposal for the continued use of English as the associate official language, and endorsed the three language formula for adoption at the secondary stage of education for the teaching language subjects.

There is very little scope for policy formulation at the local level in India. In the sphere of education, there are some institutions, mostly primary and secondary schools which are managed by District or Municipal Boards of Education. However, since most of these receive grants from the state government, they have very little say in policy matters. Nevertheless, they take into account local conditions in deciding the languages to be taught and the medium of instruction. Regarding the official language in use at the local level, the Union Government memorandum of 1956 lays down that districts having 70 per cent or more of its population speaking a language other than the official state language should have the status of unilingual areas with that language superseding the official state language.

OFFICIAL LANGUAGE OF INDIA

The unbroken history of a single language being used as the official language of the country is absent in India where the language of the rulers is known to determine the language of the government–Persian during Muslim dominance and English during British rule. Political independence in 1947 brought with it demands for cultural and emotional independence. The adoption of an Indian language for official purposes of the Union constituted a major demand in this direction.

The importance attached to the question of the official language of India is evidenced in the lengthy and detailed provisions made by the Indian constitution. The constitution distinguishes between the eighteen 'languages of India' and the 'official language' for all-India official purposes. Article 343 lays down Hindi, in the Devnagari script, as the official language of the Union. Clause 2 of the same Article stating that English "shall continue to be used" for such purposes as might be specified by law upto 1965. Article 346 provides for the use of the official language for official communication between a state and the Union or between one state and another. Article 345 leaves the choice of the state official language to the state governments. The language provisions of the constitution were the product of a heated debate and dissatisfaction and controversy over it still continues. The non-Hindi regions, in general, regard Hindi only as the first among equals and resent its being chosen the official language of the Union.

LANGUAGE ASSOCIATIONS AS PRESSURE GROUPS

Pressure groups as stated earlier exert considerable influence over policy formulation and implementation in India. In the sphere of official language policy, the various literary societies set up in the 19th and early 20th century for the promotion of Indian languages soon organised themselves into associations exerting considerable influence over the choice of the official language policy. Language groups in themselves are essentially social groups. What is significant, however, is the political mobilization of these groups for specific social and political objectives, and it is here that the various, language associations came to play a major role. Through various political parties the language associations influenced the policy-making process. It is largely due to their activities that the formulation of the official language policy has generated widespread controversy and dissatisfaction over its implementation continues till today.

The major associations that worked for the development of Hindi were the Nagari Pracharani Sabha, established in Banaras in 1893, and the Hindi Sahitya Sammelan, set up in Allahabad in 1910. Both these associations were aimed at developing and promoting Hindi in the Devnagari script, and both, in their zeal to preserve the 'purity' of Hindi turned to Sanskrit as the main source for developing and enriching Hindi. This was primarily because the leadership of the Sammelan was in the hands of literary leaders like P.D. Tandon, Govind Das and Madan Mohan Malviya. Their zeal to Sanskritize Hindi came in the way of developing the language so that it may be understood throughout the country and won the displeasure and opposition of the non-Hindi areas, which perceived a highly Sanskritized Hindi as promoting the political interests of the Hindi speakers.

Groups outside the Hindi region reviewed the Sanskritization of Hindi as a threat to their political status, and hence various associations in the other Indian languages were set up to counter this movement. The principal opponent of Hindi in North India was Urdu, and the Aligarh movement started by Sir Syed Ahmed Khan was an attempt to redress the balance and promote the political and cultural interests of the Muslims. In pre-partitioned India the major contenders for the role of official language were Hindi and Urdu.

During the national movement, there was general consensus among leaders (both from Hindi and non-Hindi areas) on the question of making Hindi the official language. However, when the question came up before the Constituent Assembly, the Hindi leadership had to face opposition on two fronts. On the one hand were supporters of Hindustani under the leadership of Jawaharlal Nehru and Maulana Azad who believed like Gandhi that a Sanskritized Hindi could not be popular on a national scale. On the other hand there was a demand, chiefly from South India for the retention of English. Within the Assembly the traditional Hindi leadership enjoyed a strong position and outside the Assembly the Hindi Sahitya Sammelan organised demonstrations and campaigns to influence the Assembly's decision on the official language question. When a vote was taken on the issue at a meeting of the Congress Party members of the assembly, the Hindi bloc won by a narrow margin of 78 against 77 votes cast for Hindustani. It was out of these controversies that Article 343 of the constitution finally emerged, making Hindi in the Devnagari script the official language of India.

THE MULTI-PARTY SYSTEM AND THE HINDI-ENGLISH CONTROVERSY

In the multi-party political system of India the various political parties have served largely as pressure groups influencing the post-independence modifications in the official language policy. For nearly three decades after independence the Congress remained dominate both at the Centre and in a majority of the states, without facing a single, strong opposition. Interestingly though, the party itself has been known for its eclectic tradition and has been composed of desperate political ideologies, groups and purposes. Consequently, the Congress Party as a whole did not have a language policy acceptable to all its members, and most of the solutions offered were in the nature of a compromise. Pressure for amending the official language policy, therefore, came as much from within the ruling party as from outside.

The two main issues now were the relative positions of Hindi and English in the official sphere and the implementation of the 1965 deadline for replacing English by Hindi as the official language of India. As the fifteen-year time limit for switching over to Hindi began to come to an end, it was feared, chiefly in the non-Hindi areas, that the removal of English as an associate official language would not only be difficult but disastrous. Apart from technical considerations, the main political objection to Hindi as the official language is that it places the non-Hindi areas (particularly South India, which belongs to a different language family) at a disadvantage in relation to the rest, English. on the other hand, being a forcign language is believed to place an equal linguistic burden on both the Hindi and non-Hindi regions.

The Official Language Commission had, in 1956, endorsed the constitutional provision thereby aggravating the non-Hindi opposition which perceived the implementation the official language provisions as a threat to the political status of the non-Hindi regions, as restriction over their participation in national politics and as disturbing the balance of power between regions.

As a result of the political significance attached to the official language question, a Special Committee of Parliament appointed to review the Commission's report, cautioned against a too hurried switch-over to Hindi. Within the Congress Party, opinion was divided. Nehru, G.B. Pant and other leaders favoured a go-slow policy, and at the Pragjyotishpur session of the Congress in 1958, Nehru pleaded for a consensus of the opinion on the language question and criticized the imposition of majority decisions on a minority. He repeatedly assured the non-Hindi areas that English would remain an associate official language as long as the non-Hindi regions wanted it. At the same time, advocates of Hindi like Govind Das and P.D. Tandon insisted on a rigid implementation of the fifteen year deadline and showed their impatience at the delay in making Hindi the official language. Their intolerance and failure to come to a compromise only served to unite the various groups from the non-Hindi areas. The latter, if previously demanding an equal role for their respective languages, now united in their support of English and opposition to the move to treat the 1965 deadline as a rigid one. The result of the agitation was the Presidential Order of April 1960 which idefinitely extended the time-limit for a final switch-over, followed by legislation in 1963 to establish the 'associate language' status for English.

The passing of the Official Languages Act, 1963 should be examined against the background of the changed composition of the Congress Parliamentary Party following the 1962 general elections. India's third general elections weakened the Hindi group within the party. While representation from the non-Hindi states of Gujarat, Maharashtra, West Bengal, Orissa and Madras increased from 100 to 124, that from the Hindi states dropped from 186 to 150. Moreover, within the Hindi states the Congress suffered significant losses, so that as pointed out by Weiner, the Hindi region was "threatened with the possibility of five years of uncertain government." Significantly, opposition within the Hindi areas was comprised largely of Hindi communalist political parties like the Jana Singh and the Samyukta Socialist Party, which identified Hindi with Hindi political interests. This adversely affected Hindi's chances of being accepted as the official language of India. The changed political atmosphere, with a weakened Hindi group in the Lok Sabha, facilitated the introduction and passing of the Bill providing for the continued use of English for official purposes after 1965. Section 3 of the Official Language Act, 1963 provides that English may be used for official purposes after 1965.

Though the 1963 Act legalized the go-slow policy of a section of the Congress, it appeared neither the pro nor the anti-Hindi groups. If champions of the non-Hindi cause such as Frank Anthony and S.K. Chatterjee objected to section 3 of the Act which provided that English 'may' be used, and not that English 'shall' be used; advocates of Hindi argued that the introduction of Hindi had been needlessly slowed down. The latter insisted that a time limit ought to have been laid down for a change-over to Hindi. Supporters of English felt that English should have been designated an associate official language for an indefinite period.

Dissatisfaction with the Official Language Act from both the Hindi and the non-Hindi groups, and the resulting agitations, necessitated an amendment. The question of amendment came up after the 1967 general elections which brought significant changes in the composition of the Lok Sabha. As in 1962, the results of the 1967 elections considerably influenced subsequent language policies in India. In the first place, the Hindi group within the Congress Parliamentary Party registered further losses. Out of a total of 211 seats in the Hindi areas, the Congress won only 120 seats in 1967. The rest of the seats went mostly to the Jana Sangh and the Samyukta Socialist Party. Secondly, and more important, the unchallenged dominance so far enjoyed by the Congress was curtailed. As compared to 1962, the Congress strength declined by 3.7 per cent and 4.3 per cent in the Lok Sabha and State Assemblies respectively. Though the Congress returned to power at the Centre; it lost control over more than half the states. In particular, the victory of the Dravida Munnetra Kazagham (DMK) in Madras (now Tamil Nadu) was significant. The DMK has already favoured an anti-Hindi policy and advocated the use of English for official purposes.

In the field of language planning, an interesting outcome of the 1967 elections was the overwhelming importance gained by the non-Hindi section among the Congress Chief Ministers. The relatively poor performance of the Congress in the Hindi states in 1967 increased the number of non-Hindi Congress Chief Ministers. This in turn strengthened the support for English as the associate official language because though in formal terms the question of the official language is to be handled by the Union Government, in recent years the state governments have been playing an important role through the Chief Ministers conference. Here the non-Hindi leaders could effectively influence policy debates because the number of Chief Ministers from the Hindi states could never outnumber their counterparts from the non-Hindi states. English thus got a boost from the non-Hindi Chief Ministers.

To sum up, the 1967 elections strengthened the non-Hindi groups both in the State Assemblies and in the Lok Sabha, and altered the composition of the Congress. A ruling party, depending on a slender majority can hardly afford to ignore the demands of its constituents. Moreover, the weakened position of the Congress made it dependent on the political support of other parties in Parliament. Thus, a favourable climate was created for evolving a compromise solution on the language question. It was under these changed circumstances that the draft bill providing for the continued use of English on a compulsory basis for official purposes came up before Parliament. Without much opposition the Official Languages (Amendment) Act was passed ensuring that English 'shall' be continued as an associate official language as long as the non-Hindi states wanted it.

The amended Act of 1967 established a two-language policy for official transactions. It provides that English shall be used for purposes of communication between the Union and a state which has not adopted Hindi as its official language. Further, where Hindi is used for purposes of communication between one state and another which has not adopted Hindi as its official language, such communication in Hindi shall be accompanied by a translation of the same in English. The compromise formula evolved by the 1967 Act has for the present settled an otherwise bitter controversy.

LINGUISTIC REORGANISATION OF INDIA

The ever-increasing number of states in India is the result of social and political pressure from the various regions for reorganizing the country into administrative areas that correspond with the main language divisions of the country. As such, the Indian states of today were not pre-existing autonomous units brought together after 1947. Before independence, most of the official boundaries had been determined by the circumstances of conquest and expansion. A demand for redrawing the state boundaries on a linguistic basis, made before independence, was reiterated in the Constituent Assembly. The Dar Commission, appointed by the Constituent Assembly in 1948 to examine the formation of linguistic states recommended against their creation for fear that it would lead to disintegration of the country and harm national units. The proponents of linguistic patriotism, however, continued their agitation and the JPV Committee (composed of Jawaharlal Nehru, Pattabhai Sitaramayya and Vallabh Bhai Patel), appointed by the Congress in late 1948 realised that the strong demand for linguistic states concentrated all government attention on that issue and delay in resolving the issue would eventually harm the unity of India. In particular, they argued for a separate Telugu-speaking Andhra. After considerable agitation and violence in 1952, a new state of Andhra Pradesh was finally created in October 1953, for the Telugu-speaking people of north Madras.

The creation of Andhra Pradesh paved the way for demands and agitation from other areas and following the report in 1956 of the State Reorganisation Commission, major state boundaries were redrawn in response to various linguistic pressures. The Indian Union was reorganised into 14 states each of which had a clearly dominant language except Greater Bombay, which remained a bilingual state.

The non-acceptance of the demand of splitting Bombay into Gujarat and Maharashtra led to riots in Bombay in January 1956. C.D. Deshmukh resigned from the Central cabinet on this issue. As a result of the States Reorganisation Act, two language front organisations came into being–the Samyukta Maharashtra Samiti and the Maha Gujarat Janata Parishad. In 1960 the bilingual state of Bombay was also split into Gujarat and Maharashtra.

Though formed on a linguistic basis, all states inevitably have a varying proportion of linguistic minority groups, with the result that whereas before Independence India had one minority problem–that of the Muslims–today there are minority problems in all the states of the Union. On the other hand, refusal to acede to the demands for linguistic states would have concentrated all political attention on this one issue, with the result that more important questions might have been neglected. In India today language has become the accepted basis for establishing state boundaries and determining their official language.

ROLE OF THE REGIONAL OR NATIONAL LANGUAGES IN ADMINISTRATION

For a decentralised, democratic form of government to be successful, it is necessary that the various regional languages are developed and used in state and local administration. Responsible participation by the people in regional and local administration is possible through the regional language. A sense of alienation and at times frustration may result when the political machinery functions in a language alien to a majority of the people. The importance of indigenous language both in administration and education at the regional level was recognised early by Gandhi who, together with his support of Hindustani as the national language, argued for the simultaneous use of the regional languages of India at the provincial level. The reorganisation of states on a linguistic basis in 1956 greatly facilitated the implementation of the regional language policy at the state level. When the constitution in 1950 left the choice of the state official language to the state governments, the majority of states were bilingual or multilingual and hence the choice of a single official language was difficult. The 1956 redrawing of state boundaries removed this practical difficulty and the movement for adopting the dominant regional language for official purposes gathered momentum. However, in spite of the reorganisation of states, some states like Assam remained predominantly bilingual. To protect the interests of the relatively large minority groups in such states the State Reorganisation Commission recommended that only states in which the speakers of one language formed 'about 70% or more' of the total population should be considered and treated as unilingual states.

Today all the states in India, with the exception of Nagaland, have chosen the dominant regional language for the official purposes of the state.

LANGUAGE POLICY IN EDUCATION IN INDIA

Education in India has been a state subject (Now it is concurrent subject), with the Centre having only advisory powers. Though individuals and private associations are allowed to set up and run educational institutions and to seek financial aid from the government, actual policy making rests in the hands of the state government. This authority is shared, in the case of secondary education, with the universities and boards of education, and in the case of primary education with local bodies. The role of the Union Ministry of Education is to plan, guide and co-ordinate state education policies. It can advise, but cannot command. This is significant as far as the teaching of Hindi is concerned, because though it is the duty of the Central Government to develop and promote that language, it does not have the legal power to make the study of Hindi compulsory in schools throughout the country. Consequently, considerable variations are found from state to state regarding the languages included in the school curriculum.

The principles which determine the choice of the medium of instruction in schools ought to be psycho-social, since it is realised that quick and effective learning is ensured if it is imparted through the medium of the mother tongue. Successive Committees and Commissions in India have recommended the mother tongue as best suited for imparting education at all states. However, practical difficulties such as the vast number of languages and the varying stages of their development make the application of this principle difficult. In view of the practical difficulties involved, the Government of India, Ministry of Education Resolution of 3 August, 1948 advocated the mother tongue principle at the primary stage only. The Resolution was endorsed by the CABE meeting in 1949. These principles were reaffirmed by the Conference of Education Ministers in August 1949, by the All India Languages Development Conference in 1953 and by the Congress Working Committee Directive of 4 April, 1954, which in particular, recommended the use of tribal languages as the media of instruction of tribal areas. In 1960, the government issued a memorandum establishing an all-India code, which as accepted by the Conference of Chief Ministers in 1961 reaffirmed "the right of linguistic minorities to have education in their mother tongue at the primary stage." At the secondary stage, in view of the practical difficulties of implementing the mother tongue policy, the CABE meeting of 1949 expected that all pupils would study in the regional language. This position was supported by the Secondary Education Commission appointed in 1953 and the Conference of State Chief Ministers in 1961. Thus, at the secondary level of education in India the accepted medium of instruction is the regional language, though there are some English medium schools also, and schools providing instruction in an Indian language other than the regional one. At the University stage there is an on-going controversy regarding the question of replacing English by the various Indian Languages as media of instruction.Though national considerations of unity, mobility of staff and students and the exchange of ideas demand the use of a single language, English or Hindi , as the medium of higher education, Universities in India are vulnerable to local political pressures for the use of the regional languages. Advocates of the regional languages received considerable support from the report of the Education Commission, 1966, which advocated a 'move energetically in the direction of adopting the regional languages as media of education at the University stages.' The use of the regional languages as the media of University education within a specified period was also endorsed by the then Union Minister of Education. Dr. Triguna Sen, thereby creating fresh controversy.

Apart from the practical difficulties, like the availability of competent teachers and textbooks, it is feared by some people that the policy of using regional languages as medium of instruction at the tertiary level would lead to a compartmentalization of the country. The educated class of each region would be able to function only within its limited area. The country as a whole would be deprived of the talents of each region and representation of the various states at the national level may be adversely affected. Such a situation may be effectively avoided if there were available a link language for communication between regions. However, falling standards in English and the reluctance of non-Hindi states to learn Hindi limit the chances of these two languages serving as a link across linguistic boundaries.

The growing importance and demand for the regional languages, the necessity to spread Hindi, the official language, and the position of English as an international language of knowledge and communication, make it necessary that the Indian students have a knowledge of at least these three languages apart from their mother tongue, if the latter is different. Hence, at the secondary level of education the government has accepted what has been popularly termed the Three Language Formula. Variously stated and variously interpreted, the formula in its simple form includes the study of the mother tongue or regional language, Hindi and English.

Originating at the twenty-third meeting of the CABE in 1956, the formula was modified and accepted by the Chief Ministers' Conference in 1961. the main considerations behind the formula were more political and social than educational since it sought to equalise the linguistic 'burden' thoughout the country. While the non-Hindi regions had to study Hindi the official language, students in the Hindi areas who learnt Hindi as their mother tongue, had to study another modern Indian language. Considerations such as the educational desirability or otherwise of learning three languages, motivation for studying an extra language, and the ability of the average and below average students to successfully learn three languages, were more or less overlooked. As a result, the formula has been neither successful nor uniformly adopted. While Hindi areas lack sufficient motivation to study another Indian language, non-Hindi areas are reluctant to study Hindi, because, in the first place they are not completely reconciled to the idea of according Hindi the status of the official language; and in the second there is fear that if Hindi became a second language, English would be studied as a third language, thereby putting them (the non-Hindi speakers) at a disadvantage as compared to the Hindi areas studying English as their second language.

As in the case of all other aspects of educational policy, implementation of the three-language formula has been left to the individual states. The reluctance of the non-Hindi states to faithfully implement the formula is best illustrated by the case in Tamil Nadu where policy has fluctuated over the years. Prior to 1956 the study of

Hindi in secondary schools was purely optional, schools being given the choice of opening Hindi classes. Between 1959 and 1965, when the Congress was in power in Madras and preparations were underway for a switch-over to Hindi as the official language of the Union by 1965, a relatively serious attempt was made to introduce the study of Hindi in secondary schools. According to the new formula, the alternative to Hindi must be a language "other than the Indian language offered as the first language" i.e., a language other than either the regional language or the mother tongue as the case may be. If the policy did not achieve the desired result, it was because of a major concession it made to local pressure by stating that the "Part II language paper (Hindi or any other Indian language) will not be considered for admission to college." There was, therefore, not much difference in the earlier policy which did not provide for the study of Hindi, and the new policy which included a study of Hindi but did not take the result into consideration. Consequently, no serious study of Hindi was undertaken. Moreover, students could select Sanskrit or any other Indian language for Paper II, and thus completely bypass Hindi. Subsequently, a decision was taken by the Madras government to do away with examinations in Hindi in high schools in the state. If this was the situation during the Congress regime, which was wedded to the principle of propagating Hindi, the victory of the DMK at the 1967 elections sounded the death-knell of Hindi in Madras, since the DMK had from the start been committed to the policy of ousting Hindi from the state.

In the Hindi states too there was not much enthusiasm to implement the formula seriously. The four Hindi states of Bihar, Uttar Pradesh, Madhya Pradesh and Rajasthan have been found to avoid the study of a modern Indian language.

According to the formula, the third language for Hindi speakers is any modern Indian language other than the mother tongue or the regional language offered as the first language. However, the majority of Biharis for instance, who return Maithili as their mother tongue, would conveniently opt for Hindi as the third language. In actual practice therefore, very few Biharis would be studying a modern Indian language other than Hindi as the third language. Similar instances have been reported from the other Hindi states. The Hindi states, therefore, have failed to include the study of a modern Indian language in their secondary education. The students of these states can consequently manage with only two scripts. Devanagari for Hindi and Roman for English, whereas a Bengali or Tamil student, if he has to study Hindi will have to master three scripts.

As a result of the difficulties and irregularities in implementing the three-language formula, the Education Commission in its report recommended a modified version of the formula as follows. *(1)* The mother tongue or the regional language. *(2)* The official language of the Union or the associate official language so long as it exists; and *(3)* A modern Indian or foreign language not covered under *(1)* and *(2)* and other than that used as the medium of instruction.

On the basis of its recommendations, the commission claims that in the Hindi areas English would be introduced as a second language from Class V and a modern Indian language as the third language from Class VIII. In the non-Hindi areas, the pattern of language study could be either *(a)* English as the second language from Class V and Hindi as the third language from Class VIII, or *(b)* Hindi as the second language from Class V and English as the third language from Class VIII.

However, what is not clear is the fact that since the official and the associate official language are put in the same group (group 2), and there is a choice between them, how will it ensure that both languages are studied either as second or third languages, as the case may be? A Tamil-speaking student, for instance, after selecting English, the associate official language, from group 2, may choose Telugu or Malyalam a modern Indian language in group 3, thus successfully leaving out the study of Hindi, if he chose to. He would still be following the formula in form, if not in spirit. These loopholes illustrate that the new formula is also not entirely foolproof. Nevertheless, the National Policy on Education advises the state governments to "adopt and vigorously implement the three-language formula."

❒

8

Caste and Class System

The exact origin of caste system cannot be traced. The system is said to have originated in India. The records of the Indo-Aryan culture contain the first mention and a continuous history of the factors that make up caste. The people, who are known as Indo-Aryans, belong linguistically to the larger family of peoples designated either as Indo-Europeans or as Indo-Germans. They comprised the Ango-Saxons, the Celts, the Romans, the Spanish, the Portuguese, and the Iranian among others. One of the branches of these peoples which reached India about 2,500 B.C. is called Indo-Aryans. There are no many theories regarding the origin of caste system. Some of them are as follows:

(i) Racial Theory. According to Dr. Majumdar, the caste system took its birth after the arrival of Aryans in India. In order to maintain their separate existence, the Indo-Aryans used for certain groups and orders of people the favourite word 'varna', 'colour'. Thus they spoke of the 'Dasa varna', or more properly the Dasa people. Rig vedic literature stresses very significantly the differences between the Arya and Dasa, not only in their colour but also in their speech, religious practices, and physical features. The three classes, Brahma, Kshatra and Vis are frequently mentioned in the Rig Veda. The name of the fourth class, the 'Sudra', occurs only once in the Rig Veda. The first two classes i.e., Brahma and Kshatra represented broadly the two professions of the poet-priest and the warrior-chief. Vis comprised all the common people. The Sudra class represented domestic servants approximating very nearly to the position of slaves. On the relations subsisting between the four classes the Rig Veda has little to say. However, the Brahman is definitely said to be superior to the Kshatriya.

(ii) Political Theory. According to this theory, caste system is a clever device invented by the Brahmans in order to place themselves on the highest ladder of social hierarchy. Dr. Ghurye states, "Caste is a Brahminic child of Indo-Aryan culture cradled in land of the Ganges and thence transferred to other parts of India by Brahmin Prospectors". The Brahminic literature of the post-Vedic period mentions certain mixed classes (Sankara jati) and also a group of outcaste classes (Antyavasayin). Among the four varnas, the old distinction of Arya and Sudra now appears as Dvija and Sudra. The first three classes are called Dvijas (twice born) because they have to go through the initiation ceremony which is symbolic of rebirth. The Sudra was called "ekajati" (once born). The word "jati" is henceforward employed to mean the numerous sub-divisions of a "varna". However, this demarcation is not rigidly maintained. The word "jati", is sometimes used for "varna". In the Brahman period the position of the Brahmans increased manifold. The three lower classes are ordered to live according to the teaching of the Brahman, who shall declare their duties, while the king also is exhorted to regulate his conduct accordingly.

As the priestly influence grew in India, complicated rules of ritual and conduct were built up and incorporated into the religious books. The Brahmans closed their ranks and tried to maintain their superiority over the other classes. It is true that in the beginning there were no rigid restrictions but slowly and gradually the idea of separation stiffened. It was first the ritual and ceremonial purity which as time went on took an exaggerated aspect. Distinction began to be made between things pure and impure. Restrictions were imposed on food and drink. When the Brahmans closed their ranks, it was but natural that other classes also should follow suit.

(iii) Occupational Theory. According to this theory, the origin of caste system can be found in the nature and quality of social work performed by the various groups of people. Those professions which were regarded as better and respectable made the persons who performed them superior to those who were engaged in dirty professions. According to Nesfield, "Function and function alone is responsible for the origin of caste structure in India". With functional differentiation there came in occupational differentiation and numerous sub-castes such as Lohar, Sonar, Chamar, Bhangi, Barhai, Patwa, Teli, Nai, Tamboli, Kahar, Gadaria, Mali, etc. came into existence.

(iv) Traditional Theory. According to this theory, the caste system is of divine origin. There are some references in Vedic literature wherein it is said that castes were created by Brahma—the supreme creator, so that human beings may harmoniously perform the various social functions essential for the maintenance of society.

(v) Evolutionary Theory. According to this theory, the caste system did not come into origin all of a sudden or at a particular date. It is the result of a long process of social evolution. A number of factors played their part in the development of the present caste system. Among these factors we may enumerate the following ones:

(a) Hereditary occupations;

(b) The desire of the Brahmans to keep themselves pure;

(c) The lack of rigid unitary control of the state;

(d) The unwillingness of rulers to enforce a uniform standard of law and custom and their readiness to recognize the varying customs of different groups as valid;

(e) Clash of antagonistic cultures particularly of the patriarchal and the matriarchal system;

(f) Clash of races, colour prejudices and conquest;

(g) Deliberate and economic and administrative policies followed by the various conquerors particularly by the British;

(h) Beliefs in re-incarnation and the doctrine of Karma;

(i) Ideas of exclusive family, ancestor worship, and the sacramental meal; and

(j) Geographical isolation of the Indian peninsula.

All the above factors conspired to encourage the formation of small groups based on petty distinctions from time to time. The lack or rigid unitary control of the state, the unwillingness of the rulers to enforce a uniform standard of law and custom, their readiness to recognize the varying customs of different groups as valid, and their usual practice of allowing things somehow to adjust themselves beyond the division tendency of groups and promoted the spirit of solidarity and community feeling in every group.

CASTE ITS FEATURES

The word 'caste' owes its origin to the Spanish word 'casta' which means 'breed, race, strain or a complex of hereditary qualities'. The Portuguese applied this term to the classes of people in India known by the name of 'jati'. The English word 'caste' is an adjustment of the original term.

Various Definitions. Various definitions have been given of the word 'caste'.

According to Lundberg, "A caste is merely a rigid social class into which members are born and from which they can withdraw or escape only with extreme difficulty". It is the type of stratification system which is most rigid in matters of social mobility and distinctness of status.

According to Maclver, "When status is wholly predetermined, so that men are born to their lot without any hope of changing it, then class takes the extreme form of caste".

C.H. Cooley says, "When a class is somewhat strictly hereditary, we may call it a caste".

According to E.A. Gait, "Caste is an endogamous group or collection of such groups bearing a common name, having the same traditional occupation claiming descent from the same source, and commonly regarded as forming a single homogeneous community".

Thus, thinkers have variously defined the term 'caste'. But as Ghurye states, With all the labours of these students, however, we do not possess a real general definition of caste. The best way to understand the term 'caste' is to examine the various factors underlying the caste system.

MAIN FEATURES OF THE CASTE SYSTEM

Megasthenes, the Greek traveller in the third century B. C. to India, mentions two of the features characterizing the institution of caste. He says, "It is not permitted to contract marriage with a person of another caste, nor to change from one profession or trade to another, nor for the same person to undertake more than one, except if he is of the caste of philosophers, when permission is given on account of dignity. Thus, according to Megasthenes two elements of caste system are *(i)* there is no intermarriage, and *(ii)* there can be no change of profession. The statement of Megasthenes, though, draws attention to two important factors of caste system, yet it does not give us a complete idea of the system. To give a complete idea of what a caste is, the following features may be described:

(i) **Segmental Division of Society.** The society is divided into various castes with a well developed life of their own, the membership of which is determined by the consideration of birth. The status of a person does not depend on his wealth but on the traditional importance of the caste in which he had the fortune of being born. No amount of wealth and no amount of penance or prayer can change his caste status. Status is determined not by vocation but by birth. MacIver says, "whereas in eastern civilization the chief determinant of a class and status was birth in the western civilization of today wealth is a class-determinant of equal or put up greater importance, and wealth is a less rigid determinant than birth". There are regular caste councils to regulate and control the conduct of all caste members. This council rules over the whole caste and is the most powerful organization which keeps the members in their proper places. The government body of a caste is called Panchayat which literally means a body of five members, but in fact there are many more who meet whenever decisions are taken. It takes cognizance of the offences against the caste taboos which prevent members of the caste from eating and drinking or smoking with members of other castes; against sex regulations which prohibit marriage outside the caste. It decides civil and criminal matters. The Panchayat was so powerful that during the British regime it retired cases which were once decided by the state in its judicial capacity. Its chief punishments were *(i)* the fines; *(ii)* feast to be given to the castemen; *(iii)* corporal punishment. *(iv)* religious expiration like taking bath in holy waters; and *(v)* outcasting. In short, "caste is its own ruler". It is a small and complete social world in itself, a quasi-sovereign body, all inclusive and marked off from one another and yet subsisting within the larger and wider society.

(ii) Social and Religious Hierarchy. The second important feature of caste system is that it has got a definite scheme of social precedence. The whole society is divided into distinct classes with a concept of high and low. Thus Brahmins in India stand at the apex of the social ladder. According to Manu, the Brahmin is the lord of this whole creation, because he is produced from the purest part of the Supreme Being, namely the mouth. By his mere birth as a Brahmin, a person is the living embodiment of the eternal law. Feeding the Brahmins is one of the acknowledged ways of enjoying religious merit. A Brahmin is entitled to whatever exists in the world. The whole world is his property and others live on his charity. Vishnu is more audacious than Manu. He observes: "The Gods are invisible deities, the Brahmins are visible deities. The Brahmins sustain the world. It is by the favour of Brahmins that the Gods reside in the heavens; a speech uttered by Brahmins never fails to come true.

In contrast to the high position enjoyed by Brahmins the Sudras were subjected to manifold disabilities. They could not use the public roads nor avail themselves of public wells, they were forbidden to enter Hindu temples to attend public school. Servitude is proclaimed to be a permanent condition of Sudras. A member of the first three classes must not travel in the company of Sudras. They were considered to impart some sort of defilement to objects like bed and seat by their touch. Severe punishments were prescribed for a Sudra in case he committed certain types of offence.

(iii) **Restrictions on Feeding and Social Intercourse.** Another element of caste is the complex of taboos by which the superior castes try to preserve their ceremonial purity. Thus there are restrictions on feeding and social intercourse and minute rules are laid down with regard to the kind of food that can be acceptable by a person and from what castes. For example, a Brahmin will accept 'pakka' food, i.e., food prepared in ghee from any community, but he can accept 'kachcha' food at the hands of no other caste. The theory of pollution being communicated by some castes to members of the higher ones places severe restrictions on the extent of social intercourse. Thus, there are restrictions with regard to distances. Among the people of Kerala, a Nayar may approach a Nambudiri Brahmin but must not touch him; while a Tiyan must keep himself at the distance of thirty-six steps from the Brahmin, and a Pulayan may not approach him within ninety-six paces. A Pulayan must not come near any of the Hindu castes. Even the wells are polluted if a low caste man draws water from them.

(iv) **Endogamy.** A person born in a caste remains in it for life and dies in it. Every caste is sub-divided into sub-castes, every-one of which forbids its members to marry persons outside it. Thus, each sub-caste is endogamous. This principle of endogamy is so strict that one sociologist regards endogamy as "the essence of the caste system". There are few exceptions to this general rule of endogamy which are due to the practice of hypergamy. Excepting the cases of hypergamy each caste has to contract matrimonial alliances within its own limits.

(v) **Lack of Unrestricted Choice of Occupation.** Members of a particular caste are expected to follow the caste occupation. They cannot change to other occupation. The abandonment of hereditary occupation is not thought to be right. No caste would allow its members to take to any occupation which was either degrading, like toddy tapping or impure like scavenging. It was only the moral restraint of one's caste-fellows that acted as a restraint on the choice of one's occupation, but also the restriction put by other castes whose members did not allow members of the castes other than their own to follow their occupation. Thus no one not born a Brahmin was allowed to function as a priest. But the records show that Brahmins did all sorts of odd jobs. During the Maratha upheaval and after they entered the profession of arms. During the reign of Akbar they were seen engaged in trade, cultivation, or any advantageous pursuit in general. At present though Brahmins are engaged in pursuits of various kinds, still the priestly profession is largely carried on by them. Similarly, the Kshatriyas and Vaishyas are now engaged in pursuits other than their original occupations, yet they still retain in varying degrees the tradition of their original calling. "Every profession, with few exceptions, is open to every description of person". Bains observes, "The occupation, again, which is common to the latter (the caste), is a traditional one, and is not by any means necessarily that by which all, or even most, of the group make their living in the present day."

(vi) Civil and Religious Disabilities. Generally, the impure castes are made to live on the outskirts of the city. In Southern India certain parts of the town or village are inaccessible to certain castes. It is recorded that under the Marathas and the Peshwas, the Mahars and Mangs were not allowed within the gates of Poona between 3 p.m. and 9 a.m. because before nine and after three their bodies cast too long a shadow, which falling on a member of the higher castes defiles him. All over India the impure castes were not permitted to draw water from wells used by the members of other castes. The public schools did not admit impure castes like Chamars and Mahars. The Sudras could not study the sacred literature. During the career of Swami Madhavrao, the Peshwa's government had decreed that Mahars, being 'Ati Sudras', beyond Sudras, could not have their marriage rites conducted by the regular Brahmin priests. The untouchable could not enter the temples. A Brahmin could not be punished with capital punishment.

COMMUNITY POWER AND FEATURES

The community is a territorial group which shares a common soil as well as shared way of life. It is no accident that people concentrate at a particular place and cluster together. Nearness facilitates contact, furnishes protection and makes easier the organization and integration of the group.People living in the same locality come to have a distinctive community life. Once a group of people gets settled, an element of space enters into the social relationship and local groupings become more important than blood relationship. People who live in the same locality though they belong to different bloods, form a community. Even an immigrant who does not belong to kinship may become a member of the local community.

The physical environment of the locality reveals the community life of the people, for example, the life of the village people is different from the life of the people in the industrial town. But it may not be assumed that there is any full correspondence between physical environment and group culture. Every social group adapts itself to a total environment of which the physical environment is but one aspect. The differences of culture of groups living in different localities are the result of numerous factors and it is difficult to isolate the influence of anyone, since they are all interactive in determining the community character.

An important aspect of the physical structure of the community to which attention may be drawn is its unplanned physical structure. No long-range pre-conceived plan stands behind the different areas of modern community, the village, the city and the region. The result has been congestion, use of physically deteriorated habitations and other buildings, unbalanced development of various areas of living and of business activity. This situation so general of large cities needs proper community planning for its solution. Some of the leading countries like Great Britain, United States, Soviet Russia have put into operation some of the proposals for planning the community. In Punjab the town of Chandigarh has been built according to a plan dividing the town into numerous sectors reramarked for specific habitations. But the task of rehabilitating the physical structure of a community is a complex one being faced with several difficulties of a practical nature like scarcity of materials, design difficulties, opposition of vested interests. It may be easy to design the shape of a new community but it is all the more difficult to redesign one already established.

Community is more than the locality it occupies. It is also sentiment. The people living at a common place and leading their lives in one another's company come to develop 'we-feeling'. The place they occupy is to them much more than a portion of earth's surface—it is their 'home'. Living together makes them share common memories and traditions, customs and institutions. It shapes their attitudes and interests. The sense of community becomes impressed in the depths of their personality. The community sentiment becomes a part of his own individuality. The individual identifies his interest with the larger interest of the group. He feels indissolubly bound up with it so that to him the community is "bone of his bone and flesh of his flesh". He carries a sense of dependence upon the community, which is both physical and physiological since his material wants are satisfied within it and since it sustains him and provides him solicitude. Every community has its own customs, interests, beliefs, superstitions, folktales, myths and folkways.

Today none of us belong to one inclusive community, but to wider communities at the same time. Man today is a member of several groups, which satisfy the diverse needs of his personality. He feels attached to these groups which replace the community sentiment. This is most observable in a large city where neighbourhood as a community may not exist at all. The development of local transport also has lessened the coherence and intensity of community sentiment. Then the developing physical contacts of the rural people with the urban people facilitated by the modern rapid means of transport have weakened the attachment to the village community and reduced the extent of dependence upon it. In short, under modern conditions attachment to local community is decreasing. Man today has tended to find it in the appeal of larger groups.

TYPES OF COMMUNITY ORGANIZATION

Human communities may be classified on the basis of many different criteria. A large number of classifications of human communities have been made and have been found useful for different purposes. A very broad and familiar classification is based on the size and density of the population, in terms of which we classify communities as neighbourhood, village, city, region and world community.The main types of community are as follows:

A. THE NEIGHBOURHOOD

City Neighbourhood. The neighbourhood is the first community with which the child comes into contact.It is a "loose integration of several family groups". In large cities it is largely a group of "neigh-dwellers" characterized chiefly by the fact that the members reside within a particular geographic area. In a city neighbourhood the people generally do not come into close contact and sometimes do not even know each other. Some of you must have experienced the difficulty of finding the house of your relative in a big city if you did not know it already. We may say that in cities neighbourhood as a community does not exist.

Village Neighbourhood. As opposed to city neighbourhood a rural neighbourhood involves persons living close to and well acquainted with each other. Though in a village neighbourhood people may not live in close proximity to each other, they may live somewhat apart, yet unlike city neighbourhood they know each other well. There are immediate contacts between the neighbours in a village.

It depends upon human nature whether the individual prefers to live in neighbourhood or he wants to live in a solitary house. There are some people who want to live near other people; while others may not like to live so.

B. THE VILLAGE COMMUNITY

The earliest human communities were perhaps the loosely organized aggregations of a few families who carried on mutually interdependent activities in gathering food and defending themselves against their enemies. These primitive bands were migratory communities. Gradually man acquired skill and knowledge in agriculture. With the development of agriculture and the consequent stabilization of the source of food, the people began to lead a settled life and human communities became more stationary. The village emerged which signified that man has passed from nomadic mode of collective life to the settled one. It is difficult to form a precise definition of the term 'village'. Generally, it is understood to mean a small area with small population which follows agriculture not only as an occupation but also as a way of life. The village is the oldest permanent community of man. Kropotkin writes, "We do not know one single human race or one single nation which has not had its period of village communities". "Human society", as Bogardus says, "has been cradled in the rural group." The most impressive of the villages said to have existed five thousand or more years ago, are the lake dwellings of Switzerland and nearby sections of Germany, France, Italy and Austria. The houses were built on platforms supported by piles driven into the lake bottom. Bridges connected these houses with the shore where fields and pasture lay.

Evolution of Village Community. The village community has passed through the following stages:

(i) Primitive Village Community. There are two peculiar features of the primitive village community; first, the part played by kinship and, second, its collectivist basis. The ancient village community was a very small group of ten or twenty families. Owing to smallness of size everybody knew each other. The feeling of familiarity was so great that if a child wandered off from the home, the parents had nothing to worry because there were numerous relatives in that village who would keep an eye on him. Since due to lack of means of communication and transport the members of the village community were separated from other communities by a great distance, considerable inbreeding occurred, so that a large part of the members were related by kinship.

(ii) Medieval Village Community. The primitive village community underwent a fundamental change by the time of the Middle Ages. Neither kinship any longer played a prominent part in binding the people nor did the land belong to the group as a whole. Instead, feudal system came into existence. The land now belonged to a lord of some sort, to the king, to a member of the nobility or to an eccelesiastical chief. It was tilled by tenants who were the vassals of their feudal lords. Their relation with the feudal lords was that of slave and master. There were, however, certain factors which bound the rural folk.

(iii) ***Modern Village Community.*** With the rise of industrialism in modern times the rural group began to lose its importance. Now urban group began to dominate civilization. However, in spite of the growth of urbanism it is a fact that even at the present time a large proportion of population lives in villages. In the U.S.A. there were approximately 4,316,000 persons in the villages under 1,000 population in 1940 and 5,000,000 persons in the villages with 1,000-2,500 population during the same year. In India, according to the census of 1961, 82 per cent of the population lived in villages.

The modern village community stands in sharp contrast to the primitive one. Urbanization, the dominant feature of the modern age has made its impact on the village community. The modern city has set the pattern of the rural way of life. Rural social forms have been changing. The rural people have taken over the urban forms of life. The kinship bond, a peculiar feature of the primitive village community has been broken due to the increased size and mobility of population. The land is no longer owned collectively or cultivated jointly. Even the methods of working the land have taken on urban characteristics.

FEATURES OF VILLAGE COMMUNITY

The village community is marked by several features. The important ones are the following:

(i) Community Consciousness. The village dwellers have a sense of unity. The relations between the village people are intimate. They personally known each other. Their customs, conventions and culture are common. They jointly take part in religious celebrations. Strucutrally and functionally the village is a unit.

(ii) Joint Family. Though in the cities the joint family system is breaking down, yet in the villages it still retains its hold. The agricultural occupation requires the cooperation of all the family members. The men plough the field, the women harves the crops and the children graze the cattle.

(iii) Role of Neighbourhood. In a village neighbourhood is of great importance. There is not enough of individuality and speed in life of the village to disable one from paying attention to his neighbour—his sorrows and joys. In the village people assist each other and thus they have close neighbourhood relations.

(iv) Faith in Religion. The people in the villages have deep faith in religion and deities. Their main occupation is agriculture which largely depends upon the vagaries of nature. The farmer acquires an attitude of fear and awe towards natural forces and starts worshipping them.

(v) Simplicity. The village people lead a simple life. It is not ostentatious. They are far away from the evils of modern civilization. They are a simple and plain people believing in God. They do not show pretensions. Their behaviour is natural and not artificial. They live a peaceful life. They are free from mental conflicts. They do not suffer heart strokes. They are sincere, hospitable and hard-working. The level of morality is high. Social crimes are very rare. Their life is governed by norms.

GROWTH OF VILLAGE COMMUNITY

The growth of village community depends upon the following factors:

(i) **Topographical Factors.** Among the topographical factors are included land, water and climate. It is obvious that these factors influence the growth of village community. Land is the most important topographical factor. People would like to settle at a place where land is fertile and plain. It is difficult to carry agriculture on land which is rocky and uneven. If the land is not fertile and is sandy the villages cannot develop there. In the rocky areas and in deserts habitation is scarce. On the other hand, in the plain and fertile lands of Punjab one can observe villages at every two or three miles. The villages settled on fertile lands are more developed and prosperous.

The facility of water also contributes to the growth and prosperity of villages. Water is required not only for drinking, bathing, cooking, etc., but also for irrigating the lands. If water is not easily available, much use cannot be made even of fertile and plain lands. Where water is not easily available as in the case of deserts the villages are far and scattered. The villages situated on the banks of canal or having tube wells are in a much prosperous condition than those which are seeking out a miserable existence in the deserts and hills.

(ii) Economic Factors. Among the economic factors we may include the condition of agriculture, rural economy and cottage industries.

Agriculture is the mainstay of the village community. As such the growth of village community depends upon the condition of agriculture. If farming yields a good crop, the economic condition of the village people will be better. If, on the other hand, they have to exert themselves to the point of exhaustion just to get enough for two meals a day, their economic and social condition will not be better. In those countries where scientific inventions and favourable natural conditions have increased the agricultural production the village communities are in an advanced stage of development. In India, the village communities are poor because of low agricultural production.

The village economy also is an important factor in the growth of village community. The farmer must be in a position to procure animals of good breed, good seeds, good manure and scientific implements.

Cottage industries play an important part in the development of village community. While the cottage industries provide a means of livelihood to landless people, they also offer means of utilization of the farmers and female labour in productive activities.

(iii) Social Factors. Among the social factors we include peace, security, cooperation and intelligence etc. For the development of the village community it is essential that there must be peace in the village. Besides peace, the village people must be guaranteed security—security from disease, and in agriculture. They also need security against natural calamities.

Community development is not possible without cooperation. In the village there are many activities which depend upon cooperation of the whole community. Such activities, for example, are public health and sanitation, peace and order, proper use of public amenities, education and recreation, etc. Through cooperation the village people can bring about their development and put the village community on the way to prosperity.

Ultimately, the growth of the village community depends upon the intelligence of the villagers. Lacking intelligence they cannot raise the agricultural output nor profit by the scientific discoveries. The village communities in the west are prosperous because they are intelligent. In India the villages are in a backward state because the village people lack intelligence to make use of scientific discoveries.

ROLE OF CASTE

Caste and the Democratic Process. The caste is the another social factor which has an impact on our democractic and political process. It is rather the most important social factor to complicate and hinder our democrate process. In its most general, but, fundamental aspect, caste can be described as a system of status and hierarchy in which the position and status of an individual depends one's over birth. In its extreme form, caste stratifcation subsumes all other stratification systems. As the caste is described by birth it is a closed system. The members of a caste group have some sorts of socio-economic and cultural similarities and a feeling of bondage. In these respects, they thinks other caste to be different from them. Over the years, in a general sense, this caste system has provided a basis interaction. Colonial rule introduced some changes in the caste system. After of social independence, the modern system of education, economic opportunities and position of power offered by new democratic institutions drew caste into its modernist network.

Class, Caste and the Democratic Process. Here it may be noted that class is different from cast in the senes that class denotes a social division based on economic considerations and not on the basis of birth. It denotes the economic power of different groups in the society. However, in India there is some overlap between caste and class. Those who belong to upper castes generally also control the economic resources of the society. And a large section of poors invariably belong to lower castes. Thus, both caste and class coincide in India. Thus, in a general sense, the person's caste indicates not only his social position but also his economic position. Thus, in many areas, the rich landlords and peasants come generally from the higher castes such as Brahmins, Bhumihars, Rajputs and Thakurs while the Harijans, tribals and other low castes constitute the bulk of landless labour, majority of the members of the middle castes such as Jats, Gujjars, Yadavas and Kurmis belong to the class of small and medium peasant. Thus, because of the social status and economic position, upper castes dominated the democratic process in India for a long time. But now the number game has become dominant for the last few years. So the persons from middle and lower castes are running ahead in the game of power politics and have threatened in real sense the monopoly of upper castes' dominance in politics.

Base of Social Structure. The base of India's social structure is caste and sub-caste. The caste system is peculiar to India. In the ancient India, there was four-fold division of society into Brahmin, Kshatriya, Vaishya and Shudra. But these were Varnas and not castes. This four-fold division was based on the division of work in the society. But later it became crystallized and rigid and came to be based on birth. This came to be known as caste. Gradually these cates got divided into various sub-castes (jatis). These castes and sub-castes were now based on birth and inter-caste marriage were forbidden completely. Thus, the caste-system, which was originally based on division of labour and occupation, over the centuries became a more or less rigid endogamous groups, based on birth. Today caste has relevance for rituals, marriages, inheritance, for many other social traditions. But what is important to note is that it is dividing our society and polity and posing a threat to the unity and integrity of our nation. It has really posed a great challenge to the task of national integration. If this menance of casteism is not curbed it will demolish our entire democratic and secular fabric and break us as a nation.

Caste as a Factor in Politics. Since independence, caste has been playing an incresingly important role in all political activities, elections, political appointments, party formations, etc. Today the caste system is basically based on jati and not on Varna or the four-fold division of the ealrier period. So far as distribution and dominance in politics is concerned, no single caste dominate all the regions. In many regions, several so-called backwad castes occupy the position of dominance in society and polity. In some other regions the upper caste dominant, sometimes with one or two backward castes. Besides, there are some caste which are basically land-based and they are very powerful and dominant in their regions. For example, the Thakurs (Rajputs), Brahimns, Jats, Yadavas, Ahirs, Gujjars and Kurmis and dominant in most of Uttar Pradesh. The Bhumihars, Kayasthas Rajputs, Yadavas and Kurmis are so in Bihar. Likewise, in Andhra Pradesh, the Reddis, the Kammas and the Velamas are land-based and dominant caste. So are Vokkaligas and Lingayats in Karnataka. Likewise, in other states and regions different caste or groups of castes are dominant.

Role. As said earlier caste has been playing an increasing important role in politics. Caste consideration has been a major factor in elections, political appointments, party formations, selection of ministers, etc., caste has become these days as an electoral constituency. Thus, caste is affecting the working of our democratic politics. Moreover, democratic facilities like freedom of speech, expression and association, participation in electoral system, formation of parties, and even legislative bodies are being misused for maintaining casteist identity. Thus while from the Indian politics is secular, its style of working has become essentially casteist. And the different caste groups have become major pressure groups in politics.

Negative Impact of Casteism on Our Political System. Thus, the negative impact of casteism on India's political system is as follows:

(i) The caste system violates the basic principles enshrined in the Constitution, namely the principles of justice, equality and above all fraternity. It is against the unity and integrity of the nation. Moreover, it is against the modern new democratic polity.

(ii) The various castes have been politicised. One caste or a group of castes counterpoise against the other.

(iii) It has vitiated the atmosphere of elections and promotes narrow loyalties, thus weakening the modernisation of the polity.

(iv) It creates tension, suspicion, fear and an atmosphere of violence, by building military on caste lines.

(v) In party politics and in ministry formation, the role of caste contributes to avoidable bickerings, narrow bargaining and jockeying for power. All this often leads to political instability and confusion.

(vi) By building caste associations and pressue-groups in politics, it has proved to be an impediment to building up of a secular society.

(vii) It adversely affects the grassroots Panchayati Raj system which becomes an instrument in the hands of dominant caste to perpetuate its domination. Thus, it frustrates the emergence of the new democratic culture of free and equal citizenship irrespective of caste creed or birth.

(viii) The caste dilutes the programmatic and ideological aspects of the parties. More importantly, it reduces the strength the activities of the business, is an, workers and other types of interest groups.

CASTE IN VILLAGE

Caste system or caste structure is an integral part of Indian Rural Society. It is based on social stratification, as a result of which the status and role of the individual member of the society is determined. In India, the caste system is still an important factor in the rural society. It has ceased to be so effective in the urban society. Because of the difference in the caste system, different people have different types of economic and social behaviour, pattern, family structure, mode of living, occupation etc. Cultural patterns are also determined by the caste system. Normally the Indian social structure or caste system is devided into four groups-Brahmin Kshatriya Vaish and Sudra. These labour divisions of conservatism, these castes have survived and continue to play an important role.

Characteristics of Caste System in Relevance to Village Society. The characteristics of the castes may be enumerated as below:

(1) ***Division of the Society into Segment or Segmental Division of the Society.*** In caste system, the society is divided into various segments. Each segment has fixed standard of membership, status and role of its members which also predominated. It is not possible to change these things.

(2) ***Social Hierarchy.*** In the caste system this is also to be found in the rural society of India various segments in which the society has been divided, have hierarchical orders. Some of these segments are considered higher while the others are considered as lower. The highest position is occupied by the brahmins and the lowest by the sudras. In rural society of India, this social hierarchy is in greater force. In it people belonging to the upper class get a higher respect while those belonging to the lower caste do not get so much respect.

(3) ***Occupational Restrictions.*** Caste and occupation are vitally linked. People of a particular caste have a set occupation. Those who transgress this reality of the caste system are generally penalised by the caste panchayat. Here no

consideration is made of the efficiency or attitude to take up that occupation. Occupation is determined by birth as is the membership of the caste. It is not possible for that man to change occupation. In the modern social order, several changes have taken place in the caste structure as well as occupational set up but generally in the Indian rural society, every caste has an occupation of its own and no one is allowed to change that occupation.

(4) ***Restrictions Regarding Food and Marriages.*** In this caste system, people have to live under restrictions in regard to food marriages etc. It means that people of a particular caste are not allowed to eat with people of other castes. Similarly, social intercourse is restricted. These types of restrictions are very much invoked in Indian rural society.

While looking at the definitions of the castes given by various authors we have seen that the caste-system is based on endogamy which means that people of a particular social group cannot marry outside tha social group. Apart from it, people belonging to the same sub caste cannot marry. Then people having blood relations are not allowed to marry. Gotra plays a vital role in the restrictions on the marriages.

(5) ***Hereditary Privileges and Obligations.*** In the caste system, certain hereditary privileges are allowed to members of the higher caste while the members of the lower caste are deprived of those privileges. Apart from it, members of different caste have certain obligations which give opportunity to certain castes to have better position.

(6) ***Universally Recognized Respect of the Brahmins.*** In the caste system as is found in India and particularly in the Indian Rural Sociaty, the brahmins have a place of respect. They are required to be respected by the members of other castes. Members of different caste have to pay respect to brahmins and also give them what has been prescribed by the religious laws. This gives them a better position.

(7) ***Economic Disparty Between Various Castes.*** Caste system is not only based on social disparity but also on economic disparities. It means that generally people belonging to the higher caste are economically well off, while those belonging to the lower caste are economically backward. Members of the higher caste have certain economic privileges. They are allowed to pursue occupations that are more secure and required less labour and get more profit.

(8) ***Birth as the Detriment of the Caste System.*** In the caste system it is the birth that determines the membership of a particular caste. Children that are born out of the members of a particular caste belong to that caste. This birth determines not only their membership of the caste but also their occupation. This is a typical feature of the caste system of India and particularly its rural society.

Role of Caste System in Indian Villages. The caste system is more to be found in the Indian villages than in the Indian towns. It does not wield the influence it once wielded. But it is still an important factor in the rural order. It also has influences in the Indian rural life. Its influence in the Indian rural life may be seen in the following ways:

1. Caste system and the economic life.
2. Caste sysem and the joint family structure.
3. Caste system and education.
4. Caste system and value pattern.
5. The problem of casteism.
6. Caste system and political life.

Let us discuss each one of the economic life.

1. Caste Sytem and the Economic Life. The rural economy even today is very much influenced by the caste structure. There even today occupations are divided on the basis of caste. Agriculture is mainly controlled by the people of the higher castes while occupations of carpenters, black-smiths, cobler etc. are performed by the members of the lower caste. Because the members of the upper class are economically well off, they control the members of the lower caste. The influence of the caste system on rural economy may be seen in the following ways:

(a) ***Indebtedness.*** In rural society the members of the lower caste are generally indebted. Those who belong to the upper class are economically well off and so they give loans to the members of the lower castes and in this manner control them. Apart from it there are certain castes that are money lenders by profession. Because of this profession they are in a position to control the members of the lower caste.

(b) ***Habitation and Living.*** In rural social structure, the habitation and living is also guided and governed by institution of the caste system. People of the higher castes have better houses and higher standard of living. Thier houses are situated in good locality. This is not the case with the members of the lower caste. These persosn are forced to live atisolated places from the main place of habitation. Their houses are also not very well built. Generally it is also seen that villages are inhabited by the people of different castes. It means that there is calssification of the villages on the basis of the caste system.

(c) ***Occupational and Social Mobility.*** This caste system has an adverse effect on social and economic mobility. It rural society profession are determined on the basis of caste. It is not possible for people to change occupations and professions. This has an adverse effect on economic condition. People of Upper classes choose any profession but members of the lower caste cannot leave their profession. Because of this they are also not able to go up socially. This restriction on the mobility retards their growth, development and progress.

(2) Caste System and Joint Family Structure. Joint family is an important institution of the rural society. It is very much encouraged by the caste system. On the other hand the caste system is born out of the collection of the joint family. Many of the social thinkers are of the view that the caste system is probably a group of the joint families and that is why caste determines the way of life of those families. In other words the caste system or the institution of the caste system also influences the joint family structure which is still to be found in the rural society.

(3) Caste System and Education. Education is also influenced by the caste pattern or caste structure, particularly in the rural society. Those who belong to so called higher class, have better education. According to the customs also they are allowed to have higher education. Such a thing is not to be found amongst the members of the so called lower castes. According to customs and tradition, the members of the lower caste were not allowed to acquire edcuation. There are economic factors also responsible for the situation. Members of the lower caste are economically hard hit and so they want a earning hand. As soon as the child grows to an extent that he is able to work with grown-up members of the family in earning livelihood, he is made to work. Because of this situation he is not allowed to go to school.

(4) Caste System and Political Life. In rural society, caste-sysem and politics have an inseparable realtion. In slave India, members of the lower caste were deprived of the opportunity of taking part in the political activities and coming to public life. They lacked education and were also handicapped socially and economically. Indian independence movement made it a part of its activities to emancipate socially and economically backward people. After independence, the members of the lower caste, in order to preserve themselves and also in order to take advantage of the opportunities provided under the law have become conscious of their castes. Apart from it the elections in free India have become caste oriented. Because of this institution, the caste has become very important in political life.

(5) Caste System and Values Pattern. The values pattern particularly in the rural society is caste-oriented. Those who belong to a particular set of values and norms are different from the values and norms of the members of other castes. This is more to be seen in rural society as compared to the urban society. For example, in rural society remariage amongst the member of the lower caste is allowed but such a thing is very rare amongst the members of the upper class. Such a thing is not so rigid in urban society.

(6) The Problem of Casteism. In modern rural society, as a result of caste consciousness, the tendency of the casteism has grown. As a result of casteism people belonging to a particular caste get organized and sometimes become aggressive to such an extent that they do not hesitate in harming the members of the other castes. Casteism is not limited to patriotism towards that caste or preserving the interest of that caste. As a result of this tendency, sometimes people do not hesitate in sacrificing the interest of other castes. Apart from it, due to casteism people have become narrow minded. They do not bother about others. They do not hesitate even if they have to do wrong things for preserving the interest of their own caste. Such a narrow parachole interest creates difficulties in the path of progress and development. It is responsible for the following obstacles in the national progress:

(a) ***Obstacle to National Unity.*** As a result of casteism, people get into narrow parachole groups. This thing has an adverse effect on national integration and unity amongst the members of different social groups. This casteism has posed a big problem for national and emotional integration which is a must for this country.

(b) ***Obstacle to New Inventions and Developments.*** Because of casteism, people develop a narrow parachole outlook. Due to narrow outlook, they other about acquiring higher education or taking to new developments. Sometimes people take to age-old profession and do not like to change the method of production. This has an adverse effect on the production of the national wealth.

(c) ***Creation of Artificial and Unwanted Social Inequality.*** Because of casteism, people think that the group to which they belong is the superior most group. They look down

upon others and in ordet to establish their superiority create artificial sitaution through which they can prove their superiority. As a result of this trend, artificial and unwanted social inequalities are created. In our Indian society which is wedded to a creation of socialist society, there is no place for inequalities. From this point of view, this caste system has beget casteism which is not in the interest of the proper development of the country.

New Trends in the Casteism. The caste system in the modern age, becaues of several new developments, has undergone several changes. There changes are to be seen in the form of new trends. The trends that are visible in the cast system are of the following types:

1. ***Decline of Caste Supremacy.*** The caste system which is in fact a form of social stratification is based on hieraruy of different castes. In this hierarchical orders brahmins are at the top and sudras are at the bottom. But in the modern set up, with the rise of the economic classes and growing importance of the wealth, the supremacy of the brahmins also added to the decline of the caste supremacy. Education has brought about dislike for religious functions and other activities in which the brahmins played the dominant role.
2. ***Relaxation in Restriction on Marriages.*** As a result of caste system, certain restrictions are imposed on marriages. People of a particular caste cannot marry outside that caste. On the other hand they cannot marry amongst blood relations and members belonging to the same gotra. As a result of the new education and certain other social and economic development, these restrictions have been removed. Inter-caste marriages are becoming more and more common.
3. ***Change in Occupational Pattern and Occupational Mobility.*** As a result of caste system, the occupation of different castes was determined. The Brahmins could not take up the business of those manufacturing and so a

Sudra could not become a teacher. Now this thing has more or less come to and end. Member of any caste can leave his traditional occupation and take to some other occupation. Brahmins who would not touch the plough are now taking to agricIture because it is very profitable. Vaishs are becoming teachers and also taking any profession that were restricted to brahmins or kshatriyas; this new trend has brought about improvement of the economic condition of the people.

4. ***Weakening of the Restrictions on Eating and Drinking.*** Due to caste system certain restrictions have been imposed on eating and drinking. Members of the so called higher class cannot eat with the members of the so called low class. Similarly, the members of the lower casts also do not eat with them. Now with the growth of education, industrialization, urbanization and due to force of social movements and legal actions, these restrictions have weakened. People of one caste freely mix with other castes and also eat with them.

5. ***Improvement in the Position of the Lower Caste.*** Normally the members of the lower caste suffer from several disabilities and handicaps. Now, as result of the new legislative measures, their conditon has improved. They are allowed several facilities that are not available to members of other castes. Certain reservations have also been made for them. Because of these things, they have improved their position economically as well as socially.

The caste system has changed its pattern. Restrictions that went with the caste sometimes ago are getting relaxed. Inspite of it, it cannot be said that the caste system has come to an end. It will undergo further changes in future. It will completely vanish only when the democratic values get deep rooted and the country makes good deal of economic progress and industrial advancement then new political and economic structure will emerge and it will change the pattern of the caste system.

CLASS CONSCIOUSNESS

Class consciousness is "the sentiment that characterises the relations of men towards the members of their own and other classes." It consists in the realization of a similarity of attitude and behaviour with members of ohter class. The workers are said to possess class consciousness when they feel that their interests as workers are common and since the interests are common they must exhibit class solidairty among themselves and common attitude towards their enmy class-the capitalists. Kari Max laid great emphasis on class consciousness among the working classes. It was his endeavour to accentuate in the working classes the consciousness of their corporate capacity.

CONDITIONS FAVOURING CLASS-CONSCIOUSNESS

What are the conditions which tend to make members of a class, conscious of their membership? Ginsberg mentions three conditions. Firsts is the ease and amount of social mobility. If movement up and down is easy and rapid, differences in mode of life disappear, if it is impossible, the attitudes of members of different classes to each other become habitual and quasi-automatic; if it is possible but not easy, the consciousness of differences is heightened.

The second condition of class consciousness is rivarly and conflict. When the members of class possess common interests, this possession is brought into consciousness by the need of defence against that common enemy, e.g., workers possessing common interests have class consciousness because they have to defened themselves agaisnt a common enemy, the capitalists.

The third factor is the growth of a common tradition, embodying common standard value and common experiences. When the members come to possess common traditions and they have common experiences, it leads to the rise of class consciousness among them.

Corporate Class Consciousness. MacIver draws a distinction between corporate class consciousness and competitive class feeling. The former involves feeling of unity and arises out of the similarity of status which the members enjoy. The latter involves disparity. It exists because of the competitive attitudes of individuals or groups of individuals belonging to a particular class. Corporate class consciousness is "a sentiment uniting a whole group sharing a similar social status." The working class exhibits most clearly corporate class consciousness which his developed under the spur of strong economic incentives and gained more strength in the struggle to maintain or destroy the pre-status. Karl Marx laid great emphasis upon the need of corporate class consciousness among the working class. His aim was to develop solidarity and organisation of the whole class of proletariat-the propertyless wage earners. According to him proletariat class is essentially homgeneous. Its interests are common and commonly subjected to the bourageoisie.

Competitive class feeling is characteristics of the competitve system that developed in modern society. It is a "personal from of class sentiment that often determines the conduct of individuals towards one another without involving on their part any express recognition of whole group to which they respectively belong." When Mr. A deprives Mrs. B from membership in this club, it does not mean that he thereby necessarily upholds the standards or the interests of a whole class or when Mr. A patronizes Mrs. B it does not mean that she necessarily feels solidarity wiht a whole order of "superiors".

Competitive class feeling, though operates within the framework of particular class, yet it acts as an important factor in maintaining the balance of interests as a whole. If the competitive class ceases to exist, the result would be that each class will stand as shortly opposed to the other. Competitive class feeling maintains indiviual hopes to rise from his own class to higher class.

Class consciousness tends to be stronger or weaker according to the degree the element of caste is present. When social conditions and customs fix rigidly a man's status by life he identifies himself with the fellows living under the same conditions. In a caste ridden living society, the class sentiment is stronger,as it is among Harijans. So when the mores of an authoritative religion holds sway, the members of the group lowly and reverently order themselves to all their superiors. But if the mores break there comes great social change. The members of the low class rise up higher in the social scale according to their individual efforts and enterprise.

ROLE OF CLASS

Class organisations work as pressure groups in the political systems and interest groups in a process of political mobilization, both stimulate and structure participation." As Myron Weiner has argued that "the greatest protection against the demands of powerful community groups is the multiplication of community and non community associations." In cae there is increase in the number of associations, "the possibility that any single community will dominate a state government is likely to decrease.

And as Hardgrave puts it, "A bargaining culture may emerge at the expanse of the wider public interests, however, as India's limited resources may be dissipated, in trade-offs and" Logrolling" between contending and self interested groups. But who is to determine the public interest, "what classes are to be served? This is the classic and fundamental dilemma of democracy-one starkly posed in the context of India's struggle for economic development and social justice."

It has been argued that the existing class structure of India displays a grave threat to "economic growth with social justice" The allege conflict between growth and justice is an expression of the more fundamental contradiction in the undergoing structural arrangments of social relations. India is fragmented by virtually every known socictal division, but while the Indian masses are beginning to respond to political appeals interest of class interests, they have no consciousness of class. Class remains and objective category imposed analytically and heterogeneity of India's contending groups. But is objective terms it is possible to ask which are the class for whose benefit the state power is exercised as indicated by the overall direction of state policy. In an enquiry to the class character of state power in India, a Marxist symposium observed that it, "is really spared by landlords and the industrial especially under the leadership of monopoly Capitalists". In view of the Communist Party of India, 'the state in India is the instrument of class rule of the national bourgeoisie as a whole in which the big bourgeoisie and landlords hold powerful influence."

These people are over three hundred million, and command comparatively, a privilege in the poor economy of India. It has been argued that, "the source of powers of these middle sectors big in the strategic combination of considerable population size with extensive economic resources and significant social status, as against the greater economic power but small number of the upper business and land owning classes and the large numbers but economic destitution of lower classes. Socialism to the middle sectors has meant apart from what may fairly be described as tokenism towards the scheduled castes, the bringing down of the upper classes to their own level. Democracy has served their classes well in these regard by facilitating the conversion of economic privilege and numerical strength into political power while at the same time giving it an aura of genuine legitimacy."

It has been found that the middle sectors gave support to the political regime in the past since it responded to their various interests. Since their position is vulnerable; they pose serious challenges to the state of political and economic certainity.

CLASS STRUCTURE

A social class is "the aggregate of persons having essentially the same social status in a given society." It is a portion of the community or collection of individuals" standing to each other in relation of equality, and marked off from other portion by accepted or sanctioned standards of inferiority and superiority." Each particular social class has its own particular social and politcal behaviour, its standards and occupations. The relative position of the class in the society arises from the degree of prestige attached to the status. Wherever the consdierations of status lower and higher, limit social intercourse, there exists social class. Status is the basic criterion of social class.

"In most societies people classify one another into categories, and rank from higher to lower. The process of defining and ranking such categories is called social stratification and the resulting set of ranked categories is called the stratification structure. The categories themselves by analogy with the different layers of rock in a geological formation are called 'strata'. More popularly, we known the as 'classes'."

Some definitions of class are the following:

(i) Ogburn and Nimkoff, "A social class is the aggregate of persons having essentially the same social status in a given society."

(ii) Lapiere, "A social class is a culturally defined group that is accorded a particular position or status within the population as a whole."

In a social class there is first, a feeling of equality in relation to members of one's own class, a consciousness that one's made of behaviour will harmonize with the behaviour of similar standards of life. Individuals belonging to the same socil class are expected to maintain similarity of standards of life, and to choose their occupations with a limited range. There is realistion of a similiarity of attitude and behaviour with members of one class. Secondly, there is a feeling of inferiority in relation to those who stand above in the social scale. Thirdly, there is the feeling of superiority over those below in the social hierarchy.

The fundamental attribute of a social class is its social position of relative inferiority or superiority to other social classes. It is the social position which determines for its possessor the degree of respect, prestige and influence.

A social class is distinguished from other classes by certain customary modes of behaviour which are taken to be characteristics of that class and may be concerned with such things as mode of dress, the modes of conveyance, the way of recreation and expenditure. The society sometimes resents the breach of these modes by that class which is expected to observe them. Some times the members of a lower social class resents any interference in their modes of behaviour by the upper class even if it is done for humanitarian reasons.

It i also to be noted that the members of a social class often put obstacles in the way of those people who wish to come up to their position. It also means that a class possessing certain privileges would like not only, to possess them exclusively but also increase them.

IS CLASS BASED ONLY ON ECONOMIC DIFFERENCES?

Acording to Karl Marx, class is based only on economic differences. He defines classs as economic groups which are divided on the basis of the possession of various instruments of production. Thus according to him the basis of social startification is economic differences. Formely there were the landlords and the agriculturists, today there are the capitalists and the proletariat.

Karl Marx explains, the cause of class formation by the middle, and low standard people (classified on the basis of the possession of capital) in the following terms:

"The lower strata of the middle class-the small trade people, shop keepers and retired tradesmen generally, the handicraftsmen and peasants all these sink gradually into the proletariat, partly because their deminative capital does not suffice for the scale on which modern Indusry is carried on, and is swamped in the competition with the large capitalists, partly because their specialised skill is rendered worthless by new methods of production.

Origin of Class. In the earliest stages of civilization *i.e.*, in the age of primitive barbaric tribs there are no social classes to be found. The reason being that the savage was not in a position to establish his superiority over his neighbaours because he was all the time engaged in the struggle for existence and lived from hand to mouth. "There is", writes Hobhouse, "always the distinction between its own members and outsider. There is also a greater or less distinction in the rights enjoyed by the two sexes. In other respects the obligations constituting its ethical life are farily uniform", In other words, equality of rank prevailed among the ancient savage tribes. There were no distinctions of rank enjoyed by particular groups.

Rise of Slavery System. But as the savage tribes grow in culture and expecially in military strength, the first result is that the conquered enemies are beaten, tortured or in any case put to death. After a while with a certain softening of attitudes captives are not killed or beaten but spared and enslaved. This was first reserved for women and children put was afterwards extended male captives. A class of slaves was thus formed who were within the jurisdiction of the conquering tribe. This class ws deprived of rights. A slave could be flogged, sold, pawned, exchanged or put to death.

Guild System. Modern classes are a development from the class structure of the Middle Ages when feudal lords or landed gentry were at the top the serfs at the bottom of society. There was another class of household servants, soldiers, fighters ro artisans in between these two classes. The artisans together with the small trades men at about the eleventh century became powerful in the towns which had remaiend indepedent organised themselves in guilds which formed the basis of economic structure of the Middle Ages. Over the above the guildmen, the lawyers, doctors and financers, who were mostly, Jews, constituted a higher class in the town.

CASTE IN THE STATE POLITICS

State politics in India has been particularly the hot bed of political casteism. Andre Betaille very candidly observes: "Caste enters much more directly into the composition of political elites at the state level... Thus, the Mysore cabinet is dominated by Lingayat and Okkaligas, the Maharashtra cabinet by Marathas and some have referred to the Madras cabinet as a federation of dominant castes." Michael Brecher remarks: "Caste plays Major role in state and local politics but it is marginal at the all-India level. Tinker observes: "...State politics will be caste politics throughout most of India for many years to come."

Bihar. Politics in Bihar has been mostly organised on the basis of castc. All those parties which happen to have a multi-caste membership have powerful functions. This was true of the undivided Congress as much as it is true of Congress (I), the Bhartiya Janata Party, and other major parties. The caste orientation of parties and groups does not mean that they are motivated only by caste interests of their members or that persons from other castes are completely barred entry or that the parties or groups actually serve any special or general interest of the caste. These are not service organisations for their castes but power machines which use caste labels for building loyalty around some personalities.

Caste Considerations. The single case of Bihar is adequate to prove the thesis that caste considerations are vital in political matters. Almost all the top leaders of Bihar Congress Party have been connected with their respective caste associations. Rajendra Prasad who held office as President of India, was for three decades connected with the All-India Kayasthas Conference and had presided over its Jaunpur

Session in 1925. A.N. Sinha, another prominent leader, was connected with the All-India Kshtriya Mahasabha. S.K. Sinha's association with the Bhumihars Brahmin Mahasabha, and his use of it to put political pressures, are also well known.

Groups. Initially, there were six groups in the Bihar Congress, *viz.*, the Bhumihars group led by S.K. Sinha, the Rajput group led by A.N. Singh, the two factions of Brahmins, one led by L.N. Mishra and the other by Binodanand Jha, the Kayasthas group led by K.B. Sahay and the backward castes led by R.L.S. Yadav. These groups were not altogether at peace among themselves. For instance, while the L.N. Mishra faction of Brahmins was supporting the powerful Bhumihar group. Pandit Binodanand Jha was supporting the Rajput faction. K.B. Sahay, the Kayasthas leader was supporting the Bhumihars till 1957, but after that he defected to the Rajput group. The backward castes leaders R.L.S. Yadav was the political disciple of Sahay and his loyalty used to change with Sahay's. After the death of S.K. Sinha, Binodanand Jha became Chief Minister. In the mean time A.N. Singh had died too, and the leadership of the Rajput faction was conferred on his son S.N. Singh. In the same manner, M.P. Sinha inherited the leadership of the Bhumihars from his father. While the Rajputs supported the 'Brahmin Raj' led by Jha, the Bhumihars, the L.N. Mishra faction of Brahmins, the Kayasthas and the backward castes opposed it. The Jha Ministry could not face such a strong opposition and the Chief Minister had to resign under the Kamaraj Plan. 'Kayastha Raj' followed with K.B. Sahay as head.

Realignment. The Congress split in 1969 meant a realignment. While at the established leaders of the Rajput, Bhumihar and Kayastha communities, *viz.*, S.N. Singh, M.P. Sinha and K.B. Sahay remained with the organisational wing, the backward castes, who had by then split into two factions—one led by R.L.S. Yadav and the other by his young competitor Daroga Rai as well as the Brahmins switched their loyalties to Congress (R) (Indira Gandhi's Congress).

Non-Congress Parties. Non-Congress parties have by no means had a clear, non-caste basis. In fact till 1967, under Congress domination, their attitude towards the ruling party depended on who representing which caste, was in power. For instance, when Bhumihar

S.L. Singh was Chief Minsiter, the then leader of the PSP Legislative Wing, Ramanand Tewari was very critical yet when Binodanand Jha came to power, Tewari's attitude softened—even as Besawan Singh another PSP leader, became more critical. Tewari is a Brahmin and Singh a Bhumihar. Thakur Prasad, the Jana Sangh Chief, use to maintain a lukewarm attitude towards the government headed by K.B. Sahay, both were Kayasthas. At the time of the Congress split, too, the so-called ideological discussion inside each political party was actually guided by caste considerations. While the Brahmins and the backward castes of most of the opposition parties fell for 'progressive idea' of Indira Gandhi, the Bhumihars, Rajputs, and Kayasthas supported the old Congress.

Clash Among Four Castes. Bihar, in fact, represents the scene of a clash among four castes, viz., Rajputs, Brahmins, Kayasthas and Adivasis. The Adivasis or the backward tribal people of Bihar-Orissa border organised themselves into Jharkhand Party which in the elections of 1957 had been able to capture most of the seats reserved for tribal and backward sections of the society and with its increased strength intensified the demand for a separate tribal state (Jharkhand) comprising all tribal areas of Bihar, Orissa and Madhya Pradesh. It afforded a potential challenge to the Congress Party. In order to face this situation, the Congress High Command deputed a Christian lady. Raj Kumari Amrit Kaur, to go to the tribal areas in order to wean away many tribes men (particularly those converted into Christianity) from the influence of this new organisation.

Kayasthas. Cases of Kayasthas (Sinha) struggling for power against the Brahmins (Jha) have also come to light particularly at the time of Ministry-making or selecting the leader of the legislature party.

Influence of Rajput. The influence wielded by the Raja of Ramgarh—a Rajput by caste—over his area and in Bihar politics as a whole despite all his acts of corruption, misappropriation, etc., has been most extraordinary. The Raja and his family interests for a decade have been the cancer of Bihar politics. In the post-1967 period, his group acquired a balancing position inasmuch as its support or denial thereof could make or unmake many of the coalition governments.

Backward Castes. The articulation of the sentiments of the backward castes during the tenure of Chief Minister K.B. Sahay and, more especially, since the time of the distribution of the Congress tickets for the general election of 1967 helped mobilize the lower-middle farmer castes of the state. It was not a mere coincidence, therefore, that of the nine governments formed in five years between the two elections as many as seven were led by leaders belonging to backward or Harijans castes. The fact that most Chief Ministers since 1967 did not belong to the 'forward castes' came to operate by 1970 as an important parameter of state politics in Bihar. The Lok Sabha elections of 1971 only sharpened the crystallization of the 'backward' sentiment and further deepened the process of mobilization of the backward classes, especially of the Yadavs, Kurmisk, and Koiris. Politics in Bihar has, thus, come to be articulated in terms of the backward *vs.* the forward.

Reservation of Jobs. In Bihar, instead of trying to attend to the pressing problems of the people, the Janata Chief Minister, Karpoori Thakur, chose in early 1978 to introduce a controversial measure for reservation of government jobs for the backward castes. It was a highly emotive issue at a time of widespread unemployment among the educated youth. There were demonstrations and counter-demonstrations and caste riots on a mass scale. The real reason behind the reservation issue was precisely a desire to create riots and caste conflicts so that there should be a polarisation between the so-called backward and forward castes. In this way, Karpoori Thakur thought he could became the leader of the backward castes and could find a solid base of support among them. Thus, the caste riots were viewed with profound satisfaction in circles close to Thakur.

Forward Castes. Atul Kohli observes, "The political struggle has been fought with unusual intensity because the forward castes of Bihar, and the Congress party that represented them, had long enjoyed unchallenged supremacy... The backward castes were eventually mobilised politically; they combined their numerical and growing economic strength under the umbrella of the Janata Party (Janata Dal). They enabled them to challenge the political hold of both the forward groups and the Congress party.

Kerala. In Kerala also caste considerations have played an important role in state politics. As Selig Harrison remarked:

> "The success of the Kerala Communist Party as the first ragional Communist party in India to capture control of a state government can be explained, above all, to its ability to manipulate politically strategic caste lobbies within linguistic boundaries...as in Andhra. The Kerala Communists were able to transform economic despair into a legislative majority because their footing on regional caste grounds, notably among the numerous Ezhavas provided the necessary margin of block strength in the necessary number of constituencies."

According to the 1971 Census, the Hindus number 59.4 per cent and the two minorities, the Muslims and the Christians, account for 19.5 and 21.1 per cent respectively. It is generally held that four major groups are contending for a dominant place in the political life of the state: Nairs, Ezhavas, Christians and Muslims. Numerically Ezhavas lead with 26.4 per cent, followed by Christians with 21.17 per cent, Muslims with 19.5 per cent and Nairs with 12.5 per cent.

Hindus. The Hindus account for 59.4 per cent of Kerala's population and caste ranking places the Namboodiri Brahmins at the peak of the Hindu hierarchy. Numbering less than 5 per cent of the population, the Namboodiris remain primarily a land-owning community. But despite the number of political leaders from this caste, such as the Left Communist E.M.S. Namboodiripad the Communists have had little political power. A far more potent political force is the Nair community—the traditional warrior of Kerala. As a land-owning and mercantile community today, the Nairs, numbering 17 per cent of the population, are a pivotal force in Kerala politics. They have traditionally held the balance, making or breaking a government by shifting sides. Economically subservient to the Nairs are the Ezhava or Tiyyar as they are called in Malabar. With 25 per cent of the population, however, the economically depressed Ezhava are perhaps the single most powerful community in Kerala. In addition to the mutually antagonistic Nairs and Ezhavas, the Christian community ranks as a major political power in Kerala. The Christians account for 19.5 per cent of the population, divided among the Syrians, the Protestants and the Roman Catholics. It is the Catholic community that numerically dominates and holds the locus of political power, largely through the organisation of the Church. The Muslims, with 18 per cent of the population and represented by the Muslim League, are a major factor politically, particularly in the Malabar region of northern Kerala where Muslims are the dominant community.

Muslims. Just as the Muslims are concentrated in certain areas of Malabar, each of the other communities dominate a particular region of Kerala. The Christians are concentrated primarily in Ernakulam and Kottayam district. The Nairs from the dominant community in the area of Trivandrum district, and the Ezhavas are particularly strong in Palghat. Each political party in Kerala must, therefore, seriously consider the dominant community, or as the Communists prefer to call it 'the social base' in the selection of its candidates. That each party tends to choose its candidates from the dominant community, however, does not cancel out community as a factor. Although there are elements of each community in all parties (except for the Muslim League), the parties in Kerala have come to be associated with particular communities, and within each party, factionalism expresses the divisions of religion and caste.

Nairs. The Nairs and even the Namboodiri Brahmins, soon followed in the creation of caste associations; the first of these being the Nair Serving Society, followed by the Uthana Kerala Nayar Samajam in Malabar and Namboodiri's Yogakshema Sabha. Caste quickly became politicised when political parties began to form. In Malabar, the lower castes (like the Ezhavas) opposed the Congress as being Nair dominated. After Independence, the Congress became increasingly a party of Christian domination, just as the Praja Socialist Party was regarded as a virtual Nair preserve. The Muslim League commands allegiance form most Muslims in Kerala, and the Communist party has drawn its strength primarily from the Ezhava and untouchable communities.

Caste Ranking. In Kerala, the elaboration of caste ranking and the generally common economic position shared by members of a caste, together with the high correlation between caste rank and economic position, have given rise to a political situation in which the most significant actors are castes and communities. While these communities are by no means wholly united, there is nevertheless a tendency toward an alignment of major communities with different parties.These socio-political constellations, reflecting a superimposition of ritual rank, social status, and economic position, represent essentially a class orientation. This is particularly evident in the social base of the Communist parties in Kerala. The Communists draw support from the poorer classes of each community—Nairs, Christians and Muslims. While the majority of the depressed Ezhavas may support of the party, the middle classes and the SNDP itself, have learned towards Congress—especially during the period of Sankar's leadership in the early 1960s. The 1965 election campaign, for example, was in large part fought by the Congress and the Communists to secure the affection of the Ezhavas. The failure of any party to secure a majority, however, only emphasised the fact that while politics of Kerala may be caste-bound no party can rule with the support of one community alone.

Andhra Pradesh. Caste politics in Andhra Pradesh seems like a game of cock-fighting between the Kammas and Reddys. The important castes in the state are the Brahmins, the Reddys, the Kammas, the Harijans, the Velamas, the Rajus and the Kapus. Politically, the Reddys and the Kammas are regarded as the dominant castes for they are numerically the strongest in the village or local area and economically and politically exercise a preponderant influence. The most important source of their power is their control over land. As the major landholders and occupants of important positions in the villages, they control the village political life. The two castes cultivated feeling of jealousy and rivalry as a result of which while the Reddys joined the Congress Party, the Kammas lent their support to the Communists. It is owing to this that Andhra Communists struggled heavily to stage Telengana rebellion in 1948. Support of the Kammas to the local Communist leaders in the first general elections became alarmingly noticeable and the Congress had to take note of this fact on the eve of second general elections of 1957 when the official High Command nominee, S.K. Patil tactfully requisitioned the support of Kamma leader N.G. Ranga and "matched caste with caste in the choice of candidates".

Landed Castes. In Andhra Pradesh, the landed castes and particularly the Reddy rural gentry constituted the backbone of the

Congress party. The Communist rebellion in Telengana, and later, a Communist bid to form the Ministry soon after Andhra state was formed in 1953, frightened the dominant castes so much that they gave extensive support to the Congress. Both the national and the State leadership of the Congress party tried to reach the voters not directly but through local influentials belonging to the dominant castes. This arrangement worked extremely well given the social status and economic power of the dominant castes and the low political consciousness of the other castes. The composition of the cabinet has reflected the same phenomenon. The Reddys, the Velmas and the Kammas held between them 45 to 58 per cent of the seats in the state cabinet, with the Reddys being the single largest group (28 to 38 per cent) till 1971.

Support Bases. After the 1969 Congress split an attempt was made to restructure the support base of the congress party. The upper middle class, landlord and peasant caste support structure of the party was considered to be a hindrance to bringing about socio-economic changes, which the new Congress, in a radical mood, was talking about. With P.V. Narasimha Rao as the Chief Minsiter, changes started. Though a Brahmin, but not from a landed caste, Narasimha Rao initiated the policy of giving greater representation to the backward classes and weaker sections in the Legislature and the Council of Ministers. In the 1972 Assembly elections, a large number of tickets were given to backward classes and minorities. The 26 members Ministry formed under his Chief Ministership had the largest number of persons belonging to the weaker sections (4 Harijans, 6 from the backward classes, 1 Girijan, 2 from the minorities—total 13). The upper castes had for the first time a markedly lower representation with only 4 Reddys, 2 Kammas and 3 Brahmins (total 9).

Impact. If caste politics, in the states of the Indian Union is examined from a comparative standpoint, it appears that Andhra Pradesh occupies the most conspicuous place. Harrison comments: "As an example of Hindu caste discipline in political motion, the post-war decade in Andhra merits special attention. Caste has played so fundamental role during this period that this examination becomes in effect a case history in the impact of caste on India's representatives institutions." A very notable feature of caste politics in Andhra Pradesh finds place in its blending with the forces of regional politics. It has added much height to the politics of the Telengana agitation. The people of a particular caste living predominantly in a particular region have given a caste-cum-regional complexion to an issue in question.

Haryana. Next to Bihar, caste exercises the single most important influence on politics in Haryana. Some of the classes and castes have a more or less set pattern of political behaviour. In a population of a little over about 10 million in the state of Haryana, Hindus are 89 per cent, Muslims less than 4 per cent and Sikhs 6.5 per cent. The four major caste groups among the Hindus are: Brahmins 12 per cent, Jats 23 per cent, Ahirs 8 per cent and Scheduled castes 22 per cent; others are Gujars 8 per cent, Rajputs 5 per cent and Banias 8 per cent. Castewise, the Jats are the toughest and constitute the single largest groups with the Scheduled Castes coming next. The latter are sharply subdivided between the Chamaras, the weavers and the sweepers. Of these, the Chamaras are the more numerous (18 per cent) and the more privileged in as much as they always obtained a greater share of political spoils.

Caste Groups. Besides being the most numerous caste group, the Jats are the land-owning class, they also supply the largest number of recruits to the army. They are traditionally imbued with the ambition of love of power and they have been basically anti-Congress, particularly because of the influence of the Unionist Party. But now there is a slight change in their voting behaviour. They vote not for a political party but for a candidate and in this respect the sub-castes become more important than caste considerations. An Ahir in the Gurgaon Mahendragarh areas, for example, would not easily vote for any party unless its candidate happens to be an Ahir. The same holds good for other caste groups in other parts of the state. There is a very telling local slogan heard during the elections which says: *"Jat ki beti Jat ko, Jat ka vote Jat ko."* in other words, just as a Jat's daughter should be married only to a Jat, a Jat's vote should go only to a Jat. The Ahirs and Brahmins, by and large (exceptions apart) are pro-Congress or anti-Congress according to the directive of Rao Birendra Singh and Pandit Bhagwat Dalyal. The refugees, by and large, were with the Jana Sangh but like the Jats, they also vote for the candidate. If the contest is between a refugee and non—refugee candidate, they will, by and large, vote for a refugee candidate whatever may be his party. If the contest is between the non—refugee candidates, then they prefer a Bhartiya Janata Party candidate. The caste influence is not confined to Hindus alone.

Jats. Thus, Jats as a community had been a political force in Haryana. They constitute about 23 per cent of the total population of the state and have a commanding position. As a community, the Brahmins have tried to Challenge their leadership. About Brahmins, it should be noted that their representation in the legislature is not very large but at the same time in the elections they have a substantial influence because in the first instance they are found practically in every village and as such they can exercise some influence. They also try to organise other non-agricultural communities at the village level and in every constituency. About the Jats, it should be noted that as a dominant community, they do not mind the leadership of other agricultural communities coming up except that of Brahmins. One of the reasons why they are not prepared to tolerate Brahmin leadership is that there is a basic conflict between these two communities at the village level.

Formation of Haryana. The result of the 1967 elections soon after the formation of Haryana in November, 1966 gave enough proof of his caste based voting. This was again the main feature of the mid-term elections to the State Assembly in 1968 in which voters did not vote for various candidates on the basis of policies and programmes of the political parties. Even the candidates also contested elections not on the basis of election manifestoes but on the basis of caste, sub-castes, agriculturists *vs.* non-agriculturists, local *vs.* refugees and among refugees, on the basis of the place of migration.

❐

9

Indian Political Process

POLITICAL SYSTEM AND FUNCTIONS

The term 'Political System' refers to a new way of looking at political phenomena which was previously covered in old texts under such terms as 'government', 'nation' or 'state.' It does not, however, mean that political system refers only to a change of name. It refers to something much more. It includes not only new names for old things, but also some new terms to refer to activities and processes which were not formerly recognised as being parts of aspects of politics. The older terms—state, government, nation—are limited by legal and institutional meanings. They referred to only the formal governmental institutions such as legislature, executive and judiciary. Political system, on the other hand, lays down that the role of formal government institutions is shaped and limited by informal groups, political attitudes and a number of interpersonal relationships. It directs attention to the entire scope of political activities within a society, regardless of where in the society such activities may be located. "When we speak of political system, we include all the interactions which affect the use or threat of use of legitimate physical coercion. The political system includes not only governmental institutions such as legislatures, courts and administrative agencies, but all structures in their political aspects.

In our modern times no political system can be either permanent or stable. If that becomes so, that is bound to degenerate itself and can conveniently be placed under the category of a state or degenerated system. Such a system is bound to create many lags in socio-economic systems as well. In fact, with the coming of awakening in every section of society all over the world, the systems have rapidly started changing and new systems quickly attract the attention of the people. It was a time when feudal system prevailed all over the world and that was gladly accepted by the people. It then became a way of life. But as the time passed religion became very powerful and even feudal lords accepted supremacy and authority of religious leaders. With the passing of time people became more conscious and demanded their share in running of administration of their own country. As is well known the old system always tries to persist and resist every change. The forces of status quo do not wish to disturb the existing order, as that does not suit to their interests. Each change is very likely to push the existing elites in the background and create a set of new set of elites who in all probabilities will challenge the dominance of the existing elites in all walks of life. This is what exactly happened with the religious elites with the passing of time. They too had to bow before the democratic system which became more and more popular. A society professing democracy in political and social as well as economic system began to be considered as the the most advanced society.

But again democratic system lost the imagination of the people. It came under severe criticism. Today, it is believed by many that democracy is in crisis. Its disadvantages have come to the front and every society is focusing its attention on these now.

With the dawn of present century socialist system and pattern of society caught the imagination of the poor and working classes. The followers of communism began to believe, rather strongly, that democracy is a method of maintaining status quo by the rich, so that they can continue to exploit the poor and weaker sections of society. The system being expensive can not be of any use to those who live from hand to mouth and have no time to get political education. It was and still is being argued that democracy never has been an instrument of peaceful socio-economic change, but a system of perpetuating the existing order which favours the rich as against the poor.

But these days there are so many new systems which are coming to the front and are being tested for their acceptability. These include Fabianism, State Socialism, Syndicalism, Anarchism, Guild Socialism, Gandhism and many others to count. Each new system, has some salient characteristics, which appeal to different sections of society. In fact, each political philosopher who expounds a new political system and ideas has an innovative mind and wants to give currency to his ideas.

No political system, both in the East as well as West, is by nature and character static but always dynamic. In fact, it can be said that it is one of the most important and universal characteristics of a political system.

Before actually discussing about political system in India, it is better to understand as to what is a political system. Why at all a political system does not remain static, what is concept of a system and what are its salient features? Other allied problems connected with a system are as to what are the functions of a system and what is meant by system persistence.

The idea of 'system' started quite some time back in natural sciences when natural scientists started using this word to establish and stress their view point. Even among the natural scientists, physicists and biologists than the others very much used this word. Among the social scientists Anthropologists as well as Sociologists started using this term and in fact they borrowed this from natural scientists. In so far as Political Science is concerned, Political Scientists used this term only in the fifties of this century. It was only in 1956 that the Society For the Advancement of General System Research was set up. But first important attempt to study political systems on the basis of systems theory was made by David Easton and Gabriel Almond. The others who made some efforts in this regard included Mitchell, Karl Deutsch, Richard Synder and Kaplan. In this way system concept became an integral part of political science.

SYSTEM DEFINED

But what is a system? In simple language system includes those individuals and articles which influence and are influenced by changes. Von Bertalanfy is of the view that system is nothing else but such facts which are close with each other under the influence of interactions. Friedrich has defined political system by saying that, "When several parts of that are different and distinct from each other compose a whole bearing, a defined functional relation to each other, which establishes a mutual dependence of these parts upon each other, so that the destruction of one entails the destruction of the whole, then such a constellation shall be called a system." According to Almond and Pawell, "The political system includes not only governmental institutions such as legislatures, courts and administrative agencies but all structures in their political aspects." In this ways system includes all actions which are inter-connected, influence as well as are being influenced by each other. Viewed from this angle the system prevails every where, may that be our solar system, circulatory, digestive or nervous system. We know that our digestive system can work well only when other parts and systems of the body inter-act with each other. Exactly this can be said about other parts of the body as well.

In a social system the individuals influence as well as get influenced from each other. A political system is linked with political roles and activities including pressure groups, participation in elections and in enactment of legislative measures. In other words, it can be said that an individual is concerned as well as very much associated with those activities which are inter linked with each-other and not with those which have either no connection or no link with each other.

Political system is a set of inter-related variables and a legitimate order for maintaining or transforming a system in the society. It is associated with the use of legitimate physical coercion in societies. But at the same time a political system cannot itself on physical force alone.

PROPERTIES OR MERITS OF POLITICAL SYSTEM

Now let us discuss the properties or Merits of political system. These are:

(1) Use or Threat of Use of Legal Coercion. Common to most defintions political system is distinguished by its power to use legitimate force in society. If Easton speaks of "authoritative allocation of values," Kaplan of "severe deprivations" Dahl of "power", "rule" and "authority." All these definitions imply legitimate, heavy sanctions; the rightful power to punish, to enforce to compel. We may as such agree with Max Weber that legitimate force is the thread that runs through the action of the political system giving it a special quality and importance, and its unity as a system. The political authorities have some generally accepted right to utilize, force and command obedience based upon it. Thus, public recreation facilities are usually supported by taxation, and violation of the regulations governing their use is legal offence. However, it must be pointed out that political system is not solely concerned with force, violence or compulsion.

(2) Interactions. The political system includes not only governmental institutions such as legislatures, courts, and administrative agencies but all structures in their political aspects. Among these are traditional structures such as kinship ties and caste groupings; and anomic phenomena such as associations, riots, and demonstrations; as well as formal organisations, like parties, interest groups, and media of communication. Almond in his book, "The Policies of Developing Areas" writes, "Political system is that system of interaction to be found in all independent societies which performs the functions of integration and adaptation (both internally and vis-a-vis other societies) by means of the employment or threat of employment, or more or less legitimate physical compulsion." The political system includes interaction between all the formal and informal institutions. The process of interaction is divided into three phases—input, conversion, and output. The inputs and outputs which involve the political system with their social system are transactions between the system and its environment. The conversion process is internal to the political system. The process of interaction roles, structures and subsystems and of underlying psychological propensities which affect these interactions may be viewed as consisting of inputs from the environment or from within the political system itself, the conversion of these inputs within the system, and the production of outputs into the environment.

(3) Comprehensiveness. Political system is comprehensive in the sense that it includes all interactions between formal and informal institutions in a given society. It includes the interaction of regionalism, regional economy, pressure tactics, party politics, social change through modernisation on the governmental institutions and the like.

(4) Interdependence of Parts. A system implies the interdependence of parts, and a boundary of some kind between it and environment. By "interdependence" we mean that when the properties of one component in a system change, all the other components and the system as a whole are affected. In political system the emergence of mass parties, or media of mass communications, changes the performance of all other structures of all the system and affects the general capabilities of the system in its domestic and foreign environments. In other words, when one variable in a system changes in magnitude or in quality, the others are subjected to strains and are transformed.

The emergence of trade unions in a political system affect the political parties, the electoral process, the legislature, the bureaucracy and the judicial system. Say, for instances, inflation has occurred in a political system. This inflation will compel the trade unions to demand more wages for their members. If this demand is not acceded to, it may lead to strike which may be even prolonged and take violent turn. Police help may be sought to restore law and order, and serious efforts made to resolve the deadlock. But, if these efforts fail, the management may declare lock-out. At this moment, government will be obliged to take active steps in bringing about reconciliation between the trade union and management. The government can appoint a tribunal or reconciliation committee consisting of the representatives of the labour, the management and the state. In order to ward off against the threat of lock-out and lay off by the management, the government may be obliged to pass legislation.

(5) Motion of Boundary. Yet another aspect of the concept of system is motion of boundary. A system starts somewhere and stops somewhere. In considering an organism or an automobile, it is relatively easy to locate its boundary and to specify the interactions between it and its environment. The gas goes into the tank and the motor converts it into revolutions of the crankshaft and the driving wheels, and the car moves on the highway. In dealing with social systems, of which political systems are a class, the problem of boundary is not easy. Social systems are made up not of individuals, but of roles. A family, for example, consists of the roles of mother and father, husband and wife. The family is only one set of interacting roles for its members, who also may have roles outside the family in schools, business firms, and churches. In the same sense a political system is made up of interacting roles of nationals, subjects, voters, as the case may be, with legislators, bureaucrats, and judges. The same individuals who perform roles in the political system perform roles in other social system such as economy, the religious community, the family and voluntary associations. As individuals expose themselves to political communication from interest groups vote or pay taxes, they shift form non-political to political roles. One might say that one election day citizens leave their farms, plants and offices to go to the polling places. They are crossing the boundary from the economy to politics.

FUNCTIONS OF POLITICAL SYSTEM

A political system performs certain functions. These are:

1. Input functions (Political functions); and
2. Output functions (Governmental functions).

1. INPUT FUNCTIONS

David Eston classifies input functions into two types—demands and supports. Almond and Powell further classify and elaborate demands and supports. They classify demands into:

(1) Allocation of goods and services, such as demands for wages and hour laws, educational opportunities, recreational facilities, road and transportation;

(2) Regulation of behaviour, such as provisions for public safety, controls over markets and rules pertaining to marriage, health and sanitation;

(3) Communication and information, such as demands for the affirmation of norms, the communication of policy intent from policy elites, or the display of majesty and power of the political system in time of threats or on ceremonial occasions.

(4) Participation in the political system, such as the right to vote, to hold office, to petition government bodies and officials, and to organise political associations;

Similarly, the examples of supports are:

(1) Material supports, such as the payment of taxes or other levies, and the provision of services as labour on public works or military service.

(2) Obedience to law and regulations;

(3) Participatory supports, such as voting, political discussion, and other forms of political activity;

(4) Attention paid to government communications, and the manifestation of deference or respect to public authority, symbols and ceremonials.

While Inputs are divided into demands and supports by David Easton, Almond calls them:

(1) Political Socialisation. Political socialisation refers to the process of recruiting individuals into political roles and to give them training in citizenship. It is a process of the induction of individuals into political culture. All political systems perpetuate their cultures and structures through such agencies as family, church, schools, work groups, voluntary associations and media of communications. Political socialisation which is the "process of induction into the political culture" results in putting in the members of the political system a set of attitudes or orientations towards the political system. The process of socialisation may be latent or manifest, specific or diffuse.

(2) Political Recruitment. Political recruitment starts where political socialisation leaves off. It recruits members of the society out of particular sub-cultures—religions, status, class, caste, and the like—and inducts them into the specialised role of the political system, trains them in appropriate skills, gives them political values, expectations and effects. It is thus concerned with the recruitment of citizens into the specialised roles of the political system.

(3) Interest Articulation. The function of interest articulation is closely related to the function of political socialisation. It is particularly important among the input functions because it differentiates clearly between the society and the political system. Almond has defined interest articulation as "the process by which individuals and groups make demands upon the political decision-makers. It is the first functional set up in the political conversion process." If groups within a society do not find proper channels, through which they may express their interests and needs, these will remain unsatisfied. Consequently, disaffection may erupt violently which may have to be suppressed the elite.

(4) **Interest Aggregation.** Every political system aggregates or combines the interests, claims and demands which have been articulated by the interest groups of the polity. Interest aggregation or combination achieved by the formulation of general policies based on the reconciliation and combination of various interests. It may also be achieved by the recruitment of political personnel who are more or less committed to a particular pattern of society.

In some systems the aggregation functions may, however, be performed by the legislature, the executive, the bureaucracy, the media of communication, the interest group (especially of the general or civic type) as well as by political parties. Party system is, however, distinctly modern structure of political aggregation.

(5) **Political Communication.** Political communication, according to Almond, is the crucial boundary maintenance function. Autonomy in the media makes for a free flow of information from society to polity and from one political structure to another, as well as an open feedback from output to input again. It can communicate the articulation of interest emanating from political parties, legislatures, and bureaucracies which themselves can correct the actions of interest groups.

2. OUTPUT FUNCTIONS

These means the functions performed by government in response to the inputs or political function:

(1) **Rule-Making.** Rule making is what was known as legislation. The term rule-making has been perferred over legislation because it depicts specialised structure and explicit process as compared with latter. Rule-making process is present in some form or the other in all political systems. In the simpler types of political systems the structures or institutions which are involved in the making of rules may be groups of adult males. These groups preserve traditions. In patrimonial kingdoms the rule-making structure may consist of political rulers such as kings or council of officials etc.

(2) **Rule Application.** Rule application is what was known as execution. Rule application means the enforcement of rules which have been made available to the society in one form or the other. The problem that arises is how to gather resources for the effective enforcement of rules and processes as well as transmit information. Application of rules means in modern society high degree of administrative capability in which role and importance of bureaucracy has considerably increased. Moreover, rule application also means search for goals and policies on the one hand and their interaction on the other.

(3) **Rule-Adjudication.** Rule-adjudication is what was known as judiciary. It means that rules are not violated. If violated, penalties must be specified and imposed. Rule adjudication is closely associated with judicial structures. Rule adjudication seeks to resolve the conflicting situation. It provides a means of resolving conflict within the system without expanding the pressure on the rule-makers to make new laws.

SCOPE OF INDIAN POLITICAL SYSTEM

Indian Political System is thus brief survey of socio-economic culture, political processes and constitutional developments operating in India since pre-Independence days. The Constitution of free India and the role of politics thereunder has developed over the last one hundred years or so giving to the parliamentary and federal institutions in the constitutional sphere alongwith the national re-awakening and separatist trends in the socio-political sphere. Quite distinct from 'Constitutional History of India', the emphasis on 'Indian Political System' now deserves to be laid on socio-political aspects ignoring not the constitutional aspect which is the legal manifestation of this phenomenon. The Constitution of the free India is be studied not from the narrative perspective but from its actual working—in its causes of amendment, the role of independent or conversely that of committed Judiciary, the reversal by the Supreme Court of its own ruling in the Golak Nath case, the role of the President in Indian Government if no political party has a clear majority in the Lok Sabha, the role of the Prime Minister since split in the Congress, the role of Governors with the inception of defections, etc.

This, however, covers only the constitutional aspect of the Indian Political System after independence. The role of socio-political forces like religion, caste, language, regionalism on the working of political institutions and forces working for and against parliamentary and federal institutions need special mention. Major attention need be paid to the party system, factionalism, defection and voting behaviour of the Indian people. In additon to political parties, pressure or interest groups also play a dominant role in Indian political system. It is not only the politicians that run a country but also the bureaucracy whose role has to be studied. But democratic administration without grassroots is always shallow and short-lived. Emphasis has, therefore, to be placed on the role of Panchayati Raj in India.

POLITICAL PARTY ELEMENTS

The rejection of the traditional view of politics as party politics, nevertheless does not mean the rejection of the view that party politics is a major aspect of politics. It is through political parties that the struggle for power takes place. Political parties, though extra constitutional in nature, always play a leading part in every political system, and more particularly in every democratic political system. These are the instruments which perform the function of interest aggregation and transform the demands into policy alternatives. They play a key role in the political functions of adaptation and integration. These are the vital channels of political communications which transmit two way informations from people to the government and vice-versa. Without political parties, elections cannot be held, government-making cannot be effectively pursued, law-making can be jeoparadised, political communication process can suffer a big decline and government can behave arbitrarily, public opinion can remain ambiguous and confused peoples support to the government can decrease and opposition to government can become anomic and harmful, and the functioning of the political system can become difficult, inefficient and unstable. No wonder then Sigmund Newmann writes, "Political parties are the life lines of modern politics." Finer observes, "Without political parties an electorate would be either impotent or destructive by embarking on impossible policies that would only wreck the political machinery." Infact, we cannot conceive a political system without political parties. Political systems are considered democratic only when people have the right to organise their political parties and only when in reality at least two parties are involved in the struggle for power. Political systems with one party system are not accepted as really democratic systems. Munro is right when he says "No Party, No Democracy" and that "Government by free political parties is merely another name for democratic government."

Political Party. A political party can be defined as a party of the people, organised on the basis of an ideology, which is always keen to get power and remains continuously involved in the process of politics. Its final aim is to secure political power in the state and to use this power for making and implementing authoritative values for the entire society. It is an extra constitutional political structure which plays an active part in a politics. Political parties are called extra constitutional structures because they grow naturally in the political system, they are not parts of the machinery of government as laid down by the constitution and yet they play an important part in the making and functioning of the government.

The following definitions, as given by eminent political scientist, project a clear picture of the meaning of a political party.

(1) In the words of MacIver, "Political Party is an association organised in, support of some principle or policy which, by constitutional means endeavours to make the determinant of government."

(2) According to Gettel, "A political party consists of a group of citizens, more or less organised, who act as a political unit, and who by the use of the voting power aim to control the government and carry out their general policies."

(3) Shumpeter, however, rejects Burke's definition and instead defines a political party as "a group whose members propose to act in concert in the competitive struggle for political power."

(4) M. Duverger defines political parties as "groups organised for the purpose of achieving and exercising power within a political system."

FEATURES OF A POLITICAL PARTY

On the basis of the above definitions of a party system, we can identify several essential features of a political party. Any organisation of people which reflects these features can be accepted as a political party.

(1) A Fairly Large Group of People. A political party is a group of people fairly large and organised. It is a whole which consists of several groups of people, young and old, rich and poor, landlords and workers, men and women, liberals and conservatists, leftists and rightists, all are members of a political party, some work as ordinary members others as active leaders and still some others as supporters sympathisers.

(2) Agreement on Basic Principles. A political party is then a group of people. The basis of unity of this group is shared political ideas, beliefs and attitudes.Faith in a political ideology provides the basis for the unity of the members of the political party. Each party considers itself separate from others because it has an agreed set of ideas, principles and programmes which are different from others. The members of a party hold similar views on public issues. Commitment to an ideology or programme, however, does not rule out the existence of differences of opinion among the groups of members which are always present in every political party. The faith in agreed principles or a common political ideology is a source of strength for the unity and operationability of the party. It enables a political party to participate in the political struggle in a concerted way and to achieve the desired goal *i.e.*, political power.

(3) Active Participation in Politics. A political party is always actively involved in the political process and at all the levels–inputs, conversion and output, local, regional and sanctional. It plays a special role in interest aggregation, which involves the conversion of demands into policy alternatives. Political parties play a key and deterministic role in elections and in the working of legislatures.

(4) Organisation. A political party is essentially an organised association of people. There is a party constitution which defines the aims, objectives, policies and organisational structure of the party. Without proper organisation no party can exist and operate in the struggle for power. Organisation gives order and strength to the members of the party through which they can pool their resources and abilities, and help the party to achieve its goal–political power or at least political support from the masses. It is the organisation which gives an enduring existence and coherence to the party that enables the members to be strong and act in concert.

(5) Promotion of National Interests. A political party always endeavours to promote national interests as distinguished from selfish interests, sectarian or communal interests. No doubt a political party has to secure material and power gains for its members yet the exercise has to be guided by self-interest viewed in the broad prospective of over-all national interests and not selfish or sectarian interests and, temporary political and material gains. Burke's conceptualisation of a political party as a body of men united, for promoting by their joint endeavours the national interests. ..." is very apt. When a political party directs its activities in furthering sectional interests and selfish ends, it degenerates into a faction. A political party has to work in accordance with the self perception that it is a part in a whole and that only through the satisfaction of national (whole) interests that it can secure its (self) interests.

(6) Faith in Peaceful and Constitutional Means of Conflict Resolution. A political party is a politically organised group of people which stands totally committed to secure the political power by peaceful and constitutional means. All political parties agree that peaceful and orderly political campaigns and movements, and finally the battle of ballot are the means for resolving conflict and for securing the goal of political power. Each political party always tries to carry out its policy by peaceful and constitutional means. Any organisation which resorts to violent and unconstitutional means for capturing power cannot be accepted and recognised as a political power.

These are the essentials of a political party. These can be used as variables for determining whether an organised association is a political party or not. Contemporary political scientists have tried to conceptualise the elements of a political party in a more explicit and realistic way. The central focus continues to consist of these five elements. Ideological unity and organisation are defined as 'partnership' and 'Separation'. Faith in constitutional means and active participation in politics is described as participation in decision making. National interest as the goal is defined as interests of the whole community. As such partnership, separation, participation in decision-making, unity in diversity, and national interests are the common characteristics of all the parties.

BASIS OF POLITICAL PARTIES

The origin and evolution of political parties is a universal phenomenon. In almost every society, political parties have been playing their due roles in their political systems.In some political systems several political parties are at work, where as in others only two or two main and some small political parties are at work. In most of the political systems with single political party it is through conscientious efforts and necessary legislation that other parties are not permitted to get organised. Party less political systems can be conceptualised but not operationalised. Even a modern dictator or military ruler and Civil Junta leader prefer to run the administration by organising and maintaining a party of their own.

The questions that need answers are. Why and how the political parties are born in a society? What is the basis of their organisation? What are the determinants of the party structure? In each society there are several determinants of party structure. Several elements provide basis for the organisation of political parties. We can study these factors by grouping them in four parts which can be described as the four basis of political parties. These are. *(1)* Historical Basis, *(2)* Psychological Basis, *(3)* Ideological Basis, and *(4)* Socio-Economic Basis.

(1) Historical Basis. In most of the societies, the emergence of political parties has been the result of the evolution of the states from monarchical to democratic states. The gradual emergence of the right to vote and consequently of the modern electorate paved the way for the emergence of political parties as the agencies attempting to capture power through the organised support of the electorate. The election system forced these agencies to organise themselves, to field their respective candidates in elections, to organise election campaigns in favour of their candidates, and to canalise voters support in their favour. Political groups or agencies as such, got the transformed into organised and separate political parties as part of process of meeting the necessities and opportunities created by historical evolution. These became mass organisations, and started performing the functions of political socialisation, recruitment, and representation, and came forward to develop institutions of their own and manage their affairs.

(2) Ideological Basis. 20th century can be legitimately described as the age of ideologies. Marxism, Communism, Socialism, Guild Socialism Fabinism, Fascism, Nazism,Democratic Socialism, Capitalism, Liberal Democracy, etc., have all been popular ideologies which have been serving as a basis for the organisation of political parties. In particular, Communism, Liberalism or Liberal Democracy and Democratic Socialism are the popular ideologies of our times, which have provided basis for the formation of political parties in almost every state. Within a state several political parties, each based on a particular ideology, are operating in the political process.

(3) Psychological or Temperamental Basis. Human nature is the first and foremost factor which gives birth to at least two types of parties–conservatives and liberals. Some persons are by temperament– conservatives, they do not go in for change but accept the change when it comes. Such persons often get organised into a political party–the conservative party. As against them, there are others who are by nature liberal, pro-change and reformists. They also organise themselves as liberals or progressives. In England, the births of the conservative party and liberal party took place on this basis.

(4) Socio-Economic Basis. Religion, race, caste, region, economic interests and needs are also determinants of party structure and these are collectively referred to as the socio-economic basis. Political parties in several states are based on religious or racial affinities among the people. Existence of such parties, like the Christian Democrates, the Akali Dal, the Muslim League and several other such parties are organised on religious or communal basis. Such parties often militate against the national spirit and develop bigotic, parochial, sectional and regional postures and outlooks.

Economic interests or conflicts of economics interests have always been a popular and more realistic basis for the formation of political parties. The different economic interests of the people– ownership of means of production, economic equality, equitable distribution of wealth resources, employment, social-economic security etc., are the vital determinants of political parties. Economic relationships or behaviour is a priority section of human behaviour. Politics has several economic roots. The ever present conflict of economic interests, individually or in combination with other sectors of conflict, provide a strong basis of division into political parties. Arthur Halcombe has rightly observed, "National parties cannot be maintained by transitory impulses or temporary needs. They must be founded upon permanent sectional interests, above all upon those of an economic character." The political parties such as Labour Parties, Kissan Dals, etc., are examples of parties organised on the basis of economic interests.

MERITS AND DEMERITS OF POLITICAL PARTIES

Contemporary human civilisation has unanimously adopted the system of differentiating between the rulers and ruled by means of election. For the conduct of real free and fair elections, the institution of political parties has naturally emerged as the means for securing the objectives of elections. In every civilised state, the elections in particular and the political process in general are basically the handiworks of political parties. There is and there can be no democratic state without political parties–Political parties are indispensable for the working of democratic government. Ranney has well said that "the political parties created democracy and that modern democracy is unthinkable without the parties." Munro has aptly remarked that "there can be no democracy without politics and no politics without parties. Political parties are the most important single links between groups, the people and the government in a democracy. These play an active part in almost every part of political system. Political socialisation, Leadership recruitment, Interest articulation, Interest aggregation, Political communication, Public opinion formulation, Elections, Law making, Law administration, Policy making, Decision making etc. Despite the fact of being extra-constitutional institutions, the political parties play a key role in all parts of the political process.

Merits. All the functions of political parties are in fact indispensable functions and can be stated as their merit. However, the following can be described as the main merits:

(1) Transformation in the Mass of Electorate into a National Force. "The parties", says Bryce, "keep a nation's mind active, as the rise and fall of the sweeping tide freshens the water of long ocean inlets. Discussions within each party culminating before election in the adoption of a platform, bring certain issues to the front, define them, express the informulas which fix men's minds on certain points, concentrating attention and inviting criticism. So few people think seriously and steadily upon any subject outside the range of their own business interests that public opinion might be vague and ineffective if the party searchlights were not constantly turned on it.

(2) ***Essential Instruments of Democratic System.*** Leacock contends that "Far from being in conflict with the theory of democratic government, it is the only thing which renders the latter feasible. For it is impossible for all the people to rule all the time taken singly. Now the only way in which any particular set of people can remain together as a majority and thus render possible a stable and consistent administration of public affairs, is that the members of the ruling group shall 'agree to agree' with one another.

(3) ***Means of Harmonising of Party Systems.*** They harmonise the organs of government. They give coherence to the very complicated mechanism of government established under the federal and state constitutions. To some extent they mitigate the disadvantages of the federal system, harmonising the policy of state and nation.

(4) ***Very Useful and Essential Role in Formulation of Public Opinion and Public Policies.*** Parties prevent popular prejudices to become incorporated in the legal code for all proposals and measures are fully discussed and criticised before they are finally passed as laws for the community. Thus it saves the state from some of the possible risks of direct legislation by the people.

(5) ***Parties Keep the Government Under Check.*** The party system also acts as a great check against domination. The parties hold the wheels of state in balance. According to Lowell, "The parties enable the people to hold the government in check. The constant presence of a recognized opposition, with a programme fairly within the limits of a possible public opinion, is a bulwark against the tyranny, not only of a despot but also of a practical majority."

(6) ***Source of National Unity.*** The parties have been instrumental in developing and maintaining a sense of national unity. The people in some political systems do not form a homogeneous unit. There are diversities of religion, of nationalistic origin and of economic interest. Political parties give order and coherence to the diversities.

(7) ***Vital Links Between People and Their Government.*** Political parties are the links, the vital channels of communication between the people and the government. They act as two way agencies–taking the demands of the people to the government and policies as the government to the people. In countries like U.S.A. where theory of separation of powers is followed, political parties have supplied the missing link among the various branches of government. Marriam also means the same thing when he says that "because of the scattering of governmental power it has been necessary for the party to gather the threads of control and bring them into a responsible Unity of Control."

Demerits. Along with having a large number of merits the parties have demerits also. Lowell refers to the following demerits of parties, particularly highlighting the inability of the political parties to form sound public opinion as the basis of the functioning of government.

(1) ***Parties are Always Dominated by Extremists or Demagogues.*** It is the extreme element that always leads the party; the moderate elements are mere hangers on. They only follow. They do not break away from the party because they can do nothing else. Hence, though disagreeing, they act according to the behest of the extreme element. This means public opinion remains falsified.

(2) ***Local Biases.*** Parties cause a bias and every voter is more or less attracted or repelled to such an extent that he is unable to form an entirely unbiased judgment either on questions of policy or on the merits of the candidates.

(3) ***Not Fully and Really Representative in Nature and Functioning.*** Sometimes the extreme element forces the hands of the leaders to do and say things which the latter do not desire. In that case too the real opinion remains unrepresented. The alternate domination of one faction over another sharpened by the spirit of revenge natural to party dissension, which in different ages and countries has perpetrated the most horrid enormities, is itself a frightful

despotism. It seems always to distract the public councils and enfeeble the public administration. It agitates the community with ill-founded jealousies, false alarms and kindles the animosities of one party against another.

(4) ***Parties cannot Reflect and Clarify Public Opinion.*** Two Parties specially involve only 'yes' or 'no' and many parties mean that a voter can say "yes" or "no" to only one proposition. This means that the differences are not integrated. Every vote is given not for the whole but for a particular cause. Public opinion thus remains distorted.

(5) ***Source of Divisions Among a Nation.*** Parties produce unnatural divisions and thus falsify public opinion. Men are not naturally separated by hard and fast lines into two or more compact groups, but present every kind of combination of opinion. Further, to maintain an outward unity, internal differences among members are not integrated; they are only not allowed to result in rupture and active dissension. Hence the apparent harmony or concord in a party is based on internal disharmony or discord among members.

(6) ***The Foreign 'Connexions' of Political Parties.*** Parties open doors to foreign influence and corruption, which find a facilitated access to the government itself through the channels of party passions.

Besides the above demerits of political parties, as pointed by Lowell, we can refer to the following other demerits:

(7) ***Unnatural Divisions in Societies.*** The parties divide the nation and the community not on basic issues but on artificially created basis. The agreement among the adherents of one party is as artificial as their disagreement with the opposing party is both artificial and unreal. Hence it encourages "hollowness and insecurity and members desert one party and join another, not because of their conviction but because of changing interests and growing desires". Moreover, the membership of each party is secured

more for the increase of mere numbers of its adherents than for the quality of membership.

(8) ***Not Fully Responsible.*** It has been asserted that party system has created double governments. The holders of governmental power and the other leaders of the party in power. The real governing power is without legal responsibility and is practically free from statutory and legal restrictions. Hence it makes a mockery of responsibility in the democratic government.

(9) ***Agencies of Corruption.*** Steffens asserts that the party system is an organisation of social treason "and the boss is the Chief traitor." People come to have confidence in him and he sells them to the magnates and corporations. This is why even some scholars repudiate the party system altogether and suggest the substitution of special and more elastic organisations for permanent and stereotyped parties–organisations which are to be limited to particular objects and which are to form and reform spontaneously according to the changing problems of life.

(10) ***Sources of Disharmony.*** It stirs up disaffection and dissatisfaction everywhere. Even Marquis of Salisbury recognised this defect of parties when he said, "Party discipline is a means to a great end, but in some emergencies and under some leaders it may be made to frustrate the end at which it aims. Take this great end away and parties become nothing but joint stock companies for the attainment and preservation of place."

(11) ***Increase the Role of Money in Politics.*** In big industrial countries party members are sometimes bought off by industrial magnates and corporations resulting in what has been called, "the invisible government" of the rich through the parties.

(12) ***Source of Undesirable Opposition and Criticism.*** Parties create factionalism as these "tend to make the political life of a country machine-like or artificial." The party in

opposition, as it is sometimes called the 'outs', is always antagonistic to the party in power or the "ins". President Washington was deadly opposed to political parties and he warned the Americans in these words. "Let me warn you in the most solemn manner against the beneful efforts of the spirit of party. Generally, this spirit unfortunately is inseparable from our nature, having its roots in the strongest passion of the human mind. It exists under different shapes in all governments; more or less stiffied, controlled or repressed but in those of the popular form it is seen in its greatest rankness and is truly their worst enemy. ... All obstruction to the execution of laws serves to organize a faction, to give it an artificial and extra-ordinary force, to put in place of the delegated will of the nation, the will of party, often a small but artful and enterprising minority of the community; and according to the alternate triumphs of different parties to make the public administration the mirror of the ill-concerned and incongruous project of faction rather than the organs of consistent and wholesome plans digested by common countries and modified by mutual interests."

ROLE OF POLITICAL PARTIES

Political parties are the major actors in the political process and the nature of political system depends, to a very large extent, on its party system. No modern political system, particularly no democratic political system worth its name, can work without a party system. As Bryce has observed, "no free and large country has been without them (political parties). No one has shown how representative government could be worked without them." Similar views have been expressed by almost all other political scientists. Allan R. Ball epitomises such a view when he observes that it is difficult even to imagine modern political systems without political parties. The conception of a party-less system of democratic government is really nothing but a utopia. The contemporary era of social evolution has accepted, almost unanimously that representative democracy is the only practical and useful way of organising the government.

'Government by the people' has come to be replaced by 'government by the representatives of the people. This transformation has made party system as the sine-quo-non of a political system, as the election of the representatives of the people cannot be effectively and really secured without the active participation of the political parties. Not only in the elections, but also in the operation of the processes of politics–law making, government-making, political communication, political modernisation and development, formulation of public opinion, political socialisation, interest articulation and aggregation, etc., the political parties play a leading role. Lowell has rightly observed, "The conception of government by the whole people in any large nation is of course a chimera for wherever the suffrage is wide, parties are certain to exist and the control must really be in the hands of a party that comprises a majority or a rough approximation to a majority of the people." Without political parties, the "disorganised mass of the people can neither elect their representatives, nor formulate principles nor even agree on a policy". MacIver accepts that without political parties "there can be no unified statement of principles, no orderly evolution of policy, no regular resort to the constitutional device by parliamentary elections, nor, of course, any of the recognised institutions by means of which a party seeks to gain or to maintain power." Parties play a crucial and all important role in involving the masses into the political process.

FUNCTIONS OF POLITICAL PARTIES

The important and absolutely essential role that political parties play in every modern political system, has been now recognised by all the political scientists. They all agree, as Herman Finer has observed that: "Parties are the power behind all thrones. Whatever the form of the states, parties govern by diverting the energy which moves the machinery (Government). Party has ceased to be the invisible government and has become not only the visible but the acknowledged government in democracies. Already it increasingly finds its place in statutes and written constitutions ..."

The role played by the parties can be examined through an analysis of the functions performed by them.

Several political scientists have tried to prepare a list of the important functions that politics performs in working of a political system. Simply stated, the political parties perform three major functions. *(1)* formulation of public opinion, *(2)* contesting elections, and *(3)* organising, running and controlling the government. S.L. Warby refers to the functions of a political parties, when he observes, "not only do parties choose candidates, they also assist in recruiting them, that is, they bring people into politics as well as help them choose between those already there. Parties not only winnow and present alternatives, but also stimulate those with view to exercise them through the vote, that is, they activate and mobilise. Another function is that of cue-giving and providing an evaluating device, the political stimuli in a complex society are so many and so complex that the average individual, who does not devote much time or (psychological) energy to politics might find himself in a chaotic situation if he had not some device whereby he could quickly label some ideas or candidates appealing, while rejecting others. The party label allows him to do this." Likewise Peter H. Merkel lists six types of functions which the political parties perform in a democratic system:

(1) Recruitment and selection of leadership personnel for government offices.

(2) Generation of programmes and policies for government.

(3) Co-ordination and control of governmental organs.

(4) Social integration of individuals or mobilisation of support by political socialisation.

(5) Societal integration through satisfaction and reconciliation of group demands or the provisions of a common belief system or ideology.

(6) Counter-organisation or subversion.

We can discuss the functions of the political parties under the following heads:

1. Formulation of Public Opinion. The first and most important function of political parties is to give coherence and meaning to the ideas, desires and ambitions and clarify the public will upon various issues and problems. In the words of Lowell, "their essential functions and the true reason for their existence, is bringing public opinion to focus and framing issues for a public verdict." They are the instruments for clarifying public opinion and thereby for making it possible for the government of the state to base or change its policies on the public opinion. "Political parties", writes Bryce, "bring order out of the chaos of a multitude of voters." Their primary task is to organise and clarify public will or opinion.

2. Agencies of Political Socialisation. Political parties play a vitally important role as agencies of political socialisation. Alongwith other agencies like, family, school and mass media, the political parties transmit the values and beliefs of the political system to the people. Mostly, it is through political parties that the people learn and act their roles as citizens and voters. Political parties play a vital role in securing the integration of an individual with his community. S. Neumann writes: "Parties transform the private citizen himself. They make him a zoon politikan, then integrate him into the group. Every party has to present to the individual voter and to his powerful special-interest group a picture of the community as an entity. It must constantly remind the citizen of this collective whole, adjust his wants to the needs of the community, and if necessary, even ask sacrifices from him in the name of the community."

3. Interest Aggregation. Political parties are the main agencies of interest aggregation. These are specialised aggregation structures of modern societies. The articulated interests are aggregated into a set of policy proposals or decisions by the political parties. They take these to the government for approval. They are the main channels of flow of aggregated demands into the political system. "In a competitive system", write Almond and Powell, "the party aggregates interests into a set of policy proposals and then attempts to gather a victory at the polls to install decision makers who will use the previously aggregated policy structure as a basis for rule formation. In non-competitive systems the party may aggregate interests in a manner similar to that of a large bureaucracy, although its structure and activities may enable it to perform other functions more effectively than a bureaucracy." Political parties, as such perform the function of interest aggregation in every political system. However, the nature of political system determines the nature and scope of such a role of political parties. "It is also true that some party systems aggregate interests much more effectively than others. The number of parties is a factor of importance. The two-party systems play a more vigorous role than the multi-party systems.

4. Interest Articulation. Though interest articulation is mostly a function of the interest groups, yet political parties, as the organised political structures working in the environment of the political systems, always play an important role in interest articulation. These help the people to sort out, clarify and specify their claims into demands. In political systems with single party systems, political parties with in built groups, act as agencies of interest articulation.

5. Political Modernisation and Development. Political parties act as agencies of political modernisation and development. This is particularly true of developing countries. In such political systems the political parties give a particular shape to government and the policies pursued by it. These provide the major links between various social and economic groups. These consolidate the human energies and resources into human power and use the organised human power for securing modernisation and development. The political parties, through their roles as agencies of political socialisation, education and training help the people to fix and then try to secure the goals of modernisation and development.

6. Leadership Recruitment. Political parties are the essential and ideal channels for recruiting leaders. In all political systems, democratic as well as totalitarian, leaders emerge through political parties. These provide necessary leadership education and training to its members, some of whom emerge as leaders. When the parties select and field their candidates, these really perform an important role as agencies of political recruitment. In two ways the political parties help this vitally important process of politics: *(1)* Political parties in offering their respective selected candidates out of a large number of its aspiring members, act as filters through which the competing type of personnel are sifted at the initial stages: and

(2) Political parties as organised and committed support associations provide the pooled resources to their candidates and help the latter to emerge as leaders. Almost all the leaders who come to occupy public offices are in a position to do so only because of the help of their respective political parties. In totalitarian political systems, only those members are in a position to emerge as leaders who are successful in completing their training at the party level.

7. Link between the Government and the People. Political parties are indispensable and crucially important links between the government and the people. These are the main channels of communication from the people to the government. They are continuously engaged in this role. These are the vehicles which carry the needs and wishes of the people to the government and in return for communicating the policies and decisions of the government to the people. They use the mass media and their local units to maintain active and continuous contacts with the local people and make them aware of various policies and programmes. Through this function the political parties, on the one hand, secure and nurse their support bases or pockets and on the other hand, educate, instruct and involve the people in the working of the political system. They constitute as many incoming connections (from the people to the government) as the outgoing connections (from government to the people)." The representatives of the people in the legislature are mostly political leaders who always use their participation in the legislative debates for voicing the needs and wishes of the people.

8. Policy Formulation. Political parties always play a major role in policy formulations. These bring order out of the chaotic mass of views and options by putting before the people their programmes and securing their approval on vital issues of policy. They plan and contest elections and endeavour to win by taking up positions on policy matters and presenting them as choices between parties. By raising issues, presenting alternative policies, taking sides and generating national debates on various issues, problems and policies, the political parties play an important role in policy making and actual implementation. They play a crucial role in opposing governmental policies which they think are not in national interest.

9. Role in Elections. A political party is an organisation committed to secure political power in the state through peaceful and constitutional means. The peaceful and constitutional means are available to them. In election a political party is always at work to contest the current elections or prepare for a future election. It is involved with the election process right from beginning to the end. It plays an active role in getting the elections held in time and in a free and fair manner. Each political party fields its candidates and actively works through an organised election campaign, to get them elected. It drafts and releases an election manifesto which forms the ideological basis for the conduct of party's election campaign. To contest and win elections is a major function of the political parties. Without elections there can be no democratic government and without political parties there can be no real elections. That is why it is usually said: "no party, no democracy."

10. Social Welfare Functions. With a view to secure and maintain popular support, the political parties work for the alleviation of the sufferings of the people during days of natural calamities like famines, earthquakes, epidemics, wars etc. They also undertake work for the eradication of social evils like dowry system, bride burning, ignorance, ill health, untouchability, etc. They take up literary drives, blood donation camps, relief camps, medical camps etc., for promoting social and economic welfare of the people. Through such non-political functions the political parties perform social welfare functions.

11. Government Making. Government making is virtually a party business. The party which gets majority in elections, gets the right to make the government in a parliamentary system. In a Presidential system, the election of the President the chief executive who runs the government, is really the handiwork of political parties. In every political system the parties act as legislators. The party leaders who get elected as representatives of the people, sit in the legislature and formulate laws. Even in totalitarian and dictatorial systems, the rulers associate, forcibly or otherwise, political parties with the working of the government.

12. To Act as Opposition. The party or parties which fail to secure majority in elections always play an active role as an opposition party. It takes up the task of criticising and opposing the policies of the government. It performs a key role in keeping the majority party in check and in enforcing the responsibility of the government to the people. Opposition is considered to be an essential ingredient of all democratic systems. It is particularly true of a parliamentary system of government. That is why, in it the leader of the opposition is granted a salary, an office and other such facilities as are considered essential for the due performance of his functions. He is given an official recognition and is respected as a possible future Prime Minister of the country. A political party, as an opposition party plays a very effective role in keeping the government on track and accountable for its acts of omission and commission.

13. Provide Opportunities for Alternative Government. In democratic and competitive political systems political parties provide alternative teams to run the government. They check the same people remaining in power too long and from looking on an office as a matter of right. A party system is a guarantee to the people that a change in government can be effected at any time if they wish it. It ensures that no group of leaders or party men are indispensable in politics and that leadership can be changed at any time. The party system always reminds the persons in power that the ultimate appeal rests with the people and they must always keep in mind those to whom they will have to account in the future as well as those who entrusted them with power.

14. Goals and Value Formulations. Parties play a vitally important role in setting value and goals for the society. Each political party works in accordance with an accepted political ideology which provides a philosophical basis to all its policies, decisions, programmes and activities. A political party, after internal discussions and debates, formulates goals and values which, it considers should be accepted and adapted by the society for undertaking guided, systematic and firm steps towards socio-economic and political, infact all round development of the people. Indian political parties, particularly the Congress, has been instrumental in setting forth the goal of Democratic Socialism before the Indian society.

15. Special Role of Political Parties in a Parliamentary System of Government. A parliamentary system of government is also called a party system of government because in it the government-making is done by the party which secures a majority of the seats in the parliament. The elected leader of the majority party is appointed as the Prime Minister and he forms his Council of Ministers, which again consists of the elected members of his party. The Council of Ministers headed by the Prime Minister wields real executive power in the state. The election manifesto and other policies and programmes of the majority party act as the basis for all governmental policies, decisions, programmes and actions. The party or parties which control minority of seats in the parliament act as opposition. The political process takes the shape of interactions between the ruling party (majority party) and the opposition (minority party/parties).

16. Special Role of Political Parties in a Federal System. In a federal system there is division of powers between the centre and states. The nature of centre-state relations depends, to a large extent, on the nature and role of party system. If the same political party is in power at the centre which is also in power in most of the federal units, the centre-state relations progress smoothly. But if the regional parties or parties other than the one which is in power at centre, are in power in the federal units, the centre-states relations are characterised by conflicts and tensions.

So, the role and functions of political parties, we would like to quote S. Neumann. He writes, "The primary task of the political parties is to organise the chaotic public will. They are brokers of ideas constantly classifying, systematising and expanding the party doctrines. They are representatives of social interest groups, bridging the distance between the individual and the great community. They maximise the voters education in the competitive scheme of at least a two-party system and sharpen his full choice." James Bryce highlights the value of political parties in the following words, "The parties keep a nation's mind alive as the rise and fall of the sweeping tide freshens the water of long ocean inlets. ... so few people think seriously and steadily upon any subject outside the range of their own business interests that public opinion might be vague and ineffective if the party searchlight were not constantly turned on." Despite the fact that parties polarise opinions, sometimes in dangerous ways, and divide the people into conflicting groups, it must be accepted that parties are essential and natural to all political systems. The demerits resulting from the operation of a party system are the demerits resulting from the weaknesses of human nature and several grave social economic limitations present in the environment of the political system and not the party system alone. These demerits, can be eliminated through conscious efforts. No political system, more so, no democratic system can work without a party system. As such, ever is attempt should be directed towards the improvement and not limitation of the party system.

POLICIES & PROGRAMMES OF BJP

The policies and programmes of the BJP may be enumerated under the following headings:

1. **Restoration of State Authority.** The B.J.P. manifesto promised to restore to out state its authority. The primary task, therefore, is to restore to the state, and to governance, its honour and its prestige—'izzat' and 'iqbal'.
2. **National Unity.** The party pledged itself to defend the unity and integrity of India. It believes that all Indians irrespective of language, caste or creed, are one people.
3. **Constitutional Reforms.** The B.J.P. will appoint a commission to comprehensively review the constitution of India, in the light of the experience of the past 50 years and make suitable recommendations. The commission will comprise constitutional experts and eminent parliamentarians.
4. **Positive Secularism.** The party stands for positive secularism.
5. **National Politics.** At the level of national politics, the party pledged to:
   (a) restore balance between the Centre and States as visualised by the Constitution.
   (b) appoint State Governors in consultation with the State Government.
   (c) enact anti-defection law.

6. **Fair Elections.** The party believes in introducing electoral reforms to make elections fair.

7. **Corruption.** The party believes that roots of corruption lie in political and electoral fields. Corruption must be put to an end particularly from the root level.

   The party promised to create an ombudsman, Lokpal and Lokayukta and to rationalise and streamline tax strucrture.

8. **Justice.** The party attaches highest importance to justice—that should be quick, expensive and just. The party promised to take effective steps to restore the independence, integrity and efficiency of the judicial system.

9. **Human Rights Commission.** The party committed to widen the scope of the present effective Minorities Commission and convert into a Human Rights Commission.

10. **Assam Problem.** The party pledged its resolve to solve the Assam Problem.

11. **Law and Order.** The party is committed to the security of life, limb, property and honour of all citizens.

12. **Police.** The party promised to implement the Police Commission's recommendations and modernise of the police force.

13. **National Economy.** In the economic there, the party pledged to:

    (a) reduce poverty, achieve full employment, maxmise production, stabilies prices, pull people above the poverty line.

    (b) encourage agriculture to attain self-sufficiency.

    (c) make public sector in industry more productive and profitable and demacrate the spheres of multi-national corporations, foreign companies, big industry and small scale industry.

    (d) Abolish octroi and sales tax and rationalise and simplify the entire tax structure.

(e) maintain price stabilty by efficient management of production and supplies and rooting out corruption.

(f) introduce nation-wide employment guarantee scheme.

14. **Facilities to the People.** The party promised a ban on cow-slaughter, provision of drinking water and electricity to all villages, more powers to Panchayats, liberal loans for house building and telephone connections to all on the waiting list.

15. **Salaried Class.** To give relief to the salaried class, it pledged to link salaries, even in private service, with the cost of living index, encourage employers to build houses for staff, progressively introduce pension schemes in all sectors of employment, lower life insurance premium, increase return on provident fund deposits, abolish compulsory deposit scheme and ensure payment of pension and G.P.F. dues within one month of retirement.

16. **Ex-Services.** The party pledged to work for the welfare of ex-servicemen.

17. **Scheduled Castes/Tribes.** The party pledged to exert its full strength in defence of Scheduled Castes and Tribes.

18. **Central Government Employees.** With regard to the Central government employees, the party desired that the Fourth Pay Commission should submit a quick interim report, order full and prompt neutralisation of all increase in the cost of living index, payment of all arrears of DA instalments and provision of residential accommodation to all government employees.

19. **Women.** The party pledged to implement the Report of the Committee on the status of women and to treat bride-burting injuries as an attempt to murder with a view to eradicating the evil of dowry system.

20. **Children.** They party pledged to do ever-thing possible for the welfare of children.

21. **Foreign Policy.** The party vowed to follow an independent foreign policy committed to world peace, disarmament and a new international economic order.

22. **Culture.** The party re-affirmed its commitment to freedom of it though and expression. It promised autonomy to All India Radio and Doordarshan.

23. **Quality of Living.** The party promised to raise the standard of living of the people. It promised to provide housing sites to the poor, free education to all children in the age group of 6-14 and to delink jobs from degrees.

INDIAN NATIONAL CONGRESS

Indian National Congress was established on 28 Dec., 1885. Sir A.O. Hume, a British Civil Officer played dominant role in the establishment of the Congress. The nature and character had not been uniform throughout its history. Early Congressmen were moderates and supporters of British Raj in India. In every annual session of the Congress, the Britishers were praised and the British Raj in India was eulogised as a blessing-in-disguise in India. The moderates believes in constitutional methods for the achievement of their objectives. They never demand independence of India from the foreign rule. What they wanted was the introduction of some administrative reforms and the Indianisation of the administration in India. After 1905, a group of extremists or revolutionary nationalists overtook the congress. The growing influence of extremists within the Congress led to its split in 1907 at Surat. The split of the Congress into two parts changed its character altogether. The reunion of the Moderates and the Extremists took place in 1916, and agian the character of the Congress underwent a profound change. Mahatma Gandhi entered the Indian political scene in 1919 and continued to dominate it till India achieved her indendence. It was Mahatma Gandhi who made the Indian National Congress a party of the masses. Alongwith it, the national struggle for freedom too became a mass movement. It was the Congress which led the national movement to its logical end and India was freed in August, 1947. After independence, the Indian National Congress ruled the country for a very long time. Though Mahatma Gandhi wanted that after the achievement of independence, the Congress should be dissolved, but this did not happen.

So far as the legacy and vision of the Congress are concerned, it can be said without any reservation that the Congress inherited a very rich legacy from its history. It is because of that legacy that the Indian National Congress has been successfully confronting many ups and downs in its political history. There is no doubt that present Congress has almost given up all those high ideals which inspired the Congressmen of pre-indepdent India. The Congress is no longer a movement in itself, rather it has become a political party like other parties. The vision of Congress of pre-independence India was largely responsible for the achievement of country's independence. It was the vision of the Congress which was largely responsible for the efficient working of the government in the initial years of India's independence. Had the Congressmen continued keeping the same vision which animated the Congressmen of pre-independence India, the country would not have seen the decline of the national values in so many ways.

COMMUNIST PARTY OF INDIA

The Communist Party of India is the "political party of Indian working class, is its vanguard and most organised detachment, the highest from of its class organization". It is the second largest party in the country not merely in terms of seats won but also in terms of votes polled. It is now the main opposition party in the Parliament with 29 seats in the Lok Sabha. It is the first political party which formed the Communist government in one of the State of India, i.e., Kerala and acquitted itself creditably from April 1957 to July 1959.

Origin. In India, the Communist Party was first founded in 1924, but was declared illegal by the Government of India. Consequently, most of the communist workers carried on their work through the Congress. They devoted themselves to the formation and organisation of trade unions and students movements. During August movement of 1942, the Communists betrayed the Congress by siding with the British Goverenment in India. This change in their attitude was due to he entry of Russia into the war agaisnt Germany. The Government of India also lifted the ban on is activities in 1943. Since then the Party has been functioning independently.

Policies and Programmes. The aim of the Communist Party has been the achievement of power by the working people, the establishment of people's democracy by the working class, based on the alliance of the working class and peasantry, and the realisation socialism and communism. It has always believed in economic equality, social justice and Marxism-Leninism philosophy. "It fights against all obstructionist conceptions and practices such as communalism, caste, untouchability and the denial of equal rights for women. The Communist Party uphods freedom of conscience, of the right of all minorities. It fights for rights and welfare of the people of tribal areas....Fighting against all separationalist and disruptionist trends and movements, the Communist Party struggles for balanced development of all regions, for equality and equal treatment for the people of all linguistic regions sure foundation of Indain unity." The Party philosophy is based on the teachings of Karl Marx and Lenin "which only show the toiling masses the correct way to put an end to the domination of exploiting classes and the establishment of a socialist. It combats tendencies of revisionism, dogmatims and sectarianism in all their manifestations."

The economic programme of the Party included:

(i) priority to development of heavy and basic industries and protection to national industries against foreign competition;

(ii) balanced economic development of various regions;

(iii) development of armament, aircraft and ship-building industries with a view to strengthen our national independence;

(iv) ceiling on profits of all big industries and taking over of profits in excess;

(v) state monopoly of foreign trade in the principal commodities;

(vi) free and compulosry education upto the age of fourteen;

(vii) provision of unemployment benefits and social insurance;

(viii) heavier taxation on corporation profits, tax on personal wealth and tax on capital gains;

(ix) fixation of minimum wages of workers, peasants and extension rural co-operatives;

(x) no compensation for the abolition of landlordism;

(xi) abolition of privy purses to Princes and reduction in the salaries of highly paid officials; and

(xii) setting up of peasants and agricultural committees to implement land reforms.

The political programme of the Party included:

(i) abolition of second chambers in the State Legislatures;

(ii) introduction of proportional representation in elections;

(iii) democratisation of administration in the Union Territories;

(iv) the right of the citiens to recal representative to legislature;

(v) abolition of Preventive Dentention Act and other repressive Acts;

(vi) active encouragement to trade unions;

(vii) encouragement to local bodies and institution of Panchayats;

(viii) making substantial provision for the welfare of backward classes.

(ix) recognising the right of collective bargaining through trade unions; and assuring trade unions rights to workers;

(x) workers' participation in industry; and

(xi) separation of judiciary form the executive.

In the foreign field, the Communist Party belives in Panchsheel and advocates peace and peaceful co-operation between all countries on the basis of full freedom and equality of all people and nations Imperialism is the chief target of its attack. A few years back, the Party believed in agitational direct strike and sabotage as the methods for the achievement of its objectives but today, because of revolutionary change in the Soviet Communist Party's thesis, it acknowledges peaceful methods and democratic means. Mr. Ajoy

Ghosh, former General Secretary of the Party, expressed his Party's agreement with the Soveit methodology at Palghal session of the CPI. The Party's constitution now provides that the Communist Party of Inida "striving to achieve full democracy and socialism by peaceful means. It considered that by developing a powerful mass movement, by winning a majority in Parliament and by backing it with mass sanctions, the working class and its allies can overcome the resistance of the forces of reaction and ensure that Parliament an instrument of the people's will for effecting foundamental changes in the economic, social and State structure."

The Party has abandoned its old policy of wholesale opposition to the Government on foreign and economic policies and has come out of it isolation to help the Congress in the implementation of planned economic development programmes. As the Party did not acquit itself well during China's agreession on tibet and India and did not condemn the agressor in unequivocal language, it suffered a great set back and had fallen in the estimation of the masses. Perhaps, it took two decades or even more before the Party could retrieve its lost prestige in our country.

POLITICAL CONSENSUS

Consensus is virtually a soul of democracy. The spirit and letter of democracy implies a certain understanding among people, about sorting out and solving their problems of life. Bullet power is replaced by the ballot power in a real democracy. Political parties come out with their principles and programmes. The make alliances on the basis of a common programme, which is another form of consensus. Conflicts are resolved either on negotiation table or through elctoral victory or defeat.

Land of Political Consensus. The working of democracy in India for about 150 years suggests that India has had a wonderful experience of democracy with a remarkable stability and continuity. Tensions and crisis that have rocked other political systems in its neighbourhood and beyond have failed to do damage to our system of democracy. The greatest achievement of Indian democracy is that it has survived unfractured for forty-eight years. More than nine hundred million people—more than the combined population of Africa and Sourth America—live together as one political entity under conditions of freedom as living model of Consensus.

As Nani Palkhivala wrote in his book, "We, The Nation": Never before in history, and nowhere else in the world today, has one-sixth of the human race existed as a single free nation. "The achievement is all the more creditable, since no other democracy has had such diversity in unity, such a mosaic of humanity." There are twelve great religions in the World and all the twelve flourish in India. We have eighteen major language wirtten in different alphabets and derived from different roots; and, for good measure, our people—whom you can never call taciturn—express themselves in 250 dialects. English, which is not included in the major language listed in the Constitution, yet continues to be the only link language for the whole country.

Constitutional Features of Consensus in India. The word 'Democratic Republic' in the Preamble of the Constitution denotes in the first instance that India is a democracy. This implies free and fair periodic elections of people's representatives on the basis of universal adult franchise by an impartial electoral machinery, and the government is responsible to these elected representatives of the people. Thus, we have, of course, a representative democracy and there are in our Constitution no agencies of direct control by the people, such as 'referendum' or 'initiative'. The people in India are to exercise their sovereignty through a Parliament at the Centre and a legislature in each state, which is to be elected on adult franchise and to which the real executive, namely, the Council of Ministers, shall be responsible. Though there shall be an elected President at the head of the Union and a Governor nominated by the President at the head of each state, neither of them can exercise any political function without the advice of the Council of Ministers which is collectively responsible to the people's representatives in the respective legislatures.

Social and Economic Consensus. The Indian Constitution promises not only political but also social and economic democracy. The justice in real sense can hardly be achieved if the democracy envisaged by the Constitution were confined to a 'political democracy'.

In the words of Pandit Nehru, "Democracy has been spoken of chiefly in the past, as political democracy, roughly represented by every person having a vote. But a vote by itself does not represent very much to a person who is down and out, to a person, let us say, who is starving or hungry. Political democracy, by itself, is not enough except that it may be used to obtain a gradually increasing measure of economic democracy, equality and the spread of good things of life to others and removal of gross inequalities."

Political Justice. Again we have adopted the universal suffrage and complete equality between the sexes not only before the law but also in the political sphere. In order to ensure the 'political justice' held out by the Preamble, it was essential that every person in the territory of India, irrespective of his proprietary or educational claims, should be allowed to participate in the political system like any other person. Universal adult suffrage, without any qualification, was adopted with this object in view. Again, this means that every five years, the members of the legislatures of the Union and of each state shall be elected by the vote of the entire adult population, according to the principle—'one man, one vote.'

Working of Indian Democracy. Under the leadership of Nehru and others, that vision took shape in the form of new political institutions. Arrangements were made to keep the armed forces out of politics. We adopted the British style of Parliamentary democracy. More, the diversities of the Indian people were carefully considered in designing the new federal system. The Congress Party took upon itself the task of fulfilling the democratic aspirations of the people. It reached out into village India to incorporate the previously immobilised masses. India's first elections were also held and they were held periodically thereafter. The Congress dominated the scene and dominance by a single party thus provided stability. It also accommodated the new forces in the society. The party's five-year plans stressed a mixed economy model of development that sought economic growth, self sufficiency and a modicum of wealth redistribution. The Congress Party professed the twin principles of nationalism and democratic socialism. So it hoped to bring the poor and the oppressed masses into the mainstream of India's democratic process. But these were the euphonic times in India, as new beginnings often are.

Erosion of Consensus. Successive governments, however imposed mindless socialism on the nation, while the spirit of social justice was left to chance. We built up state-owned enterprises, called the public sector in India. Most of these enterprises proved to be the black holes, and the money guzzlers and were festooned with red-tapism and corruption. From the very first decade of the republic, the permit-licence-quota raj were laid upon the national economy and even today their grip continues. Legal redress became time consuming and a law suit one started in India is the nearest thing to eternal life. As a result, nothing moves except the river Gangas. The recent spirit in public interest litigation cases and the arising judicial activism in India show how difficult it has become to rectify the things.

Decay of Political and Administrative Institutions. There has been decay and decline of political as well a administrative institutions. Thus there are very few mechanisms still infact of the resolution of conflicts in the society. There is rampant corruption at the highest level as is evident from a series of scams covering up in recent years. Even the Parliament has not functioned as a significant political body and there has been decline of ethical value amongst the members of Parliament. Many of them are corrupt, opportunists, defectors and criminals in some cases. All this has undermined discipline within the bureaucracy. the civil and police services have been politicized. There has been a breakdown of the civil machinery intended to enforce the land and maintain law and order. In order to protect themselves, the citizens in some parts of the country have begun organising private armies. The growing political violence has periodically brought the armed forces into India's political area and they are increasingly being used for suppression of the violence and the non-combatant roles.

Erosion of State's Authority and Power to Govern. In 1950s and 1960s, India was widely regarded as one of the few stable democracies in the non-western world. But today, the state's capability to govern has declined. Along with this decline, order armed authority have been fast eroding. Today, the Congress Party, India's major political institutions has lost its hegemony over Indian politics. The decline of Congress Party has not been offset by the development of an alternative national party.

Divisions of Social Structure and Political Violence. There has been communisation and criminalisation of politics. There have been growing attempts to build power bases and vote banks by dividing the people into narrow groups on the basis of religion; caste region, language and the like. Earlier, we could blame the British for their policy of 'Divide and Rule'. But now, after independence, our politicians are doing the same thing. They have developed vested interests in perpetuating various divisions in the society. Besides, the role of money and muscle power has also increased. There has been rampant violence and terror in several parts of the country. The new social groups have entered the political arena and pressed new demands upon the state. The agitation and violence that have resulted from these demands have been difficult to control. The result has been a dramatic increase in political violence in India.

No Parliamentary Democracy. It may be noted here that we adopted the British Parliamentary system. But it is not easy to transplant foreign institutions on native soil. Moreover, it is not necessary that a system that succeeds in our country would succeed in another as well. For the success of the representative Parliamentary democracy of the British type there are certain essential prerequisites which did not exist in India at the time of the commencement of the Constitution. The first requisite, for example, is that people should have become a nation. But even today we are struggling to become one and there is danger to the unity and integrity of us as a nation. Secondly, for success of parliamentary system of government, there must be a general commonality of interests and agreement on fundamental national issues. But it is difficult to interests and agreement on fundamental national issues. But it is difficult to pin-point any issues on which there is national unanimity or consensus. Thirdly, there should be a well-organised two-party system. But a healthy two-party system has not developed so far. Fourthly, there must be some economic stability and a certain level of prosperity. But we have nothing of that sort. There is still an object and mass poverty in

India. The leadership seems to have developed a vested interest in keeping the people poor, illiterate and backward. Unless the common man is provided economic security, right to vote is meaningless. Those who are educationally and socially backward and economically dependent, how can they be politically free or equal. When voters cannot understand the value of their votes and cannot appreciate national problems, to talk of representative Parliamentary democracy is a farce. In such a situation, representation goes to various vested interests—group leaders and gang leaders only.

Concentration of Power. There is also concentration of power in the hands of few leaders only. India's democracy is an elite-dominated democracy. And so when these elites fight to power, they mobilize different socio-economic groups. This mobilization is not the result of industrialization, urbanization, modernisation, literacy and so forth. Thus, whereas social mobilization is generally produced by economic development and modernization, elite-led mobilization often reflects pattern of inter-elite conflict. Thus, Indira Gandhi discovered India's poverty when she was pressed politically by other members of the Congress elite. Dev Raj Urs, Karpoori Thakur and then V.P. Singh discovered the backward castes when the desperately needed to establish new ruling coalitions. The Akalis began emphasising issues of Sikh nationalism only when thrown out of power. Now Kashi Ram has discovered Manuvada to be fought out.

CASTE AND MODERN PERSPECTIVES

The predominant feature of the social structure in India is the caste system. The caste system in its most general but fundamnetal aspects is an ascriptive system of status and hierarchy. It is pervasive and all embracing and is known for controlling and defining all social, economic and political realtionships, for the individual M.N. Srinivas opines : "Caste is so tacitly and so completely acceepted by all, including those most vocal in condemning it, that it is everywhere the unit of social action." A sociologist would define caste as a hereditary, endogamous and localised group having a traditional association with an occupation and a particular position in the local hierarchy of castes. It is a group of actual kins where every member of the group can be shown as the kin of another on a genealogical chart.

Caste at Political Level. The point which needs to be emphasised here is that for purposes of socological analysis of distinction has to be made between caste at the political level and caste at the social ritual level. The latter is a much smaller unit than the former. The policy of the British government providing a certain amount of power to local self-governing bodies and concessions to backward caste provided new opportunities. In order to be able to take advantages of these opportunities castes group entered into alliances with each other to form bigger entities. Gradually, the characteristics of and occupation of castes are weakening in cities and towns. Even the villages are experiencing a certain amount of change. This process has, however, been accompanied by the greater activity of caste in administration and politics. Adult franchise and Panchayati Raj have provided new opportunities for castes. In the course of exploitation of new opportunities, the caste system has undergone a certain degree of change. Numercially large castes have become important pressure groups in politics at the district and state level. The politics of Rajasthan will not make sense if we do not take into account the rivalry between Jats and Rajputs. Similarly in Karnataka there is rivalry between Okkaligas and Lingayats; in Andhra Pradesh, the chief competing castes are Reddis and Kammas; in Kerala, there is a triangular struggle between Nayars, Izhavas and Syrian Christians; in Maharashtra, Maratha Brahmin and Mahar; in Gujarat Banias, Patidars and Kolis, and in Bihar between Bhumihar, Kayashta and Rajput.

Caste in Historical Perspective. The word 'caste' derived from the Portuguese word 'casta' signifying breed, race or kind: humem de boa Casta is "a man of good family." The first use of this this word in the restricted sense dates from 1563 when Gercia do Orta wrote that "no one changes from his father's trade and all those of the same caste of shoe-makers are the same." To define a caste is more difficult than to give the derivation of the term. Risley defines it as "a collection of families or groups of families bearing a common name; claiming a common descent from a mythical, ancestor human or divine; professing to follow the same hereditary calling and are regarded by those who are competent to give an opinion as forming a single homogeneous community." The caste name is generally associated with a specific occupation. A caste is almost invariably endogamous to the extent that it is further divided into a number of smaller circles each of which is endogamous, so that a Brahmin is not only restricted to marrying another Brahmin, but to marrying a woman of the same sub-division of Brahmins. The words 'caste' and 'sub-caste' are not absolute but comparative in significance. The larger group will be called a caste while the smaller group will be called a sub-caste. Senart asserts: "A group which has the power to maintain its authority by means of a jurisdiction which, though rather attenuated, is capable of making the authority of the community effectively felt by the imposition of various penalties....such in epitome, as it seems to us, is a caste."

Varnas. According to Hindu tradition the caste system owes its origin to the four Varnas, derived from the Brahmin, who sprang from the mouth of the deity; the Kshatriya who was created from his arms; the Vaishya, who was formed from his stomach; and the Sudra who was born from his feet. The Brahmins were declared to be the chief because of their creation from the mouth. The Kshatriya were deemed vigorous because they were created from vigour. The Vaishyas were meant to be businessmen because of their creation from the stomach, the receptacle of food. The Sudra, because of his creation from the feet, were deemed to be the transporter of others. In this particular account of the creation, not only is the origin of the the classes interpreted theologically, but also a divine justification is sought to be given to their functions and status.

Aspect of Social Structure. Caste as a fundamental aspect of the social structure of India and the economic foundation upon which it is based, is a major parametric variable of the Indian political system. In the opinion of many thinkers, castes are assuming new functions like influencing politics and their role in political dynamics is gradually increasing. It is almost playing the role of an effective interest or pressure group at various levels of the decision-making apparatus.

Natural Product. Earlier European observers of the caste system were content to regard caste as an artificial creation, as a device of a clever pristhood for the permament division and subjection for the masses, or even as the creation of a single law-giver. Abbe Dubois speaks of it as the ingenious device of Brahmins and clearly regards it as made by, and for them. But is is not admissible to accept such an extremist view because so deeply rooted a pervasive social institution at the caste system could hardly have been imposed by an administrative measure. Nesfield regards occupation as the exclusive basis of caste distinction. It is the nutural product of society in the creation of which religion played no part at all. Dahlmann feels that caste sprang not from the four varnas but from the infinite number of corporations and of groups of realtives into which these four Varnas were divided. He argues that there was a steady progress of development from classes to corporations and from corporations to castes. Chandra traces the origin of caste to race and function; colour or race difference, real and fancied, together with hereditary functions, gave birth to the caste system. Whatever may be the history of the origin of the caste system, the institution of caste has been one of exclusive characteristics of the Indian society since early ages. Inspite of great changes in the history of India, caste has continued to be an important feature of Indian social life.

Caste in Modern Perspective. It is recognised that the traditional social system in India is organised around caste structures and caste entities. Hence, it is particularly interesting to study it implications on politics. Politics is a competitive enterprise, its purpose is the acquisition of power for the realisation of certain goods and its process is one of indentifying and manipulating existing and emerging allegiances in order to mobilise and consolidate positions. For that what is needed is organisation and articulation of support, and where politics is mass based, the point is to articulate support through the organisations in which the masses are to be found. It follows that where the caste structure provides one of the principal organisational clusters along with the bulk of the population is found to live, politics must strive to organise through such a structure.

The relationship between caste and politics reveals the politicised nature of caste in the context of Indian politics:

Politicisation

1. Caste provides an extensive basis for organisation of democratic politcs. The need to organise and articulate support in an open polity inevitably turns those engaged in political competition towards organisations and solidarity groups in which the masses are found. In a society such as India were caste remains the principal basis of social organisation and activity, this means turning towards caste groups and associations. In this way caste identity and solidarities became the primary channels through which electoral and political support is mobilised within the political ssytem. Thus, as Kothari puts, it, "it is not politics that gets caste ridden, it is caste that gets politicised.
2. Caste is used more extensively in mobilising support in rural than urban areas.
3. Political parties find it easier to mobilise support directly from the members of a caste community by appealing to them.
4. The communication of ideas is strong within a caste and generaly the members of a caste share the same view in relations to political parties, politics and individuals.
5. The present political system itself encourages or inhibits the use of caste as a means of breeding followers.
6. It has been recently argued that caste enables the illitetrate and politically ignorant masses of India to participate in the modern democratic process.

Political Mobilization. According to Rudolph and Rudolph, the relationship that caste bears to politics can best be understood in terms of three types of political mobilization, each suggestive of different phases of political development : vertical, horizontal and differential. Vertical mobilization is the marshalling of political support by traditional notables in local societies that are organised integrated by rank mutual dependence and the legitimacy of traditional authority. In India traditional elites were characteristically the leaders of locally dominant castes. They responded to representative government and popular politics by mobilising what local notables in Britain called their 'interest. Horizontal mobilization inovles the marshaling of popular political support by class or community leaders and their specialised organisations. Differential mobilization involves the marshaling of direct or indirect political support by political parties from viable but internally differentiated communities through parallel appeals to ideology, sentiment and interest.

Political Dimensions of Caste : Rajni Kothari's Approach. Everyone recognises that the social system in India is organised around caste structures and caste identities. In dealing with the relationship between caste politics however, the tendency is to ask the question : Is caste disappearing ? In reality, however, no social system disappears. A more useful qeustion would be : What form is caste taking under the impact of politics, and what from is political taking in a caste oriented society? Those who 'complain of casteism in politics' in India are really looking for a sort of politics which has no basis in society. They also probably lack any clear conception of either the nature of politics or the nature of the caste system. The process politics is one of identifiying and manipulating existing structures in order to mobilise support and consolidate positions. Where the caste structure provides one of the most important organisational clusters in which the population is found to live, politics must strive to organise through such a structure. The alleged casteism in politics is thus no more and no less than politicization of caste. By drawing the caste system into its web organisation, politics finds material for its articulation and moulds it into its own design. In making politics their sphere of activity, caste and kin group, on the other hand, get chance to assert their identity and to strive for positions.

Integration Dimension. Second, there is the integration dimension. The caste system not only determines the individual's social station on the basis of the group to which he is born but also differentiates and assigns occupational and economic roles. It thus gives a place to every individual from the highest to the lowest and makes for a high degree of idetification and integration. At the same time, it is an integration structure of a specific type, namely, one that is more intense in its small group orientation and particularistic loyalties and where wider loyalties operate only when they are structured through the prevailing differentaitions. This aspect is important in understanding the structural impact of democratic nation-building. For the competitive style of democratic politics involves group action and cohesion; democratic politics is as much a process of fusion as of fission.

Dimensions of Caste System. It the context of interactions between caste and politics, Rajni Kothari has pointed out that three aspect of the caste system call for special attention :

The first is what may be called the secular dimensions. In emphasizing caste as a stratification system in which distances are rigidly maintained through endogamy, pollution and the legitimacy of rituals, caste as a system of conflict and interaction has received sparse attention. Yet the fact is that functionalism and caste cleavages, patterns of alignment and realignment always been prominent features of the caste system.

Dimension of Consciousness. Third, there is the dimension of consciousness. Caste enters politics through the 'Consciousness aspect' highlighted by its symbolism and value structure. This is where symbolic gestures for cultural mobility such as 'Sanskritisation', 'Westernisation' and 'Secularisation' assume or disguise political overtones in their manifestation. According to Rajni Kothari, "It is not politics that gets caste-ridden; it is caste that gets politicized." The operation of competitive politics has drawn caste out of its a political context and given it a new status and identity.

GOOD EFFECTS OR MERITS OF CASTE-SYSTEM

It is customary to attack caste-system vehemently and to aspire for its abolition root and branch. But despite all this it has survived through ages. The very fact that it continues in spite of these attacks as before goes to prove that the system is not so bad as it is thought to be. It is definitely endowed with some virtues and it has left a good deal of wholesome effect on Indian society. To quote J.S. Furmovall, "The caste-system has afforded a place in society into which any community, be it racial, social occupational or religious can be fitted as a co-operating part of the social whole, while retaining its own distinctive character and its separate individual life". In short, mention may be made of its following good points:

1. **Helpful in the Preservation of Hindu Religion and Culture.** The first service of caste system has been that it has protected Hinduism against all kinds of odds. It is the caste-system that has been largely responsible for the preservation of Hindu religion and culture. The caste brotherhoods, on account of their policy of exclusiveness did not mix with the foreigners. So Greeks, Huns, or Muslims could not conquer Hindu Culture.
2. **Means of Social Insurance.** The caste provided a means of social insurance and promoted social-service activities. It made the individual learn the lesson of self-sacrifice and of subordinating the individual will to the collective will. Along with the guilds the castes enforced social and economic discipline among their members. Explaining this social function of the caste Hutton writes, "He is provided in this way with a permanent body of association which controls almost all his behaviour and contacts. His caste canalizes his choice in marriage, acts as his trade union, his friendly or benefit-society, his State-club and his orphnage, it takes place for him of health insurance and if need be, provides for this funeral".
3. **Helpful in Fostering the Spirit of Co-operation.** It has fostered the spirit of co-operation and fellow-feeling among members of the same caste. By helping the poor and needy, it has avoided the necessity of the State supporting the poor. It minimises envy and unhappiness and thereby promotes social harmony among the people.
4. **Sound Basis for Division of Labour.** The caste-system is based on the sound economic principle of division of labour which ensures efficiency of production. A person from his birth knew what profession he was to follow later

on. So from the start he devoted all his energy to the one profession of his forefathers. It was because of this reason that in every period of Indian history, there was no dearth of highly skilled workers and scholars.

5. **Provides for Various Functions.** Caste-system provides for the various functions necessary to social life. It divides society in different functional division ensuring the efficient performance of all kinds of functions. People of different castes perform their assigned functions and none of them ever seeks to deviate from their inborn functions whether high or low. Consequently all the functions in society ranging from respectable functions of priesthood down to the low function of sweeping the dirt are performed efficiently and automatically. To quote Hutton in this connection, "The caste-system does provide for the various functions necessary to social life, functions ranging from education to scavenging, from government to domestic service of the most menial kind and it makes this provision under the sanction of a religious dogma, the belief in Karma, which tenders the superficially inequitable distribution of functions acceptable as being part of the divine order of the universe and a transient episode in the prolonged existence of the individual soul, which by acquiring merit in one existence may rise in the scale in the next, or which may suffering from a degradation in caste merely by reason of its transgressions in a previous life".

6. **Helpful in Preserving Racial Purity.** It has preserved the racial purity of the higher castes by forbidding indiscriminate intermarriages. It has also greatly fostered the habits of cleanliness by insisting on ritual purity. There is no wonder that the caste-system has been responsible for preserving the purity of blood among the various groups of Hindus even up to this day. Each caste made rigid rules for marriages. Inter-caste marriages were forbidden and in this way India was able to preserve racial purity to a large extent.

7. **Influence on Intellectual Make-Up of the Individuals.** It influences the intellectual make-up of an individual. Since the caste dictates to each member customs to be observed in the manner of diet, the observance of ceremonies and whether he may marry a widow, his views on the social and political matters are bound to be influenced by his caste customs.

8. **Development of Country's Integration.** It develops class consciousness without breeding class struggle. It has created an efficient organization of Hindu society without giving any chance to class frictions and factions. It was the best device organised within one society people of different castes with different cultural levels. It prevented the country from splitting up into warring racial units. It integrated Indian society into one vast and variegated community whereby a stable and orderly organization of society could be possible. Commenting on this fact Hutton has said, "It will be understood then that one important function of caste, perhaps the most important of all its functions and the one which above all other makes caste in India a unique institution is or has been to integrate Indian society, to weld into one community the various competing, if not incompatible groups composing it".

9. **Helpful in Cultural Diffusion.** It helps in cultural diffusion within the group. The caste-customs, beliefs, skill, behaviour, the trade secrets are passed on from generation to generation. Culture is thus carried from one age to another. The ancient culture of India is alive till modern time and the credit of it is given to the caste-system. According to A.R. Desai, "It is the caste that rigidly determines the place of its members in religious life of the people".

10. **Separation of Social from Political Life.** It has separated the social from political life and has maintained its independence from political influences. S.C. Hill says, "His intimate life, the life which to the Hindu really matters is

altogether independent of the political conditions, which happen to prevail". It serves as a great church and maintains its own religious system by providing for the worship of caste gods. R.P. Masani beautifully writes "The concept of organic unity and interdependence ran through the whole caste-system even when it was sought to deduce divine sanction for the ascendancy of the superior orders on the hypothesis that the four castes had emanated from four different limbs of the creator of the universe, the underlying idea was not one of detachment but of union. Each unit formed part of the whole. Every one had, therefore to perform his duty towards himself and society at large while none was allowed to remain in want, each was under an obligation as long as he was able to contribute his share of labour, according to his capacity and calling for the benefit of society. Such an attitude brought all the castes, their beliefs, customs and activities under one common system. Every one found a place appointed for him; everyone had his legacy of the common tradition, common creed and common ethical code in addition to the special legacy of hereditary skill for the fulfilment of the part to which he was called. The system conduced to the solidarity of castes as distinct units of the social organization; it prompted effective association not only of the different members of each group but also of group and groups.

DEMERITS OF CASTE SYSTEM OR ITS EVIL EFFECTS ON HINDU SOCIETY

It is believed that the caste-system and particularly, the caste-system as it stands today has done more harm than good. Sir Henry Maine describes the caste-system, "as the most disastrous and blighting of human institutions". It has in fact given rise to a number of evils and there by it has rendered great disservices to Hindu society. This fact will become explicitly clear from the following arguments:

1. An Anti-National Institution. The fundamental draw-back of caste-system is that it has proved to be an anti-national institution. Caste prejudices and caste feuds have always dominated our history. At the time of grave foreign dangers, only a section of the people, the Kshatriyas fought against the enemy. Other castes, being ignorant of fighting, stayed away in their homes. This led to many great disasters. Caste rivalries were also responsible for many troubles in the days of the Rajputs and the Marathas. Rawlinson remarks, "By splitting the people into a number of water-tight compartments, the caste-system rendered the growth of a national spirit almost impossible and it was one of the reasons why India for centuries was at the mercy of foreign conquerors".

2. Social Division Based on the Principle of Birth Undesirable. A caste system based on the principle of birth is undesirable. The social divisions, according to Gita, should be based on "Guna and Karma", *i.e.* character and functions. The present grouping of Indian castes is based on birth and so it makes no provision for low born talents to rise and high born incompetents to occupy a low position. In this way, it is also open to grave and genuine criticism.

3. Obstacle to National Unity. It has proved an obstacle to the growth of national unity in the country. The lower classes feel discontented at the behaviour meted out to them in society. As Dr. G.S. Ghurye states, "It is the spirit of caste-patriotism which engenders opposition to other castes and creates an unhealthy atmosphere for the growth of national-consciousness".

4. Impediment to Co-operation Between Indians and Foreigners. According to V.A. Smith, one of its chief defects is that "it shuts off Indians from free association with foreigners"thus making it difficult for Indians to understand them. The upper caste particularly the Brahmans would not mix with foreigners and consequently created innumerable difficulties and often hindered hearty co-operation between the Indians and foreigners during the various periods of Indian history.

5. Obstacle to Social Progress. It is a great obstacle to the social and economic progress of the nation. Since the people believe in the theory of 'Karma', they become conservative. Again because their economic position is fixed, they are led to inertia killing their initiative and enterprise.

6. Cause of Narrow Outlook Among Indians. The caste-system has been responsible for the narrow outlook and caste exclusiveness. Till recently, the Indians lived according to caste customs and never bothered about the general affairs of the country. Castes hindered the growth of nationalism. On account of these reasons an average Indian is conservative and stay-at-home.

7. Root Cause of Untouchability. The caste-system has led to the evil of untouchability. In a caste-ridden society the low caste people are treated as untouchables and the high caste people do not like to have any sort of social intercourse with them. This problem is more particularly prevalent in India and has been eating into the vitals of Indian society. The Govt. of India has been forced to take special measures to eradicate this evil.

8. Responsible for Stagnation in Society. Some critics are opposed to caste-system on the ground that it has denied mobility of labour. Since the individual must follow the caste occupation and cannot change it according to his likes or dislikes he cannot progress in life according to his capacity and desire. This leads to stagnation in society.

9. Wrongful Placement of People Possible. The caste-system often results in putting man on wrong occupation. There is no guarantee that a priest's son would also like to be a priest or would possess the qualities for a successful priest. Under the caste system he cannot take up any other profession even though he may possess the skill and liking for that. It does not utilise fully the talents and capabilities of the population and is, therefore, a barrier to optimum productivity.

10. Opposed to the Spirit of Democracy. Caste system is anti-democratic and denies equal rights to all. A man cannot join any profession or calling. Nor does every man, high or low, enjoys the same privileges. Nor can he marry the woman of his own choice. All these are opposed to the spirit of democracy. It is quite unfortunate that social barriers are erected specially in the way of lower class individuals, who are not provided with opportunities for their physical and mental development. The low caste people enjoy no freedom of any kind and they have to lead very hard and restricted life. It is not in keeping with the present day democratic set up of society and this is why with the dawn of democracy in India caste system is fast losing ground.

WELFARE OF BACKWARD CLASSES

The term 'Backward Classes' is used to include Scheduled Tribes, Scheduled Castes, Denotified Tribes and other Backward classes. These sections of the community have laboured under distinct disadvantages in consequences of the rigid case ridden hierarchy that prevailed in the past in Indian social structure. They have suffered both from social and economic disabilities and have come to be known as Backward Classes. The population of the Scheduled Castes was estimated at 5.53 crores and that of Scheduled Tribes at 2.25 crores as a result of the issue of revised lists under the Scheduled Casts and Scheduled Tribes Lists Modification Order, 1956. Denotified Tribes numbered has given about 40 lakhs. It was fully realised that special arrangements would have to be made for them in order to bring them to a position of equality with other citizens. The Constitution of India, therefore, prescribed protection and safeguard for Scheduled Castes, Scheduled Tribes and other Backward classes, either speciafically or by way of general rights of citizens, with the object of promoting their educational and economic interests and of removing certain social disabilities, they were subjcts to.

Constitutional Provisions for their Safeguards:

(1) The abolition of 'untouchability' and the forbidding of its practice in any form. (Art. 17)

(2) The promotion of their educational and economic interest and their protection from social injustice and all forms of exploitation. (Art. 46)

(3) The throwing open of Hind religious institutions of a Public character to all classes and sections of Hindus. (Art. 25)

(4) The removal of any disability, liability, restriction or condition with regard to access to shops, public restaurants, hotels and places of public entertainment, the use of wells, tanks, bathing ghats, roads, and places of public resort maintained wholly or partly out of state funds or dedicated to the use of general public. (Art. 15)

(5) The obligation of the State to consider their claims in the making of appointments to public services and reservation for them in case of inadequate representation. (Art. 16 and 335).

(6) Special representation in Parliament and State Legislatures for a period of twenty years. (Art. 332, 333 and 334)

(7) The right to practice any profession or carry on any occupation, trade or business. (Art.19)

(8) The forbidding of and denial of admission to educational institutions maintained by the State or receiving aid out of the State funds. (Art. 29)

(9) The setting up of advisory councils and separate departments in the States and the appointment of a special officer at the centre to promote their welfare and safeguard their interests. (Art. 164, 338 and Fifth Schedules)

(10) Special provision for the administration and control of scheduled and tribal areas. (Art. 244 and Fifth and Sixth Schedules)

It may not be out of place to point out that out of total 543 Lok Sabha seats 79 have been reserved for Scheduled Castes and 79 for the Scheduled Tribes.

Besides reservation has been extended from time to time. Recently Mandal Commission envisaged more representation to the backward classes then they already enjoyed. this entailed violent agitation by the students & self molation, by them. It shook the very fibre of V.P. Singh's Government (J.D. Govt.) The Congress Govt. headed by Narsima Rao also stand for reservation though it takes into consideration economically backward classes as well. Reaction to this also is not very favourable. Twice, thrice, the students have resorted to closure colleges & schools and 'Bundhs'. It is yet too early to conjecture the outcome of Govts' move.

IMPLEMENTATION OF THESE PROVISIONS

(1) Measures to Eradicate Untouchability. Untouchability and disabilities arising out of it has been a peculiar problem of the scheduled castes. At the beginning of the twentieth century, the appaling, living and working conditions of scheduled castes and the growing realisation of the fact that the barriers preventing their growth and development are man—made, aroused human sympathy and the leaders of the country took initiative and interest in the emancipation of lower castes. Gandhiji, in particualr, focussed the attention of the people on the degrading effects of untouchability. He tackled the problem and brought in a great evolution in the minds of the people.

Untouchability has been legaly abolished. Various laws have passed by the State Governments to punish certain kinds of actions involving its practice. The Centre has passed the Untouchability Offences Act, 1955, which has made the offence cognisable and punishable under law, uniformly throughout the territory of India. But untouchability is still practised in many parts of the country particularly in the rural areas. It has been appreciated that while legislation alone will not achieve the results because the evil is intricately woven in the social fabric itself, it must be backed and regularly followed up by persuasion and propaganda for educating public opinion.

Since 1954 the Government of India has been accordingly giving financial support to the movement to eradicate untouchability. Both official and non official agencies are being utilised for the purpose. The State Government have instructed their district officials, who deal with the public to stress need for and the urgency of doing away with this evil. 'Harijan Days' and 'Harijan Weeks' are observed to focus public attention and enlist people's co-operation in the eradication of untouchability. Most of the States have appointed small committees to enforce, where necessary, the provisions of the

Untouchability Offences Act, 1955. Publicity media such as books, pamphlets handbills and audio-visual aids have also been pressed into service.

The assistance and co-operation and voluntary organisations such as the Harijan Sewak Sangh, the Bharatiya Depressed Classes League, the Bharat Dalit Sangh, Hind Sweepers' Sewak Samaj and Iswar Saran Ashram have also been obtained. A sum of Rs. 61,50,476 of which Rs. 14,77,200 came from the Centre, as given as grants-in-aid to these organisations during the First Plan period. The Second Five Year Plan envisaged an expenditure of about Rs. 208 lakhs as aid to non-official agencies for this programme of which Rs. 138 lakhs were provided under the States' sector and Rs. 70 lakhs under the Central Sector of the Plan. A sum of Rs. 125 lakhs was earmarked in the Third Plan for financial assistance to non-official agencies of all India status. To take the winds out of the sails, the Congress (I) Govt. has on Sept, 24, 1991 decided to maintain the 27% reservation in Central Govt. employment for socially and educationally backward classes (SEBC) giving preference to the poorer of the lot.

The Govt. has also expanded the field of reservation beyond the Central Govt. service to the fields of education and other economic opportunities in the spirit of totality of the Mandal Commission recommendation. Eight per cent of the quota of BCs would be reserved for the minority communities. Three per cent of the reserved quota for the poor among the upper classes would be kept for the higher castes among the minorities. Thus the Congress Govt. has retained 27% reservation formula of V.P. Singh's Govt. Just to steal the Janata Dal thunder. Yet it has sought to introduce the economic criterion in determining who among the BCs should qualify for the position discrimination introduced by the State. This seems more sensible and is certainly an improvement over the V.P. Singh's Govts. hurriedly announced policy based on the Mandal Report. However, the proposal does not take into account the sentiments of the student community which a year ago reacted violently to the earlier proposal. The Govt. has failed to live up to its promise of ensuring social harmony while seeking to hand down social justice.

	In Parliament			*In the State Legislatres*		
State/Union Territory	*Total No. of seats in the House of People*	*Scheduled Castes*	*Scheduled Tribes*	*Total No. of seats in Legislative Assembly*	*Scheduled Caste*	*Scheduled Tribe*
States						
Andhra Pradesh	43	6	2	301	43	11
Assam	12	1	2	108	5	26
Bihar	53	7	5	318	40	32
Gujarat	22	1	3	132	10	17
Jammu & Kashmir	6	...	...	75	2	...
Kerala	18	2	0	126	11	1
Madhya Pradesh	36	5	7	288	43	54
Madras	41	7	...	205	37	1
Maharashtra	44	6	2	264	33	14
Mysore	26	3	...	208	28	1
Orissa	20	4	4	140	25	29
Punjab	22	5	...	154	33	...
Rajasthan	22	3	2	176	28	20
Uttar Pradesh	86	18	...	430	89	...
West Bengal	36	6	2	252	45	...
Union Territories	...	...	...	...	...	15
Delhi	5	1	...	...	...	...
H. Pradesh	4	1	...	...	...	...
Manipur	2	...	1	...	...	...
Tripra	2	...	1	...	...	...

Representation in the Services. Twelve and a half per cent of the vacancies for which recruitment is made by open competition on all-India basis and $16\frac{2}{3}$ per cent of the vacancies to which recruitment is made otherwise are reserved for the Scheduled Castes. For the Scheduled Tribes the reservation is 5 per cent in both cases.

To facilitate their adequate representation, concessions such as exemption in age limits exemption in examination fees, relaxation in the standard of suitability and of qualifications, selection subject to fulfilling the minimum standard of efficiency and inclusion at least in the lower category for purpose of promotion where promotion is otherwise than through a qualifying examination have been provided for. The principle of reservation has been extended also to services filled by promotion through competitive examination, limited to departmental candidates are available for the reserved posts, they are to be treated as reserved for scheduled tribes and vice versa. It is only when suitable candidates are not available from either that a post is treated as unreserved. In such cases, an equal number of reservations are carried forward to two recruitment years. The employing authorities are required to submit annual reports of recruitment for scrutiny by the Government. To bring about a greater awareness for ensuring effective implementation of the special representation order liaison officers have been appointed in the different ministers of the Government of India. Arrangements have also been made for intensive training and coaching facilities at certain educational institutions to enable Scheduled Caste and Tribes candidates to compete on merit for All India services.

Educational Facilities-Scholarships. Measures to provide increased educational facilities to Scheduled castes. Tribes and Backward classes have been taken, the emphasis being on vocational and technical training. The concessions include free tution, stipends, scholarships and the provision of books, stationary and other equipment. Mid-day meals are also provided at many places.

Of all the schemes introduced by the Government for the benefit of backward classes, the one regarding the grant of scholarships is perhaps the most extensive in coverage, liberal in practice and far reaching in significance. The Government of India started the schemes for the grant of Scholarships to Scheduled Castes in 1944-45. After four years this was extended to Scheduled Tribe and in the following year 1949-50 to backward classes. The amount set apart for scholarships has registered a remarkable rise in 1951-52. At the commencement of the First Plan, it was a small sum of Rs. 15.41 lakhs. By 1956-57, it had risen to Rs. 187 lakhs. By the beginning of the Second Plan in the year 1956-57, the original allocation for post-matric scholarships to backward class students was of the order of Rs. 150 lakhs. To this another sum of Rs. 86 lakhs was added in order to meet the increasing demand.

The Central Government's scheme to award scholarships to deserving students from these classes for studies in foreign countries came into force in 1953-54. From 1955-56, the number of such scholarships was increased to 12. four for each of these groups. Overseas scholarship to students belonging to backward communities are also awarded by the State Government of Assam and Bihar.

Reservation of seats, lowering of minimum qualifying marks and raising of maximum age limit for admission of members of these classes in all technical and educational institutions were among other steps recommended by the Union Government to all educational authorities.

Other Welfare Schemes. Other welfare schemes include the grant of house sites free or at nominal cost, assistance by way of loans, subsidies and grant-in-aid to local bodies for the construction of houses for their Harijan employees and monetary assistance to co-operative building societies specially for the benefit of the Scheduled Castes and Scheduled Tribes. A system of legal aid to Scheduled Castes is also in operation in many States.

Commission for the Scheduled Castes and Scheduled Tribes. We know that our constitution provides for several safeguards for the backward classes. While the Ministry of Home Affairs of the Government of India is incharge of overall responsibility of ensuring the proper working of these constitutional safeguards, the responsibility for investing and evaluating the progress in respect of all matters relating to these safeguards rests with the Commission for Scheduled Tribes. This officer is appointed by the President of India under Article 338 of the Constitution, and he enjoys an independent status.

His Functions. As laid down in the Constitution, it shall be the duty of the special officer to investigate all matters relating to the safeguards provided for the Scheduled Tribes under Constitution and report to the President upon the working of those safeguards at such intervals as the President may direct, and the Presidens shall cause all such reports to be laid before each House of Parliament. The Commissioner is at present performing the following functions:

(i) evaluating the progress of the welfare schemes undertaken by State Governments and non-official organisations with grants-in-aid received from the Government of India;

(ii) giving advice on schemes received for grants-in-aid from the State Governments and non-official agencies for the amelioration of the condition of backward classes;

(iii) serving as a nominee of the Central Government on the Managing Committees of the Non-official organisations receiving grants direct from the Centre; and

(iv) examination of accounts of the non official organisations receiving grants direct from the Centre.

The Commissioner is assisted in his work by 11 Assistant Commissioners. The duties of the Assistant Commissioners are:

(a) to investigate cases which may be referred to him by the Commissioner or which may be brought to his notice by the local residents;

(b) to establish close contacts with the Scheduled Castes, Scheduled Tribes and other backward Classes, with a view to gaining first hand knowledge of the disabilities under which they live and to educate them about the measures that they should adopted for their welfare;

(c) to submit to the Commissioner periodical reports, showing the various facilities available for the Scheduled Castes and

Scheduled Tribes in his region and the disabilities under which they live;

(d) to report on the progress of expenditure and of the achievement of the prescribed physical targets from time to time and to investigate and advise on how best the collection of statistical data can be improved;

(e) to report on the adequacy of the resources and personnel employed on the various schemes by State Government in whom the responsibility for the implementation of sanctioned schemes in backward classes sector is vested;

(f) to help the State Governments to remove the bottlenecks as may be noticed in the actual implementation of the sanctioned schemes and undertaking schemes, where necessary, in the light of local needs; and

(g) to ensure that co-operation is forthcoming in an adequate measure from public where the schemes involves public co-operation.

NEO-EMERGENCE OF OBCS

The Other Backward Castes (OBCs). Broadly speaking, the three 'twice born' Sawarna Castes have dominated the religious, political, economic, social life of this country. Even today, it is very common to say that the politics of this or that state is being controlled by the Brahmins or the Thakurs. Occasionally, Kayasthas have also thrown up fairly influential Chief Ministers and party bosses. But it may come as a bit of a surprise to most people to learn that the Brahmins constitute only about 5.5 per cent of the country's population and the Kshatriyas hardly 4 per cent.

Proportion of Castes. In fact, the overall proportion of forward Hindu castes does not exceed 17.6 per cent of the total population of India. On the other hand, the share of Scheduled Castes (SCs) alone is 16.48 per cent. And if you lump SCs with Schedule Tribes (STs) they outnumber the forward Hindu Castes by 24 per cent. In between these two aggregates lies the vast cluster of the so-called 'other Backward (Hindu) Castes', which constitute nearly 52 per cent of our population.

Caste Contours. Another notable feature of our scenario is that the South has very different caste contours as compared to the North. In the North we have the classical Varna model of four castes. But in the South there are only three castes groups—Brahmins, non-Brahmins and SCs and STs (There are particularly no Kshatriyas in the South) and whereas the Brahmin domination in the services and the cultural life of the South, especially the Tamil region, was far more pronounced than in the North, they numbered only 3 per cent of the population.

Caste Antagonism. Thirdly, Caste antagonism have tended to be much more fierce and violent in the North than in the South.

And Fourthly, in West Bengal and the north-eastern states, the hold of caste is much weaker. Regional and ethinic loyalties are much more important in the north-east.

It is, indeed, a fact that the caste conflicts have become much fierce after independence, and the caste factor has come to play a very important role in Indian politics. But it could not be otherwise. After all when the forward castes comprising 17.6 per cent of the country's population corner 70-80 per cent of its positions of power and patronage, the backward castes care bound to protest and agitate, and demand a more equitable sharing of the national cake.

Rise of OBCs. The most important post-Independence development on the caste front has been the rise of the 'Other Backward Castes' (OBCs). As the label itself indicates, it is a sort of residual category. Whereas Scheduled Caste, Scheduled Tribes and the Sawarna Hindu Castes are quite clearly differentiated, OBCs embrace a very large spectrum of nearly 3,000-4,000 intermediate castes. The more advanced amongst them owe their rise to power primarily to the abolition of Zamindari after Independence. With the conferral of ownership rights on various categories of tenants, a new class of peasant proprietors was born. These cultivating and herding castes were generally very hard-working and after becoming peasant proprietors, they acquired both prosperity and social status.

Political Potentials. Ram Manohar Lohia was the first national level leader who realised the political potential of OBCs and advocated the view that the surest way to dislodge the Congress from power was to mobilise these backward castes against it. After him Devraj Urs and Karpoori Thakur, two eminent backward class leaders, rode to power on the back of OBCs, but they could not weld them into a stable power base.

Now that the Congress (I) has become jitery about its traditional constituencies, and the opposition is trying to annex all the floating votebanks, the OBCs have become the primary object of courtship by both sides. After all, these caste constitute nearly half the population of the country.

Mobilisation. As OBCs are too numerous and dispersed, the first concrete steps towards their mobilisation were taken in the form of grouping cognate or related caste by forming 'Caste association's Described as 'horizontals stretch' by Prof.. M.N. Srinivas, this 'fusion' process has resulted in the rise of powerful caste conglomerates as Izhavas and Naris in Kerala : Nadars and Vanniyars in Tamil Nadu; Vokkaligas and Lingayats in Karnatka; Jats, Gujars and Minas in Rajasthan; and Yadavas, Ahirs, Kurmis and Koeris in Bihar and U.P. Further the size of the spread of a caste grouping depends upon the level of which pressure is sought to be exerted. For instance, the Ahir Kshatriya Mahasabha speaks for the Ahirs of U.P., whereas All-India Yadavas Mahasabha operates at the national level. AJGAR (Ahir-Jat-Gujars) in the Hindi belt and KHAM (Kshatriya-Harijan-Ahir-Muslim) in Gujarat are the extreme instances of this process of jumboisation on sectarian lines.

Lohia's Thesis. The eclipse of the Congress in the 1967 elections seemed to vindicate Ram Manohar Lohia's thesis, SVD ministries in UP, Bihar and some other states were formed with the backing of OBC MLAs who had been elected in large numbers than ever before.

Caste Calculus. Perhaps nothing shows the complexity of caste calculus more clearly than the case of the "Yadava quarter"; in U.P. Both the Congress (I) and Janata Dal are bending upon backwards to win over this highly influential intermediate peasant caste. After the Congress (I) had appointed Balram Singh Yadava as its P.C.C. Chief, it successfully hijacked Chandrajit Yadava and Ram Naresh Yadav to its ranks, thus strengthening its OBC base. The Janata Dal, on the other hand, has appointed the crafty Mulayam Singh Yadav to head the state unit to attract the Yadav.

UF Experiment. "The most significant face of the United Front experiment is its strong caste base. Although the Mandalisation of politics began in earliset in 1989-90 during V.P. Singh's regime, this is (1996) the first time that the country not only has a Backward caste Prime Minister but also most of his ministerial colleagues belong to either the Backward, Dalit or minority. Even outside the ministery, anti upper caste politics is clearly reflected in the dominance of Laloo, Mulayam, Naidu, M. Karunannidhi and G.K. Moopanar.

Caste Conflict. A major example of this phenomenon is the growing caste conflict between the "backward" and the "forward" castes. Leader in State after state have utilised "reservations" as a means to gain the electoral support of numerically significant backward castes. Higher Castes, feeling that their interests are threatened, have resisted there moves. Conflict has often been the result.

Cast Tactics. Caste associations and caste tactics have thus, contributed significantly to the success of political democracy by providing bases for communication, representation and leadership. They have taught illiterate masses how to participate manfully and effectively in politics. Neo-emerging backward castes, whose large number give them advanage in competitive democratic politics, have in many areas been granted influences, access and power in state and society. They can change the tide of power in their favour and influence decisions regarding the allocation of resources and distribution of privileges and honours.

Negative Impact. To summarise, the negative impact of casteism on India's political system is *(i)* that it violates the basic principles in the constitution for promoting a new democratic polity; *(ii)* that it has politicised the castes as a divisive factor; *(iii)* that it has vitiated the atmosphere of elections, by projecting predemocratic ascriptive identities, promoting narrow loyalties, thus weakening the modernisation of the polity; *(iv)* that by building caste associations, pressure groups and lobbies, it seeks to retain outmoded and outdated caste cohesion in national and state politics, which is an impediment to building up a secular society; *(v)* that in party politics and in ministry formulation its role contributes to avoidable bickerings, narrow bargaining and jockeying for power, which often leads to political instability and confusion.

WELFARE OF TRIBES

The Directive Principles of State Policy, as enshrined in the constitution have a bearing on social welfare. They enjoin the State to ensure that, the health and strength of workers, men and women, and the tender age of children are not forced by economic necessity to enter avocations unsuited to their age and strength', and that 'childhood and youth are protected against exploitation and against moral and material abandonment.'

Constitutional Provision for Scheduled Tribes. The Constitution of India has a part which deals with the special provisions relating to the scheduled castes and schedulted tribes. Article 342 lays down that "the President may by public notification, specify the tribes or tribal communities or part of or groups within tribes on tribal communities or parts which shall for the purposes of this Constitution deemed to be Scheduled Tribes...

According to this provision, President of India has specified these communities through Constitution (Scheduled Tribes) Order 1950, S.R.O. 510. The tribes so specified are in number about one hundred and sixty leaving out the schedulted tribes of Assam. In 1953, under the provision of Indian Constitution, Backward Tribes Commission was appointed under the chairmanship of Shri Kaka Kalelkar. The Commission submitted its report on 31st March, 1955.

Representation in Legislatures and Panchayats. The Constitution of India prescribes protection and safeguards for schedulted tribes with the object of promoting their educational and economic interests. Under Articles 330, 332 and 334 of the Indian Constitution, seats have been reserved for schedulted castes and scheduled tribes in Lok Sabha and State Vidhan Sabhas. Under Article 334, this concession was to end on January 25, 1970, but Parliament, by passing the Constitution (Twenty-third Amendment) Bill 1969, has extended the period of reservation till 1980.

Besides the reserve seats, members of the Scheduled Tribes also represent some general constituencies in Lok Sabha and Vidhan Sabhas. There is no reservation of seats in Rajya Sabha and Vidhan Parishads.

Following the introduction of Panchayat Raj, suitable safeguards have been provided for proper representation of the members of the Scheduled Tribes by reserving seats for them in the Gram Panchayats and other local bodies.

Reservation in the Services. Government has given adequate representation in the services. On January 26, 1950 the Union Government decided that 5 per cent of the vacancies for which recruitment is made by reserved for scheduled tribes to facilitable their adequate representation certain concessions have been provided, such as:

(i) Exemption in age limits.

(ii) Relaxation in the standard of suitability and of qualifications.

(iii) Selection subject to fulfilling the minimum standard of efficiency, and

(iv) Inclusion at least in the lower category for purpose of promotion is otherwise than through qualifying examinations.

The principle of reservation has been extended to those services in which recruitment is made by department candidates through competitive examinations. It is only when suitable candidates are not available for the reserve posts, then the post is treated unreserved. Annual reports required to be submitted to the employing authorities for scrutiny by the Government.

Administration of Scheduled and Tribal Areas. Some areas have been 'scheduled' in the states of Andhra Pradesh, Bihar, Gujarat, Madhaya Pradesh, Maharashtra, Orissa and Rajasthan. Governors of the respective states submit a report annually to the President on the administration of the 'scheduled' areas in their state. District councils have been set up in the districts of united Khasi-Jainti Hills, Garo Hills, Mizo Hills, North Cachar Hills and Mikir Hills.

Each of these district councils consists of not more than 30 members, threefourths of them being elected by adult suffrage.

Tribes Advisory Councils. The fifth schedule to the constitution provides for the setting up of a Tribes Advisory Council in each of the State having scheduled areas. According to this provision, Tribes Advisory Councils have been set up so far in the States of Andhra, Bihar, Bombay, Madhya Pradesh, Orissa, Punjab, Rajasthan and West Bengal. The duty of these councils is to advise the Government on such matters concerning the welfare of scheduled tribes and development of Scheduled Areas. Advisory Boards for the Scheduled Tribes have been set up in Assam, Kerala and Mysore to advise the State Government. Tribes Advisory Committees have also been formed in the union territories of Andaman and Nicobar Islands, Himachal Pradesh, Manipur and Tripura.

Commissioners for the Scheduled Castes and Scheduled Tribes. Under Article 338 of Indian Constitution, a Commissioner has been appointed by the President of India. The main duty of the Commissioners for the Scheduled castes and scheduled tribes is *(i)* to investigate all matters relating to the safeguards for scheduled castes and scheduled tribes under the Constitutions and *(ii)* to report the President on the working of these safeguards. At present there are ten Assistant Commissioners to assist the Commissioner.

WELFARE SCHEMES

Under Article 339 (2) of the Constitution, the Union Government can give directions to States in the formulation and execution of schemes for the welfare of the scheduled tribes in the States. Under Article 275 (i) the Centre is required to give grants-in-aid to the States for approved schemes of welfare and for improving the administration is Scheduled Areas.

Plan Outlays. During the First Second, and Third Five Years Plans, Rs. 26 Crores, Rs. 78 Crores and Rs. 102 Crores respectively were spent in the Backward Classes Sector. In the Fourth Plan, an outlay of Rs. 142.38 Crores, Rs. 60 Crores in the Central Sector and Rs. 77.43 Crores in the State Sector has been earmarked. In the Fifth Five Year Plan (1974-79) a provision of Rs. 288.88 Crores has been made. This, in addition to the provision made by the State Government in their non-plan budgets.

Scholarships. The Central Government award scholarship to deserving students from these classes for higher studies in foreign countries. This scheme is into foce since 1953-54. Now since 1955-56 Government have increased the number of such scholarships to 12 for each of the three groups. Besides this, tourists class sea passages are given to students who receive foreign scholarships without travel grants. Seventeen and half percent of the merit scholarships granted by the centre to deserving students of lower income groups for studies in institution which are members of the Indian Public Schools Conference, are reserved by backward communities.

Educational Facilities. Measures to provide educational facilities have been taken by the Government. The emphasis is being given to vocational and technical training. According to these measures concessions, free tuition, stipends, scholarships are provided as well as books, stationery and other equipments. In many places mid-day meals are also supplied.

Economic Opportunities. Besides educational facilities, Government have give great importance for economic development of tribal population. Out of 225 lakhs, about 26 lakhs persons practise shifting cultivation annually over an area of 22,55,616 acres. This problem is in its acute form in the State of Andhra Pradesh, Assam, Bihar, Madhya Pradesh, Orissa and the Union Territories of Manipur and Tripura. A scheme to control shifting cultivation was started during First Five Year Plan Period. Sixteen pilot project centres so have been started in the Assam and 4 colonisation schemes have been started in Andhra Pradesh.

Besides this, Andhra Pradesh, Bihar, Bombay, Madras, Orissa and Uttar Pradesh, have launched schemes to improve irrigations facilties to reclaim waste land and to distribute it among members of the scheduled castes and scheduled tribes. In addition, facilities for the purchase of live-stock, fertilizers, agriculutral implements, better seeds etc. are also extended to them. Some States have also set up demonstration farms for training them in methods of scientific cultivation.

The Government of Andhra Pradesh, Assam, Bihar, Bombay, Uttar Pradesh and West Bengal are encouraging the development of cottage industries through loans, subsidies and training centres. Multipurpose co-operative societies which provide credit in cash and kind to the scheduled caste and scheduled tribes have been established in Andhra Pradesh, Bihar, Madras, Mysore, Orissa, Uttar Pradesh and West Bengal. In some such as Bombay and Andhra Pradesh contracts for forest produce are being given to the scheduled tribes through labour co-operative societies.

Tribal Research Institute. Tribal Research Institutes, which undertake intensive studies to tribal arts, culture and customs have been set up in Bihar, Madhya Pradesh, Orissa, Rajasthan and West Bengal. The Gauhati University has started the study of the social and cultural life of the tribes of Assam. In Bombay tribal research is being conducted by the Anthropological Society of Bombay. In West Bengal the cultural research Institute has produced reports on several aspects of tribal life in the State. Studies in the culture and languages of the people of NEFA are being undertaken by the Research Department of NEFA. The Bihar Institute has also completed studies on Santhal Parganas. The Bhartiya Lok Kala Mandal, Udaipur is a pioneer non-official organisation which has conducted survey of the tribes in the former Madhya Bharat State Rajasthan.

Fifth Plan and Tribal Welfare. In the Fifth Plan, a new strategy has been adopted for the uplift of scheduled tribes. Greater emphasis has been placed on the role of general sector for proving a major thrust to the development for back ward classes.

With regard to the scheduled tribes it has been decided that all those areas which have more than fifty percent tribal population should be clearly identified and sub-plans should be prepared for these areas. The sub-plan represents the total effort of the region of the central ministries, the state governments and other institutions.

CHARACTERISTICS OF TRIBES

Since pre-historic times, India has been country of multi-racial stocks. Its different parts are occupied by the various groups of people having their distinct cultural traits and levels of development.

Among them, a number of groups are still in primitive stage and are far from the impact of modern civilization. Therefore these people are called aboriginals. India's mythological accounts desbribe that Aryans invaded this country and came in contact with the aboriginal people of this country.

According to Sri L.M. Shrikant, "there are a plenty of indications in the mythological stories of Ramayana and the Mahabharata and even in the pre-Christian era that the indigenous people had to reasist the impact of foreign culture. But in the course of time, those all races mixed into one composite whole. The modern form of Hinduism comprises many elements of such cultural admiture. But apart from this fact, there are groups of people representing the primitive stage of life. Therefore, people represeting to these stages are called aboriginals. In the Indian constitution they are termed as "schedulted tribes".

Tribe has been defined into various ways. The following are some of the notable definitions of tribe:

Notes and Queries on Anthropology, "A tribe may be defined as a politically or socially coherent and autonomous groups occupying on claiming a particular territory."

Imperial Gazetteer of India, "A tribe is a collection of families bearing a common, name, speaking a common dialect, occupying or professing of occupy a common territory and is not usually endogamous, though originally it might have been so."

Jacobs and Stern, "A cluster of village communities which share a common territory, language and culture and are economically interwoven is often also designated as tribe."

Characteristics of Tribe. The above definition throw light on the characteristics of a tribe into the following categories:

(1) ***Common Territory.*** A tribe has a definite territory in which its members reside. In the absense of common territory, a tribe cannot sustain its peculiarities.

(2) ***Feeling of Unity.*** The other characteristics of a tribe is the feeling of unity among its members which results on account of common geographical backgronds.

(3) ***Common Language.*** The members of a tribe speak a common language which develops their community feeling.

(4) ***Blood Relationship.*** All the members of a tribe claim themselves to be connected by blood relationship. They claim their origin from a common ancestor.

(5) ***Endogamy.*** The next characteristics of a tribe is that it is endogamous in character. All members marry within their tribe and marriage relations outside the tribe are prohibited.

(6) ***Common Culture.*** Apart from endogamy, it is also notable that all the members of a tribe share a common culture pattern. This culture similarity is one of the principal factors which integrates the organisation of tribal community.

(7) ***Common Religion.*** Religion has got an important place in a tribe. It is observed in the form of ancestor worship which develops the habits of obedience.

(8) ***Common Name.*** Every tribe bears a common name through which it is known to others.

CLASSIFICATION OF INDIAN TRIBE

In India, the aboriginals, who under the constitution are designated schedulted tribes, can be classified into various categories. On the ground of language area of inhabitation and physical features, we may have the following classifications.

(1) Territorial Classification. On the basis of territory, Indian tribes may have the following four divisions:

(a) ***Tribes of Northern and North-Eastern Zone.*** This zone comprises the sub-Himalayan region and the mountain valley of eastern frontiers.The tribes inhabiting in Kashmir, East Punjab, Himachal Pradesh and northern U.P. are within this zone. The Aka, Defla, Miri and Naga are some of the principal tribes of this zone. The Naga tribe consists of five major groups namely the Rengma, the Sema the Angami, Aolahota, the Phom, the Chang and the Kacha.

(b) ***Tribes of Central Zone.*** The central zone consists plateous and mountainous belt between the Indo-Gangetic plains to the north and the Krishna river in south. Trives inhaviting in Madhya Pradesh, Hyderabad, Northern Rajasthan, Southern Bombay and Bastar are included under this zone. The principal tribes of this zone are Savara, Gadada. Borido, Khone, Bhumij, Bhuiya, Mundas, Santhals, Oraons Hos and the Birthors. Among these tribes Gonds from the largest groups and occupy the area which is known as 'Gondwana'.

(c) ***Tribes of Southern Zone.*** The southern zone comparises the area which falls between Krishna river and Cape Commorin. Hyderabad, Mysore, Coorg, Travancore, Cochin, Andhra and Madras fall within this zone. The tribes of these areas are considered to be the most ancient and primitive. Among them Kanara, Teruvas, Todas, Kadars, Kenikkars and Malvadan are most important.

(d) ***Tribes of Andaman and Nicobar Island.*** Apart from the other zones, there is small isolated zone comprizing Andaman and Nicober Islands. The principal tribes inhabiting these zones are Jarava, Andmanese and Nicobaries.

(2) Linguistic Classification. Besides territorial classification, Indian tribes can be classified on the basis of their affiliation to the various families of languages:

(a) ***Dravidian Linguistic Group.*** This tribal group is popular in Central and Southern India and includes Gonds, Maler Polia, Soara, Koya, Paniyan, Kadar and Malakurwan.

(b) ***The Austro-Asiatic Linguistic Group.*** This group comprises Kols, Mundas of Central and Eastern India, Khasi of Assam and Nicobaries of the Nicobar Island.

(c) ***The Tibeto Chinese Group.*** This group includes all the tribes belonging to southern slopes of Himalayas from Northern. Punjab to Bhutan and Assam. The Nagas, Kuki, Dafla and the Khasi are some of the principal tribes of this linguistic group.

(3) Occupational Classification. We may also divide the Indian tribes on the basis of their occupation and distinctive economy. This classification depends on the level of economic development from food gathering and hunting stagtes to shifting and settled cultivation. According to the stages of stages of economic development, Hutton has classified the Indian tribes into three major groups:

(i) Primitive tribes collecting forest produces.

(ii) Primitive tribes in the pastoral stage.

(iii) Primitive tribes practising agriculture, hunting, fishing and industries.

(4) Classification According to the Physical Characteristics. On the basis of outstanding characteristics, Indian tribes have been classified into three major groups:

(a) ***Mongoloid Group.*** The principal element of aboriginal population of India is Mongoloid which is found in all the tribes inhibiting the sub Himalayan region. Light skin colour, straignt and dark hair, flat nose and prominent-cheek bones, medium stature with long head, scanty hair growth on body and face and almost shaped eyes are some of the main characteristics of this groups. This group is well represented by the Nagas, Chakmas, Lepchas, Tharusand, the Bhatias.

(b) ***Proto-Australoid Group.*** The tribes of Central Zone are marked by Negrito strain and confirm the Australoid character. They have short to medium stature, long head, broad and flat nose depressed at the root, and everted lips. This group has been represented by the Chenchus, Kurumbas, Malayans, Manda, Kols, Santhals and the Bhils.

(c) ***Negrito Group.*** The Negrito strain is indicated by frizzly hairs marked among the Andmans, Paryans and the Kadars of the south west. These tribes are greatly intermerged.

(5) Classification According to Culture Contact. Beside the above classifications, we may also classify the Indian tribes on the basis of culture-contact. According to Elvin, the aboriginal population is distributed into four cultural divisions. The first two divisions consist of the comparatively small black primitives living in the hills. Their religion is characteristic and alivet; their tribal organizations unimpaired and their traditions and mythology still vitalizes the organism of their tribal life, geographical conditions have largely protected them from the contacts of the outsiders.

(1) This in the first group we may include those triber which are living in the most primitive stage. The tribes which represent this group are the hill Marias of Bastar, the Juangs Keomjihar; the Gadabas and Bondos of Orissa. These tribes are entirely isolated from the people of plains. The members of these tribes represent the following major characteristics:

   (i) All members live a communal life.

   (ii) All members share a similar economic structure.

   (iii) All membners are concentrated round a peculiar form of agriculture.

   (iv) They are honest, simple, innocent and are very shy before strangers.

(2) In the second group, we may include those tribes who on one side are associated with the old traditions, but on the other side they have begun to change. The major tribes who represent this group are the Marias, Bhumias, Binijhwere and Baigas. Their chief characteristics are as follows:

   (i) Individualistic village life.

   (ii) Non-participation in common affairs.

   (iii) Adoption of the order mode of life and the absence of primitive simplicity.

In the fourth group, we may include those tribes who represent the ancient aristoeracy of this country. For examples, the Bhils; the Naga chieftains; the Gond Rajas; Bhuiya landlords; Korku noble men and the wealthy Santhals. These tribes retain their old tribal name and practise their tribal religion. But apart form this they has also adopted the faiths of modern Hinduism and modern mode of living.

(6) Classification by Tribal Welfare Committee. The Tribal Welfare Committee constituted by the Indian Confernece of Social Work, has divided Indian tribes into four main divisions:

(i) Tribes who confine themselves to the original forest habitant and are distinctive in their pattern of life. These may be termed as 'tribal communities.'

(ii) Tribes who have migrated to urban or semi-urban and rural areas and are engaged in industries and other vocation adopting the traits and culture of people. These may be termed as acculturated tribal communities.

(iii) Tribes who have settled down in rural areas and practise agriculture and other allied occupation. This category of people may be termed as 'semi tribal communities'.

(iv) Totally assimilated tribes.

DISTINCTION BETWEEN CASTE AND TRIBE

These are basic difference between the caste and the tribes. The caste rests on the assumption that men are born unequal and their present social position is determined by birth. Like the tribe, the caste is an endogamous group or collection of such groups which bears a common name and practice a common traditional, occupation. The membes of a tribe are linked together by various ties, such as the tradition of a common origin, worship of a common deity, and same social and ceremonial observances. They all have family priests and form a singel homogeneous community.

On the other hand, according to Kelkar "A caste is a group having two characteristics, *(i)* Membership is confined to those who are born of members and include all persons so born. *(ii)* The members are forbidden by an inexorable social law to marry outside the group." Similarly a tribe is also a collection of families bearing a common name, culture, language territory. But inspite of this similarity we may distinguish caste and tribe on the following grounds :

(1) Both the caste and the tribe are collection of families and bear a common name. But in case of a tribe, this comon name does not indicate a community of function.

(2) The title of a caste implies that all its members follow the same occupation, for instance, Lohars, or Blacksmiths and malis or Gardeners. But the title of a tribe does not indicate a common occupation.

(3) The caste claims a comon descent from a mythical ancestor while the tribe sometimes traces its origin from some animal which may be treated as its 'Totem'.

(4) Thirdly the caste is a social group while the tribe is a territorial group. The tribe is supposed to occupy a well defines areas while the members of a caste may be scattered all over the country.

(5) Listly, the caste always observes the strict law of endogamy But in case of a tribe it does not apply always. Its members may find wives from the members of another tribe. Thus the caste is always endogamous divided into exogamous sections or subcastes.

ROLE OF RELIGIOUS AND CULTURAL ORGANISATIONS

In India, community associations, party due part in the politics of the country. These associations have 'their bases in religious, caste, tribal linguistic and ethnic factors.' The student's organisations, can be covered here, though briefly, as they have a community of their own. The membership of these associations is constituted of the communities in which individuals are born, or grow up. The associations are classified into four distinct categories : *(i)* institutional, *(ii)* associational, *(iii)* non-associational, and *(iv)* anomic. The importance of these associations become more practical in view of the fact that most of political movements present in India "are political overflows of community tensions."

(A) RELIGIOUS ASSOCIATION

The Religious associations that play noticeable part in the national politics are Shiromani Akali Dal and Arya Samaj in Punjab, Muslim League in Kerala, Anglo-Indian Association, Associations of the Roman Catholics and Jamaat-e-Islam and Majlis-e-Mushawarat and many more.

(1) The Akali Dal. The associations like the Shiromani Akali Dal should be treated as "more of a religious pressure group than a political party" since it has been concerned more with the mission of protecting the sikh community 'from being absorbed into the ocean of Hindu society than in fighting for the cause of 'Sikh Homeland' and, as such, any movement in the direction of having a Sikh State should be considered as "a device for etablishing cultural boundaries." The demand for Sikhistan was manufactured by the Akali leaders belonging to the old order like Master Tara Singh who once defined the case of Sikh homeland in terms of a separate and sovereign state of the Sikhs, while it had a softer and nobler form when the leaders of new order like Sant Fateh Singh redefined it in terms of having an autonomous State of the Punjabi-speaking people within the Indian Union. With the creation of the Punjabi-speaking state in 1966, the Akali Dal could get much of what it really desired.

(2) The Arya Samaj. The Arya Samaj was drawn into politics for the Hindus and the problem was solved by the creation of Haryana. In this way the creation of the State of Haryana may be considered as the outcome of the Arya Samaj's participation in politics that could save the predominantly Hindi speaking areas from being absorbed into the Punjabi-speaking State. Not merely this, the Arya Samaj struggled against the imposition of Punjabi language by the Government of Punjabi in its D.AV. schools and colleges.

(3) The Muslim League. Muslim League, after the creation of Pakistan, reappeared "in the State of Kerala where it, by virtue of being a constituent of the CPM-dominated coalition government under E.M.S. Namboodripad, could have two Muslim districts carved out and that it could see to it, later on, in the CPI-led coalition government under Achutha Menon that certain references to the communal character of the Muslim League made by Nehru (relating to the pre-partition days) were expunged from school text books as these hurt the sentiments of the Muslim community." Later, the League expanded its area of activity and its role in the local politics of Bombay Municipal Elections of 1973 appeared astonishingly when it won more than expected seats. The League forced the local administration to abandon the practice of reciting 'Vande Matram' in the municipal schools. Apart from Muslim League, there are other organisation as Jamaat-e-Islami and Muslim Majlis-e-Mushawarat.

(4) Association of the Roman Catholics. This association has a very little importnace as the Christians are very small in number. The Christians being a peace loving people, 'believe more in getting through humble petitions made to the men in power than in resorting to the techniques of pressure politics.' When a Bill of Freedom of Religion was introduced by O.P. Tyagi, Janata M.P. the Christians stood together for the defeact of this Bill. This Bill sought to prohibit religious conversion by any means but it lapsed due to the dissolution of Lok Sabha in Aug. 1979.

(5) The Anglo-Indian Christian Association. On account of special reservations and safeguards given to the men of this community it is slightly in a better position.

(B) CASTE ASSOCIATIONS

Caste influences have been great in affecting the political behaviour in India. Caste in narrow sense refers to segment of society. In the comprehensive sense, it covers a religious body as a whole. "The politics of caste associations presents a strange as well as a complex phenomenon of being in the form of distinct political party like that of the Jharkhand in Bihar or having different factions fighting against one another as Jharkhand (Hul) And All-India Jharkhand in Bihar and Orissa. Dravida Kazhgam, Dravida Munnetra Kazhgam, Anna-DMK in Tamilnadu or a caste organisation fully supporting a political party like Reddies backing the Congress and Kammas doing the same for the Communists in Andhra Pradesh, or a case organisation assuming the form of a political pary Akali Dal in the Punjab or a caste organisation by all means having the character of a political party but bent on concealing its ideological trimmings like Peasant's and Worker's Party of Maharashtra." The organisations are based on an ad hoc basis. Such organisations are seen at the time of local elections. The caste factor may influence the poltics even in an unorganised form.

In Tamilnadu there is a distinctively anti-Brahmin caste organisation. The Justice Party and the Dravida Kazhgam built on its debris under the leadership of E.V. Ramaswami Naicher constitute the glaring instance in this regard." The DMK wanted a separate and sovereign state of the Dravindians as Dravidisthan. After a split that occurred in Dravida Kazhgam in 1949 led to the organisation of Dravida Munnetra Kazhgam (DMK) under the leadership of C.N. Annadurai for 'the cause of an autonomous and prosperous State of the Tamil speaking people within the Indian Union.' Being supported by the electorate this party captured power in the state assembly election of 1967 and 1971. This party again faced division in 1972 and under. M.G. Ramachandran a new party Anna-DMK was formed. This party charged DMK of gross mismanagement and corruption after the demise of Annadurai in 1969. DMK saw another split in 1975 under Muthu and formed an organisation called the Tamilnadu Toilers Party (TMK). Many members of the caste organisations joined the Congress Party at the instance of Kamaraj Nadar. The caste association of these people was called as Vanniyakul Kshatriya Sangam. Apart from this, the Scheduled Castes Federation established by Dr. B.R. Ambedkar had played important role in the State of Maharashtra.

(C) THE TRIBAL ASSOCIATIONS

Tribal associations have been found operating in the backward "region of Bihar, Orissa, West Bengal and Assam. Though some of the tribal-associations may be treated as a composite caste organisation (as Jharkhand), several other have a peculiarity tribal character in view of the fact that their membership is open to the men of the same tribe articulating their interests in the form of demands from the point of more and more reforms to that of session from the Indian Union." The organisations of Jharkhand consist of major five tribes, namely Munda, Ho, Oran, Bhumi and Kharia. They have been fighting for "separate and autonomous state covering the areas of Chotta Nagpur and the contiguous predominatly tribal areas of Orissa and West Bengal, the Naga National Council has been at the cross-roads, that is, while extremist leaders of the NNC drawing inspiration from A.Z. Phizo (now in England) has been demanding nothing short of complete independence, moderate elements have found everything to their satisfaction in the State of Nagaland created in 1963." Meghalaya was created owing to the agitation of certain tribal associations in the State Assam as 'an autonomous State within the State of Assam' and in became a full fledged State of the Indian Union in 1971. In North-Eastern India was reorganised to create the Union Territories of Mizoram and Arunachal Pradesh. Under the process of re-organisation the Union Territories of Manipur and Tripura were granted statehood owing to agitations of several tribal organisations."

(D) PRESSURE GROUPS CREATED BY LINGUISTIC AND ETHNIC FACTORS

The role of pressure groups under this category has led to the creation of provines based on regional language and the first wast he creation of Teleugu-speaking State of Andhra in 1953. The movement for this purpose was launched by Andhra Pradesh Sabha. The Government of India appointed State Re-organisation Commission to review the political map of India to the basis of linguistic composition of the country, with due consideration to the administrative efficiency economy and regional political and economic development factors. There emerged a controversy over the creating of the bilingual state of Bombay and from here came into being the Sampooran Maharashtra Samiti in 1956. And the movement for the unilingual state eleminated when Bombay was bifurcated into the State of Gujarat and Maharashtra in 1960. As already mentioned, the language problem was behind the bifurcation of the Punjab in 1966, one more example is the name of Nag Vidarbha, Ethnic groups like Gorkha League consisting of the Gorkha people employed in the tea plantation industry of Darjeeling-less a political party, more a pressure group playing its part in the politics of West Bengal sometimes independently and sometimes with support of other parties like the Congress and the Communists." Recently these people have started demanding a new state of 'Gorkha land'.

Role of Student's Organisation During the Post-Independence Era. Immediately after the independence, most of the students joined the All-India Students Congress (Students wing of the Indian National Congress) Whereas the Communists made effort to strengthen their Students Federation, the socialists sponsored

'Young Socialist League' the Samyukta Socialist Party started its Samajwadi Yuvjan Sabha and the RSS organised its Hindu Students Federation which later became Akhil-Bhartiya Vidyarthi Parishad. When the Bharatiya Jana Sangh came into being, and the Maxists Communists set up Progressive Students Union. When Congress came into power, the All-India Students Congress, was dissolved and the National Union of students (NUS) was organised as "an ancillary wing of the Indian National Congress with a programme in the form of a non-political federation of various students unions in the country.

Role of Students Unions in Indian Politics. The role of the students organisation in independent India, particularly after 1967 is of highly anomic character. These has been a steep rise in "their vulgar politicisation and their more and more advancement in the direction of indiscipline. The organisations of the students have made strikes on every other day. Any demand from non-enhancement of tuition fees and provision for essential facilities to that of participation in management of institutions may become a matter of pastime." Now the grave indiscipline among the students, led by unions indulge in the breaking of furniture, window panes damging the premises by activites and resorting to hooliganism and arson very after assumes monotrous nature. It has rendered the teachers snd authorities running colleges and universities so helpless "that the adminsitration of educational institutions looks like an insoluble problem. "What, however, became the most serious problem was the role of the students bodies called Nava Nirman Samitis in demanding the dissolution of popularly elected governments." The State of Gujarat and Bihar were the worst sufferers at the hand of this organisation and it forced the government to resort to stern measures. Despite some efforts by the government, the situation has not undergone any remarkable change and the potentiality of student's power has not been successfully tapped for the positive and constructive purposes. Recently Delhi University which has been running in huge deficit thought of enhancing examination fee which was far less than the fees kept by the CBSE or Delhi School Board but the Students Union President resolved to hunger strike and the students threated agitation. The matter has gone to a committee.

HINDU-MUSLIM COMMUNALISM

In an attempt to examine the causes responsible for communalism in the post indenpendence era, it would be appropriate to understand what is meant by communalism. In common approach the communalism meant a sentiment of enemity towards other religious communities with prejudice against and possible aggressiveness towards the individual belonging to them or the attachment to one's own community and to its preservation and concern for the uplift of its members. But in real sense communalism was a much more than a phenomenon and was generated by a 'variety of factors. For instance during the period of British Rule Hindu-Muslim communalism was due to deep diversities in respect of places of worship, holy books, method of worships, religious festivals, social customs and ways of daily life, language and standard of living'. In addition to this the British policy of 'Divide and Rule' played a very important role. After the British rule some elements of discord were added. These factors are being discussed below.

1. The Sentiment of Separatism and Isolationism Among Muslims. The leading reasons for Hindu Muslims unrest was the tendency of Muslims to keep themselves away from the majority community as well as isolate themselves 'from the secular nationalistic politics of India'. Immediately after independence, some Muslim leaders felt that the support of the demand for Pakistan by the Muslims of non-Muslim majority was a blunder. In their bid to retrieve the situation they told their co-religiousnists that they should co-operate with those political parties and individuals who stood for secularism and economic justice. The Muslims were also exhorted to join national mainstream because their future lay not in separation from the rest of the Indian people.

Unfortunately, despite such efforts many Muslim organisations and leaders advocated that the Muslim 'community should organise itself separately to protect its interest, culture, language and religion. The organisations like the Jamati-ul-Islam 'exhorted the Muslims to refrain from the First General Election being held under the Constitution of Independent India. A section of Jamait ulmai Hind, an organisation or Muslim divine and intellectuals played the same tune. The remanants of Muslim league went ahead and demanded in 1948 separate electorate for Muslims. However, it disappeared during the 1950's but surfaced again on the eve of the Third General Election. On 29.10.1961, a split within its ranks led Mohd Raza Khan to leave the parent body and he formed new All India Muslim League and preached Muslims to support the Congress candidates because according to him the Congress was the best protector of Muslim interests. On the contrary the General Secretary of the original League, Ibrahim Suleman Sait reiterated his claim even during the 1960s that his organisation was the only representative body of muslims and that no other organisation could speak for the Indian Muslims. The Muslims from every corner of India held a Political Convention in New Delhi on the eve of midterm poll for Lok Sabha in March 1971. This convention adopted half a dozen resolutions stressing the interest of Muslims, including security of life and property of Muslims, protection of Urdu, reservation of posts in services preservation of stauts of Aligarh Muslim University and elections on the basis of proportional representation.

2. Economic Backwardness and Poverty Among Muslims. Economic backwardness of the Muslim masses is the backlash of religious orthodoxy and obscurantism among the Muslims. The fall of Mughal empire drove them to poverty and starvation. The Industrial Revolution during British rule in India deprived the Muslim artisans and craftsmen of their means of livelihood. Though the British reversed the policy around the last quarter of the nineteenth century, yet their position did not improve because of their indifference to change. The situation remained *status quo* even after Independence. Due to illiteracy Muslims could not secure an adequate share in public services or in trade and industry filling them, in consequence with frustration and demoralization which often burst forth in the shape of violent and lawless activities against the Hindus who are comparatively better placed in the society.

3. Religious Orthodoxy. Religious Orthodoxy and obscurantism was another factor which bred communalism in the post Independence period. The Muslim Organisations like the Jamaat-e-Islami, Majlis-e-Mushawarat, Muslim League and Muslim Majlis preached anti-modern ideas and hailed the obscure and medieval glories of Islam. The supremacy and importance or religion in individual life was also advocated. They also stressed upon the 'mental differences between the Hindu and Muslim cultures, personal laws, and ways of living and thinking.'

4. Role of Pakistan. The existence of Pakistan on the two sides of India was another factor which goaded, communalism in this country. In every eventuality of Hindu-Muslim flare-up, the Pakistani radio and the press and leaders "blurted out stories of genocide of Muslims by the Hindus, and accused the Govenment of India of 'connivance' in the 'crime'. For instance, when there was a riot at Aligarh Muslim University in 1972, President Ayub Khan said the riots "could not have happened without the connivance of the Indian administration." In the similar tone spoke the then High Commission of that country in New Delhi, Agha Hilaly, about it is 'organised killing' of Muslims by 'Militant Hindu Communalists,' and called it an 'act of barbarism.'

Pakistan did all this with nefarious designs to wean the Indian Muslims away from secular-nationalistic forces in India. It was also directed towards Hindus living in Pakistan and to create fear in their minds to force them to run away to India. But these designs were not understood by the illiterate Indian Muslims who carried the impression that Pakistan was their true-well-wisher and Pakistan would save them if need be, "against the onslaughts of Hindu fanaticism." Loaded with orthodoxy and such a frame of mind, they did not hesitate to unleash in violence and rotting whenever there was an opportunity. Pakistan, once again tried to inflame the situation in Jammu and Kashmir in 1990. Its foreign minister subsequently after his return from India made derogatory speeches leading to many Pakistani people vainly attempting to cross the international border. The Kashmir militants and sikh terrorists of Punjab are being actively supported and equated with adequate training of sophisticated weapons causing torture killing and kidnaping of innocent people in Kashmir, Punjab, U.P. and Haryana.

5. The Factor of Hindu Chauvinism. Hindu community became Chauvinistic, in wake of Muslim religion's orthodoxy and hostility. During the pre-independence period, it was then fomenwed by the Hindu Mahasabha, the Arya Samaj and the Rashtriya Swayam Sewak Sangh (RSS). Great emphasis was laid on Hindu culture by these organisations in a "predominantly Hindu land," stressed Hindutya, Hindu Rashtra and Hindu Bhasha (Hindi), and glorified Aryavarta the land of magnificent culture and ancient civilization, an depicting British as well as Muslim culture as 'alien'.

Their Chauvinism became more intense after the partition of the country, the Hindu beliefs, values and institutions were vigorously emphasized planned movements by these organisations were popularised. The Hindu Mahasabha in October 1950 started enrolling the non-Hindu minorities, on the condition that only those who had "stakes" in the mother-land and were prepared to safeguard them under the system of "Hindu Rashtra" would be granted membership of the Organization.

The leadership of the Hindus came into the control of the Jan Sangh, the political wing of the RSS. On the eve of the Second Gerneral Election. The Jan Sangh demanded the annulment of partition and restoration of "Akhand Bharat" on the eve of the Second General Election in 1957. In the next General Election (1962) it stressed upon Bhartiya Sanskriti and Maryada (culture and civilization).

Owing to the prevailing political consideration, the Jan Sangh made a casual reference to its anti-Muslim slant in its Fourth General Election Manifesto and stated that Congress Government "appeared separatist, disruptionist and anti-national forces". At the All-India Delegate's Session of the Jan Sangh at Patna in December 1969 demand was put forward for the "Indianisation" of all fissiparious elements, especially those overtly or convertly believing in the "two-nation" theory. One of the leaders of the Jan Sangh, Balraj Madhok, said on 12 February 1970 : "Islam will have to be Indianised if Indian Muslims are to become nationalists." "The present face of Islam," he said, "is most dangerous." He also observed that so long as "the biggest den of communal and anti-national activities, "was allowed to function, the Indianisation of the Muslims was not possible." Militant attitude towards the Muslims was kept continued by the RSS, and its chief leader, M.S. Golwalker, who in his book, A Bunch of Thoughts, sought to establish Indian nationality was founded on Hinduism. At one place he stated that India meant "Hindu Rashtra" and that Indian culture, was basically Hindu culture.

The All-India Muslims Political Convention in December 1970, demanded separate electorate for the Muslims. To this the Hindu Mahasabha reacted and held that the move was fraught with grave consequtences. In a resolution, it stated that those Muslims who still sought separate privileges on the basis of 'two-nation theory' should be sent to Pakistan "on a Government level." The Hindu leaders endeavoured in January 1971, to form a "Hindu Sena" to counter the "Muslim Sena." Ranjan Baba Satyarathis, the convenor of the All India Hindu Sena said the Sena would be "closer" to Jan Sangh which was a "nationalist party." "The Shiv Sena in Maharasthra, originally directed against Communists and trade unionists, adopted in mid-1970, a violently anti-Muslim stance." Its chief leader, Bal Thackeray, denounced the "green menace of Islam." In the Shiv Sena journal be wrote: "Hindus should not only remain Hindus, but be fanatic Hindus and dedicated crusaders of their religion. I am not ashamed to say that I am a fanatic Hindu." The issue of Ram Janma Bhumi and Babri Masjid has also caused unrest in the communal quarters of Indian society. The Rath Yatra organised by the BJP also resulted in Hindu Muslim riots in certain party of the country. It was said to be a vote catching device on the eve of General Elections after the fall of Chandra Shekhars' Government. The 'Shila Pooja ceremony' conducted by the Vishwa Hindu Parished in 1989 created a great upsurge and temperaments went high.

6. Inefficient Handling of the Menace by the Government. The failure of Union and State Government in tackling the problem efficiently was one of the causes of the persistence of Hindu-Muslim Communalism. The problem was never handled rationally, and each time 'there was a flare up the non-Congress were made the scapegoat and were blamed for it. The tendency of the rulers was to treat the Hindu-Muslim riots as a law and order problems while the malady had its roots in economic disparity, social backwardness and religious and cultural diversities of the two communities.'

Very often, the administration failed in controlling the riots. The Muslim community often alleged that the police, and even its intelligence wing, never took appropriate action whenever there was a flare-up to stop it. The Muslims also alleged that the government officials, "mostly Hindus, connived when the majority community was on the offensive, that the government did not provide adequate relief and assistance when they (the Muslims) were the victims of onslaughts, and that even after those who indulged in communal violence had been caught were not punished." Likewise the sikhs who became victim of 1984 riots after Mrs. Indira Gandhi's assassination by the sikh guards in Delhi and adjoining areas still nurse a grouse that the culprits have not been brought to book. The sikh psyche feels hurt and sikh militancy exploits the situation.

CASTE AND POLITICS

Before we explain the role of caste in Indian politics it is essential to define the term caste. Caste signifies a population with a common general culture divided by social barrier into endogmous units each of which possesses some peculiar cultural specialities. These units are heirarchial according to the rank of purity. Caste in India may be defined as a homogenious endogamous social control organisation performing different rituals especially those pertaining to a religious purity. Each caste and sub-caste is accorded an offical status rating high or low according to the date of its origin, its suffered one time occupation and the structurers of its moral and religious codes. Caste is an endemic feature of Hindu life and is exclusively an Indian phenomenon. An indigenous word for caste is 'jati' in Sanskrit or 'Zat' in persian meaning race, a fact which has led some scholars to point a racial or tribal origin for castes. There are orignially four castes based on division of labour viz. Brahmins, Kashtriyas, Vasiya and Sudra. The Brahmins constituted the priestly class, Kashtriyas the warrior class, Vaisya the traders class and Sudras the class of labourers together with the outcastes termed as Harijans by Gandhiji. Birth decided the entry of a person into a caste. In the initial stages the casge system became exclusive.

Prof. G.S. Ghurya has explained features of caste as below:

(i) Castes are groups each with a well developed life of its own the membership whereof unlike that of voluntary associations and classes is determined not by selection but by birth.

(ii) To everybody in India there is a definite scheme of social precedence among the castes with a Brahmin at the head of social hierachy.

(iii) There are restrictions on feeding and social intercourse.

(iv) There is a lack of unrestricted choice of occupation.

(v) There are restrictions on marriage.

(vi) Segregation of individual castes and groups of castes in a villages is the most abvious mark of civil privileges and disabilities and it has prevailed in more or less defined forms all over India.

As referred in, 'Social Service in India' edited by E. Blunt, "A Caste is an endogamous group or a collection of endogamous groups bearing common name membership of which is hereditary imposing on its members certain restrictions in matters of social intercourse either following a common traditional occupation or claiming a common origin and generally regarded as framing a single homogeneous community."

However, the traditional concept of caste has undergone a change. A fairly sizable number of differentiations have come to the force within the caste groups resulting in deviation from caste norms with impurity. The elder for instance cannot exercise authority over the youngers with the same degree of command and confidence as was the case previously. Besides educational attainments service status and financial position assign a person very respectable position irrespective of caste attachments. This is a sort of caste transformation. However that does not amount to termination of caste system. The lower castes have striven to emulate the ways of higher ones. Professor Srinivas remarks, "There is a wide-spread impression among educated Indian that the caste is on its last legs and that educated urbanized and westernized members of the upper classes have already escaped its bond. Both these impressions are wrong.

CASTE AND INDIAN POLITICS

There is no denying the fact that, the caste system which is operational in Indian political system is no longer traditional. It also cannot be denied that reservations and safe guards as provided in the Indian Constitution, for certain castes and tribes has given caste system an opportunity to operate as well. It is gradually gaining tighter groups on Indian body politic. Caste in fact has been politicized. In parliamentary democracy like that of ours caste considerations have influenced the political behaviour of the people at the time of distribution of election tickets and also composition of ministries. It has been generally observed that the persons of a particular caste vote enblock for a candidate of their own caste or for some other candidate as per decision of their caste panchayat. It has been seen that irrespective of merit and demerits of a particular candidate the members of his caste have exercised franchise in his favour. Hence the parties concerned have been particular that such a candidate is given a ticket who could get votes of his caste inhabiting the constituency tame consideration weighs on the minds of party leaders while choosing party office beares. Even alliances of parties are sometimes formed on the basis of caste consideration by mutual give and take.

It may also be said that caste politicisation is not a one way traffic. If caste orientation involves politics, politics also leaves its effect upon caste solidarity. A caste conscious of social stratification makes an effort for modernizing the life of its members and for saving itself from social injustice. For instance the Shanans—low caste south Indian—had indulged in riots till the feudal potentate of Travancore conceded that their women folk could cover their bosoms in any way but different from the women of the upper castes. Independent Indian has added to the vigour of politicization of caste. Hence it has started manifesting itself at regional level as well. The top leaders do proclaim a casteless society but the newly unfranchised rural masses are aware of the language of traditional politics. Hence as said by Morris Jones, ".... Behind the formal list of party candidates nominated for the contests there is probably as an inside story of careful calculations in terms of caste appeal." For instance inspite of a clear directive issued at the Avadi session of 1955 the congress leadership particularly in Andhra Pradesh on the eve of second General Elections postponed the selection of candidates until the C.P.I. had finalised its list.

Political articulation of caste attains climaxty when a certain party is set up to protect and promote the interests of its members. Caste associations thus establish an institutional means of their own to capture power and compel other political parties to recognise their existence. The Justice Party of Madras and Independent Labour party of Bombay are such examples of pre-independent era: Getting fed up with the achievements of their caste associations the Vanniyars of Madras convened in 1951 a meeting of Vanniyakulu Kahattriye Sangam on a state wide basis and resolved that they should contest elections in co-operation with the toiling masses. This led to the formation of Tamilnadu Toilars Party whose assistance was sought by the congress led coalition government of Rajgopalachari followed by Kamraj Nadar. The Jharkhand Party of Bihar is another such example.

CHARACTERISTICS OF CASTE IN INDIAN POLITICS

An analysis of Caste in Indian Politics reveals following characteristics:

(i) Caste politicization has been a two way traffic. One has affected the other and opened a new direction for the study of politics in our country.

(ii) Caste associations strive for the protection and promotion of their specific interests like separate electorates, reservation of seats in educational institutions, public services, removal of disqualifying classes etc.

(iii) Caste politicization shows its glaring presence at the time of elections Jat for Jat, Ahir for Ahir, Brahmin for Brahmin, Bania for Bania are the election cries and slogans. Various caste associations induce their respective members to exercise vote for their caste member. A powerful caste like Jharkhand in Bihar may nominate its candidates and marshall support in their favour.

(iv) The relationship between the Caste and Politics has been determined by the factor of expediency and pragmatism. It has been changing with the rise and fall of innovators of politics. The scheduled castes who are congress vote bank did not vote for congress in 1977. In 1980 they again voted for congress led by Mrs. Gandhi despite the fact that the Janata-the ruling party was led by a great Harijan leader-Jagjiwan Ram.

(v) Traditional Caste rivalries have impact on the politics of our country. In Andhra Pradesh Congress has always banked on the support of Reddies and the Communists have sought the support of the Kammas.

CASTE AND STATE POLITICS

Caste politics plays major role at local and regional levels. It is marginal at all India level. Caste politics has been of maximum intensity in south of Vindhya mountains where is post independent era struggle took place to dispossess Brahmins of power and position. However that phase has now come to an end and a struggle between newly dominant middle classes and the submerged mass of lower castcs and untouchable has just begun. A birds eye view of the role of caste in state politics will be evident after making an appraisal of the state politics in some of the leading states of India.

(A) Bihar. It represents the scene of a clash among four major castes-Brahmins, Rajputs Kayasthas and the backward tribals. Jharkhand Party comprising Advasis of backward tribal people of Bihar and Orissa border could succeed in capturing most of the seats reserved for tribals and backward section of society in 1957 elections. This enabled them to intensify their demand for a separate tribal state of Jharkhand consisting of all tribal areas of Bihar, Orissa and Madhya Pradesh. It proved to be a potential danger to the Congress Party. The Congress High Command deputed Raj Kumari Amrit Kaur to visit the tribal areas to wean away tribesmen particularly Christians (as she was Christian) from the growing influence of this organisation. Congress succeeded in dirving a wedge as Jharkhand party stands divided into two parts-Jharkhand and Hul Jharkhand.

(B) Maharashtra. Marathas, Brahmains and Mahars have been playing significant role in the politics of Maharashtra. Brahmins being more highly educated have played more conspicuous role in urban areas in particular. The Marathas on the other hand have been equally effective in the rural areas Satara and Kolhapur in particular. The Mahars (untouchables) have assumed a privilege position as a vote bank as they have been working as Labourers in the industrial units and commercial ogranisations and joining army services. The Congress has tried to maintain a balance between these castes still at times it has failed in its mission.

(C) Kerala. The role of caste in the politics of Kerala suffered a set back on account of open confrontation of the Hindus with the Christians on the West Coast and with the Muslims in the northern part of the state. The amalgamation of Travancore-Cochin princely states resulted into the emergence of Kerala—the biggest Malyalam speaking state comprising an overwhelming majority of Hindus divided into castes-Brahmins (Namboodripas) Nayyars and Izhavas or Tiyyans (a backward class)

(D) Tamil Nadu. In pre-independence era the Dravidians organised justice party and there Commenweal and Toilers Party. Most of them forged a front under the banner of Dravida Kazhagam of Naicker-an anti-Hindi anti-Hindi and anti-Hindustan organisation. A large section of the party under the leadership of C. Annaduraj joined the Dravida Murnnetra Kazhgam. In the recent past another faction get separated from the DMK and became Anna DMK under the leadership of M.G. Ramachandran. All these Dravidian Organisations drew sustenance from caste. The extremists amongst them demanded a separate sovereign state-Dravidisthan. The moderates amongst the demanded an autonomous province of their own, now existing as Tamilnadu.

(E) Karnataka. In this state traditional rivalary between Lingayats and Vokkaliyas has been going on since long. The Vokkaligas who predominat in Mysore and are worshippers of Lord Vishnu have apprehensions that they would always remain dominated by Lingayats in Kannade speaking state. They have asked for a seperate state-

Dakshina Pradesh. The Lingayats worshippers of Lord Shiva hold sway in Banglore areas. They are opposed to Dakshina Pradesh and desired the formation of Kannada speaking state. The fall of K. Hannmanthayya can be attributed to traditional rivalry between the two dominant castes of Karnataka.

(F) Madhya Pradesh. In the state the Kammas dominant in Krishna Godavri delta known by the nickname of 'Kamma Rashtra' and Reddies dominant in other areas (Royalseema) play vital role. The communists bank upon the support of Kammas whereas the congress has enjoyed the support of the Reddies. Brahmins have reaped political gains out of prevailing rivelry between the two dominant castes. On the eve of second General Election held in 1957 the Congress High Command duputed S.K. Patil to visit the areas and weaken the grip of the communists. He could win the support of a Harijan Kamma Leader N.G. Ranga. The position of Reddies got-boost with the inclusion of Telangana in Andhra Predesh and this went in favour of congress.

(G) Punjab. In case of Punjab the element of caste remained in the sphere of religion and furnished a new dimension to the study of caste politicization. The example of sikhs is worth quoting. The sikhs claim separate entity as well as they constitute part of Hindu community as well. They claim sikh is a caste a community and religion. The privailing rivalry and skirmishes between the sikhs non-sikhs and emerging Akali and non-Akali politics is worthy study. A sizable section of extremists termed often as militants demand a separate and sovereign state for sikhs called Khalistan. The moderates had felt satisfied with the creation of a Punjabi Suba named later punjab-as a autonomous state within the Indian union. To begin with the sikhs fought for Punjabi language whereas non-sikhs expressed zealousness for Hindi. Thus Gurdwara Politics was pitched against Arya Samaj Politics. The Akali Dals have been more secure in rural areas. Hence they banked upon rural vote whereas the Hindites banked upon urban voters. Thus Jan Sangh now BJP and Arya Samaj who espoused strongly the cauuse fo Hindi were ever sure of votes of urban areas people worthy the traders, the shopkeepers, the upperclass businessman.

(H) Haryana. 'Jat' Politics has reigned supreme in Haryana which came into existence in 1966. Jat community has been solidly to coming the line of top Jat personalities like Ch. Bansi Lal and Ch. Devi Lal and forging a united front. Likewise Ahirs have stood togehter and have always sought guidance either from Rao Brindar Singh and Col. Ram Singh. Brahmins have followed the lines laid down by Pt. Bhagwat Dayal Sharma. The Punjabis had divided line of action. Some of them stood for congress others for BJP. Now they are getting united. Whosoever may be dominant they want their pound of flesh for being a sizable chink of vote bank. The Banias too have been either supporting BJP being the traders or toeing the line of leader of their community if he happened to be at the helm of affairs or in the coterie of top leaders. Sh. B.D. Gupta once Chicf Minister has been able to assert on this account. The Harijans is a divided lot. They accepted Ch. Chand Ram as their leader, who has been a turn coat. He has been however most of the time a congressite. Ch. Devi Lal has been a founder of Janata Dal prior to its split when J.D. Samajwadi came into existence. Ch. Devi Lal and his protegy stand for JDS. Bishnois as a caste are all out for Ch. Bhajan Lal-the present Chief Minister of Haryana who claims to be a refugee from west Pakistan. Hence the Refugees-the Punjabi settlers in Haryana have almost always stood for him. K.R. Punia ex IAS is the new Harijan leader who formerely belonged to Janta Dal later on resigned and untimately switched loyalties to congress.

Thus a study of a role of caste in well meaning states of the Indian Union makes us conclude that caste has exerted its influence on the political processes though in unison with the vicious forces of communalism regionalism and linguism. Certain clever astists have given a caste cum communal cum regional complexion to the issues in question. Besides caste politicization has been in perpetual flux of changability. At times one party gained at the expense of others. However congress has been the chief beneficiary.

An appraisal of role of caste in Indian and state politics reveals that caste is everywhere the unit of social action. We state below the good and had aspects of caste politicization.

❐

10

Foreign Capital and Indian Politics

ROLE OF MNCs

A multinational corporation (MNC) is a company, firm or enterprise with its headquarters in a developed country such as the United States, Britain, West Germany, Japan, etc. and also operates in other countries, both developed and developing. They are spread not only in the LDCs of Asia, Africa and Latin America, but also on the continents of Europe, Australia, New Zealand, and South America. They are enagaged in mining, tea, rubber, and cocoa plantations: oil extraction and refining, manufacturing for home production and exports, etc. Their opeations also include such services as banking, insurance, shipping, hotels and so on. Thus "like animals in the Zoo, MNCs come in various shapes and sizes, perform distinctive functions differently and their individual impact on the environment."

Sanjaya Lal and Streeten define the MNCs from economic, organizational and motivational viewpoints. They economic definition lays emphasis on the size, geographical spread and extent of foreign involvement of the MNC. According to this definition a typical multinational company is one with net sales of 100 million dollars to several thousand million dollars having direct foreign investment in manufacturing usually accounting for at least 15 to 20 per cent of the company's total investment.

The organisational definition stresses on some organisational aspects of an MNC, besides the economic ones. In this respect a truly MNC is that which "*(a)* acts as an organisation maximising one overall objective for all its units, *(b)* treats the whole world (or the parts open to it) as its operational area, and *(c)* is able to co-ordinate all its function in any way necessary for achieving *(a)* and *(b)*.

The motivational definition highlights "corporate philosophy and motivation in laying down criteria for multinationality. Thus, 'True' multinationality is generally indicated by a lack of nationalism, or a concern with the firm as a whole rather than with any of its constituent units or any country of its operations." On this basis firms are distinguished between ethnocentric (home-oriented), polycentric (host-oriented) and geocentric (world-oriented), on the basis of attitudes reveald by their executives.

Lal and Streeten define MNCs in general as very large firms with widespread operations which are clearly in character and have more than five foreign subsidiaries or more than 15 per cent of total sales produced abroad, and acting in a cohesive manner to achieve maximum profit or growth.

Spread of MNCs. MNCs overwhelmingly dominate not only global investment but also international production trade, finance and technology. But adequate and reliable up-to-date data regarding the spread of MNCs in terms of subsidiaries, production, trade, finance and technology are rarely published and hence are not available. A poineering study, Sovereignty at Bay (1971), by Raymond Vernon listed 100 colossal MNCs whose total production (not sales) of goods and services totalled $350 billion a year. Of these, 187 were US controlled raw material producers and manufacturing concerns, half of the remaining third were British and Dutch, and the other half European and Japanese. Among the first ten, eight were American and the remaining two were British-Dutch combines, the largest being General motors with the total world sales of $25 billion which exceeded the GNP of all but a dozen countries in 1970.

An American magazine Forbes (November 15, 1971) published a list of 50 major American corporations which revealed that on an average 40 per cent of their total revenue came from their fields like tea (115 branches), pharmaceuticals (24 branches and subsidiaries), cosmetics, food products, manufacture of industrial products and consumer goods of wide range, oil exploration, book publishing, automobilies, chemicals, fertilisers, etc.

MERITS OF MNCs

The advantage flowing from the MNCs to the LDCs are based on the theories of direct foreign investment. Such theories are related to oligopolisitic interdependence and monopolistic behaviour of the MNCs. Henc they confer the following advantages on MNCs.

1. MNCs are financially very strong and hence provide large and cheap capital to the LDCs by way of direct investment.
2. They undertake great risk in investing their funds in LDCs in the face of imperfect infrastructural facilities like power, transport, skilled labour, etc., low market demand and short supply of inputs.
3. MNCs bring in new techniques of marketing in LDCs through market research at their headquarters. They adopt novel advertising and promotional methods which impart information to buyers and create demand for particular brands and products.
4. They start new ventures and bestow the advantages of superior management, training, education and entrepreneurial ability in LDCs.
5. They transfer superior technology to LDCs based on R & D in the parent concerns because they are able to spend huge funds on R & D. This leads to the discovery and introduction of new processes and new and differentiated products in LDCs which tend to raise the standard living of the people in LDCs.
6. Above all, MNCs are socially desirable in LDCs because they lead to a net increase in capital formation output and employment.

DEMERITS OF MNCs

MNCs have come to be regarded as agents of exploitation in LDCs because of their invidious operations which are highlighted in their modus operandi.

The US-based MNCs insist on per cent ownership in LDCs and they have succeeded in this in Singapore, Mexico, Hong Kong, Brazil and Taiwan. With low rates of taxation in these countries, they have been exporting "super profits" to America.

In countries like India where since the 1960s, the MNCs are allowed to operate as joint ventures with 25 to 40 per cent participation, they enjoy a number of privileges which again tend to increase their profits manifold. Such consessions or privileges are in the form of dividends, payment for installation fee, royalty on the use of patents, payment on know-how fee, payment for imported equipment whose price is 30 to 40 per cent higher than the competitive international price, and tax holday for a number of years of the concern belongs to the priority sector industry.

Besides, the staff which comes in the wake of an MNCs is paid very high salaries. Some of their top executives get much more than the highest paid executive head of the state in which they serve. Not only this, the MNCs pay to the locally employed labour twice and even three times more than what they might earn in local firms. This not only leads to social inequality but also breeds discontent and unrest among the workers employed in indigenous industry.

The MNCs are pre-empting local savings by overpricing the imports and underpricing the exports of LDCs. In cases where there is competition from local entreprenuers, the MNCs undercut them by charging low prices for their products. As a result, the local firms are squeezed out of business.

The MNCs transfer second rate and overpriced technology to LDCs. More often, they try to minimise the transfer of technology to such countries by *(a)* carrying out R & D in the parent company located at the headquarters; *(b)* neglecting the training of local personnel for R & D posts; and *(c)* holding closely the techology itself. Moreover, the technology which the MNCs transfer into the LDCs is capital-intensive and hence unsuited to their capital-scarce and labour-surplus economies.

The MNCs set up their plants in big towns and cities in LDCs where infrastructural facilities are easily available. Thus they accentuate sectoral inequalities and strengthen dualism in such countries.

Besides, the long-term effect of direct and indirect investment by the MNCs on the balance of payments is usually negative, as they repatriate huge amounts in the form of royalties, profit, interest, dividend capital, etc.

Last but not the least, the MNCs influence the internal politics to the deteriment of the LDCs by bribing the legislators not only directly but also indirectly. They offer posts in the higher echelons of their companies to the privileged sections of the society, especially to the friends and relatives of the local politicians, bureaucrats and the economic oligarchies. They also subvert domestic fiscal and monetary policies in LDCs.

It is not that the MNCs are simply the agents of exploitation, they also act as agents of development. By establishing manufacturing plants, providing production, managerial, technical, organisational and marketing skills, and by harnessing their resources, the MNCs have helped in augmenting the GNP of Singapore, Hong Kong, Taiwan and Canada. But as pointed out earlier, these benefits accuring to such countries have been the outcome of the self-interest of the MNCs, that is, the need to meet the US domestic market.

The problem before the other developing countries like India is how to control and curtail the damaging effect of MNCs and harness them for their maximum benefit. All this depends upon the "will" to control the working of these global gaints. Given this, the LDCs should have stringent anti-trust laws, as we have in India the twin institutions known as the Monopolies Commission and the MRTP Act. The MNCs should be encouraged to enter into 'licensing agreements' with a local manufacturer who may be taught the use of the patented processes in lieu of a fixed royalty.

The LDCs should also take advantage of the expertise and superior technical know-how of the MNCs by entering into 'turnkey agreements' with them whereby a foreign company undertakes to build a plant or help in exploiting their natural resources, imparts training to local personnel, provides technical know-how, starts production and then leaves the country for good by entrusting the entire operations to the local firm. In lieu of these services, the MNC should be paid either a fixed fee or cost-plus fee.

Further, there should be joint venture agreements on 60-40 basis at the maximum by the local concerns with the MNCs. All joint ventures with the foreign concerns should be based on specific agreements to manufacture the product within the country with indigneously produced and procured raw matrials (provided they are available), to train and employ nationals in high jobs, to carry on R & D within the host country and to reinvest a certain percentage of prifits wihtin it.

It is advisable, as suggested by Streeten, that the governments of LDCs should not press the MNCs to pay specially high wages to local labour. Rather, the MNCs should be asked to employ local people at the prevalent rates for the same jobs in the country. On the other hand, they should tax the MNCs more heavily so that the people of the country benefit rather than the few people who work for them. This increased tax revenue may be spent of providing greater infrastructrual facilities to the people which will benefit all sections of the society including the MNCs.

Given the conditions laid down above, the MNCs should be encouraged to establish plants in backward areas or regions of LDCs so that regional imbalances are ironed out.

GLOBALIZATION, EFFECT OF MNCs

Multinational Corporations (MNCs) are huge industrial organisations which extend their industrial and marketing operations through a network of their branches or their Majority Owned Foreign Affiliates (MOFAs). MNCs are also known as Transactional Corporations (TNCs). Instead of aiming for maximization of their profits from one or two products, the MNCs operate in a number of fields and from this point of view, their business strategy extends over a number of products and over a number of countries. At the onset of the 1990s, there were 37,000 TNCs whose tentacles straddled the international economy through 1,70,000 overseas affiliates. They possess staggering resources as would be clear form the fact that the revenue of 200 top corporations stood at $ 3,046 billion in 1982 which rose further to $ 5,862 billion in 1992. Their share in world GPD rose from 24.2 per cent to 26.8 per cent over at the same period. Their aggregate profits stand at a mammoth $ 73.4 billion. Of this, the share of the largest 10 corporations is as much as $ 34.8 billion—a towering 47 per cent of the profits of the 200 mega corporations.

The above data show the massive control exercised by the MNCs on the world economy. In fact, because of their huge capital resources, latest technology and worldwide goodwill, MNCs are in a position to sell whatever product they choose to manufacture in different countries. The fact is that people in underdeveloped countries are 'crazy' for the products of these corporations and prefer their products to the products produced indigenously.

REASONS FOR THE GROWTH OF MNCs

Reasons for the growth of multinationals are manifold, the important ones being as follows:

1. Expansion of Market Territory. As the operations of a large sized firm expand and as its international image builds up, it seeks more and more extension of its activities beyond the physical boundaries of the country in which it is incorporated.

2. Financial Superiorities. A multinational firm enjoys the following financial superiorities over the national firm; *(a)* It has huge financial resources with which it can easily turn all circumstances in its favour; *(b)* It maintains a high level of funds utilization by generating funds in one country and using them in another; *(c)* It has easier access to external capital markets; and *(d)* Because of its international reputation it is able to raise more international resources. Even investors and banks of the host country are eager to invest in it.

3. Marketing Superiorities. A multinational firm enjoys a number of marketing superiorities over the national firms; *(a)* It possesses a more reliable and uptodate market information system, *(b)* It enjoys market reputation and faces less difficulty in selling its products; *(c)* It adopts more effective advertising and sales promotion techniques, and *(d)* It has efficient warehousing facilities due to lower inventory requirements.

4. Technological Superiorities. The main reason why MNCs have been encouraged by the underdeveloped countries to participate in their industrial development is on account of the technological superiorities which these firms possess as compared to national companies. The underdeveloped countries regard transfer of technology from MNCs useful on account of the following reasons: *(a)* Industrialization represents the most important way out of underdevelopment and the resources of these countries are insufficient to sustain the industrial progress on their own; *(b)* Local manpower, materials, local capital equipments etc. have to be optimally exploited and these countries are unable to accomplish this; *(c)* Depending totally on local companies would require heavy imports of raw materials, capital equipment, machinery and technical knowledge whereas MNCs bring these on their own; and *(d)* The underdeveloped countries have to face stiff competition for selling their products in international markets. Unless their goods meet international standards and quality specifications, they cannot sell. MNCs help them in producing such goods.

5. Product Innovations. MNCs have Research and Development Departments engaged in the task of developing new products and superior designs of existing products. Therefore their production opportunities are far greater as compared to national companies.

DOMINATION OF MNCs

MNCs have a strong hold over the Indian economy. In fact, even two decades ago these corporations controlled 53.7 per cent of the assets of the giant sector in India. According to the Industrial Licensing Policy Inquiry Committee, there were 112 companies in India in 1966 with assets worth Rs. 10 crores or more. Of these, 48 were either foreign branches or Indian subsidiaries of foreign companies. In addition, 14 Indian companies had extremely heavy loans and equity capital and, therefore, were virtually foreign controlled. These 62 companies had Rs. 1,370 crores worth of assets which constituted 54 per cent of the total companies were also under foreign domination in one way or the other. In return for technical assistance, they had promised an assured market of machines and spares to their foreign associates. Some companies were heavily dependent on international financial institutions for economic assistance.

An interesting thing about the operations of MNCs in India is that they have raised a major part of investment resources from within the Indian economy. A study on the sources of finance of MNCs was conducted by Sudip Chaudhuri for the period 1956-75. The sample selected for study included 50 largest foreign subsidiaries. His analysis revealed that for the period 1956-75 as a whole, foreign sources (in the form of foreign share capital and foreign loans) contributed only 5.4 per cent of the financial resources of these companies, 94.6 per cent being contributed by the domestic sources. Directly comparable data are not available for the period after 1975. However, Table 5.4 of John Martinussen's study shows that the amount of capital issues consented with foreign participation declined from 61.5 per cent of all consent to public limited companies in 1976 to a mere 29.5 per cent in 1980. John Martinussen indicates that 20 TNC affiliated companies even reduced their foreign funding. Several of these companies obtained no foreign funds at all during the period from 1974 to 1983. This fact about the financing behaviour of MNCs explodes the myth that they bring in large amounts of foreign capital with them.

FOREIGN COLLABORATION AND MNCs

A common form of MNC participation in Indian industry is through entering into collaboration with Indian industrialists. Foreign collaboration agreements are made between Indian companies and foreign parties, involving sale of technology, as well as use of foreign brand names for the final products. The enormity of foreign collaborations entered into by the Indian companies would be clear from the fact that in nearly all of the new industries in the large or medium size group, privately or publicly owned, set up after Independence, some collaboration agreement was present. Trends of liberalisation in the 1980s gave a substantial spurt to foreign collaborations. This would be clear from the fact that of the total 12,760 foreign collaboration agreements approved in 40 years between 1948 and 1988, as many as 6,165 (i.e. 48.3 per cent) were approved during the eighty years between 1981 and 1988. As a result of liberalised foreign investment policy announced in July-August 1991, there has been a further spurt in foreign collaborations. The value of approvals of direct investment proposals rose considerably from $ 325 million (Rs. 739 crores) in 1991 to $ 4.3 billion (Rs. 13,591 crores) in 1994. The total direct foreign investment proposals approved since 1991 till September 1995 amounts to $ 15.0 billion (Rs. 46,580 crores), against just under $ 1.0 billion (Rs. 1,274 crores) approved during the whole of the previous decade (1981-90).

A study of the foreign collaborations reveals certain interesting results. Thus, a large number of agreements were concluded for the manufacture of products which were non-essential or which could be produced with the help of local technology. These items included vacuum flasks, lipstick, toothpaste, cosmetics, brassiers, ice-cream, gin, beer, biscuits, dry batteries and readymade garments. Not only were collaborations granted for these products, they were often in multiple numbers and were renewed on expiry.

In addition to this 'orientation' of foreign collaborations, they also suffered from a number of other drawbacks as is clear from the following considerations.

(i) The government permitted multiple collaborations, i.e. repetitive import of the same or similar technology. This resulted in repetitive payments without adding to the stock of technical knowledge in the country;

(ii) The terms of agreements were mostly weighted in faovur of the foreign collaborators and were against Indian interests. This arose on account of the lack of bargaining power in the Indian side and the government's eagerness to acquire foreign participation in the fact of foreign exchange shortage;

(iii) The practice of multiple collaborations led to the introduction of standards of various countries (in raw materials, spare parts, deigns, specifications, and even terms of measurement) into the Indian industry even for very similar products or within the same firm. This multiplicity led to large inventory accumulation and uneconomic locking up of working capital. It also hindered standardisation and variety reduction which are so essential for raising industrial productivity;

(iv) Since the responsibility of specification and supply of equipment was entrusted to the foreign collaborators, there was close tie-up between the designers and suppliers resulting not only in price mark-up but also in over-import of equipment. Sometimes equipments were imparted even when they were available locally, sometimes they remained idle for want of spares, and often the processes were more highly mechanised and sophisticated than was desirable or necessary. At times, obsolete technology was imported;

(v) The terms of payment were also drawn up so as to squeeze out the maximum payment under one head or other. Generally 5 per cent of the annual turnover for 10 years as royalty plus 5 per cent of the imported plant cost as technical fees in the case of royalty-cum-technical fees, or 10 per cent of the issued capital as lumpsum payment for technical fees alone, were the limits of official policy. However, these tended to become routine;

(vi) The most important part related to the presence of various restrictive clauses in the agreements. Some restrictions imposed were: *(a)* the technology cannot be passed on to any one else, in some cases even after the expiry of the agreement; *(b)* manufacturing is to be carried out according to the specifications laid down by the collaborator and no local adaptations can be made; *(c)* control over overseas purchased was exercised through the provision that it had to be made directly or indirectly through the collaborator; *(d)* production was tightly controlled at times through the posing of foreign technicians; *(e)* controls over the pricing and marketing of the products were exercised by requiring that a part of the production was to be sold to the collaborator's subsidiary in India at a fixed commission or that specified firms were to be made the sole selling agents; and *(f)* right to export was also restricted by provision that exports could be done only to specific countries or on certain preconditions; and

(vii) Foreign collaborations have helped the growth of monopolies and concentration. They joined hands with the big business houses and the latter were only too eager to enter into understanding with them since the presence of foreign links often conferred certain strategic advantages (patent, resources, foreign exchange, etc.) enabling the big business houses to diversify and expand.

HARMFUL EFFECTS OF THE OPERATIONS OF MNCs ON INDIAN ECONOMY

The operations of MNCs open up the possibilities of interference in the industrial (and other) activities of the recipient country and are thus resented by the 'nationalist' thinkers. Their arguments against the operations of MNCs can be summed up as follow:

1. Payment of Dividends and Royalty. A large sum of money flows out of the country in terms of payment of dividends, profits, royalties, technical fees and interest to the foreign investors. For instance, remittance made abroad by private sector companies stood at Rs. 72.26 crores in 1969-70. This rose to Rs. 398.9 crores in 1981-82 and further to 813.5 crores in 1989. A study by N.K. Chandra shows that over three fifths of private corporate, or about two fifths of factory sector dividends were paid out by the foreign firms in the mid-1980s.

2. Distortion of Economic Structure. MNCs can inflict heavy damage on the host country in various forms such as suppression of domestic enterpreneurship, extension of oligopolistic practices (such as unnecessary product differentiation, heavy advertising, or excessive profit taking), supplying the economy with unsuitable technology and unsuitable products, worsening of income distribution by distorting the production structure to meet the requirements of high-income elites, etc. Modern Marxist economists (Paul Baran, for example) argue that foreign investment (especially through multinational corporations) opens up the doors of 'neo-imperialism' and 'exploitation'.

3. Technology Transfer not Necessarily Conducive to Development. As far as transfer of technology to underdeveloped countries is concerned, the behaviour pattern of MNCs reveals that they do not engage in R & D activities within the underdeveloped countries. Their R & D efforts are concentrated in laboratories in the home county or in other industrialised countries. Though R & D activities continue to be centralized in the parent country, the host countries have to bear the bulk of their costs since the affiliates of the MNCs in these countries remit payments on this account generally in relation to their sales volume. Such payments by the affiliates are generally over and above those remitted in the form of royalties and technical fees to the parent firm. The satisfaction expressed on technology transfer is partly misconceived also on account of the fact that MNCs which generally command a semi-monopolistic position in their product lines do not transfer their first-line or most advanced technology until foreign firms compel them to do so. In many cases, the technology transferred is of a capital intensive nature which is not useful from the point of view of a labour surplus economy. In fact, continued insistence on the import of such technology can have serious consequences for the economy of the host country since unemployment will increase.

4. Political Interference. Because of their immense financial and technical power, the MNCs have gained the necessary strength to influence the decision making processes in underdeveloped countries. Though they do help in transferring technology to underdeveloped countries. It has been often found that models and patterns of industrial development and technologies transferred are not in harmony with the interests of the host countries. The governments of underdeveloped countries have also felt threatened by the direct and indirect interference of MNCs in their internal affairs. The autonomy and sovereignty of the host countries is in danger. Because of these reasons, the governments of various countries have sought to restrict the activities of MNCs in their economies through a battery of administrative controls and legal provisions.

CONTROL OVER MULTINATIONAL CORPORATIONS

The responsibility of controlling the activities of Multinational Corporations in India rests on different government agencies. These agencies are: *(i)* the Ministry of Company Affairs, *(ii)* the Reserve Bank of India, *(iii)* the Ministry of Industrial Development, and *(iv)* the Ministry of Finance. However, these agencies do not work in close cooperation with each other. As a result, there is no coordination in their functioning. Each case is discussed on its own merits by the authorities.

As a result of a study of Michael Kidron entitled Foreign Investment in India published in 1965 (and the follow up discussions in which many economists participated) and the appearance of the Industrial Licensing Policy Inquiry Committee Report in 1968, the belief got strengthened that imports of foreign technology were overpriced and were designed to perpetrate dependence. As a consequence, the government policy was progressively tightened in the following directions: *(1)* Some industries were not allowed to import technology at all, the underlying principles of the policy being that *(a)* no 'inessential' article should be produced with fresh imports of technology (this gave the existing domestic and foreign producers automatic protection against fresh imports of technology) and *(b)* where domestic capacity was 'adequate' no technology should be imported; *(2)* Among industries where technology imports were allowed, the maximum rate of royalty was laid down; *(3)* In some designated industries, foreign investment was allowed in principle, but sanction in individual cases was a matter of administrative decision; *(4)* The normal permissible period of agreements was reduced form ten years to five, and renewals were generally frowned upon; *(5)* Exports and other marketing restrictions were generally not allowed, and often an obligation to export a certain proportion of the output was insisted upon; *(6)* A clause was often inserted in the agreements granting permission to the importer to sub-licence the technology; *(7)* The CSIR was allowed to look at applications for approval of technology imports, and if it expressed willingness to supply the technology, approval was withheld or at least delayed.

GOVERNMENT POLICY OF FOREIGN CAPITAL

In view of this low inflow of foreign investment, the Government of India has announced a liberal policy towards foreign capital. The new Industrial Policy announced in July 1991 contains the following provisions with regard to foreign investment:

(1) As against the past policy of considering all foreign investment on a case by case basis and that too within the normal ceiling of 40 per cent of total equity investment, the new policy provides for automatic approval of direct foreign investment upto 51 per cent forein equity holding in 34 specified high-priority, capital intensive, high technology industries provided the foreign equity covers the foreign exchange involved in importing capital goods and outflows on account of divident payments are balanced by export earnings over a period of seven years from the commencement of production;

(2) In order to avail of professional marketing activities for systematic exploration of world markets for foreign products, foreign equity holding upto 51 per cent will be permitted for trading companies as well;

(3) Foreign technology agreements are also liberalised for the 34 industries with firms left free to negotiate the terms of technology transfer based on their own commercial judgement and with out the need for prior Government approval for hiring foreign technicians, and

(4) A special Board viz., Foreign Investment Promotion Board has been set up to look into large foreign investment projects where higher foreign equity limit of more than 51 per cent may be permitted.

With an eye to attract Foreign Direct Investment (FDI) of $10 billion annually, the NDA Government, in a major policy shift, threw open (February 1, 2000) most of the Industrial sectors (barring defence, aeronautics, explosive, alcohol, tobacco products) for FDI an automatic route to NRIs and overseas corporate bodies. The main features of the latest liberalised FDI regime are : 100% FDI in *(a)* mining (including coal and lignite supply to private Indian power companies) prospecting of gold, silver diamonds and other minerals *(b)* pollution control-related equipment *(c)* films (in addition to high priority areas, export houses, trading houses, hotels and tourism-related industries, projects for electricity generation, transmission and distribution, roads and highways, parts and harbours and vehicular tunnels and bridges, which are already covered under automatic route) : 74% FDI in *(a)* advertising *(b)* Bangolore international airport joint venture *(c)* prospecting and mining of gemstones.

FOREIGN INVESTMENT IN THE POST-LIBERALISATION PERIOD

The response to the new industrial policy and the liberalisation measures enunciated in that with respect to foreign investment has been encouraging. Inflow of foreign investment which was barely $133 million in 1991-92 and $559 million in 1992-93, jumped to $ 6008 million in 1996-97 after which it come down to $ 5025 million in 1997-98. Internal factors such as favourable growth prospects, exchange rate stability and bettter profit expectations compared to other industrial countries contributed to increased inflows.

The foreign capital inflow in India comes in two forms viz., *(a)* Portfolio Investments and *(b)* Foreign Direct Investment (Foreign Collaborations). Portfolio investment has been the largest single source of foreign investment whose volume has increased from $4 million in 1991-92 to $3824 million in 1994-95 but then its flow was reduced to $3312 million in 1996-97 and $1828 million in 1997-98.

The other source of investment inflow is Foreign Direct Investment. Foreign investment under the equity participaton schemes which was only $129 million in 1991-92 rose to $3197 million during 1997-98 and to $ 4.2 Billion in 1999-2000.

LIBERALIZATION AND IMPACT

The recent policy of the Government is that of liberalisation. The policy has been pursued with a view to have rational and fuller utilisation of resources in the different sectors of the economy, promotion of exports, development of backward areas, development of small-scale sector, larger opportunities to the new enterprises, etc.

Steps Towards Liberalisation. The Government, in the recent past, has announced a number of concessions and incentives which tend to lieberalise the different producing sectors of the economy. Some of the major concessions in this direction are given below:

1. Except for a short list of industries in the high priority ares, all other industries have been deregulated. Industrial licensing would be compulsory only for 15 industries in the high priority sector.
2. Fully-owned foreign enterprises will be allowed to set up gaint power project without thc requirement to balance dividend payments with export earnings.
3. Automatic approval up to 51 per cent equity extended to trading companies primarily engaged in export activities, to hotels and tourism-related industries, exploration/ development, refining and marketing of petroleum oil and gas.
4. The list of the industries exclusively reserved for the State has been pruned. Only 6 industries have been reserved for the public sector. In the Union Budget 1993-94, even the generation of power and processing of minerals has been left open to private sector.
5. Automatic approval by the Reserve Bank for foreign direct investment up to 51 per cent for foreign equity in 34 selected areas.
6. NRIs and overseas corporate bodies predominantly owned by them are permitted up to 100 per cent foreign equity in high priority areas.

7. Foreign Exchange Regulation Act companies have been brought at par with Indian companies. The existing FERA companies have also been extended the facility of 51 per cent equity. Companies have also been allowed to use foreign brand names and trade marks on goods for sale within the country.
8. Condition of dividend balancing thorugh export earning has withdrawn except for 22 industries under the consumer goods category.
9. Automatic approval for technology agreements related to high priority industries, if such agreements do no require the expenditure of foreign exchange.
10. Free float of Indian ruppee in the international market.
11. A concessional tax rate of 10 per cent on short-term capital gains for foreign institutional investors was introduced to enhance the level of foreign investment in Indian stocks.
12. Threshold limits of assets (Rs. 100 crores) in respect of MRTP companies and dominant undertakings stands withdrawn. This eliminates the requirements of prior approval of Central Government for establishment of new undertakings, expansion of undertakings, merger, amalgamation and takeover and appointment of directors.
13. All existing registration schemes (Delicensed, Registration, Exempted Industries Registration, DGTD Registration) have been abolished.
14. Investment in fixed capital by SSI unis raised to Rs. 60 lakhs, in case of ancillaries to Rs. 75 lakhs. and for tiny sector units to Rs. 5 lakhs.
15. New export-import policy announced for the five-year period 1997-2002, has made a major thrust towards trade liberalisation. The new policy substantially eliminates licensing quantitative restrictions, and other regulatory and diseretionary controls. Exports and imports are allowed

freely, subject only to a negative list of imports and a negative list of exports. The list of canalised items imported and exported through public sector undertakings drastically curtailed.

16. A five-year tax holiday for new industries in industrially backward States and Union Territories and for power generation anywhere in India was produced.

All these measure suggest liberalisation of the Indian economy in a big way. In spite of certain defects associated with liberalisation, it is likely to accelerate the pace of economic development in the Indian economy.

ROLE OF MNCs IN INDIA

International flow of funds to the less developed countries takes the form of either *(i)* Direct Foreign Investment or Private Foreign Capital which is the investment made by foreign companies or Multinational Corporations in various economic sectors of the less developed countries, or *(ii)* Official Development Assistance or Foriegn Aid provided by the donor countries or multilateral institutions like IBRD, IDA, etc. to the less developed country's governments in the form of concessional loans and outright grants. The first one i.e., direct foreign investment is called Foreign Capital and the second one i.e., international loans and grants is known as Foreign Aid.

Multinational Corporations (MNC's). Private foreign investment or foreign capital takes the form of direct foreign investment by huge multinational corporations. These are the mighty big firms with their headquarters in North America, Western Europe or Japan who have their massive network of subsidiaries spread over many nations. These firms are so big that in many cases their annual sales turnover is greater than the entire GNP of the nations in which they operate.

Advantages of Direct Foreign Investment. Direct foreign investment coming from these MNC's having much experience, standing and efficiency can confer great benefits on the less developed countries where they operate. They by providing capital, supplement the domestic resources, provide the much needed foreign exchange resources for essential capital goods imports; provide necessary and up-to-date technology and knowledge and general employment and incomes in the countries where they operate. They can benefit the consumers by offering better quality goods at lower prices due to the high levels of efficiency in their production processes. In brief, foreign capital supplements domestic savings to achieve higher levels of investment and facilitate import of capital goods and technology, which are not domestically available and thus promote the diversification of economic structure and its efficiency. Apart from finance and technology, foreign capital brings with its marketing and management skills which are so scarce and undevelopd in the underdeveloped economies.

Drawbacks of Direct Foreign Investments. Our distrust of MNC's. However as the experience in India under the British rule has shown, foreign capital has not been of much help. No doubt, many of our industries own their growth to British Multinational firms, but the fact is that such foreign investments have only developed our export items like tea, jute, rubber, etc. where the clientele were foreign and profits were high. Not much was done to develop those industries that provided necessary goods to the teeming millions of poor Indians. The pattern of development that took place was essentially dualistic where some packets were growing while the rest of the economy remained backward.

Because by nature the MNC's are big industrial gaints, they can exercise their semi-monopoly power to oust local producers and exploit the consumers. They, through massive publicity and propoganda, promote inappropriate products and cause misallocation of country's resources. By using inappropriate technology brought from and suited to their home country resource endowments, cause unemployment to rise and dualistic structure to rigidity. By their sheer money power they can corrupt the politicians and bureaucrats and seek large concessions for themselves. They cause drain on our resources in the form of repatriation of their large profits and export of goods made form raw materials which may be scarce in the country and hence needed to be preserved for our own development.

(1) Reasons for Preferring. Since our experience with foreign capital has not been satisfactory in the past, the Government of India showed a distinct preference for the other means of international capital transfers viz., foreign aid. Over the years India has received massive foreign aid from various countries and international agencies. The good thing about foreign aid is that India can use it in accordance with its own plans and priorities. None of the evils that accompany direct foreign investment are found in foreign aid. We can invest according to our own plans, produce the goods that we think to be necessary, use the technique that is most suited to our conditions and keep the profit within the country to prevent drain of resources.

(2) Problem of Foreign Aid. But the problem with foreign loans (most of the foreign aid is in the form of loans) is that they have to be serviced, i.e., interest has to be paid on them and the loan returned in instalments. Besides, most of the loans are tied loans, that is they can be used for specific projects for which they are given and equipment for those projects has to be purchased in the country that gives the loan. This reduces the freedom of the borrowing to use the loan the way it likes.

(3) Mounting Indebtedness. Indiscriminate borrowings have led to growing international indebtedness. Total external debt of India outstanding as at the end of 1991 was around $83801 million. This increased to about $ 99008 million at the end of 1995 but came down to 93908 million by the end of March 1998.

As a ratio of GDP at current market prices, India's external debt which was 28.0 per cent in 1991, rose to over 33.1 per cent at the end of March 1994 but declined to 26.3 per cent in March 1996 and further to 23.8 per cent at the end of March 1998.

International Debt Trap. Since a country that takes loans has to return that in instalments and pay interest on that loan regularly, it means every year a part of our foreign exchange earnings will have to be used for debt servicing, *i.e.*, amortisation and interest payment.

And when the country contracts large amounts of loans year after year, then a situation may arise where the country has a raise to new loan to pay the interest and instalments of the old loans. In such a case the new inflow of aid (gross aid minus debt servicing) will become small and hence development process would suffer.

Lately such a situation has emerged in India. Every year almost one half to two thirds of gross foreign aid received is used for debt servicing thereby reducing the net aid to extremely low levels.

Debt Service Ratio. Debt service payment take away a substantial part of our foreign exchange earnings. Debt service payments as a ratio of country's current receipts are an important indication of its international indebtedness. A situation where a country may have to pay about 40 to 45 per cent of its current receipts for debt servicing is an indication that it has virtually been caught in a dept trap. In India the Debt Service Ratio i.e., the ratio of debt servicing to export of goods and services (current receipts) increased from 9.3 per cent in 1981 to about 35 per cent in 1991. Though this ratio gradually declined after that year, it was still high at 26.4 at the end of March 1998. This shows that a quarter of country's foreign exchange earnings were used to meet repayment obligations.

India's mounting external indebtedness and increasing debt servicing obligations have caused tremendous strain on our balance of payments position. There was a virtual crisis in 1990 and 1991 when India's position to meet its external commitments became precarious and the country had to rush to IMF and World Bank to bail it out. Due to such mounting pressures on balance of payments and foreign exchange rerserves, the Government of India decided to liberalise its policy towards direct foreign investment with a view to encouraging its inflow.

One great advantage of direct foreign investment to the recipient countries lies in the fact that servicing of this capital begins only when the investment reaches a profit-making stage unlike foreign loans and commercial borrowings where servicing begins shortly after disbursement. While borrowing go to augment investible resources in the short-term and medium-term, direct investment in the form of equity capital provides reasources on a much longer basis.

In view of this, the Government has announced liberal terms and incentives to foreign investors. According to the Industrial Policy announced in July 1991, there will be automatic approval for direct foreign investment upto 51 per cent equity holding in 34 specified high priority industries. Many additional concessions have been given to attract foreign direct investment in India.

India, undoubtedly, has a number of advantages to offer to the potential foreign investor. Among these are political stability in a democratic framework; and economy characterised by steady growth; a vast domestic market; a large and growing pool of trained manpower; fairly well developed physical and social infrastructure; a vibrant financial system and a diversified industrial base.

❑